PSYCHODYNAMIC GROUP PSYCHOTHERAPY

Psychodynamic Group Psychotherapy

Third Edition

J. Scott Rutan
Walter N. Stone

THE GUILFORD PRESS
New York London

Library of Congress Cataloging-in-Publication Data

Rutan, J. Scott.
 Psychodynamic group psychotherapy / J. Scott Rutan, Walter N. Stone—3rd ed.
  p. cm.
 Includes bibliographical references and index.
 ISBN 1-57230-518-5
 1. Group psychotherapy. 2. Psychodynamic psychotherapy. I. Stone, Walter N.
 II. Title.
 RC488 .R88 2001
 616.89′152—dc21   00-061756

About the Authors

J. Scott Rutan, PhD, is a past president and distinguished fellow of the American Group Psychotherapy Association. He founded the Center for Group Psychotherapy at the Massachusetts General Hospital and was a Founding Father of the Boston Institute for Psychotherapy.

Walter N. Stone, MD, is Professor of Psychiatry at the University of Cincinnati College of Medicine. He is a distinguished fellow and past president of the American Group Psychotherapy Association and currently a board member of the International Association of Group Psychotherapy. His broad-ranging interests in group psychotherapy include application of self psychology and dynamic treatment of chronically mentally ill persons. He has published more than 50 articles and book chapters relevant to group training, dynamics, and psychotherapy, including *Group Psychotherapy for People with Chronic Mental Illness.*

Acknowledgments

Just as groups are cooperative efforts, so was this book. We are deeply indebted to our many friends and colleagues who have selflessly toiled over this text in order to make it better. Anne Alonso, Earl Hopper, Robert Kunkel, Cecil Rice, and Steven Saeks gave freely of their scholarship and time, and their contributions are woven throughout the text. Mark Ettin was particularly helpful while we wrote the material on the sociocultural context. Special mention should go to the members of the group described in Chapter 13, who willingly gave permission to record and transcribe their words for publication.

Of course, our wives, Jane and Esther, have endured the many long hours we spent at the computer rewriting this edition. We are forever grateful for their encouragement, tolerance, and good humor during this time.

Preface

What a piece of work is a man! How noble in
reason! how infinite in faculties! in form and
moving how express and admirable! in action
how like an angel! in apprehension how like a
god! the beauty of the world! the paragon of
animals!

—WILLIAM SHAKESPEARE, *Hamlet*

The world of health care, psychotherapy, and group
therapy continues to evolve and change since the first
edition of this book appeared in 1984. At that time
group therapy was ascending and finding legitimacy in the world of psychotherapy, psychodynamic theory was dominant, and long-term therapy was
the standard. Today, especially in the United States, there is an alarming
trend toward viewing discrete symptoms as unique pathologies for which
there are specific treatments. There is less reliance on the importance of *relationship* in healing, despite the research by Luborsky (1985) which documents
that the ability to form a relationship with a patient is the major criterion for
predicting a successful outcome. This holds true whether one is practicing
psychoanalysis or psychopharmacology.

Group therapy, which uses the power of relationships so fully, offers
unique advantages in this era. Further, psychodynamic theory, with its emphasis on looking beneath symptoms in order to understand them, continues to
offer an antidote to the cultural temptation to view symptom reduction as the
sole goal of treatment.

Though under attack, psychodynamic theory has by no means lost its appeal. There are well over 4,000 members of the American Psychological Association who are affiliated with divisions relating to dynamic theory (including *Psychoanalysis and Groups*). On the other hand, students in the mental health fields are no longer getting the grounding in psychodynamic theory that was previously the case. Alan Stone recently noted:

> A computer search of Harvard course catalogs for classes whose descriptions mention either Freud or psychoanalysis turned up a list of 40, not counting my own two courses. All of them are in the humanities, particularly literature, no course is being given in the psychology department and next to nothing is offered in the medical school. (1999, p. 36)

In this edition, we have attempted to address how to use the power of psychodynamic group therapy in today's world. Along with bringing the literature references up to date, adding a great deal of material about advances in theory, and adding many new clinical examples, this edition includes a new chapter on the use of psychodynamic principles in time-limited groups (Chapter 15) and one that provides a clinical vignette (Chapter 13). In the latter chapter, both authors respond to the clinical data in order to bring our thoughts alive.

Contents

ONE

Groups in Today's Society

Our individual lives cannot, generally, be works
of art unless the social order is also.
—CHARLES HORTON COOLEY, *Life and the Student*

H uman beings are group oriented. We begin in small
groups, our families, and live, work, and play in various
groups. The formation of our personalities is
predicated upon our experiences with the different groups in which we interact, and the opportunities for modification and change of our personalities
are very much affected by the groups in which we are involved. As Harry
Stack Sullivan (1953) maintained, it takes people to make people sick and it
takes people to make people well again.

While much has changed since the first edition of this book appeared in
1984, it remains true that the structure of modern society makes groups
uniquely important. Modern society still seems to have lost much of the capacity to build or maintain intimate relationships. The tendency is to change
partners rather than to resolve conflict.

CULTURE AND MENTAL ILLNESS

Psychopathologies confronting modern clinicians are different from the ones
that confronted Sigmund Freud and his colleagues. Freud (1914) analyzed the

pathologies of the members of the society in which he lived, and through that examination he made revolutionary discoveries about the formation and complexion of personality. The pathology that most fascinated Freud was hysteria. This disorder became the lens through which he focused his conceptions of individual psychodynamics.

In modern time, classical hysteria is not the pathology around which theory is formed. Masterson (1976), for instance, noted that today's patients usually do not come to psychotherapy "with a specific discrete symptom picture, such as an obsession or a phobia. Rather, their complaint is more general and vague—of getting too little satisfaction in their lives" (pp. 10–11). The cutting edge of modern psychodynamic thought has to do with character disorders, especially narcissistic and borderline conditions. Pathology is manifested in the disturbed quality of relationships with others. However, there is a trend, subsequent to the ascendancy of managed care in the United States, of trying to fit patients into discrete symptom formations and to find specific treatments for each of those diagnoses. In fact each of these specific diagnoses is a different way of coping with difficulties in gaining and sustaining viable relationships.

These "new" pathologies have been accompanied by other post-Freudian developments in our understanding of psychopathology and our practice of psychotherapy. Giovacchini (1979) observed that as psychoanalysis began to treat character-disordered patients, this "shifted our focus from a predominantly id-oriented psychology to an ego psychology. . . . It highlighted the importance of early development. The subtleties and vicissitudes of early object relationships have assumed paramount importance" (p. 3).

The etiology of psychopathology is multidetermined. Elements of genetics, biology, and temperament go into the human experience, along with the intrapsychic and interpersonal forces that are the province of psychodynamic theories. Unfortunately, most theory and research focus on one side of this interactive axis rather than trying to understand how these forces interrelate.

The search for a link between cultural factors and mental illness began as early as 1897, when Emile Durkheim (1897/1951) wondered about the connection between suicide and social conditions. In 1939 Faris and Dunham suggested a causal relationship between schizophrenia and the living conditions in Chicago slums. Leighton (1959), in his well-known Stirling County (Nova Scotia) study, discovered an overall correlation between mental illness and social disarray, as well as correlations between specific sociocultural settings and particular types of psychiatric disorder. A number of clinical syndromes, such as *koro, latah,* and *amok* are clearly culture bound (Leff, 1988). *Koro,* for example, is the strange syndrome in which there is a belief that a man's penis will disappear into his body and relatives are prepared to take action to prevent this from occurring. At times this belief has reached epidemic proportions in native populations. Dohrenwend and Dohrenwend (1974) found that while schizophrenia seems to be present in all cultures, there is considerable discrepancy in the types of schizophrenia that dominate in different cultures. Likewise, Y. A. Cohen (1961) demonstrated cultural factors in the etiology of depressive reactions.

Thus, the notion that there is a connection between cultural factors and the formation and expression of mental disorder has already been examined in some depth. For our purposes, the fact that cultures and ages have their own characteristic and dominant pathologies is of particular relevance. In the modern world, for example, there is evidence that individuals have difficulty obtaining and sustaining intimate interpersonal relationships. Ours is a culture which emphasizes individual gratification. We shall pursue these ideas by comparing the cultures, focal pathologies, and psychodynamic formulations of Freud's day and our own.

EARLY VICTORIAN CULTURE

The early Victorian era was stressful and comforting to people in specific ways. Victorian society offered far fewer choices than does current Western society. Although it was vastly more open than societies which preceded it, members of Victorian culture were nevertheless born into roles largely determined by class, church, ethnicity, and gender. Because there was little opportunity to go beyond those roles, the individual's hopes and aspirations were sources of frustration. On the other hand, individuals were spared the burden of ambiguity and choice. Acceptable behavior was highly codified, typically by a strong church morality, with the result that sexual and aggressive drives in particular were restricted. (The presence of a vigorous body of Victorian pornographic literature suggests that sexual drives were not thwarted altogether.)

In Victorian society individuals had a definite place, though not necessarily a place they chose or relished. Concomitantly, individuals had an identity that was clear. Relationships were set within the framework of the nuclear family, the extended family, the neighborhood, the world of work, and the church, all of which provided most people with natural sources of support and stability.

Individuals in Victorian times were presented with fewer choices about how to live their lives and with whom to live them. This is not to imply that there was an absence of frustration and pain. If few complained about being "bent out of shape," it was only because being shaped was so universal. It is reasonable to assume that the restrictiveness of that society might lead to pathologies that express conflict between individuals' powerful innate impulses and the introjects of a superego-ridden society.

VICTORIAN PSYCHOPATHOLOGY: HYSTERIA REVISITED

Freud's theories developed as he treated his patients, many of whom were neurotic hysterics. Students of Freud are familiar with the case of Anna O, the young woman Josef Breuer treated from December 1880 until June 1882. She suffered from classic hysteria, or "conversion reaction." While nursing her dying father she developed paralysis of three limbs, contractures and anesthesias, a nervous cough, and other symptoms. Breuer conducted his first analysis of Anna O using hypnosis throughout the treatment. In the course of this treatment it was discovered that Anna O had two quite distinct personalities. Further, during the treatment the patient developed toward Breuer what later became known as a transference love (Freud, 1937).

Freud and Breuer often discussed this case, and out of these discussions came many of Freud's original formulations about the existence of unconscious material and the structure of personality. Shortly after this Freud saw Emma von N, and in this case he had the opportunity to observe firsthand the strange behaviors present in hysteria.

Freud postulated four major premises about personality: first, all behavior is determined, not random; second, behavior is purposeful and serves to protect the self (*der Ich*), with even the most bizarre symptoms serving such an adaptive/compensatory purpose; third, there are unconscious urges, memories, wishes—a vast reservoir of information outside the individual's awareness; and, fourth, Freud eventually suggested that there are two basic drives within personality, the libidinal (pleasure-seeking) and the aggressive—personality was presumed to be formed in the thwarting and harnessing of these two drives. These four postulates are, of course, a most summary attempt to distill the essence of Freud's theories.

Do we psychotherapists see patients like Anna O or Emma von N in our offices today? Probably not, unless we work in highly contained ethnic communities where the role of nuclear family, extended family, neighborhood, and church still hold sway. When these patients do appear, they often come to our colleagues in neurology or internal medicine. The fact that the *types* of psychopathology present in our society are different than those observed by Freud suggests a powerful correlation between society and mental illness.

Freud not only observed the patients of his day, he observed them within the framework of that society. People in the Victorian era had a conviction that "structure" could harness the very forces of nature. This belief in the ultimate dependability of matter led to unprecedented productivity, wealth, and hegemony over peoples of a more "primitive" nature around the world. It is little wonder that Freud began to hypothesize about the "parts" that make up personality—it fit comfortably with the science of the era.

In the intervening years, more modern psychodynamic theories began to refer not so much to faulty parts as to dysfunctional relationships and dissatisfying ways of living. Modern concepts of pathology are cast less in terms of mismatched or improperly fitting parts than in terms of disrupted developmental processes. However, in the current atmosphere there is a press to return to a more Victorian approach—of understanding our patients as "broken," suffering from a specific and discrete illness for which there is presumably a specific and discrete treatment.

Whereas modern psychodynamic theorists chart the evolution of personality through social systems, Freud viewed the ego as essentially the product of intrapsychic conflict. Though individual personality was understood to be affected by interactions with significant others (especially the mother), it was nonetheless not seen as predominantly formed in those interactions. Rather, personality was understood to be the result of a thoroughly inward process. The ego was conceptualized as a rational, unemotional arbiter between the instinctual urges common to all people and the acceptable mores of the particular society in which they lived. The superego was "the alien *it* which tyrannizes the ego" (Binstock, 1979).

It is difficult to criticize Freud for this focus, given the genius required to hypothesize as much as he did about human development. Rather, we should simply understand that he did not have time or opportunity to expand all his observations to their logical conclusions, though he began this quest in *Civilization and Its Discontents* (1930). That was left to later authors, who elaborated on Freud's observations about the impact of human interactions and developed theories about personality resulting from interpersonal interactions. The apex of this trend is seen in modern theories of object relations and self psychology, where the need for human relationship is understood to be common to all people and fundamental to the forming of personality.

If it is true that personality is formed in, through, and by relationships, then a therapeutic modality that uses the interactions of networks of individuals should be capable of altering disturbed or disturbing personalities.

In modern culture the traditional sources of identity and continuity are waning or gone. It is as if the Victorian and modern eras are opposites on many important axes. Mainstays of the community and identity, such as the extended (or even nuclear) family, the neighborhood, the church, and the ethnic group are all diminishing in stability and dependability. The rate of change is now so accelerated that each generation would seem to have its own culture. For example, mass media, including the growing influence of the Internet, penetrates the nuclear family while mass transportation explodes it, and those central places that once gave individuals a sense of themselves are changing dramatically.

There was a certain dependability about the future in Victorian times. If a goal could not be attained in an individual's lifetime, there was always the reasonable expectation that it might be attained in the lifetime of his/her children or grandchildren. This is not the case today. Changes in technology are exponential, occurring at a faster rate than at any time in history. If that were not enough, technology has contributed even more lethal weapons of mass destruction, and there is little in human history to inspire confidence that at some point this awesome capacity will not be used. The value of working for and investing in the future has been diminished and modern individuals "live for today."

If Victorian culture provided stability at the cost of choices, in modern culture individuals are confronted with a bewildering array of choices (Toffler, 1970). Along with choices come ambiguity and uncertainty. If Victorian culture provided secure but restrictive relationships at the price of internal conflict, modern society underestimates the importance of maintaining and sustaining relationships.

MODERN PSYCHOPATHOLOGY

The ability to enter into cooperative, loving, interdependent relationships has always been a sign of psychological maturity and health. However, it is particularly so today. Indeed, one quick but accurate indicator of mental health is the degree to which individuals allow themselves to know how important others are to them.

Given the changes that have occurred since Freud's time, it is quite understandable that the stereotypical pathologies of today involve the ability to effect, experience, and enjoy intimate and sustaining relationships. Consequently, psychopathologies that confront modern clinicians are character disorders (such as borderline and narcissistic personalities) and mood disorders (such as depression and anxiety). These conditions may be understood as relational problems. The borderline patient is *too* aware of the importance of others, whereas the narcissistic patient appears incapable of knowing how important others are. Depression and anxiety can both be understood as adaptive responses to the terrors of intimacy. Fairbairn (1952a) was among the first to state that it is the relationship with the object (another), not the gratification of an impulse or drive, that is the fundamental fact of human existence. It is as though modern patients do not disable physical "parts" of themselves, as did Freud's patients, so much as they disable their relationships (Kernberg, 1976) and are unable to adequately relate to others (Kohut, 1971).

GROUP THERAPY

Our understanding of the structure, functioning, and objectives of therapy groups is consistent with our description of modern society and the pathologies it fosters.

Freud's patients lived in a structured and mechanistic world. This both affected the ills that beset them and determined the form and focus of the cure that would work for them. The focus of the cure for hysterical patients was abreaction, catharsis, and access to repressed wishes and memories. Given the strong sense of what were acceptable thoughts and behaviors in Freud's time, the form of treatment was one to one and very private. Freud's patients did not lack social connections. If anything, the social element was all *too* present, and therapy offered a much needed *private* place where one could explore the feelings, wishes, and behaviors that society prohibited.

Typically, the situation is reversed today. Individualism is so dominant that social connections are not formed or, if formed, soon unravel. The requirements and goals of psychotherapy are different. Modern patients need authentic human relations, the skills for building them, and the ability to make the compromises necessary to live intimately with others. They need less help with the *structure* of their being than with the process of relating. From this perspective, the benefits of group therapy begin to become clear. Therapy groups are supportive yet, in a way, restrictive communities. They incorporate some of the Victorian values of dependability, and it is expected that group members will *work at* their relationships with others in the group. The easy out of changing relationships is highly discouraged in favor of resolving conflict. Rutan and Alonso (1979, p. 612) have written:

> Group therapy, by its very format, offers unique opportunities to experience and work on issues of intimacy and individuation. In such groups the community is represented in the treatment room. It is usually impossible for individuals to view themselves as existing alone and affecting no one when in a group therapy situation over any significant period of time.

TWO

History of Small Group Theory and Practice

The whole past is the procession of the present.
—THOMAS CARLYLE

Differences between the way individuals think, feel, and behave when alone and when in groups have interested observers for many years. Gustav LeBon and William McDougall, both in 1920, were among the first to write about the impact of groups on the behaviors of individuals. Sigmund Freud, F. H. Allport, Harry Stack Sullivan, Kurt Lewin, and Carl Rogers are just a few of the well-known authors who have contributed to this field of interest. If we are to understand more fully the ways in which participation in groups is currently thought to be curative, we must examine the history of our interest in group psychology.

GROUP THERAPY THEORY

Aristotle referred to man as a "social animal," and he considered man's affiliative needs to be a source of strength. Rigorous scientific exploration of the effects of group upon individuals began as early as 1895, when Gustav LeBon, a French social psychologist, referred to the phenomenon of the "group mind." As with the other early authors in this field, LeBon was concerned with groups of very large numbers. Having been impressed by the primitive nature of crowd behavior, he used the word *foule* ("crowd") to denote the object of his study. LeBon hypothesized that once individuals become part of a crowd, a type of hypnotic power engulfs them and causes their behavior to change. Individuals lose their sense of responsibility, and a group mind assumes control.

LeBon's (1895/1920) main thesis was that when individuals are in groups they experience a diminishing of human functioning. He described large crowds as regressive, primitive, and uncivilized. He stated:

> By the mere fact that he forms part of an organized group, man descends several rungs in the ladder of civilization. Isolated he may be a cultivated individual; in a crowd, he is a barbarian—that is, a creature acting by instinct. (p. 36)

LeBon accounted for this change with three factors. First, he believed that by virtue of group membership individuals in groups experience a sense of increased strength, even invincibility. Second, he noted that *contagion* occurs in groups. He described contagion as akin to a hypnotic state induced by the group on its members. Finally, and for LeBon the most important, he felt that suggestibility was greatly increased in groups:

> We see, then, that the disappearance of the conscious personality, the predominance of the unconscious personality, the turning by means of suggestion and contagion of feelings and ideas in an identical direction, the tendency to immediately transform the suggested ideas into acts; these we see are the principal characteristics of an individual forming part of a group. He is no longer himself, but has become an automation, who has ceased to be guided by his will. (1920, p. 35)

This is not an auspicious or optimistic appraisal of the potential benefits of groups for therapeutic purposes! But more and more succeeding authors have postulated that the power of groups can be effectively turned to therapeutic use.

William McDougall (1920), an Englishman, published *The Group Mind* at the same time that LeBon published his work. As the title suggests, McDougall had come to the same conclusion as LeBon regarding the premise that something "extra" occurs when individuals find themselves in groups. However, McDougall contributed an important new notion, for while agreeing that groups have the potential for degrading the level of civilized behavior of individuals, he also saw the potential of groups to enhance individual behavior. McDougall is perhaps the first theorist to see the potential of groups as a means of helping persons change their behavior for the better.

The key for turning the power of groups into a positive force, according to McDougall, is *organization*. Of unorganized groups he was no more optimistic than LeBon, thinking them "excessively emotional, impulsive, violent, fickle, inconsistent, irresolute, and extreme in action." But, he stated that his book would

> show how organization of the group may, and generally does in large measure, counteract these degrading tendencies; and how the better kinds of organization render group life the great ennobling influence by aid of which alone man rises a little above the animals and may even aspire to fellowship with the angels. (p. 28)

McDougall further stated that clear goals and purposes are essential to the effectiveness of a group.

> There is . . . one condition that may raise the behavior of a temporary and unorganized crowd to a higher plane, namely, the presence of a clearly defined common purpose in the minds of all of its members. (p. 67)

Thus two of the earliest authors on the impact of groups upon individuals identified several important phenomena: the power of groups to affect the behavior of individuals; the presence of "contagion," or the capacity of groups to fill each of the members with feelings; and the importance of organization, group agreements, and goals.

Sigmund Freud (1921) added a great deal more. (Freud did not directly refer to the operations of small groups. Rather, his observations concerned large groups such as armies and nations. Much later Fritz Redl, 1963, related Freud's work to group psychotherapy.) Freud was intrigued by the effect of the group on the individual, and his study of group dynamics was a step in his further conceptualization of the superego, which had been thought of as the ego ideal. As he considered what constituted a group, in contrast to a collection of people, he posited that group formation necessitates having a sense of purpose (a goal) and the emergence of clear leadership. Using the theory available to him at the time, Freud suggested that groups form when members develop libidinal ties to the leader and to one another.

The nature of the ties of the members to one another and to the leader differ. Freud (1921) speculated that group members identify with one another as a result of their libidinal ties to the leader. He used the example of the army to illustrate his hypothesis:

> It is obvious that a soldier takes his superior, that is in fact, the leader of the army, as his ideal, while he identifies himself with his equal and derives from this community of their egos the obligation of giving mutual help and for sharing possessions which comradeship implies. (p. 56)

Inherent in these formulations of identification between members is a regression and dedifferentiation of each individual, who is no longer seen as having individuality except to meet a common goal. This phenomenon helps explain some of the attraction as well as some of the fears experienced in entering group life.

A second dynamic emerging from Freud's formulations concerned the process by which an individual relinquishes his ego ideal and accepts instead the group leader's goals and ideals. Freud compared the members' relationships to the leader with being in love, a situation in which the loved one is overvalued and idealized. He suggested that "when we are in love a considerable amount of narcissistic libido over-flows on to the object. It is even obvious in many forms of love-choice that the object serves as a substitute for some unattained ego-ideal of our own" (1921, p. 66). This mechanism linked individual psychology to processes operating in groups and offered an explanation of the behaviors observed by LeBon (1920) and McDougall (1920).

Freud pointed the way toward resolution of the regressive phenomena occurring in groups in his frequently quoted reference to empathy. He wrote, "a path leads from identification by way of imitation to empathy, that is to the comprehension of the mechanism by means of which we are enabled to take up any attitude at all towards another mental life" (1921, p. 66). This pathway suggests that individuals, following the initial regression associated with group formation, can reverse the process by learning temporarily to identify emotionally with others. This process, empathy, enables a reidentification of each individual and, for the purpose of group therapy, learning about one's own emotional life and the emotional life of others.

The closest Freud came to conducting an actual therapy group was probably the famous Wednesday Evening Society. During the first decade of this century, his group of analysts met regularly and discussed the theoretical concepts of psychoanalysis, with highlights from their work with patients. Early analysts such as Alfred Adler, Lou Andreas-Salome, Paul Federn, Max Graf, Wilhelm Reich, Hermann Nunberg, Alfred Saenger, and Frank Wittels attended regularly. The group was initially an educational group; however, the founder of the group, Wilhelm Stekel, had been a patient of Freud's, and thus the legacy of using Freud for therapeutic purposes was built into the fabric of these sessions. The members regularly engaged in mutual personal sharing, but Freud remained in the role of group leader. Ultimately, as documented in the minutes of the Vienna Psychoanalytic Society, the meetings became exceedingly emotional and passionate. The group ceased meeting when the conflict between Adler and Freud reached its crescendo.

This concern with the power of groups to be destructive is echoed in Virginia Woolf's *A Room of One's Own* (1929, p. 22): "Great bodies of people are never responsible for what they do."

GROUP THERAPY PRACTICE

While scholars were theorizing about how groups affect individuals, practitioners were already experimenting with the use of small groups as therapeutic agents.

Joseph H. Pratt (1906), an internist in general medicine at the Massachusetts General Hospital in Boston, is widely credited with being the founder of group psychotherapy. In July 1905 he established a group of 15 of his tuberculosis patients. Pratt's groups did not provide group therapy as we know it today. The format of these meetings was primarily lecture presentations. For purposes of citing a beginning point for group therapy, Pratt's groups were considered therapy groups for two reasons: they represent the initial known attempt at having patients discuss and learn about their common problems in a small group setting, and they involve a set of agreements that each member had to make before being allowed to join the group. Each participant had to agree to give up working and to live essentially out of doors as part of the treatment. Pratt reported very positive results from this new type of treatment.

Other early pioneers who experimented with the effectiveness of small groups for therapeutic purposes included Edward Lazell, who was the first to see psychiatric (largely schizophrenic) patients in groups, which he did at St. Elizabeths Hospital in Washington, DC, in 1919; Trigant Burrow, who saw neurotic patients in groups in 1920; Alfred Adler, whose theories about man's being entirely a social creature led him to use groups with patients as early as 1921; Julius Metzl, a pioneer in group techniques for alcoholics, began using groups by 1927; Cody Marsh, who presided over lecture-type groups in New York City in 1919; Rudolf Dreikurs, who, in 1930, conducted the first private therapy groups; J. L. Moreno, who used groups in psychodrama in the 1930s; and S. R. Slavson, an engineer by profession, who at the same time began seeing disturbed children in "activity group" therapy.

It is evident that small group psychology bears a strong American flavor. Not only was America receptive to the use of groups, but adverse conditions in Europe at this time meant that many eminent Viennese psychologists immigrated to America, bringing with them their interest in small groups.[1]

HISTORY OF SENSITIVITY GROUPS

The sensitivity group movement, developing approximately parallel with the development of group therapy, is another wellspring of theory and experimentation about the potential uses of small groups. Kurt Lewin was the man

---

[1]See Cartwright and Zander (1960, pp. 9–30) for a more complete discussion of these preconditions.

most responsible for using small groups for the enhancement of human growth and development rather than for the specific alleviation of psychopathology.

In order to place Lewin's contributions in context, one must understand the scientific tenor of the time. This was an era in which scientists were severely questioning the reductionistic model of scientific investigation. As smaller and smaller units of matter were discovered, it was postulated that the universe might not be nearly so ordered as had been previously assumed. A specific example is found in the theory of light.

Sir Isaac Newton's time-honored corpuscular theory of light had originally won favor over a wave theory proposed by Christian Huygens because it seemed to explain more of the characteristics of light. However, in succeeding years scientists discovered increasing evidence in support of *both* the diverse theories. Max Planck finally offered a resolution by formulating quantum theory, which conceptualized light not merely in terms of waves or corpuscular units but in terms of both. He spoke of a *field* of forces.

Lewin, along with Freud and others, applied the concept of a field of forces to personality development. Just as in physical sciences it is too restrictive to posit simple one-to-one relationships in most instances, Lewin maintained that in personality development we must consider whole fields of influences that touch upon each person. Perhaps the most important forces in each person's field are other persons. Given this interest it was natural that Lewin would become interested in the interaction of people in small group situations. Primarily a researcher and theorist, Lewin experimented with groups as a means of enhancing decision-making power, increasing group effectiveness, and increasing group morale. After World War II Lewin continued his work at the Massachusetts Institute of Technology in the Research Center for Group Dynamics, the first academic project specifically designed to study the dynamics of small groups.

In 1947, the year Lewin died, three of his students—Kenneth Benne, Leland Branford, and Ronald Lippett—initiated a series of workshops at Bethel, Maine. These workshops culminated in the formation of the National Training Laboratories (NTL), the first of the sensitivity group, or T-group, organizations. (NTL referred to their groups as T-groups, for "training groups.")

Another school of small group practitioners was being developed concurrently by Carl Rogers at the University of Chicago. This project began as a means of training counselors for the Veterans Administration shortly after the war. A major difference between Rogers's and Lewin's groups was in their goals: "The Chicago groups were oriented primarily toward personal growth and the development and improvement of interpersonal communication and relationships, rather than having these as secondary aims. They also had a more experiential and therapeutic orientation than the groups originating in Bethel" (Rogers, 1970, p. 4).

Thus by the 1940s the sensitivity group movement can be identified as a separate entity with at least two distinct traditions: one, which traces its roots back to Kurt Lewin, uses the small group as a forum for improving individual and task effectiveness; the second, which traces its roots to Carl Rogers, uses the small group as a primarily emotional education for individual growth.

MODERN THEORIES OF GROUP THERAPY

In the beginning group therapy was conducted on a trial-and-error basis, with practitioners trying to meld the observations of LeBon, McDougall, Lewin, and others on how groups function with the individualized theories of psychotherapy, notably Freud's. However, a satisfactory integration was not forthcoming, and theorists varied in their emphasis. Some focused on the individual, whereas others examined groupwide phenomena. Imbedded in the theories was the proposition that multiple interpersonal transactions could illuminate the individual's inner conflicts or expose groupwide processes. Although we still have not achieved a unitary theory, therapists have come to use a combination of group dynamic, interpersonal, and intrapsychic psychodynamic theories as the foundation of group psychotherapy practice.

Group-as-a-Whole Approaches

Bion: Group-as-a-Whole

Wilfred R. Bion made his contributions from work done during the 1940s. This decade, which encompassed World War II, was a time of extensive attention to small groups by many great thinkers. For a very short time, Bion conducted a few psychotherapy groups composed of 56 patients as well as some colleagues interested in learning about group processes. Although his work with these groups did not last long, his writings about his experiences have had enormous influence. In fact, "Bion" has become synonymous with one theoretical view of groups.

Bion (1960) conceptualized every group as having two levels. At the overt level groups have a purpose and a task, and the group works toward those ends. The leader is not the only one with skills; he leads only as long as he can serve the task of the group. The members are discreet individuals who contribute to the task and, in short, operate at a level of secondary process. Bion referred to this as a *work group*. In Bion's (1960) view, "the work group is constantly perturbed by influences which come from other mental phenomena" (p. 129). These phenomena are the *basic assumptions*, which represent a second level of group functioning. However, "the work group is very powerful, and it is noteworthy that it survives with a vitality that would suggest that fears that the group will be swamped by the emotional states proper to the basic as-

sumptions are quite out of proportion" (p. 98). While this level of group operation is always present, Bion's theory is primarily about the other level of
group functioning, the basic *assumption group.*

Bion posited that, in addition to their attention to the designated tasks,
all groups operate on fundamental unconscious assumptions, as if they are
meeting in order to fulfill emotional needs and/or to avoid dreaded relationships among their members. Bion hypothesized three basic assumption
groups:

1. In the *dependency group* behavior is as *if* the members can gain security
and protection from one individual, the leader, who is omnipotent and omniscient. Although this fantasy is unrealizable, the members act as *if* they really
can create a situation that will conform to their wishes.

2. In the *fight–flight group* behavior is as *if* the members gain security and
preserve the group through battle or escape. Action is essential and individual
needs may be sacrificed in order to preserve the group. This is a group that
may "fight" the ideas of self-examination; the group may flee the therapeutic
task by engaging in trivial talk. Members may demonstrate other overt flight
behavior such as tardiness, absence, or even premature dropping out of the
group.

3. The *pairing group* operates as *if* it were to produce a messiah. The discussion often appears intimate or sexual and is future oriented. Two people
create something in the future; the hope is that what is produced will save the
group from intense feelings in the present.

Bion indicated there may be additional basic assumptions. Turquet
(1974) tentatively proposed a basic assumption of "oneness." Writing in the
context of work with large groups, he suggests members "seek to join in a
powerful union with an omnipotent force . . . to surrender self for the passive
participation and thereby [to] feel . . . well being . . . and wholeness" (p. 357).
The stimulus for the basic assumption of oneness is thought to be the threat to
the individual's identity. Out of his work with traumatized people and groups,
Hopper (1997) proposed that this basic assumption of oneness is really bipolar. He argues that the severely traumatized suffer from the fear of annihilation and develop an internal oscillation between fear of "fission and fragmentation" and fears of "fusion and confusion. " For the group, the proposed
basic assumption is shared "incohesion: aggregation/massification" (p. 453).
He contrasts that with a mass which is "characterized by a maximal degree of
mutual attraction and involvement among . . . people who . . . share the illu-
sion of solidarity, usually for a brief period of time" (p. 452). Hopper's contribution seems particularly valuable in the dynamics of more developmentally
arrested individuals.

Bion used two additional concepts to account for group interaction that follow from the application of Melanie Klein's idea of *projective identification.* One concept is *valency,* which he uses to refer to an individual's primary tendency to enter into group life with one of the basic assumptions mentioned above. Individuals differ in their valency to the three basic assumptions. *Valency* implies the instantaneous and involuntary nature of each individual's tendency (Bion, 1960, p. 24). Bion, who was analyzed by Klein, also understands and interprets unacceptable wishes as the disowned and unacceptable aspects of self which are projected into another, who then contains those projections and is influenced by them. Both the leader and other members of the group are deeply affected by these projective processes and can barely keep from identifying with them.

Bion visualized group life as alternating between basic assumption group and work group status. He did not posit a developmental model in which basic assumptions led to maturation. The model emphasized the members' relationships to the leader and to the group at archaic levels, but it did not address interpersonal relationships. Brown (1992) suggests that group dynamics are not fully explainable from only authority relationships, but "unmodified basic assumptions result in groups from avoidance of genuine personal encounter, so that difficult feelings in relationships are disavowed" (p. 216).

The therapeutic goals for Bion were to enable people to learn about their earliest problems with authority, to free individuals from their historic bonds through an understanding of their natural valences and basic assumptions, and subsequently to enable individuals to enter into more satisfactory peer relationships. This theoretical orientation results in a particular style of leader intervention that sometimes has the flavor of noninvolvement punctuated by mystic pronouncements. In the Bion tradition the leader sits on the group boundary and attempts to make interpretations aimed primarily at helping the group members examine the manifestations of the basic assumptions under which they are functioning. Probably no group therapist functions exclusively in this mode, but Bion's influence on understanding the unconscious aspects of group life has had a major effect on therapists utilizing group-as-a-whole concepts. Furthermore, Bion's work illustrates the group processes that are at work in all groups. Although some therapeutic styles opt not to focus on these processes, they exist and are at work nonetheless.

Ezriel: Psychoanalytic Group Therapy

Henry Ezriel (1973) became interested in groups through his membership in Bion's first group. Soon, however, he found that Bion's theories, which were based upon Melanie Klein's work, were not to his liking and he formed his own theory based upon the work of W. R. D. Fairbairn (1952a, 1952b) and H. Guntrip (1969). Ezriel began with the hypothesis, derived from object relations theory, that individuals seek to reinforce repression and avoid contact with frightening unconscious fantasies. The reinforcement is accomplished through the development of object relationships that help deny the unconscious fantasies; such a relationship is labeled the *required relationship*. In this view such relationships or transferences take place in many situations and are not a developmental process, as in the formation of a classical transference neurosis, although there may be developmental issues. The required relationship is precisely that, required, in order to bypass the *avoided relationship;* entry into the avoided relationship would result in a calamity (the *calamitous relationship*). These three object relationships constitute the tripartite model associated with Ezriel's work.

A common group tension (which is unconscious) emerges as patients try to express the three relationships. Since no two patients have identical intrapsychic conflicts, each tries to express something different and impose his/her own pattern on the group. Tension at a latent level then develops among the members. As the process evolves in the here and now of the meeting, the therapist demonstrates the common group tension and each individual's contribution to it. Essential to this approach is the idea of "communicating by proxy," by which Ezriel meant that a patient may not say anything but unconsciously or silently identifies with another patient.

Ezriel stated that no interpretation is complete without elucidation of all three relationships for the group-as-a-whole and, in addition, as thoroughly as possible for each individual. For example, if members were involved in a highly intellectualized discussion about there being insufficient emotional sharing in the group, Ezriel might suggest that the group is talking about there being too much analysis and not enough feelings (the required relationship) in order not directly to criticize the therapist, who represents the analytic point of view (the avoided relationship), because they fear that he/she will not feed them or care for them (the calamitous relationship). Ezriel would then elucidate how each member's personal conflicts were woven into the discussion. Ezriel preferred a group size of five patients.

For Ezriel, all interpretations are rooted in the here and now, and the therapist restricts his/her activity solely to interpretations. Indeed he/she may remain silent until he/she is able to clarify the common (unconscious) group tension and the individual's contribution to it. A successful interpretation frees individuals so that they can more successfully face the avoided relationship. Then memories and associations from the past will spontaneously emerge. However, Ezriel also believed that avoidance of the past may be used as a defense, since revelations of past conflicts might expose an avoided relationship in the present.

In this purist approach, Ezriel has no contact with patients outside the group meeting and limits himself entirely to interpretive comments. Other interventions are conceptualized as gratifying the required relationship, lowering anxiety, and undermining the work of the group. The therapist is central in this approach, and peer transference is viewed as a displacement from the therapist (rivalry among group members is required because to struggle with the therapist could be calamitous). Interpretations are made to the group-as-a-whole, at the level of the common group tension, and to each individual member. Overall, this method attempts to integrate object relations theory with group-as-a-whole concepts.

While Ezriel has many fewer followers than Bion in contemporary group therapy, he remains important as one of the first in the group-as-a-whole tradition to pay attention to the individual members as well as to the group itself.

Foulkes: Group Analysis

Group analysis is the name applied to the therapeutic approach of S. H. Foulkes, a British analyst who finished his analytic training in Vienna in the 1920s and who wrote his text on group analysis in 1948. Foulkes was heavily influenced by classical Gestalt psychology, and from that source he maintained that the group is more than the sum of its parts. No individual can be studied successfully in isolation, since individuals exist only in networks that are their social groups. The original social structure is the family in which each individual derives his/her personality and identity. The neurotic person, according to Foulkes, is isolated from the family network and is unable to communicate his/her distress accurately. Foulkes speaks of the process of the person's changing from a nodal point in a network to becoming a focal point. Utilizing the classical Gestalt notion of figure–ground, Foulkes maintained that individual pathology would appear as the *figure* in the midst of the group's ground. For Foulkes, the individual and the group both required the therapist's (conductor) attention.

"What distinguishes group analysis from other approaches is its unique integration of psychoanalytic concepts within an open-system, Gestalt framework that underpins both its theory and practice" (Pines & Hutchinson, 1993, p. 31). For all group analysts, the notion of the *open system* is central. This refers to an awareness of the place where communications and relationships take place. "It is a common shared ground which ultimately determines the meaning and significance of all events and upon which all communication and interpretations, verbal and nonverbal rest" (Foulkes, 1964, p. 292). The concept of *resonance* describes reverberation of a theme among the members who may react at different levels of consciousness and regression, according to their needs, developmental level, and regressive state. *Mirroring* is the aspect of the self that is reflected in others. Through identification and projective mechanisms members become aware of unknown (unconscious) parts of themselves (Zinkin, 1983). At times, with difficult patients, a therapeutic impasse or potentially destructive group process emerges when members are unable to own the split-off and projected parts of themselves.

The therapist has the task of widening and deepening communication. This may take into account differing psychological levels that "range from the more conscious objective 'everyday' relationships to increasingly subjective and unconscious fantasy relationships, from more to less clearly differentiated and individual relationships" (Brown & Pedder, 1979, p. 129). The therapist is actively engaged in the group and is not the austere observer-authority placed on the group boundary. Both group and individual dynamics are taken into account, and interventions to individuals will reverberate through the matrix and affect all present. The group analytic therapist models communication, in addition to assisting members, through interpretation, with the goal of increasing communication. The members are actively involved in the analyses of events occurring within the group. Group analysis, as Foulkes (1975) has stated, is "psychotherapy by the group, of the group including its conductor" (p. 3).

The group provides opportunities to discover similarities and differences through each member seeing him-/herself in others (the mirror). At times the individual is speaking for the group, and at other times the individual's needs are represented by the group. Taking into account the members' differing communicational levels, the therapist recognizes that group interpretations may not be accurate for each individual.

Group analytic teachings have been a major force in group work in Europe. The Institute of Group Analysis, which began in London, has developed a network of training centers in a number of major European cities as well as in Australia and Israel.

Whitaker and Lieberman: The Group Focal Conflict

The group focal conflict approach is an integration of the work of Thomas M. French (1952) and group dynamic theory. First described by Whitman and Stock (1958) and elaborated in a monograph by Whitaker and Lieberman (1964), the central notion suggests that all or almost all of the verbalizations and behavior of patients in a session can be understood as efforts to solve an intragroup conflict. By definition, the focal conflict is closest to the surface (i.e., preconscious) and will account for the observable data. The theory further posits that as conflicts are integrated, deeper material becomes exposed for interpretation, enabling patients to learn about themselves.

In this approach it is postulated that a wish (the disturbing impulse) becomes generated in the group but cannot be directly exposed for fear of some negative consequence (the reactive motive) and therefore is expressed in a compromise fashion (the solution). Focal conflicts may be elaborated into themes, which may then be expressed during a series of sessions, or certain solutions in themselves may stimulate further conflicts. After conflicts are actively clarified and worked through, the group may enter a conflict-free period during which more personal material can be examined, responded to, and worked on without stirring unmanageable anxiety or resistance.

An individual patient may or may not respond to any particular conflict; however, as in other theories, the notion is advanced that silence is not lack of interest but is often a cover for significant emotional participation (resonance). Therefore the therapist may make appropriate groupwide interpretations that would affect each member, including the member who seemed not to be participating in the discussion.

Notions derived from group dynamics include those of the group culture, which are used in this context to describe how the group deals with the focal conflicts—that is, either by enabling or by restrictive solutions. The enabling solutions allow the group greater safety so that conflicts can be worked through at great depths. If conditions become unsafe for the individual, he/she may attempt to alter the group culture through habitual defensive maneuvers, thereby setting in motion another focal conflict. An enabling group culture provides the patient an arena in which it is possible to understand and relinquish habitual maladaptive patterns.

In utilizing the group focal conflict model the therapist is in emotional touch with the group but stands apart in a space where he/she can interpret it. The therapist observes the group process and attempts to interpret restrictive group solutions. The framework (which is quite similar to the tripartite model based on object relations as proposed by Ezriel, 1973) is interpretation of the disturbing motive (the wish), the reactive motive (the fear), and the solution.

Successful interpretations alter the group solution and increase the safety of the group culture, which in turn will benefit the individuals within the group. The therapist's strategies are directed at the focal conflict and may include translating an individual problem into one that applies to the whole group. An intervention to one member may address the group conflict (Whitaker, 1989, p. 248). However, in an earlier publication Whitaker and Lieberman (1964) caution that the therapist needs to be aware of the potential effects, both negative and positive, of such interpretations. Their main point is that all therapists' interventions have an impact on the group process. Awareness of response to interpretation enables the therapist to follow the group struggles toward new and hopefully enabling solutions to focal conflicts.

Michael Balint, a Hungarian psychoanalyst highly influenced by Sándor Ferenczi as well as by his involvement with the Tavistock Clinic in London, incorporated both the group-as-a-whole model and the more personal and interactive therapeutic style espoused by the Hungarian psychoanalytic movement. Like Bion, his groups were not therapy groups. Rather, Balint worked with groups of physicians. His premise, which is highly relevant in today's world, was that it was the relationship between physician and patient that was primarily healing (Balint, 1957).

Interpersonal Theories

Irvin D. Yalom (1985), in *The Theory and Practice of Group Psychotherapy*, elucidates his theory of interpersonal learning as it occurs in group therapy. Yalom
trained in the Sullivanian tradition, and many of his notions derive from that
interpersonal orientation. He believes that the major therapeutic thrust for
change occurs in the group interaction as it takes place in the here and now.
He does not preclude discussion of outside ideas or events, but the main arena
for learning is the therapy group. With proper structuring this evolves into a
social microcosm, a miniaturized representation of each patient's social universe.

Through repeated experiences in the group settings, patients learn about
their maladaptive interpersonal transactions and their perceptual (parataxic)
distortions that elicit negative or undesirable responses from others. The
mechanisms involved in helping patients learn are feedback from others (consensual validation) and self-observation. During this process patients learn
that their fears may be groundless in the present and that their anxieties arise
from perceptual distortions. As patients learn about their behavior patterns in
the group, they become more able to observe comparable behaviors, both inside and outside the group, thereby increasing their ability to manage themselves successfully. The ultimate responsibility for change rests upon the patient. Increased insight alone will not guarantee change.

Interpersonal learning takes place at several levels, according to Yalom.
As in other theories the therapist is a representative of prior family (parental)
relations, and the group members represent both authority and sibling relationships. Transference and insight are considered aspects of interpersonal
learning, but they are considered of less therapeutic value than the "corrective
emotional experience" of authentic human interactions that occur in the
group. Transference is understood, in the Sullivanian tradition, primarily as
an interpersonal perceptual distortion, and the work of the group involves
working through these distortions. Insight is categorized as learning at four
different levels: (1) how others see the patient, (2) what the patient is doing in
relationship to others, (3) why the patient might be doing what he/she is
doing, and (4) genetic insights.

For most patients Yalom feels that the first three levels of insight are sufficient for change. He suggests that intellectual understanding (insight) is a critical element for change, but he does not feel that this must extend into the patient's past in order to be useful (depth of interpretation and insight is not
correlated with potency).

The therapist's role in this model is that of a person whose tasks include
the creation of an appropriate group culture where interpersonal behaviors
can be examined. The group therapist, by attending to the development of
group cohesiveness and appropriate norms, shapes a social system. Yalom be-

lieves that the greater the group cohesion the more likely will be the influence of interpersonal feedback; thus he emphasizes this dynamic. Rothke (1986) specifies the elements of useful feedback: it is clear, has a high degree of immediacy, focuses on the sender of the message, is an affective nature, is risky self-disclosure, deals with the sender–receiver relationship, and is minimally evaluative (p. 228).

Particularly in the early sessions, the therapist must be attentive to tardiness, absences, subgrouping, extragroup socializing, and scapegoating. The therapist's task is primarily as gatekeeper, and he/she shapes the norms of the group through his/her use of authority and by presentation of a rationale for his/her work. At various stages in the group the therapist utilizes different techniques. The therapist models the group's behavior by offering feedback, by clarifying the concept of responsibility, by disconfirming fantasied disastrous consequences, by reinforcing generalizability of learning, and by encouraging risk taking. The therapist also attempts to demystify his/her power and reinforces the members' capacities to help one another (Leszcz, 1992). Yalom does not exclude group dynamics and group-as-a-whole phenomena, but he relegates them to a secondary position. He maintains his focus on the interpersonal interactions and transactions within the group setting.

Intrapsychic Approaches

This approach to group therapy emphasizes the principles of intrapsychic conflict and the translation of the psychoanalytic model into the group therapy situation. The paradigm is that of an individual-within-the-group—psychoanalysis in a group setting. Group dynamics in their pure state are seen as resistances and interfere with the basic therapeutic task. This orientation was central to the work of S. R. Slavson (1950). Alexander Wolf and Emmanuel K. Schwartz (1962) give a scholarly exposition of this position. Theoretically the group provides a situation where regression takes place and allows for elucidation of transferences and resistances that then become available for interpretation. Regression may take place in libidinal, object relations or cognitive lines of development. Libidinal regression to oral dependent or anal controlling power phases is very common. Emergence of preoedipal patterns of object relations is manifest in fears of fusion and loss of self. Defenses consistent with the early object relations include splitting, projective identification (see Chapters 11 and 12 for further elaboration), projection, and denial (C. A. Rice, 1992). Cognitive processes may regress from secondary to primary forms. However, it is uncommon for psychotic mechanisms, such as hallucinations, delusions, or loss of time–space orientation to appear (Ashback & Schermer, 1987, p. 46). Scheidlinger (1968) distinguishes between *group-formative* regressions, which are responses to the group interactive patterns (i.e., the members' manifestations of dependency as they orient themselves to a new group) and the *transferential expressions* of the individuals' earlier developmental modes of functioning.

The presence of other members enhances the possibilities for exposing a variety of relationships, thereby broadening the context in which the patient's intrapsychic problems can be examined. The group provides unique opportunities for development of parental (vertical) and sibling (horizontal) transferences. The value of the peers includes their representation not only as siblings but also as parental transferences. Initially peer displacements may be easier to analyze than more commonly identified therapist–parental transferences. Furthermore, the presence of peers means more affective stimuli to elicit associations, memories, and affect.

There is controversy as to the depth of the regression and transference that can occur in group psychoanalytic therapy. Therapists at one end of the continuum maintain that the group setting provides a special matrix in supporting the individuals and creating a safe environment, which along with all the stimuli of the other members enables an in-depth regression. At the other end, clinicians maintain that the presence of others and the need to share time is a significant limitation to the depth of the regression, and as a consequence a limitation to the depth of therapeutic benefit. Either possibility may account for the differences in transference and resistance observed in group and in dyadic therapy. However, the basic premises remain that significant transferences develop and that through interpretation of these transferences neurotic conflicts and character styles can be analyzed.

Exploration of genetic material is seen as crucial in helping patients develop thorough self understanding. According to Wolf and Schwartz (1962), the group analyst is not "concerned so much with the collective effort as he is with the emerging wholesome individual ego. He is not preoccupied with how the mystique of the group feels, an irrational projection, but with how the individual within the group thinks, feels, fantasizes, dreams and behaves" (p. 246). Thus, for these authors, the therapist in group psychoanalysis helps patients explore the latent motivation behind their current interaction: the here and now is suffused with the there and then, and the interpersonal is translated into the intrapsychic.

The group psychoanalyst interprets the nature of the unconscious processes among patients and between therapist and patient. The patients learn to understand the latent meaning of their interactions and make interpretations among themselves, thereby acting as auxiliary therapists. The therapist does not allow any single member to become the sole focus of the analytic action but shifts attention from one member to another. The analyst searches for transferential material or defensive operations he/she believes to be appropriate to work on at a certain time. He/she exercises judgment in these individual choices and pays less regard to the reactions of others. As

Wolf and Schwartz (1962) state, "If he didn't, he would fail to function effectively as an analyst" (p. 269).

Most contemporary psychoanalytic group therapists do not adhere exclusively to this individual-within-the group model but utilize their awareness of group dynamics to help explore issues that may be relevant to more than one individual.

General System Theory

In the past 25 years or so, many practitioners and theorists have found an incompleteness in psychodynamic theory and have explored a broader theoretical basis for understanding human behavior. This has led to the application of general system theory (GST) to group psychotherapy. The work of von Bertalanffy (1966) served as the foundation upon which to build GST as a new approach to the practice of group psychotherapy. GST provides a model for examining the interrelationships among the intrapsychic, interpersonal, group-as-a-whole, and social aspects of the treatment group.

A number of important assumptions make GST an attractive conceptual model. For example, GST maintains that though a wide diversity of form and behavior are exhibited by systems, fundamentally all systems possess a common underlying structure, *isomorphy*. Additionally, there are similarities in organizing processes, which are conceived of as self-organizing and are labeled *living structures*. (J. E. Durkin, 1981, p. 28). Further, GST holds that transformation or change takes place across boundaries that each system or subsystem can autonomously control.

GST is a growth or change theory, not a conflict or deficit theory. In GST transactions are seen as occurring across boundaries. The nature of these boundaries is a critical concern for GST (A. K. Rice, 1969). It is at the boundary level that attention should be paid, whether it be between group members and group members, group members and the leader, or even boundaries separating aspects of an individual. Boundaries must be permeable enough to take in and give out what is necessary, and yet impermeable enough to offer protection and separation. The opening of boundaries (e.g., to allow a transfer of information or emotion) is essential for the system (individual or group or any structure) to survive. Gaining the capacity to open and close boundaries appropriately is an important goal for members of groups. Thus group therapists should focus their attention on various levels of boundaries, depending upon which boundary is the focus at any given moment in the life of the group.

The therapist in GST is seen as a boundary regulator (though not the exclusive regulator—a group member could take on this role as well) and a boundary observer (Astrachan, 1970). Therapists monitor boundaries and make interventions that are appropriate to their diagnosis about the permeability or impermeability of boundaries.

Clearly, from this perspective the precise level at which therapists opt to intervene is related to their conceptualization along the lines described by the other psychodynamic theories. But GST provides a unifying approach that does not require a major shift of conceptual levels when moving from intrapsychic to group levels of inquiry and observation.

One of the problems tackled by GST theorists is that of energy exchange. The transmission of information and emotion across boundaries implies a shift of energy. Systems, in order to remain alive, must counter entropy, the process by which systems gradually become disorganized. Negentropy, the inherent self-organizing activity of systems, counters entropy and is fueled by energy shifting across boundaries. Although this aspect of the theory is incomplete, it suggests an avenue for exploring the flow of emotions that occurs in group situations.

Agazarian (1997) has applied systems thinking to clinical work with groups. She has emphasized the hierarchical nature of the system within which the group is embedded (the group-as-a-whole, subgroups, and the individual), and within that framework she conceptualizes the subgroup as the basic unit to be examined. For Agazarian, the major task is to increase communication across boundaries. She actively works to establish subgroups that will contain the splits inherent in individuals. Communication within and across the boundaries of the subgroup is the therapeutic focus: "*how* the group communicates is always more important than *what* it is communicating about" (Agazarian, 1989, p. 176; emphasis in original). Subgroups form naturally as an expression of the "inherent opposition to differences" (p. 191). Within "homogeneous" subgroups the therapist attempts to demonstrate that members can be alike and still be different. If differences are disruptive, then the clinician demonstrates the members' covert likenesses. These strategies open the boundaries (at individual, subgroup, and group-as-a-whole levels, as an example of isomorphism) for increased communication and understanding of resistances to learning about the walled-off aspects within the self.

RECENT INTEGRATIVE ADVANCES

Originally, group therapy was founded on established psychodynamic theories. However, those theories were based on dyadic practice. A great deal of attention has been given to the task of finding an authentic integration of individual and group therapy theory.

Group Psychodynamic Formulations

Efforts at integrating group and individual processes and theories are exemplified in the work of Helen E. Durkin (1964) and Henrietta T. Glatzer (1953). These authors focused upon the transferences and resistances in group psy-

chotherapy, utilizing the interactions that emerge to help clarify those phenomena. They took individual psychoanalytic theory and made initial inroads
in establishing a meaningful integration with group psychodynamics. According to these authors, in addition to transferences to individuals, transferences
to group phenomena exist as well. An example of the latter would be a situation where one patient is the focus of attention, which stimulates rivalrous
feelings in other members. Analysis of the transference or the resistance to
this sibling transference becomes the focus of the group's inquiry.

An additional integrative model has been proposed by James P.
Gustafson and Lowell Cooper (1979, 1992; see also Cooper & Gustafson,
1979a, 1979b; Gustafson et al., 1981) in a series of publications describing
"unconscious planning in small groups," which has more recently been re-
named the higher mental functioning hypothesis (HMFH; J. Weiss, Samson,
& the Mount Zion Psychotherapy Research Group, 1986; J. Weiss, 1993).
Elaborating the control mastery theory of Weiss et al. (1986), Gustafson and
Cooper propose a general theory integrating individual member behavior
and group dynamics. They posit that individuals enter into groups with unconscious and conscious expectations of what will be dangerous and what will
be protective. Patients execute a series of tests (their unconscious or preconscious plan) to determine if they will be traumatized in the present as they had
been in the past. If conditions of safety are met, they will risk exposing previously "withheld" information. In this process members align themselves with
subgroups that will provide safety. Gustafson and Cooper suggest that three
major plans are utilized: (1) *transferring* in which the therapist is treated as a
parent figure—the test is to determine if the clinician will behave differently
from the traumatizing parent; (2) *turning passive to active*—the test is to determine if the therapist, or another member, will have a more constructive solution than the patient initially had (thus growth takes place through identification); and (3) *remembering*—the test is to see if connections from the past can be
integrated into the patients' experience of internal continuity.

Inevitably clashes take place between subgroups when there are conflicting plans. The therapist must then steer between the two plans recognizing
the validity of both as necessarily arising from the individual member's historic past. For example, one member (representing a subgroup) might need to
idealize the therapist to test the degree of protection before risking an autonomous behavior, whereas another subgroup might need to maintain their
independence (test to determine if that is acceptable) before exposing their
wishes for caring from a parental figure.

The model is a growth model, and according to Gustafson and Cooper
can be applied to drive, object relations, or self psychological theories. Stone
(1996b) described the overlap between self psychology and the HMFH as
both theories stressing individuals' attempts through an "interpersonal" experience to change. Gustafson and Cooper believe that Bion's theories are a spe-

cial instance of conflicts between, for instance, basic assumption groups or between a basic assumption and a work group.

Hierarchical Integration

Integrative efforts have also been approached from the perspective of the group-as-a-whole. Kernberg (1975), who was heavily influenced by Bion's concepts about object relations, suggests that group-as-a-whole interventions address one developmental level of psychopathology—that of preoedipal development. In contrast, more individual transferences (and resistances) are at a more advanced level of object relations development, representing dyadic (envy) and triangular (oedipal) conflicts. Thus Kernberg posited that the group therapist may choose the intervention most appropriate to the group and individual levels of functioning.

A technical integration has been suggested by Horwitz (1977). Trained in a group-as-a-whole tradition, Horwitz modified his initial position and suggested that the group therapist conceptually must maintain a hierarchy of group-as-a-whole to interpersonal to intrapsychic formulations. With this in mind the therapist assesses the group members' abilities to examine their functioning within a group. Horwitz suggested that in most instances group members are emotionally able to understand comments about themselves before understanding comments relating to their relationships to the groupwide issues. This approach represents a technical advance because it highlights the need for collaboration and alliance between the group therapist and each individual group member. The more traditional group-as-a-whole approach does not sufficiently value or utilize the importance of the therapeutic alliance.

CONCLUSION

In general, group-as-a-whole theorists have highlighted authority (parental) relationships in contrast to the interpersonal theorists who have paid closer attention to peer (sibling) transactions. Relationships with both authorities and peers are obviously very important considerations in psychotherapy, and most patients referred to group psychotherapy have difficulty in each sphere. Therefore an integrative conceptualization is necessary for the psychodynamic group therapist.

The social structure of the group and the impact of the social forces must be kept in mind at all times. Just as in the world at large, individuals in groups exist within social systems, complete with leaders, followers, and colleagues. Furthermore, not only do the social forces affect and impact upon each individual in the group, but each individual in the group affects the group-as-a-whole. Thus the group therapist has the considerable task of keeping complex, interacting forces in mind. Sometimes the group-as-a-whole factors are the most significant (as, e.g., when a new member enters a group) because whenever the group's basic boundaries are changed or endangered, the entire group reacts and individuals are best helped by careful attention to the group-as-a-whole process. At other times the group-as-a-whole processes may fade into the background, though never disappear. We must always remember that, despite the powerful influence of the group dynamics, the job of the group therapist is to treat individuals who are seeking help, not groups. We choose to understand the forces within the social systems in order to maximally assist our individual patients. The uniqueness of each individual should never be lost in our eagerness to understand the workings of the group. The purpose of this book is to help the group therapist understand and harness the forces at work in a therapy group in order to move effectively across boundaries from group-as-a-whole to interpersonal to intrapsychic foci with proficiency, thereby taking advantage of the therapeutic power residing in therapy groups.

There will continue to be innovative shifts in emphasis as long as our understanding about human beings is broadened. Three primary considerations emerge from examining the diversity of approaches subsumed under psychodynamic group psychotherapy. First, there is an emphasis on the individual's internal life (the *intrapsychic*). This component examines the patient's character formation, typical defenses, problem-solving techniques, internal object relations, and so on. The second component is the *interpersonal,* which gains information from analyzing relational styles and deducing what internalized conflicts are replayed in the interpersonal field. This component includes inquiry about individual role, style, and externalization of the internal role through projection and projective identification. These are elements subsumed under Sullivan's term "parataxic distortions." Finally, the *sociopsychological* component is the broad context in which the group occurs, including but not limited to the social structure of the group. In this component the group-as-a-whole dynamics are explored, including group norms, values, assumptions, and restrictions. However, each is completely intertwined with the others.

THREE

Group Dynamics and Group Development

There was that law of life, so cruel and so just,
that one must grow or else pay more for
remaining the same.
—NORMAN MAILER, *The Deer Park*

Even a neophyte group therapist observing two groups, one having been in existence for three or four sessions and another for several years, would quickly be able to determine which is the older and functionally more mature group. A process has taken place that is the result of what are called group dynamics and group development. In this chapter we will address these two elements, which may be considered as the "basic sciences" of group formation and function.

GROUP DYNAMICS

Group dynamics, a term coined by Kurt Lewin, are the interacting forces that define how the whole group functions. When we refer to group dynamics we are viewing the group in its totality, and hence our perspective differs from one in which there is a summation of individual personal psychodynamics. A group is similar to a family, in which parents pass on to their children their personal values. This is not always a conscious process since the values are influenced by the subgroups and the culture to which the family belongs. As children grow they have an impact upon the parents' values. Family customs and attitudes evolve as children grow and their developmental requirements change. Children also influence their parents to change.

Group values and norms also evolve, and changes are observable in how members interact with one another or with the leader, what they find interesting, and what they ignore. Careful observation will show that some ideas are reinforced and others ignored. One group might report many dreams (if the therapist is a person known to have an extensive interest in dream analysis), and another group might focus on relationships among the members. The variations are countless, but they represent the norms and culture of the group. The group dynamic perspective explores the group as a social field in which elements of leadership, status, roles, structure, climate, standards, pressure, and communication are in interaction (H. E. Durkin, 1964). We now examine the elements of leadership, culture, and roles as central in the understanding of group dynamics and processes.

Leadership

Leadership can be understood from a social systems perspective as the responsibility for defining the tasks and goals of the group (Skolnick, 1992). Having determined the basic purpose of the group, the therapist defines the structure, time, place, frequency, duration, and size of the meetings. With these elements in mind, member selection and preparation can be made based on the availability of patients who may potentially be able to use the therapeutic processes compatible with the group tasks and goals. From a systems perspective, these tasks can be viewed as managing the external and internal group boundaries.

The leader's attention to internal group boundaries includes defining the nature of the relationships among members and with the therapist and how members are to proceed in order to achieve their (and the therapist's) goals. Many of these elements are spelled out in the group agreement (see Chapter 8) and include how communication will take place (in words not actions) and what level of communications will be addressed (conscious/unconscious). The boundaries among the members, subgroups, and with the therapist are also defined in order to optimize the therapeutic interactions (i.e., subgrouping among members should be openly discussed). One powerful aspect of the therapist's "education" is helping members consider their in-group experience as a microcosm of their external lives (Slater, 1966). This phenomenon is also described by Garland (1982), who attempts to have members take the so-called nonproblem ("non-problem" in Garland's paper) seriously; the term *nonproblem* here refers to members' reenactment of their problematic relationships within the group, which may differ from or replicate their complaints for which they sought treatment.

The structure of psychodynamic therapy groups, paradoxically, includes both strong direction and nondirection from the leader. Psychodynamic therapists tend to *follow* the group process rather than *initiate* it. The leader uses real authority in establishing viable therapeutic boundaries and mechanisms. However, within that therapeutic framework, the leader invokes a nondirective leadership role that enhances regressive fantasies and projections. Group leaders become objects of members' fantasies. According to Wilfred R. Bion (see Chapter 2), affective responses to the therapist evoke dependency, fight–flight, and/or pairing basic assumption behavior. In a regressed state, members experience and respond to their therapist in polarities: benevolent/malevolent, faultless/flawed, omnipotent/powerless, or omniscient/unknowing. They communicate with the therapist through projective processes, subjecting him/her to powerful feelings such as hate, envy, or love. The therapist's role includes containing and internally processing (metabolizing) these powerful affects in order to use them for therapeutic purposes.

A major role task is management of boundaries. The challenge for the therapist is creating flexible boundaries that can ensure the integrity of the group but are not so loose that structure and safety are sacrificed. Generally there is little negotiation regarding external functions and structure. The therapist initiates the agreements regarding group structure, and the patients accept them as a precondition for group membership. While external events or situations may result in these agreements changing, it is up to the therapist to enact these changes. Norms and values change as a group matures, and the manner in which members address the group boundaries become more flexible in more advanced groups.

Newton (1973) compares the therapist's tasks to those of a parent, and by extension he views the parental role as an opportunity for particular transference configurations. He asserts that paternal transference is evoked by the therapist's role of managing the external relationships–providing a safe space. Maternal transference is evoked by the internal group tasks–monitoring relationships among members and with the therapist. Thus, the dynamics and structure of the group are conceptualized as influencing the emergence of transference, which is not solely a response to the gender of the clinician.

Group Culture and Norms

In the course of time, particular ways of handling conflicts or affects become ingrained within the interactional patterns of groups. Groups develop particular kinds of culture, which help define what individuals can and cannot do as well as how they express themselves or deal with affects.

For example, two beginning phase groups may attend to the issues of joining in quite different ways. The members in the first group look to the therapist for solutions to the problems of joining, whereas members in the other talk primarily to one another and ignore the therapist. These represent

two differing group cultures; members are negotiating the same tasks of joining and forming a group but are doing so in different ways. The study of a
group culture helps define how the members relate to one another, to the
therapist, and to the group. It is a way of viewing the organization of the
group. Every group develops norms (both conscious and unconscious) regarding appropriate behavior. These norms begin with the expectations of the
members and the therapist.

Because the therapist serves as a regulator of the group boundaries and
initially defines what is of interest to the group (Astrachan, 1970), he/she is a
powerful contributor to group culture. For leaders who focus on the here and
now and the affects raised in the therapy room, a description of a childhood
event would be a distraction; and, soon, members would no longer relate
childhood events. For therapists who value the metaphorical value of a childhood story, such a memory might throw light on group dynamics in the immediate setting. Such a therapist might delight in hearing such a story from
childhood and thereby reinforce the likelihood that other members would
share comparable stories from their pasts. For a therapist who values the place
of genetic exploration, this might represent an important piece of personal
work. Since the therapist is a potent initiator of group norms, reinforcement
through interest or noninterference serves to establish appropriate ways of interacting within the group. Often a dichotomy exits between therapists who
emphasize transferences to the leader, thereby helping individuals learn of
these inner fantasies, and therapists who focus on peer transactions, which
highlight the learning of social skills and the giving and receiving of feedback
but diminish exploration of the unconscious (E. Klein & Astrachan, 1971).
Groups led by therapists from these different theoretical positions might be
equally effective, but they would carry on their work quite differently.

The therapist is not solely responsible for normative behavior and the
subsequent group culture. The individuals who constitute the group are constantly changing and altering ways in which norms are expressed. These are
not usually major changes because, once established, norms are rather difficult to alter. In a study of T-groups, Lieberman, Yalom, and Miles (1973)
found the expectations that members brought with them were a powerful set
of constraints that were unlikely to be reversed in the actual state of affairs.
Furthermore, in determining eventual outcome, the impact of the individual
upon the group norms is as potent as the leader's.[1] Recognition of norms and
the resultant culture provides another perspective for the therapist to begin
exploration of the members' personalities and to understand differences in
group development.

As the group culture develops there are forces operating that lead to co-

---

[1] Since this was a study of groups limited to 30 hours' duration, the opportunity to alter the norms
through analysis of groupwide and individual resistances was diminished.

hesion or lead to dispersal. The attractiveness and sense of belonging to a particular culture has been labeled group cohesion (Day, 1981). The ability of a group to influence behavior and, indeed, for members to identify with its values and goals is in part a product of its attractiveness. Unfortunately group cohesion has been thought of as a static phenomenon, whereas in truth it is dynamic and changing. What might make a group attractive in a beginning developmental stage (e.g., sharing stories of outside experiences) would be seen as a distraction for a mature-phase group. Implicit in the notion of cohesion is a basic trust that members will not willfully injure other members and that there will be an effort to understand others' inner world and their interactions. This formulation is the group equivalent to the holding environment in dyadic therapy (Winnicott, 1965). Developmental progress is signaled by members' capacities to recognize individual differences and idiosyncrasies, a recognition which increases group attractiveness. Patients learn to hear what others are feeling and experiencing, even if it differs from their own perceptions. Put simply, a member might ask, "Where else can I go and have emotionally meaningful exchanges in an atmosphere where I can trust and be trusted?"

Roles

In business an owner hires others and assigns tasks for them. These may be specialized functions such as factory worker, salesperson, advertising executive, and so on. In the beginning the only clear function (role) in a therapy group is that of therapist. As groups develop, specialized functions emerge that serve to manage the emotional and work tasks. This was noticed very early by Benne and Sheats (1948), who classified three types of group roles: task roles, maintenance roles, and ego-centered roles. As in business, some individuals have particular talents to fill specific roles that successfully interact with the group culture and norms. Others are "assigned" roles that fail to fulfill their own personal needs but may serve the group (Astrachan, 1970). When the concept of role is used to describe behaviors in a therapy group, it is important to distinguish between specialized functions within the group itself and characteristic behavioral patterns of a particular individual. The fact that groups often typecast their participants, using personal roles to fill certain group functions, simply confuses the matter further.

Examined from the perspective of the whole group, roles serve both emotional and task functions. Some roles seem to facilitate the group effort to work on problems by encouraging exploration of affect or important topics. Others serve to maintain restrictive culture and norms (Benne & Sheats, 1948). A host of specific titles may be assigned to the roles, but basically a groupwide function is being addressed. MacKenzie (1990) condenses the multitude of labels into the following four roles:

1. The *structural* role focuses on understanding the group tasks and is primarily a leadership role. Some individuals who enter treatment with a history of skilled leadership may serve the group effectively, whereas others may demonstrate ineffective (e.g., overly controlling or dominating) leadership. Some members gradually learn how to adopt leadership roles and benefit from these skills in their lives outside the group.

2. The person occupying the *sociable* role is one who is attuned to the quality of feelings in interpersonal relationships. These individuals tend to regulate the amount and kind of affect. For example, group affect can be modified or lessened by certain types of humor and joking. Such functions can facilitate or inhibit group movement. Too much feeling may overwhelm and fragment the group; too little feeling may produce a group that becomes stuck intellectualizing. Members certainly are capable of accurate empathy, labeling emotions, or merely inquiring for more direct expression of feelings, which serve to move the group forward. However, the individual who characteristically quashes emotions may not serve a group function and may be forced into another role—that of deviant or scapegoat.

3. The *divergent* role most often is associated with a scapegoat, which is unfortunate because this role serves a very valuable function of providing differing perspectives. This is the oppositional or rebellious person who does not ordinarily comply with group norms or values. It becomes apparent that all persons have such affects, and indeed one of the core conflicts of entering a group is that of joining while still maintaining one's own values. The deviant role serves the therapeutic function of potentially bringing to the fore oppositional, rebellious, or deviant emotions or ideas for examination. It would be a dull and nontherapeutic group indeed if everyone agreed! The role carries a danger to the individual, who may be scapegoated and extruded. The group then loses the potential for examining hidden or "unacceptable" aspects of its membership. The leader in such a situation has an important role in helping the group understand that the scapegoat is expressing universal, though perhaps unacceptable, feelings. Further, it is important that the leader help the group understand that the scapegoat is fundamentally trying to protect and help the group, albeit in a way that may not be productive.

4. The *cautionary* role is often first identified in the silent person. All of us have secrets and fears that we wish to keep private. From that perspective the function of this role becomes clear. The cautionary member demonstrates the potential humiliation and shame that is possible in any interpersonal encounter. While the cautionary member is less likely to be scapegoated and extruded than the deviant member, he/she may end up being ignored. Attention to the group function being served by this individual may help free members to risk sharing shameful or guilt ridden aspects of themselves.

It is important to understand that groups might use a particular individual in a specific role or several individuals might be required to fill the function. For instance, in a situation where intense emotion is present, the group members may regulate the intensity through joking, direct soothing, or diverting. It is the function that is important, rather than the individual or perhaps even the specific mode. On occasion, under intense affective stimulation a person might (unconsciously) be called upon to fill a role that is quite alien; this process is labeled "role suction" by Redl (1963).

Members enter a group with their own specific repertoire of roles, which they have used in other life situations. Albert Einstein is reputed to have once mused that "insanity is using the same process repeatedly in the fond hope that the results will be different." Only rarely are roles generated solely by group processes. One of the purposes of gaining personal historical information is for the therapist and patient to become aware of these stereotypic patterns. However, it is not unusual for an individual to take on a role with past determinants unknown to either patient or therapist. When this happens, the opportunity for therapeutic gain is great, since unconscious conflicts are observable in current behavior.

To illustrate overlapping between groups and individual behaviors, we can look at common early group behaviors. Often one or more "hosts" or "hostesses" will initiate the introductions and will fill up silences. This function may become "assigned" to one person who will routinely handle affects surrounding newness, beginnings, or silences, or the role may be divided among a few individuals. Individuals who routinely accept the host and hostess role may come to this role from a variety of sources. It may be a lifelong pattern of bearing the emotional burden of their families, or it could represent exhibitionistic needs to be the center of attention no matter what the psychic cost, or perhaps a need to be the favorite child in the family. Whatever the derivation of the role, it is generally quite facilitative to the beginning group.

Often some members are essentially mute in the initial meetings. Their silence also is not a new behavior generated specifically for this difficult situation (Gans & Counselman, 2000). Individuals bring out habitual responses of silence to cope with this new stress. Again, the source of this behavior can be quite diverse: It may represent a passive–aggressive position, commanding attention through the power of passivity. It may be the youngest sibling once again playing out the role of waiting until last to be fed. It may represent a chronic altruism, an assumption that the needs of others must come first. It may represent a martyr role. Or, of course, it could be the manifestation of terror in this interpersonal arena.

Another subset of behaviors, often labeled roles, are unique to an individual's character (Benne & Sheats, 1948). These behaviors satisfy individual needs and are fundamentally irrelevant to the group development, but they may become a dominant force operating within the group. Individuals who take on these roles are viewed negatively, and members often have a strong wish to extrude them from the group. These roles include the monopolizer, the help-rejecting complainer, the naive one, the supplicant, and the playboy.

The therapeutic management of some of these roles will be discussed later in this book.

Of course, not every behavioral pattern or role is self-destructive or pathological. At root all such behaviors are adaptive and serve some purpose. The therapist needs to discriminate between the useful and adaptive aspects of these roles for the individuals themselves and the potentially destructive and constraining aspects of these roles for the group. The same role can be both healthy and, if pushed to an extreme, pathological. Moreover, the group therapist needs to alternate continually between the group and the individual developmental perspectives (see Chapter 9). A role that may be productive for the group may be constricting for the individual, and vice versa. A balance must be struck as to which aspect to explore and in what order so as to maximize the therapeutic effectiveness of the group for all members.

GROUP DEVELOPMENT

Understanding the broad outlines of predictable group evolution, complete with the tasks involved in the various stages of that evolution, provides an anchor for the therapist. Just as a knowledgeable individual therapist can gain a deeper understanding of his patients' ideas and associations by having an appreciation for the developmental levels and the associated tasks for individuals as they grow, so group therapists are helped by an understanding of the usual stages of group development. However, groups, like individuals, do not move forward in a linear fashion: they are subject to forward and backward movement. Furthermore, these fluctuations do not take place automatically or by any set timetable.

Not everyone endorses the concept of development within groups. Slavson (1957) attempted to expunge group processes from psychotherapeutic groups; he focused purely on interpersonal interactive processes. Slavson's position represents an effort to transpose classical dyadic psychoanalytic concepts (transference and resistance) into the group psychotherapy settings. By linking group interaction closely to dyadic therapy, Slavson and others (see A. Wolf & Schwartz, 1962) stressed the continuity of psychodynamic/psychoanalytic concepts. This historic bridge made group therapy acceptable, if not attractive, to the mainstream of the American psychotherapeutic community.

Most of what we know about group development emerged from studies of time-limited, closed-membership groups (Bennis & Shepard, 1956; Tuckman, 1965). Generalization of these ideas to ongoing, open-membership psychotherapy groups has often been done indiscriminately. There is overlap, but the two situations are not identical. For instance, a psychotherapy group has only one actual beginning. Yet, with each addition of one or more new members there is a modified new beginning, usually accompanied by reemergence of themes and modes of relating similar to those at the time of the initial sessions. Moreover, events inside or outside an ongoing group may set off recrudescence of power struggles characteristic of the second phase of development. The repetition of various developmental phases provides an opportunity to rework previously traversed ground, sometimes in greater depth and with increased insight, and therefore has considerable therapeutic potential.

Group development is a product of the individual members, their interactions among themselves and with the therapist. Accurate assessment of the developmental level of groupwide functioning can aid the therapist in assessing the progress patients may be making. For example, less advanced patients may make major gains while working on the early issues of joining, trust building, and belonging to a group. A group of such patients will likely remain at early levels of development for prolonged periods, which would be quite beneficial to that population. Consistent movement to the next level would indicate an important achievement. Patients who have conflicts at a more advanced developmental level often make less therapeutic gain at early levels of group development. If healthier patients were to remain stuck for a prolonged period in an early stage of group development, this would constitute a case of either misdiagnosis or significant problems of transference or countertransference.

Thus far no schema describing group development has been able to do justice to the complexity of internal fantasies and behavioral transactions that occur when a small group of individuals organize and begin to work together. The tradition of linking individual psychodynamics of oral, anal, and phallic development to similar phases of group development (Savaray, 1975; Gibbard & Hartman, 1973) does not do justice to the complex phenomena. A somewhat more complete model linking the two fundamental elements present in a successful group—attaining a goal and attending to members' emotional needs—is present in Bion's model of group functioning. The *basic assumption* group is one in which the members are responding primarily to their emotional needs. In contrast the *work group* is rational and functions to achieve goals. This model is more descriptive than developmental. The group focal conflict model takes into account development in the formulation of restrictive and enabling solutions, which are fueled by conscious and unconscious emotional needs of the members.

As discussed in Chapter 2, some therapists reify group development and focus on little else. The stages of development, however, are best used as indicators to help the therapist more fully understand what is going on in the group. One stage is not inherently more valuable than another. A common misconception among therapists is that in order to have a "good" group, it is imperative that the group attain and maintain the most advanced developmental level. For many patients this would be asking the impossible. Rather, there should be a reasonable fit between the level of group development and the dynamic issues salient for the members.

Group development can be seen as occurring in four phases: reactions to joining and forming the group, reactions to feelings of belonging, the stabilization of the mature working group, and separation/termination. Therapists need to remember that the ultimate goals of therapy—improved intrapsychic functioning and self-learning—can occur during any of these four stages. Keep in mind that these are schematic presentations; only careful study of the processes and the individuals in each particular group will provide the base for meaningful therapeutic change.

Stage 1: The Formative Phase

The overriding characteristic of the formative phase is the members' unique responses to the emotional and work aspects of group formations. Within expectable variations, members try to orient themselves to the task of learning the ground rules for making group therapy work. Each member will attempt to establish a level of intimacy that has been historically safe, and levels will vary dramatically among members. The themes then revolve around gaining information—asking the leader or inquiring among peers to see if there is an expert on how to make the group work. When such information is not readily forthcoming, which it never is, self-protective mechanisms and reactions to frustration are manifest. The frustration and ambiguity inherent in the task exert a regressive pull upon the members. The emotions stimulated by this situation then dovetail as all the members struggle to form a group that feels safe enough for them to do their work.

There have been a plethora of contributors to understanding group formation. Yalom (1975) labeled this first phase "orientation, hesitant participation, and search for meaning" (p. 303) Hill and Grunner (1972), Fried (1971), and Schutz (1958) have stressed the issue of inclusion. Those espousing a psychoanalytic framework (Bennis & Shepard, 1956) emphasize the dependency aspects in this initial phase. Savaray (1975) likened this early phase to that seen in the childhood progression of oral drives. Day (1981) emphasized both the patients' dependency needs and their inevitable competition with one another during this initial phase. Slater (1966) suggested that the main concern of the new group is the fear of being controlled or engulfed by the group, and thus he viewed the deification of the leader as the normative and characteristic response. Common to all the contributors is the notion that a series of expected processes routinely take place in a new group, processes involved in the task of joining and forming a group.

A major task facing patients is orienting themselves through trial and error to see what will be useful and safe. Every member approaches this task with his/her own personal history, developmental needs, and conflicts. Still, there are some common experiences in our culture. Growing up has provided each person with prior experiences in small groups, beginning with the family and then continuing in schools and a host of religious, business, or social institutions.

In psychodynamic group therapy clues regarding how to proceed are purposefully minimized, leaving the members, either in a newly formed group or as entrants into an ongoing group, in the emotional position analogous to that of meeting strangers. All the usual concerns about trust and safety, quite appropriately, are central in the minds of the participants.

When the task at hand includes sharing the most intimate details (and secrets!) about one's life, the stakes are very high. Revealing these data implies loosening one's personal boundaries and trusting that they can be reestablished. However, fears are often expressed that boundaries, autonomy or the "self" will be lost in the group. Joining stimulates each person's conflicts between, on the one hand, wishes to belong and the implied surrendering elements of his/her individuality and, on the other, the desire to maintain complete control of him-/herself, which carries with it the potential for feeling isolated and alone.

Members' anxieties are further stimulated by the relatively unstructured, ambiguous situation, creating a situation rife with possibilities to evoke regression. Each member tends to regress to a personally important developmental stage, and his/her response in the group may represent either a successfully or an unsuccessfully completed task. The regression induced in this situation is clinically useful to the therapist in gaining understanding of a member's manner of managing anxiety.

While it is expected that patients will regress when they join a group, it should not be expected that all patients will respond to this regression identically. For some this is a time for gaining insight into the nature of their relationship to their parents, since many patients respond to joining primarily in terms of feeling dependent, helpless, and confused. Perhaps most patients, due to the interpersonal nature of group psychotherapy, turn away from the therapist and approach peers in their efforts to determine the best way to proceed. These patients are often mislabeled as counterdependent. Such processes often replicate important aspects of members' relationships to their parents and demonstrate important transferential reactions to the therapist. Others regress to developmental stages of fear, self-dissolution, annihilation, or intense desire for merger and engulfment, along with the consequent response of fight–flight behaviors.

The very processes that set regression in motion also contain the seeds for solutions. Gustafson and Cooper (1979) assert that members enter a group planning a series of tests. These tests, containing both conscious and unconscious elements, revolve around the individual's anxiety: will he/she again be traumatized by the group as happened in early childhood or with significant others in the past? Patients are not only testing, they are actively trying to master and resolve earlier conflicts around trust and safety.

Typically, new members look to the therapist to determine how they should proceed, what they should talk about, and what behavior is "good" group behavior. The same information may be sought from peers. Common questions are addressed (though not always overtly): What information is relevant? Are past events significant or do we just focus on what happens in the meeting? How do outside relationships fit in with what is happening here? How far can we take these relationships after the therapy hour ends? Am I expected to share all my secrets with these people? These and many other questions generally produce interaction among members, stimulating a variety of opinions and conflicts. Affects are stirred, and how these affects are managed becomes embedded in the group norms as well as providing valuable therapeutic information. Some members may not be ready to face angry encounters and therefore may establish a norm, "Let's be friendly and not angry." Others may not be ready to face intimacy and prefer a norm of angry, confrontational exchanges. One individual may fill a sociable role by joking whenever angry feelings are likely to erupt. Another might shift the topic of discussion. Allowing these patterned distractions by the other members indicates that a group norm is operating.

Patients not only ask questions, they also tell about themselves and their experiences. Under the pressure of getting to know one another and the anxiety about how to proceed, patients usually "tell their story" (often demonstrating through behavior rather than reciting verbally), including informing the group about why they have come and what they hope to gain. This may take the form of a "go-around," with one member acting as the conductor. Patients experience intense pressure to conform, and seldom will they refuse to tell something about themselves. They might tell about anxiety-laden or frustrating situations they have encountered or are encountering. These stories also should be heard as unconscious metaphors for the individual's experience of being in the meeting.

Patients reveal themselves both verbally and nonverbally. Many therapists emphasize the members' need to tell their story, but exclusive focus on verbalization misses significant information about a person that emerges in the manner in which he/she interacts. Members relive their difficulties and demonstrate their maladaptive styles. They reenact rather than recollect. For example, a member might feel envious of the attention received by a member's particularly engaging story and respond by becoming competitive, destructively envious, or withdrawn. These responses, labeled enactments, often are outside the individual's awareness, but their presence provides an avenue to gaining self-understanding.

The anxiety and apprehension regarding the formation phase also represent the first commonly shared experience of the group. Everyone (including the therapist) approaches the unknown with his/her own internal fantasies and his/her own mechanisms of defense and mastery. This is particularly true before the first meeting of a new group. Since there is no reality for this group as yet, there can only be fantasies. The sharing of anxieties represents the first in-group experience of being involved and less isolated; and it represents a beginning step for experientially based group cohesion. For the individual joining an ongoing group, the same is true because the veteran members observe and perceive the new member's anxiety and are reminded of their own initial anxieties upon entering the group. They also have their own anxieties about meeting a stranger. As those anxieties are shared, a common beginning point is again forged.

An important task that patients need to accomplish is the development of a sense of basic trust in both themselves and others. Slater (1966) observes that groups go through cycles in which members exhibit their conflicts at progressively deeper levels. Trust at each level is necessary before threatening information is revealed. Some individuals with early developmental conflicts may verbalize their distrust and appear to have made gains managing their feelings only to have another's absence expose a deeper level of the same anxieties. Members may express their problems verbally or behaviorally. The therapeutic opportunities afforded by these experiences inherent in the working-through process are detailed in Chapter 4.

Members try to determine the optimal anxiety-free way of entering a group. They want to do it "right." Yet, it is hard to join a group "wrong," since whatever happens becomes a part of the group history. Whatever a new member does in an attempt to join is clinically relevant because it represents an opportunity for learning. No patient generates totally new behavior just for this situation.

The therapist, acting to help establish the most therapeutic environment, contributes to the process through keeping the group alert to the goals and by attending to members' and the groupwide emotional climate. As we will discuss in Chapter 5, the therapist's actions and nonactions are often used by members as behavior models with which they can identify. These identifications may lessen anxiety and promote openness and directness as a desirable group norm. Such norms become fully established only as they are experientially validated.

The following brief examples illustrate ways members of a newly forming group manage and communicate their initial anxieties.

CLINICAL EXAMPLE

A new group met for the first time. Seven of the eight members were present on time and they began anxiously introducing themselves. They each alluded to how difficult it had been to get to the group on time, some citing work conflicts and others citing traffic problems. About 10 minutes into the group, Allen, the final member, arrived. His entrance was noisy and intrusive, as he stood in the middle of the group and carefully took off his coat, arranged it neatly on the floor beside his chair, took off his beeper and placed it conspicuously on the floor as if he were expecting a call. After this ritual he sat down and said, "Sorry I'm late. I was in an important meeting. What did I miss?"

*   *   *

Allen was the youngest—by some 10 years—in his family. He experienced his entrance into the family as an unwelcome intrusion, not only by his siblings but by his parents, who routinely reminded him that he was a "mistake." His late arrival in the group not only replicated his "late" entrance into his family, it set the stage for the group to respond to him in much the same way as his family had. His entrance was a very important communication about central aspects of his personality.

CLINICAL EXAMPLE

A group that had met only a few weeks began one meeting with a period of silence. The silence was broken by one member telling about a recent vacation in which he was learning to ski. He had found it a frightening experience, both because of the novelty of the sport for him and because of the various stories he had heard about skiers breaking bones. Moreover, he was quick to point out, the instructor had given them too difficult a slope to begin with, and in general had done such a poor job that many of the class had quit.

*   *   *

This vignette highlights the anxiety of the new group enterprise, adding the specific fear of being injured. The blame for this traumatic experience is placed directly on the instructor's (therapist's) shoulders for picking too difficult and dangerous a task and for not instructing them properly in advance. An implicit threat to quit was present. One could imagine a new group getting caught up with such a story and giving advice such as "change instructors" or "choose a less steep hill." Indeed advice giving is a characteristic of early group formation. Yet another response from the group might have been for the other members to begin associating to similarly harrowing experiences in their own lives or to comparable times of insufficient instruction or assistance. If the members were particularly insightful, they might see the metaphorical aspects of the story and begin discussing their fears in the group and their concern with the amount of preparation that they were or were not receiving from their therapist.

Depending upon their theoretical orientation, different group therapists might handle this early group vignette quite differently. A therapist who wants the norm to be that the member will examine *only* the in-group interactions might point out that the member had taken the focus outside the room. For this therapist the member's story is a resistance, and he/she would exert pressure for members not to talk about events outside the group itself.

A psychodynamic therapist, on the other hand, might welcome such a sharing as a metaphor for the patient's feelings within the group itself, complete with references to the perceived danger of the new venture and questions about the skill of the leader. By linking the story to possible groupwide feelings, the therapist helps set the norm of curiosity about potential deeper meanings of communications, placing out-of-group and in-group events in juxtaposition with each offering possible elaboration and insight into the other. Yet other therapists, still within a psychodynamic frame of reference, might understand the member's sharing in the manner suggested but decide to make no comment at all. That approach serves to enhance the members' dependence upon one another for input and sharing. If the discussion felt positive and the members seemed to enjoy the interchange, they might feel more positively about the group, thereby enhancing cohesion. By keeping the overt input of the therapist to a minimum, the opportunities for the patients to make assumptions about the therapist's point of view based on their own history and basic assumptions are enhanced.

The therapist's role in the formative stage, as in all phases of group development, is to help establish useful norms so that the members feel safe enough to be spontaneous in their participation. Then his/her role is to help the members learn from their feelings, behaviors, reactions, and memories so that they may resolve their interpersonal and intrapsychic difficulties.

The therapist and members all contribute to the movement from one phase to the next. The resolution of conflicts over joining is never complete, and a variety of stimuli or stress may reactivate conflicts over belonging. Nevertheless, transition to the second phase becomes manifest when issues of trust diminish and reactions to belonging are prominent.

Stage 2: The Reactive Phase

If in the formative phase the focus was on joining and finding commonalities, in the second phase of development members are preoccupied with their reactions to belonging to the group. In the reactive phase the individuality of each person becomes more apparent and important as members try to determine how they can retain or develop their own identities and remain members of a group. They may react to their experiences of the group, the therapist or to fellow members, either in response to particular "noxious" characteristics or as displacements from the therapist.

This phase is characterized by emotional outbursts and unevenness of commitment to the group. The norms that arose in the initial phase are now tested and modified. The group agreements will be tested. This is a time when members often arrive late or not at all, threaten to quit or actually do so, or become tardy in payment of their bills. The therapist's competence is severely and at times aggressively questioned. Emotionality is rampant, making it difficult for members to think clearly and rationally; obvious distortions in perception occur, and members experience transactions within the group as controlling, demanding, or otherwise injurious. Anger and sadness, two of the affects most accepted in our culture, are expressed and shared.

Some authors (e.g., Gustafson & Cooper, 1979; MacKenzie, 1994) have suggested that rebellion is characteristic of this phase. Schutz (1958) noted that individuals seem to share a common purpose of maintaining control, and he labeled this phase as one of "power." Authors (e.g., Savaray, 1975) emphasizing the comparison between group and individual development refer to the anal quality of the transactions during this phase; that is, transactions are characterized by alternating withholding and outbursts. Tuckman (1965) succinctly labeled this the "storming" phase.

The tasks of this phase revolve around moving from a sense of "we-ness" to a sense of belongingness that includes "I-ness." As with the growing child, members often react as if they are saying "Me do it!" Yet, just as with the child, this should never be interpreted as a wish to no longer belong to the family. Members are freeing themselves from the enthrallment with the therapist and the group. The honeymoon has ended. Early norms are now experienced as rigid and inflexible. Members try to exert their individual mark upon the group by testing how far they can bend, break, or more constructively alter the norms. Other individuals are not seen as having their own needs or wishes but are viewed as exerting control and power. It is during this phase that many patients experience their presenting problems most powerfully within the sessions. This is often a painful reality for the patients, and we frequently hear comments such as, "This group is no different from my family!" or "Why should I stay here? I have as much trouble talking in here as I do in the world outside!" It is important that therapists help patients understand that the change in attitudes about membership during this phase is very helpful for their therapy, since therapy groups are much more effective when individuals are actually experiencing their problems within the group itself.

It is common in this phase for one or more members to abruptly threaten to quit while vigorously complaining either about the therapist or the group for not meeting their expectations. Typical complaints are "This group won't solve my problems!," "Everything is so superficial—nothing is happening," or "These people are not all like me." Sometimes, the therapist is labeled incompetent, uninvolved, or disinterested. These members are not only expressing their own concerns but are also voicing groupwide fears. The threat to quit may represent an expression of the control/helplessness affects of this phase. The disaffected member accuses the others of discussing trivial or irrelevant issues, and the threat to drop out is an effort to control and change the direction of the meeting. Such protests may also represent a test to determine how safe it is to express such feelings. However, these protests may reach such a level of intensity that for a time it appears that the group may dissolve.

The reemergence within the therapy of early internalizing styles of object relationships enables members to learn a great deal regarding their developmental problems and tasks. There can be very important congruencies between individual development and group development, and the growth potential stimulated in this rebellious/differentiation phase is very important in helping individuals resolve comparable problems in their individual development. Fried (1970) distinguished among various types of anger shown in groups. One type is the anger shown in response to disappointment and hurt. Another, very salient to this developmental phase, is the equivalent to normal assertiveness.

Patients' historic patterns of handling angry feelings, whether originating within themselves or coming from others, are characteristically exposed during this phase. For some patients regressive processes expose deeply buried character problems not apparent earlier. These persons may lead group destructive processes (Nitsun, 1996).

Not all patients experience or demonstrate overt anger, rebelliousness, or assertiveness. For some the emotional response is withdrawal, passivity, and compliance. Many patients do not have direct access to more active forms of aggression and use passive aggression instead. For these individuals crucial developmental tasks may be accomplished during this phase as they learn to balance anger and withdrawal with assertiveness and compromise.

Powerful group processes affect individuals in this phase. The rebellion or hostility may be concentrated exclusively in one or two "difficult" individuals, and the remaining members may seem peaceful and even scornful of the troublesome ones. Often the difficult member is the spokesperson for similar affects felt by others, and the therapist must never assume that quieter members do not share the affects verbalized by the more overtly troublesome member. Indeed, the hostility may be increased or aggravated in the rebellious member as the others unconsciously project their feelings into him/her and disown the feelings themselves. This is the commonly observed process of projective identification and reflects how group process is capable of creating difficult members (Gans & Alonso, 1998).

A converse situation arises when the anger is not universally shared. In order to maintain the appearance of togetherness, thereby protecting against retaliation or rejection, angry members try to recruit others to their point of view. Powerful forces for conformity are unleashed under these conditions.

This is also a time of conflict among members. Some of their fighting may be a displacement of anger felt toward the leader, because in our society hostility and assertiveness is more condoned when directed toward peers rather than toward authorities. And some of the fighting may be to demonstrate who among the members is the most powerful. Although culturally these power struggles are generally thought to take place among men, careful observation will reveal that women are either encouraging the men, or, as shifts in the tenor of gender relations have recently evolved, women may now actively enter into the fray.

Not every group has a volatile storming period, just as not all 2-year-olds are "terrible 2's." Theories of development offer guidelines based upon common behaviors seen in many groups. But groups go about the tasks involved in development according to the unique mix of individuals, not according to an inexorable set of unvarying steps. If a group were not experiencing the storming phase overtly, its therapist would be mistaken should he/she persist in viewing this as a sign of grave dysfunction.

Nonetheless, most groups do seem to move from a stage of giving information, advice, or opinions to a stage of exploring emotional reactions within the meeting. They seem to move from a stage when the members are preoccupied with belonging, of developing we-ness, to being preoccupied with themselves as individuals, competing to have their needs met. In the emotional transactions that occur in this period, members bond to one another in much more authentic ways than had been possible before. This is vitally important if groups are to gain maturity, where the curative factors are predominantly within the membership and not the leader.

The therapist's tasks in this phase are different than in the formative stage. Not only is the therapist personally challenged, but the entire enterprise is often depreciated as members try to free themselves from what they perceive as the domination and imprisonment of the group. The clinician needs to appreciate that this is a developmental phase and reflects members' transferences to their experience of restrictive group norms. Norms may be concretized in the image of the group, the leader, or peers.

The therapist must appreciate that fundamentally members are not intent on destroying the group. Rather, they are insistent in asserting their individuality. The group dynamic of using one or more receptive members as carriers of the critical or rebellious feelings creates an atmosphere conducive to group-destructive processes. The therapeutic task is to avoid the temptation to focus on individual dynamics or transference. Rather, the clinician tries to engage others in expressing feelings carried by the scapegoat. They are helped to reown disavowed aspects of themselves.

CLINICAL EXAMPLE

A group of eight members had been meeting for about 3 months. They had proceeded along an expectable path in forming a group, working on trust and openness, and beginning to address intragroup differences. Attendance had been excellent, with members arriving promptly. However, signs of difficulty were emerging, as in each of the two sessions prior to the one to be described a member failed to attend without notice.

On this evening, all members were present, although Joan arrived 10 minutes late. She apologized for her tardiness. Bill, who had missed the preceding session, began by saying that he had attended a golf outing for work. Ruth immediately followed by recounting a recent experience of attending advanced administrative training for her job and getting into conflict with the faculty because of their rigid rules. Several members commiserated with her, and they wondered why she would remain in a job that seemed so controlling and unsatisfactory.

At that point, Hank vociferously complained about the group. He said that all they talked about was superficial things. Hank complained that the group therapist did nothing to help, and the group seemed to just go in circles. Martha said she had talked with Hank about this after the last two meetings. They had gone for coffee, and she agreed that they seemed not to be getting anywhere. Joan said she had been asked to join Martha and Hank, but she had needed to go home.

The therapist wondered if some of what had taken place in the group was a reflection of members' dissatisfaction with the group. Perhaps Ruth's story about the inflexible rules at her conference was a communication about similar feelings about the group.

Ruth replied that there were a lot of feelings about what happened in the group, and that it was very helpful to talk with Hank after the meeting. Another member wondered if Hank was thinking about quitting the group. Hank responded that he didn't know, but the group was not being helpful.

*   *   *

This vignette illustrates some of the manifestations of a group rebellion. The theme of resentment at what are perceived as strict rules is clearly articulated by Ruth. Hank is more direct about the failure of the group to meet his needs, and indeed he had acted on his dissatisfaction by forming a subgroup with Martha and by maintaining secrecy, clearly altering the group boundary.[2] Joan's failure to discuss this in the group points to her collusion in the process.

Other data suggesting that the group was protesting the developing norms of being on time and examining reasons for missing a meeting were apparent in the failure to explore the choices involved in Bill's decision to go golfing or Joan's lateness to the session. The potential for Hank being seen as uncooperative and the "wish" to extrude a troublesome person was expressed by a member's inquiry as to whether Hank was going to quit the group. Such a question may represent a projection into Hank of others' feelings about the group and can be experienced by the therapist as threatening to the integrity of the enterprise. Taken together these individual acts (both active and passive

[2]One of the essential elements in the group agreement [structure] is to discuss in the group salient extragroup meetings among members.

components) represent a more widespread resentment of the group norms, and are members' expressions of their wish to establish more autonomous "rules of behavior." The leader needs to remember, however, that the expression of affect, including dissatisfaction with the group agreements, represents an important *acceptance* of a fundamental group norm of openly talking about all feelings.

CLINICAL EXAMPLE

A group of eight members had met for an extended period. They had made progress in their capacity to experience a feeling of belongingness and inclusion, but they had remained stuck in that comfortable stage for many months. The underlying themes of competitiveness between members and concern about the power of the therapist began to emerge initially through a seemingly innocent argument about whether or not a window should be opened! Some members wanted the window opened, while others did not; and all seemed quite concerned with the therapist's opinion in the matter, since they feared his power and did not want to offend or anger him by their actions. In the middle of this debate, as fate would have it, the therapist canceled several meetings in order to fulfill various professional obligations. The therapist, concerned about the number of sessions missed, suggested that the group meet for a double session to replace one of the missed sessions (see Chapter 11 for a discussion of a variety of responses to leader absences). This offer was experienced by the group as an effort at control and domination by the therapist: "You just need our money, Doc!" was the way one irate individual put it. The initial intense rejection of the idea of a double session was modified because the group was quite cohesive and members found it pleasant and helpful to meet. Moreover, the members were trying their best to understand their feelings and reactions rather than simply acting on them.

In the discussion prior to the proposed double meeting, one member abruptly announced that this was to be his last meeting. "My insurance has been discontinued for some time, and I've been thinking about stopping treatment," he said by way of explanation. In reality, he held a relatively high-paying job, lived alone without undue overhead, and could easily have managed the financial obligations. The remaining members were enraged, but they could neither help him explore the meaning of this sudden flight nor deter him from actually terminating. One of the primary interpretations the group offered this member was the notion that his sudden desire to leave was directly in response to his feelings about the power and control of the leader.

The theme of power and control was also evident in another way just prior to the double session. The members joked about the extended session, and they explored the need for an intermission, for bringing in food, and for allowing time to feed parking meters (despite the fact that the group met at night, when the meters did not require feeding). There was also sufficient feeling of belongingness and togetherness among the remaining members to stimulate curiosity regarding their worries about what might happen in the longer session.

The remaining seven members all appeared on time for the 3-hour session. The meeting was characterized by considerable fear of overinvolvement, which dominated the first 90 minutes (the usual length of the group). Within 5 minutes of the halfway point, one man ostentatiously juggled his coins and left the room to buy a cola. Upon his return two men in succession left the room, announcing they were going to the bathroom. When all the men were back in the room, the group discussed these events, and the exploration clearly showed both conscious and unconscious rebellion by the men who left. As one man said, "I sit through business meetings and sporting events that last three hours or more without having to go to the bathroom." Moreover, the group began to recognize that there was subtle encouragement by the women. One woman, for example, said, "I saw him get those coins, and I hoped he would get up and leave."

*   *   *

In this instance a change in format provided an opportunity to bring simmering rebelliousness into the open. In the context of the emerging conflicts, this rebellion was not a protest against the loss of a maternal object (the therapist) but rather an opportunity to test one's power to control one's fate. The members' fear of the strength and power of the therapist, along with their wish to take the therapist on, was manifest in their responses to the double session. The terminated member's rebellion was clearly echoed in the less self-defeating rebellions of the remaining members.

Understanding the members' behaviors in the context of group development protects against potential scapegoating by both therapist and other members.

For the therapist, experienced or not, this storming phase often brings about a crisis of confidence. The harmonious group that had been such a joy has suddenly become an uncomfortable, affect-laden group that occasionally calls the leader's credentials into question. The release of these affects represents a sign of progress, not failure, for the group and the group therapist.

Stage 3: The Mature Phase

The mature group is a performing, working entity that appears goal directed. In the schema used here, this phase represents the apex of group effectiveness. Members interact spontaneously, and they easily carry themes along from session to session. Leadership is shared, and members assume important tasks and emotional leadership roles. Personal growth is indicated by members' capacities to assume a variety of roles. Strong emotions and seemingly intense conflicts can be tolerated and are not prematurely cut off. There is sufficient flexibility to allow for a shifting focus from intragroup to extragroup to personal or group historical events. Conflict in the group is explored not only from an individual perspective but from that of all members. Thus a true group enterprise.

Descriptions of a mature group reflect various authors' theoretical perspectives. Bion's (1960) description of the *work group* is similar to that of a mature group. Some characteristics of a work group are goal-directedness, an ability of the individuals to cooperate in an activity, and the ability to relate to reality. For Whitaker and Lieberman (1964) group maturity is attained when no focal conflict is evident: "Under these special conditions of safety, the patient may take steps to test the necessity of maintaining his old maladaptive solutions" (p. 166). MacKenzie (1994) emphasizes members' decreased need for stereotypic and forceful role behavior and the emergence of more "distributed leadership."

In general system theory (GST) terminology the mature group exhibits a balance between open and closed boundaries (J. E. Durkin, 1981). Boundaries that are too open do not protect the individual sufficiently, and boundaries that are too closed stop the necessary exchanges of information and feeling. H. E. Durkin (1981) maintains that this strictly systems point of view is incomplete without adding a psychodynamic understanding of the individual. In an earlier work, contrasting individual psychoanalysis and ordinary living, she suggested that the former almost completely cancels reality and focuses on transference whereas the latter obscures transference in the reality interchange (H. E. Durkin, 1964). Group therapy falls in the middle, where reality is present but diminished and transference is present but available for examination. Mature groups for both Durkins are those in which free interaction is made possible by a permissive and safe atmosphere, and this free interaction is the basis for the expression of multiple defenses and transferences that are then analyzed and understood.

Gustafson et al. (1981), utilizing Mahler, Pine and Bergman's (1975) stages of separation and individualization, suggest that a mature group is like the practicing toddler: members periodically return to the leader for reassurance and support, but they can continue to practice on their own and do so with increasing effectiveness. In addition, members' ability to tolerate differing points of view and conflicting feelings are signs of a maturing group.

For Day (1981) the mature state is characterized by the members' mutual appreciation of and trust for one another. In turn, members gain the flexibility to understand themselves more completely in relation to the other members and the leader; they become able to process rather than merely experience transferential relationships. Berman and Weinberg (1998) describe the dynamics of an advanced-stage group along the personal axes of symbolization, internalization, and containment, and along the interpersonal axes of self and self–others development and of differentiation and individuation.

Garland (1982) defines one aspect of a working group as that in which members have become less interested in the problems they entered the group to solve and more interested in the group interactions that were initially viewed as *not* a problem—the "non-problem" (in Garland's terminology). Within such an environment patients are able to expand their views of their respective difficulties to include elements of their lives that they did not know were problems but in fact are essential in understanding the initial problem.

With this general review, we can more closely examine some of the indicators of a working group environment.

1. Mature working groups emphasize the intragroup responses and interactions as the primary source of learning and cure. A sense of history develops so that current episodes are linked to prior events, and members become sensitized to repetitive patterns in themselves and other group members.

2. Despite the primacy of in-group interactions, flexibility develops that allows discussion of relevant outside events in the members' lives. Groups develop the capacity to distinguish between outside events brought into the discussion as resistances and outside events discussed as part of the therapeutic quest. Where possible, members seek to bring such outside material into the group in order to clarify issues. For example, an individual who complains about his interactions with a significant person in his life might be helped to understand his contributions to the problems if members are able to link the outside problem with their in-group awareness of the individual's behavior.

3. In mature groups the members develop a more collegial relationship with the therapist. The therapist is viewed as an authority and expert, but he/she is demystified and not imbued with magical powers. In other words a therapeutic alliance has been established that allows for a more realistic appraisal of the leader as well as a more complete conviction that he/she is an ally in the therapeutic venture. While transference reactions are still cooperative, members are able to help one another gain objectivity on distorted perceptions of the leader and each other.

4. Members have developed confidence in their ability to tolerate anxiety and to examine problems themselves. They no longer look solely to the therapist as the primary source of caring, concern, guidance, and understanding. They have learned that no permanent harm will result from intense affective interactions, and they do not consistently interfere with heated exchanges. The members are more able to trust that it is helpful to share spontaneously the affective responses they experience during the meetings without undue regard for politeness, rationality, or embarrassment. At times individuals remain unable to tolerate specific affects, but such instances are used as opportunities for self-understanding. Members have learned to distinguish between expressing feelings and attacking with intent to hurt.

5. Through repeated experiences members gain a deep understanding

and appreciation for one another's strengths and weaknesses. Compassion and tolerance are founded upon the knowledge that unconscious factors operate for everyone and often adversely affect interpersonal relationships. Members in mature groups have also learned that the most abrasive aspects of behavior are often defenses designed to protect against pain, not indications of inherent malice in the individuals in question. Members have an appreciation of the unconscious, even if they do not understand its sources, and they attempt to understand the behavior of their fellow members as well as their own. Similarly, the therapist's strengths and weaknesses can be appreciated or accepted without overwhelmingly intense or prolonged affective swings.

6. Finally, members have learned that transactions inevitably involve two distinct components—the interpersonal and the intrapsychic. They know that behavior is not always what it appears to be and that there are personal meanings which might produce particular behaviors. They further appreciate that identical behaviors might have very different meanings for different individuals. Members strive in a consistent manner to respond to behaviors from two perspectives—as the recipient of behaviors (external observer) and as the empathic listener of the more personal meanings of the behaviors (internal observer).

The therapist in the mature group faces new tasks. Using the metaphor of the parent of toddler or adolescent children, the therapist must balance members' capacities to experiment and explore without undue interference or intrusion. Moreover, the therapist's own level of maturity is tested in this phase, not only out of concern for control but out of envy (Stone, 1992a). As members share moments of play or great intimacy, countertransference forces may strain the therapist's capacity to remain in role.

Stage 4: The Termination Phase

Termination, which represents the final phase of group development, is of such significance that it will be discussed in detail in Chapter 16. In time-limited groups, the final meetings of the group are completely devoted to the ending of the group. Even in those groups where the members seem not to speak about the ending of the group, dynamically we must assume that all group content is related to the forthcoming ending. In ongoing psychodynamic groups, the termination phase occurs whenever an individual member decides to terminate membership in the group.

The affects associated with the sense of graduation and saying good-bye to the group are seldom easily managed either by the departing or the remaining individuals (including the therapist). Terminations are emotionally painful and joyous, but never simple.

One vital aspect of the development of group maturity is the *successful* termination of a member. In the early months members struggle with their fears that this treatment might not be truly therapeutic. Indeed, the first terminations usually are therapeutic failures–patients who flee the group prematurely. It is often quite a long time before any patient successfully completes the work he/she set out to achieve and leaves with a sense of well-being and accomplishment. It is not unusual that members will refer to such a patient for many years, using that memory as an antidote to doubts and worries about the effectiveness of the group. Mature groups almost invariably have had at least one termination that was perceived as successful by the great majority of the members.

New members also become symbols of successful or unsuccessful treatment, because new members fill seats formerly occupied by individuals who have terminated. Groups develop oral legacies whereby history is remembered for a long time. The ways in which various members leave take on powerful meanings for groups. During a period when a number of members leave happy and fulfilled, the sense of confidence and maturity is raised greatly. Perceptions of new members are obscured by the shadows of the members who left before. A new member who happens to fill a seat occupied by a member who left prematurely is greeted differently than someone who fills the seat of an honored member who left with work completed. Both situations have their problems. Examination of the impact of terminations on feelings about the replacement member or the group-as-a-whole provides one more opportunity for members to differentiate reality from the affective response, which contributes considerably to group maturity.

THE EFFECTS OF GROUP DYNAMICS
AND DEVELOPMENT

Repetitive events may be handled differently at different stages of development. In order for the therapist to maximize learning, it is important to understand the differences in how groups respond to similar events at different developmental stages. For example, throughout the life of a group, individuals will from time to time break the agreement regarding prompt attendance at all meetings. Such breaches are inevitable, but members use those breaches for learning in quite different ways, depending upon the stage of group development.

In the formative stages lateness is often ignored or only cursorily addressed. Commonly, reality reasons are offered to explain the tardiness, and these reasons are quickly accepted by the others. Thus a late member might casually announce, "The bus was late," or "My boss kept me in a meeting," or even "I misplaced my car keys." Such explanations, accompanied by a sincere apology, are usually satisfactory to the others, and the attention of the group moves on to some other subject. These responses are multidetermined. At one level members do not know how to explore or appreciate such behavior. Sometimes members offer advice about how to avoid such situations in the future, but there is little permission in the group to express feelings about such situations. If a member has an intense affective reaction, such as anger, it is usually kept under wraps out of an even more pressing need for acceptance. Furthermore, members at this stage seem to view the lack of condemnation or attack from the therapist as a sign that they, too, should offer no strong response to the tardy member. They are still looking to the therapist for direction about how to behave. Finally, there is a powerful but subtle unconscious pressure *not* to comment upon breaches in the group boundary, since at this stage of development members may feel a need to employ the same behaviors. The members behave as if no one wants to bolt the door too securely lest they, too, be forced to stay in the group and experience intense emotions.

As members develop a sense of belonging and thereby move to a different stage of development, there is usually increasing pressure to arrive on time, as well as to honor the other agreements. Lateness now occurs at the expense of potential censure from one's peers, and it may represent either a displaced expression of dissatisfaction with the developing group norms or a more direct expression of rebelliousness and assertiveness. Whereas lateness in the forming stage may represent some response to anxiety about joining, such as a fear of being engulfed or becoming dependent, arriving late now represents a move toward individualizing, of fighting for fulfillment of one's own goals potentially at the expense of the others in the group. Often the rebelliousness begins as an attack on the leader, and this can include overt and covert collusion by the other members. Patients in this mode may pay no more attention to the tardiness than do patients in the earliest stage of development, but in this case the affective tone is quite different. Whereas in the initial stage the nonattention is out of naïveté or unwillingness to try to understand a defense that others might want to employ, now the unwillingness is an angry, belligerent struggle with the leader and his/her rules. As one patient angrily expressed it, "Russ comes for 80 minutes. Why focus on the 10 minutes he *isn't* here?"

Given that norms are often very rigid during this stage, the affective responses to the perceived or actual tyranny of the group are understandable. A member's breach of the agreements frequently produces strong emotions, which then are directed either toward the offending member or toward the leader. At the same time recognition is dawning about the existence of underlying or even unconscious motivation for lateness. No longer will the excuse "I misplaced my keys!" be accepted without question. Following the therapist's lead, and by now having had occasion to see the fruit such inquiries have borne in the past, members begin to explore lateness for hidden meanings.

They are freer to communicate emotions, not just thoughts, and they have begun to internalize the curiosity about behavior as a means of learning very important information about themselves and their colleagues. Furthermore, exploration of unconscious feelings is no longer simply an opportunity for humiliation—it is an opportunity for learning.

In mature groups the members have begun to examine the meaning of breaches of the agreements, both for the individuals who come late or not at all and for themselves. Such behavior is understood as potentially powerful communication. The members may still be enraged by the fact that an individual arrives late or occasionally does not come to the group at all, but they have begun to accept that not all individuals are the same and that absolute conformity is neither just nor fair. Thus members can use such interactions to study both their own external and internal responses and concurrently the inner meanings for the latecomer. Finally, members begin to explore the possibilities that such behavior on the part of one individual member is in fact a group event. It is commonly observed that lateness and absenteeism tend to increase as a therapist's vacation approaches, and these breaches of the agreements are in fact a groupwide commentary about the therapist's impending absence.

Many variations on this example occur, but common to mature groups is the capacity of the group to establish a norm of viewing behavior as communication and therefore one more pathway to knowledge. Understanding the multiple determinants of behavior (which would include recognition of processes impacting on the entire group and exploration of the reactions various individuals have to that behavior) becomes a powerful therapeutic tool when the members are attuned to exploring these arenas.

SUMMARY

Group dynamics represent the foundations of understanding whole-group processes. Concepts of goals and structure orient clinicians to phenomena that are supraordinate to the individual. The dynamics of leadership, norms, and roles result from the interaction among participants and impact upon their behavior and feelings.

The concept of group development is valuable in orienting therapists to a number of processes common to group psychotherapy. Familiarity with the phases of development helps anchor therapists in their work and provides a road map to help them understand what is occurring within their groups.

A great deal of valuable therapeutic work can be accomplished in each phase. Indeed, each phase offers unique opportunities. Further, since groups are dynamic organisms composed of living beings, the phases are not rigid and steadfast. The stages are best considered guidelines, not laws. As groups grow and are confronted with crisis and change, the phases will be revisited regularly.

As development takes place, each group forms its particular culture and norms that have a major impact upon how the group goes about fulfilling its goal of helping the members solve their problems. The therapist has considerable importance in the evolution of the culture, but the members also contribute greatly. The concept of role is linked with the group's requirements for building and maintaining its culture as well as the individual's past habitual methods of handling stress and anxiety. Both aspects of role require consideration and frequently can be observed as overlapping within the group.

The developmental stages we have delineated refer specifically to open-ended psychodynamic groups. Time-limited groups go through the same stages, though the stages are compressed. Furthermore, the reality of a forced ending creates a special emphasis on termination issues. Indeed, most time-limited groups begin making references to the end of the group in the first meeting. Furthermore, from the halfway point in the group until the end, the entire process of the group can usually be understood as stimulated (usually unconsciously) by the approaching end of the group.

FOUR

Therapeutic Factors in Group Psychotherapy

To teach a man how he may learn to grow
independently, and for himself, is perhaps the
greatest service that one man can do another.
—BENJAMIN JOWETT

A multitude of therapeutic factors are at work in therapy groups—so many, in fact, that different therapists successfully use some while deemphasizing or not using others at all. In addition to the usual factors, groups in particular invoke sociocultural factors. These latter important elements often are underappreciated. In this chapter we begin with a brief consideration of how group dynamic theories have been influenced by the culture in which they arose. In the second portion we examine the question, "What makes groups therapeutic?" Sorting the factors that are of presumed mutative importance has concerned clinicians and researchers alike.

THE SOCIOCULTURAL CONTEXT

The word "culture" conveys different concepts. It represents "high art," and it also represents "a way of life." We are concerned with the latter definition here. People do not enter therapy as blank slates. Not only do they have their highly individualized personal histories, they also have their "cultures," the assumptions that come with their various sociological backgrounds.

For Wilfred Bion culture refers to basic assumption or work group life whereas for S. H. Foulkes, who was influenced by the sociologist Norbert Elias (Pines, 1997) and by Gestalt psychology, culture refers to the influence of the world outside of the group and its impact on what members bring into the group. Culture may refer to more general national or international values or ideas, to values of specific subgroups (e.g., Jewish, African American, Hispanic, Asian), or to familial values (e.g., "Don't expose any family business to outsiders"). Moreover, culture can refer to the *Zeitgeist* and the influence of the politically correct or prominent in current events (e.g., focus on diversity, feminism, the men's movement, or political events). For example, Conyne, Wilson, and Shi (1999) recently studied differences between comparable groups of Americans and Chinese. They found that "U.S. group members spoke more frequently and the length of their speeches was shorter" (p. 45); also, "Chinese members spoke directly to the group leader 33% of the time, whereas U.S. members spoke directly to the leader 11% of the time" (p. 45). They conclude that leaders should respond differently to these two populations, for example behaving more authoritatively with Chinese populations and including written materials in those groups (p. 46).

From a broad perspective it is possible to trace cultural, social and personal influences upon psychodynamic group theory as it emerged in Britain and the United States. Foulkes, who lived and worked in Britain, emphasized "holistic forces and human embeddedness, the location of members in the context of the communications and relations and the *a priori* preference for intersubjective rather than interpersonal interpretations" (Ettin, 1997, p. 45). In addition, reflecting the evolution of the theory during World War II, Foulkes emphasized the hopeful and growth-promoting aspects of group life and generally neglected to address potentially destructive forces (Nitsun, 1996). Neither could Foulkes fully separate himself from his psychoanalytic background. Dalal (1998), commenting on Foulkes's understanding of clinical events, states, "True, Foulkes does describe group specific mechanisms, but in his clinical comments, he always appears to understand them from an individualistic and psychoanalytic basis" (p. 68).

Eric van Schoor characterizes the development of group psychotherapy in the United States as arising in a context of pluralism, emphasizing individualism and self-realization, an optimistic tradition that tends to create a schism between the individual, the group, and the pluralistic culture. As in Britain, group psychotherapy emerged from the psychoanalytic tradition and many initial formulations were transpositions from that dominant dyadic culture, a "strategy that may have served to gain acceptance and simultaneously restricted the broader group and social context" (van Schoor, 1997, p. 29, see also Slavson, 1957, and A. Wolf & Schwartz, 1962). American eclecticism may be reflected in efforts to meld dyadic theoretical perspectives (object relations, self psychology, and interpersonal theory) with whole group formulations. American stress on individualism, however, has deemphasized the group-as-a-whole in American group therapy.

A central tenet of dynamic group psychotherapy is the notion that members, through their group interactions, re-create their social situation and so the group becomes a microcosm of their external lives (Slater, 1966). They bring with them their social and cultural values and attitudes (Ettin, 1994a). Yet, the contributions of "culture" to their personalities are likely to remain unexplored (Brook, Gordon, & Meadow, 1998). Hopper (1996) observes:

> The effects of social facts and forces are more likely to be unconscious than conscious. The concept of the social unconscious refers to the existence and constraints of social, cultural and communicational arrangements of which people are unaware, in so far as these arrangements are not perceived (not "known"), and if perceived, not acknowledged ("denied"), and if acknowledged, not taken as problematic ("given"), and if taken as problematic, not considered with an optimal degree of detachment and objectivity. (p. 9)

The clinician must struggle to find a balance that includes exploration of the personal and the cultural elements (sociopolitical, sociocultural, and familial values), particularly those "cultural" elements that are deeply embedded within the self, as they emerge and influence the interpersonal transactions of the group.

Members' personal and sociopolitical values (conscious and unconscious) are evident in the group interactions. For example, it is not unusual for a clinician to enter the group room and find the members in a discussion about a current political or social event. This discussion stops when the therapist enters the room, and yet the members have communicated attitudes and values in the discussion which are likely to have an impact upon the subsequent interactions.

Another example of how social or cultural issues influence the group process would be the impact of "politically correct" attitudes on the spontaneity of members. Social constraints (Hopper, 1996) may act to suppress or support ideas and affects. Clinicians also need to be introspective and explore their own stereotypical attitudes, which are often influenced by political and social forces (Grunebaum & Smith, 1996). Another example would be a therapist's discomfort with a patient who holds a political view much more conservative or liberal than his/her own.

Unexamined stereotypical attitudes can have devastating effects on the ability of participants to trust the group. Multicultural or multiracial groups do not fare well when attitudes of both the members and the therapist interfere with learning details of one another's culture. Fenster and Fenster (1998) focus on problems of xenophobia and developing basic trust which arises both from the culture and from the individual. They propose a continuum model of paranoia, ranging from "good enough trust" to "nontrusting towards group members of all backgrounds" (p. 83). The latter position is usually incompatible with successful group participation.

The following clinical example illustrates patients' interactions as they "construct" a group atmosphere:

CLINICAL EXAMPLE

The members of an outpatient group suffered significant problems in forming trusting relationships. The previous sessions had been filled with contentious bickering as members attempted to integrate a newcomer, who defensively demeaned the group. This meeting followed a 2-week interruption due to the therapist's vacation. One member was absent when the therapist entered the room. There was a moderate period of silence, and then Diane described her mother's recent visit, which she had anticipated with some dread. Diane said that her mother slept away the morning, and the two of them spent their afternoon talking superficialities and being active. There had been no intimacy. Diane had often railed about her mother's insensitivity and "endless criticism" and seemed relieved that the visit had been "benign." There was a lengthy pause, and Tony said that he would ask questions of Diane but that would not get anywhere. A silence followed, and Colleen said she had visited her family for the Fourth of July and much to her surprise there had not been any of the usual arguments, and her mother had been subdued. Colleen conveyed a sense of relief that no disaster had taken place; its absence had created a positive tinge to the visit. She went on to say that she had been very relieved with her annual review at work, and she had received a substantial pay raise. She would now remain at her place of employment rather than search for a new job. Again there was an absence of overt response. David recalled the prior Thanksgiving family dinner when his grandmother had been very weird, and he said he had avoided visiting her after that.

*   *   *

The group process was one of telling parallel "stories" followed by pauses. It was as if the members had re-created a noninteractive "family." They were responding as if superficial involvement would preclude arguments and criticism.

This meeting occurred just at the time when President Bill Clinton was admitting an inappropriate sexual liaison with a White House intern after having publicly denied such actions. Although the societal contributions to the discussion were not examined, it would not be far fetched to wonder if the serious questions of the President's trustworthiness was an added element limiting the interaction. A possible perspective would be that the atmosphere had been suffused by the culture of distrust of authority. It would be an oversimplification to merely describe this example in personal dynamic terms without appreciating the potential of the culture also "having spoken."

Integration of the social and group perspectives with the intrapsychic is incomplete. There is also an interactive effect whereby personal psychic functioning and experience impact on the group atmosphere so as to form a group culture, which in turn influences the members (Ettin, 1994a). In this fashion, the recursive nature of these interactions becomes apparent.

With this background, we now turn to the traditional formulations of the dynamics of individual change. The ultimate aim is for the clinician to retain the notion that group and societal forces are inside and outside the members and these forces may exert influence on the treatment process.

THE DYNAMICS OF CHANGE

All theories of psychotherapy have explicit and implicit convictions about how best to help people grow. Psychoanalytic theory belongs to the philosophical tradition which holds that "the truth shall make you free" (John 8:32). That is, people make psychological changes as they gain information and understanding. Freud recognized that a great body of information is unconscious and that emotional knowledge (and therefore freedom) requires making the unconscious conscious. The fact that psychoanalytic theory belongs to an educational philosophy has many implications in this era, when mental illness is more and more defined in medical, symptom-relieving ways. Whereas the nomenclature of the fourth edition of the American Psychiatric Association's *Diagnostic and Statistic Manual of Mental Disorders* (1994; DSM-IV) conceptualizes psychopathology as separate from the personhood of the individual (e.g., a patient "has depression"), psychoanalytic theory is more holistic (e.g., the patient "is depressed"). According to psychoanalytic theory, "pathology" represents an earlier adaptive response to inner pain which is counterproductive today.

Through a variety of windows into the world of the unconscious, we may deduce a great deal about the conflicted aspects of our patients' lives and histories that have led to these counterproductive patterns. The windows include free association, slips of the tongue, body language, character styles, dreams, repetition compulsions, transferences, and resistances. In the effective therapeutic process, it is posited that patients will regress to a level where they have not mastered a developmental task or have become fixated because of intrapsychic conflict (Rutan, 1992).

In classic psychoanalysis the patient's regression and development of a cohesive transference are fostered by the dependent position on the couch, the absence of visible stimuli from the analyst, and the use of free association. In group psychotherapy regression is stimulated in part by stranger anxiety, by a nondirective therapist, and by the group process. When group therapy first appeared there was considerable debate about whether transference could really appear in a multiperson field where consensual validation might serve to limit projections to the therapist and other group members. While transference is limited in certain ways by the presence of others, transference is also enhanced in other ways through intense although short-lived experiences with peers, the therapist, and the image of the group (H. E. Durkin & Glatzer, 1973). Change is effected by assisting patients in gaining emotional understanding of their reactions inside and outside the therapy situation and by examining the basic assumptions which support their characteristic perceptions and behaviors. For psychodynamic group therapists, the opportunity to see patients actively involved in interpersonal matrixes offers unique opportunities for gaining insight into the patients' unconscious worlds.

Modern modifications of classical Freudian theory stress the interpersonal aspects of personality formation and the etiology of psychopathology. Object relations theorists (e.g., Fairbairn, 1952a; Winnicott, 1965; Guntrip, 1969) hypothesize that the need to be in relationship with others is the primary drive that forms personality. Stressing the importance of authentic and healthy human relationships as therapeutic factors, object relations therapists pay special attention to the quality of patients' relationship styles. The presence in groups of a network of human relationships, rather than just the single relationship to the analyst, provides a forum for examination of the relationship style of each patient.

Ego psychologists (e.g., A. Freud, W. Hartmann, E. Kris, L. Lowenstein, and G. Blanck and R. Blanck) further underline the importance of relationships in rebuilding fragmented and flawed egos. In ego psychology theory, health is defined by the quality and developmental level of defenses employed by the individual. Groups offer ideal settings for therapists and patients to explore the types of defenses patients use to protect themselves from interpersonal pain. Kauff (1997) commenting on recent advances in theory and technique questions whether "regression is a *requirement* of 'true' analytic work in treatment generally, either in the group or in the dyad" (p. 208).

Self psychologists (e.g., H. Kohut, E. S. Wolf, A. Goldberg, and P. H. Ornstein and A. Ornstein) stress the importance of viewing others along a continuum from archaic selfobjects, which are used to fulfill developmental functions, to distinct and separate individuals. In this tradition, therapy groups offer marvelous opportunities for analyzing the degree to which others are selfobjects or separate entities for each group member. More recently self psychology has incorporated the notion of intersubjectivity: the subjective worlds of therapist and patient interact to create an intersubjective field. This notion emphasizes both participants emotional contribution to the therapeutic exchange (Atwood & Stolorow, 1984; Stolorow, Branchaft, & Atwood, 1987).

Within each of these psychodynamic frameworks important commonalities appear. All presuppose a supportive, warm, but neutral, fairly unobtrusive therapist who strives to create a safe, supportive, and therapeutic relationship. The elements contributing to support in group psychotherapy will be discussed below.

The therapist's nondirective stance, along with the anxiety created by the group setting, promotes regression. This allows the pathologies and defensive mechanisms of the members to emerge in the interpersonal transactions in the group. The regressive re-creation of the patient's inner world may simulate the family of origin, and/or it may resemble the patient's current interpersonal world or the broader social environment. The stereotyped fantasies and responses are the transferences from which members may gain an understanding of their repetitive responses. These responses (either behavioral or in fantasy) may have been necessary for self-preservation in childhood or at other periods in the patient's life but are counterproductive in the present. Yalom (1985, p. 45) considers transference as a component of the patient's disturbed interpersonal transactions. However, we would add that it is omnipresent and particularly obvious in the fantasized recapitulation of the primary family group.

Each of the theoretical variations cited emphasizes the importance of emotionally charged interchanges taking place within a safe environment. Through these exchanges individuals gain opportunities to understand and alter their inner responses and previously unexamined hypotheses about life and interpersonal relationships.

GROUP THERAPEUTIC FACTORS

Not all change takes place as a result of gaining knowledge into one's unconscious life; learning factors (education or modeling), so-called nonspecific or supportive elements, and the corrective emotional experience have all been found to contribute to behavior change in conjunction with or in the absence of self-knowledge. This gave rise to extensive efforts to develop categories of "therapeutic factors," which Crouch, Bloch, and Wanlass (1994) define as "element[s] of group therapy that contribute to improvement in a patient's condition and can be a function of the actions of the group therapist, the other group members, and the patient himself" (p. 270).

Beginning with the work of Corsini and Rosenberg (1955), categories of therapeutic factors have included the dimensions of interpersonal/intrapsychic, support/insight, and cognitive/affect. Efforts to determine group-specific factors, that is separating those particular to the group setting remain incomplete (MacKenzie, 1997a). As will be discussed in the following chapter, these factors may be processed either consciously or unconsciously and may take place at a "dynamic-contemporaneous" or "genetic-regressive" level (Scheidlinger (1982a, 1997).

Categorization assists the clinician, but the boundaries between the categories are not tightly drawn and a multidimensional perspective is necessary to grasp the full breadth of the opportunities for understanding patients in a therapy group (Dies, 1997; Fuhriman, 1997).

In the interpersonal tradition of Harry Stack Sullivan, Yalom (1975) developed a list of "therapeutic factors" derived from observations of individuals, their interactions, and the group system. Modifications over the succeeding two decades led to a listing of 11 factors:

1. Instillation of hope
2. Universality
3. Imparting of information
4. Altruism
5. Corrective recapitulation of the primary family group
6. Development of socializing techniques
7. Imitative behavior
8. Interpersonal learning
9. Group cohesiveness
10. Catharsis
11. Existential factors

MacKenzie (1997b) has modified and rearranged these elements into four factors:

1. *Supportive:* a sense of belonging to the group, including universality, acceptance, altruism and hope; this factor includes the support of group cohesion
2. *Self-revelation:* self-disclosure and catharsis, which are separated on the basis of cognitive and affective dimensions
3. *Learning:* education, guidance, vicarious learning, and modeling
3. *Psychological work:* interpersonal learning and insight (self-understanding)

These categories may be roughly viewed as paralleling the schema of group development. Supportive and self-revelation factors are prominent in the early developmental stages. Similarly, elements in the learning factors may be present throughout, but they are more prominent in the earlier phases whereas psychological work is more characteristic of the mature phase.

In an overview of the research of therapeutic factors, Fuhriman and

Burlingame (1994) state that "some factors (cohesiveness, interpersonal learning, catharsis) are universally valued across diverse clientele, while others have differential value depending on the specific population" (p. 27). Illustrative of the variability is the finding that for populations of more impaired individuals (i.e., those attending day treatment centers) universality and the installation of hope have greater importance in effecting improved functioning (Butler & Fuhriman, 1980). This notion is echoed by Dies (1997), who asserts that "there are no universal mechanisms of change, but rather a range of key dimensions that interact with clinical settings, diagnostic compositions, and forms of group therapy. Different patients may benefit from various therapeutic ingredients within the same group, and the availability of multiple sources of learning within sessions may be even more important than any limited set of common dimensions" (p. 164).

The Supportive Environment and Group Cohesion

The dichotomy between insight and support has gradually eroded, as supportive interventions are present in all forms of psychotherapy. The traditional separation of the two therapeutic formats arose as a way of thinking about treatment for patients who seemed to have serious personality deficits (or psychotic processes) that impaired their ability to gain self-understanding. Historically, supportive interventions have at times been thought to be too gratifying of infantile needs, and as a consequence they have been viewed as undermining the patient's motivation for change. Analytic technique has focused on interpretation of the transference as the mutative treatment element. This has meant that less attention has been paid to the supportive elements intrinsic to all dynamic therapies. This view seems all too narrow and is an unfortunate misunderstanding of the nature of both support and psychotherapy groups. Support and acceptance are the essential bases from which patients can risk exploring other ways of relating or of examining their inner world. Indeed, for some this may be sufficient, and therefore, in our schema, support is not only a therapeutic factor but also represents a therapeutic *process* (to be discussed in Chapter 5).

The accumulation of treatment experiences with developmentally less mature individuals has broadened the application of analytic theory and technique to this population. In order to hear and make use of an interpretation and gain insight into their behaviors, these patients in particular need to feel a sense of safety, which includes the respect, interest, and optimal responsiveness of the therapist. The strict analytic posture, which in any case probably only existed in rare instances, did not provide sufficient psychological *oxygen* (to use Kohut's [1980, p. 481] felicitous expression), for patients to grow. The research at the Tavistock Clinic (Malan, Balfour, Hood, & Shooter, 1976), where the therapist attempted to limit all interventions to interpretations, supports this notion with the finding that the main beneficiaries were patients with prior treatment who could withstand the austerity of the approach.

Pine (1985), comparing the treatment setting with children's developmental needs, stated, "Children develop under conditions of optimal strain, optimal demand, optimal frustration. Too much strain gets in their way, leading to anxiety or anger or frustration or helplessness at levels that are not constructive and too much to deal with; but too little strain, too much gratification, also stands in the way of development" (p. 166).

These experiences have led us to recognize what should have been obvious all along: all patients do better if they experience the therapy setting as fundamentally supportive, no matter what theoretical orientation is being used. From the perspective of the individual, the supportive climate implies a place where he/she has a sense of safety, where there is emotional "space" to contemplate, where others make an effort to understand and respond, where unique and common attitudes are respected, and where others are experienced as authentic.

CLINICAL EXAMPLE

Jamie, a new member, had sat silently for several weeks. Her first real contribution to the group came when she said, "I agree with Rick. At times this group feels very critical." Rick seemed touched and replied, "I'm glad you spoke up, Jamie." The discussion then seemed more lively. The therapist, wishing to make sure that Jamie knew he had recognized her, said, "The tone in the group seemed to change and the members became more active after you agreed with Rick."

*   *   *

Such a process intervention acknowledges Jamie's contribution and encourages her to take additional risks. From a dynamic perspective, by Jamie speaking up, she had reassured the others of her ability to participate, and that had led to a loosening of the process.

Support comes from a patient feeling understood or from knowing that the therapist is paying attention to what he/she has said. An early definition of cohesion was, "the attractiveness of a group for its members" (Frank, 1957, p. 54). Evans and Jarvis (1980) differentiate between members' attraction to the group, which is the usual manner in which cohesion is measured in research studies, and group cohesion. Attraction to the group is understood as members' feelings *about* the group. More broadly, Crouch et al. (1994) state, "The core of cohesiveness (a condition for change) is the commitment of group members to the aims and the work of the group which can be distinguished from the compatibility of the members (which may or may not be therapeutic) and from the satisfaction of being a group member" (p. 276). Thus, cohesion refers more to the properties of the group, whereas attraction addresses the individual's goals in remaining in the group. This useful distinction adds to our understanding of group cohesion.

Cohesion is a dynamic concept. What might make a group attractive at one stage of development would be antithetical to cohesion at a different stage. For instance, an individual entering a group wants to be accepted and liked in spite of whatever defenses he/she may present. Thus the therapist must be aware that confrontations or hostility, which would evoke a sense of emotional danger, might be perceived by a new member (or a new group) as a sign that this is not an attractive, "safe" group. At a later stage, when members are more prepared to manage conflict and to learn from affect-laden interactions, a group atmosphere that would limit free expression may well be experienced as saccharine and constricting. As Yalom (1985) observes, "Cohesiveness is not, for example, synonymous with inter-member acceptance and understanding, but is interdependent with these factors" (p. 50).

Pines (1985) suggests that the term "coherence" is more descriptive than "cohesion." For Pines, cohesion alludes to being "stuck together" and seems insufficient to describe a level of group development where members are working together toward their goals. However, Hopper (1997) argues that coherence is only one dimension of cohesion and is relevant mainly when communication is the basis of the group's cohesion.

The therapist plays an important initial role in providing support, which eventuates in cohesion. In establishing a clear group boundary and by reinforcing certain group behaviors the therapist is "informing" the group about the safety of the setting. However, in long-term dynamic groups, members who view their group as successful point to the helpfulness of member-to-member interaction (Dies, 1994, p. 138). As we discuss in Chapter 8, the group agreements serve to establish a boundary between the treatment room and the outside world. A respectful examination of boundary infractions, such as tardiness or absences, is experienced as supportive, since ignoring such violations may convey to the members that neither the therapist nor the group is ultimately dependable. Of course, the therapist's manner of addressing these and other attempts to alter the group boundary carries multiple complex meanings that eventually have to be understood for the patient's benefit. It is usually best if the therapist adopts an attitude of curiosity rather than one of a superego.

Many therapeutic interventions are supportive—such as linking group members' feelings or ideas, connecting present feelings to history, and inquiring what others feel (this implies that the therapist is able to listen and care about such matters). The demeanor the clinician conveys through eye contact, posture, and mannerisms carries messages that can be interpreted by the patients as supportive. Many ordinary courtesies initially serve to promote respect, a sense of safety, and a desire to belong. In object relations terms this is the "holding environment." The therapist through his/her verbal or nonverbal behavior provides an initial model for support. Subsequently, members and the group-as-a-whole contribute their share to the support and cohesion. The interpersonal setting of a group is not conducive to a stone-faced, inhuman therapeutic stance.

The therapist is aware of and can readily observe the universal anxiety and apprehension that people have in joining a group of strangers. However, the therapist is not the only source of support. Members soon learn to identify similarities among themselves, which helps to reduce their sense of isolation and aloneness. As we will address in subsequent chapters, the experience of being a singleton (an isolate) in a group can be alienating; the opposite, that of linking and being similar to others, is soothing. This is even more powerful when there is a sense of belonging to an enterprise in which all participants have certain similarities. Of course, in group therapy a common denominator is that people have come to solve their problems.

CLINICAL EXAMPLE

One of the therapist's tasks is to hear commonalties in members' seemingly disparate associations and then be able to link two or more individuals together on a common theme.

Joe spoke with considerable shame about his recent foray into riverboat gambling and his loss of $12,000. Seemingly changing the topic, Lorene spoke about her concerns with her weight. She had gained 30 pounds in the past 8 months. Several members inquired if Lorene had been to Weight Watchers or had any success with any diet. She sadly replied, "No."

The therapist suggested that Lorene seemed to understand Joe's problem. Both were struggling with similar issues: they could not control their impulses, for Joe the gambling, and for Lorene the eating. This intervention not only linked the two members, and lessened Joe's shame, but it served to stimulate others to examine their own manifestations of "greed."

*   *   *

Other elements that contribute to the supportive and sustaining group environment are altruism and hope. Altruism, the experience of offering something of value to another without the expectation of something in return, occurs at various levels. To be genuinely helpful can be a deeply satisfying experience, and one that many patients have not experienced before. Initial efforts to be useful may consist of members giving advice and suggestions. If they are accepted, there is a sense of being of value to others and to the group. However, often in early phases of group therapy advice contains a self-protective function by limiting the adviser's self-revelation. Moreover, suggestions may be rejected and concomitantly lower self-esteem.

Hope occurs when change takes place. A relatively common experience is for several members to report a symptomatic change ("My stomach no longer bothers me," or "I'm getting along better with my wife") after only a few sessions. We see these changes and recognize that they are likely the consequence of nonspecific or supportive factors. Members, however, may see them as the group interaction working for them. This reinforces the general sense of belonging. In order to endure, change often requires considerable work, and not all change is easy. Hope emerges from successful navigation of conflict. Of course, the experience of working over extended time periods and observing fellow members make substantial changes is an ultimate signifier of hope.

Object relations theory postulates that everyone is fundamentally trying to be *in* a human relationship, not trying to destroy such relationships. This is a fundamentally supportive notion. As members adopt this premise, they are able to examine even the most vile interpersonal styles from a position of empathy and understanding.

Self-Revelation Factors

Catharsis and self-disclosure are patient behaviors that expose aspects of each individual. Catharsis, succinctly defined as the purgation of emotions or the release of tension, can bring considerable, if only temporary, relief from pent-up affects or experiences. Sometimes experiences are blurted out and the person feels that there is an untimely and precipitous self-revelation. Yalom (1966a) observed that this can be an element that might lead to premature termination. Nevertheless, in most instances patients judiciously disclose information about themselves, often after subtly (either consciously or unconsciously) testing to determine if the group is safe. In our view, self-revelation both *follows* assessment of the atmosphere and is a result of increased safety (another example of the difficulty in separating therapeutic factors from the therapeutic process).

CLINICAL EXAMPLE

Anita, an alcoholism counselor, often complained about feeling isolated and having few friends. During a several-week period Roger told about the excruciating experiences of watching his wife going through another hypomanic episode and the efforts of her psychiatrist to maintain her in the community. In the third session Anita revealed that she had a diagnosis of bipolar disorder. She had never told anyone outside of her immediate family. She went on in great detail, explaining to the group and to Roger the essence of her experience while manic, and fortunately how she was unable to recall many of her behaviors during the acute phase of her illness.

*   *   *

Anita thereafter felt considerably freer to speak about herself, and Roger felt very supported as he gained more insight into the nature of his wife's experience of a manic episode.

Learning Factors

Most elements of the learning factors are at some level cognitive. The emergence of cognitive-behavior therapy has demonstrated that significant change can take place with therapeutic emphasis on cognition as an avenue to altering emotional responses. Clearly, some patients gain a sense of personal control by having a degree of cognitive mastery prior to risking exposing emotions. There are at least four types of learning that occur in groups: education, suggestions (advice), vicarious learning, and trying out new behaviors.

The initial structuring of the group by the therapist is educational. Patients are informed of the ways to make the treatment useful. An example of such education is the instruction to express one's thoughts or feelings rather than ask a question. Such a simple educational maneuver can often have significant impact on the subsequent treatment process.

Members offer one another suggestions and advice; in general most of the advice has already been offered but failed prior to a patient seeking therapy. However, several elements may now make the suggestion useful: it occurred in a trusting, nonintrusive setting; subtle phrasing may have made it more palatable; and the recipient may have changed sufficiently to "hear" the idea. Not only is there potential for the recipient of information to learn something new, a great deal may be learned by the manner in which advice and suggestions are provided or received. An essential key is the attitude and relationship in which advice is provided. Words may make a difference, but patients learn the potential pitfalls of giving "mixed signals" through body language, lack of eye contact, or tone of their voices.

Vicarious learning through observing others is an aspect of therapy that is particularly relevant to group therapy. Group therapy has been referred to as a hall of mirrors because patients see aspects of themselves in others. They see the valuable ways others interact, and they can observe the self-defeating and destructive interactions. It is common for patients to comment that "John, you are behaving like I do, and I get the same responses." As we discuss in Chapter 5, vicarious learning can take place consciously and unconsciously, the latter through processes of identification and internalization.

The fourth element in learning process is more "active" group dynamics. Members try new behaviors. They practice approaching or interacting with others in new ways. Using what they have learned, for instance, members may refrain from asking questions and may instead comment directly about their response to another's behavior. The potential for positive reenforcement is substantial. If the behavior is purely imitative, it may be more difficult to generalize than if it is transformed and integrated into the person's personality. The most valuable practicing seems to be in the context of trying to interact in a new manner in the group. Kohut's (1984) notion of twinship phenomena and transferences places modeling in a frame of depth psychology. The need for another person from whom one can learn skills (whether cognitive or behavioral) is self-strengthening.

Psychological Work

The central emphasis in this book is to examine the ways in which psychodynamic group psychotherapy can assist patients perform psychological work and gain self-understanding. We also wish to emphasize that the most effective psychological work takes place where there has been activation of emotions and members are able to integrate cognitive understanding with emotional experiences.

Insight may take place along several dimensions: the here and now of the session, the contemporaneous, or the past. The depth or value of insight is not specifically linked with any one of these dimensions. Traditionally the concept of reconstruction, linking here-and-now, external contemporary events and the past into an integrated whole, has been considered the standard for effective change. Experience has shown that well integrated self-understanding along any of the dimensions may lead to important and enduring change.

In group therapy a great deal of insight can be gained in the here and now of the meetings. Insight may accrue either from the content of a person's words or from the manner of interacting. What patients say reveals attitudes, motivations, and assumptions. Patients' behaviors are equally, if not more important, in exposing aspects of themselves. These include behavioral patterns (when do they withdraw, when do they speak up, with whom do they seem competitive, with whom are they seductive, when do they miss meetings or come late); nonverbal behaviors (where do they sit, what facial expression or body language are they showing); or paraverbal behavior (speech patterns, sound images, rate, tone, and the manner of discourse).

Clinical Example

Adrian, a woman with a diagnosis of borderline personality, would often dominate the group. If someone commented to her about "talking in circles," Adrian would quickly reply that no one else seemed to want to talk. She might also say that she was just trying to comment on what had been said. The therapist wondered if Adrian had "heard" what was said, because she seemed to respond so quickly there was little time to process the information. Adrian was startled. She thought for a few minutes (while the others sat quietly), and then she said that she was very afraid of being controlled. The insight into the behavioral process in the here and now became a central piece of self-understanding in Adrian's successful integration into the group.

*   *   *

Groups also serve as a stimulus for insight into one's current and past relationships. The group, with its social/family-like atmosphere, provides opportunities to evoke associations to current life relationships or to family of origin experiences. The familiar associations—"This group is just like my family," or "I'm reacting to you just like I did with my mother [or father, brother, or sister]"—are links from current responses to those from the past.

Clearly there are multiple avenues for accessing unconscious aspects of each person. Insight may follow from feedback from others or from self-reflection.

Considerable overlap exists between therapeutic factors and processes. Research addressing the importance of each element is incomplete. However, the framework of therapeutic factors provides a way of thinking about what transpires in the group and what may be useful or counterproductive in the conduct of group treatment.

SUMMARY

In this chapter we have examined aspects of what makes psychodynamic group treatment therapeutic. Groups are embedded in a social matrix that includes the values and attitudes members bring to treatment from their backgrounds, but contemporaneous social and political events stimulate discussion and evoke deeply held attitudes and beliefs. These elements contribute to the ambience and the dynamics of the treatment.

Traditional (dyadic) psychodynamic theory posits that the treatment situation provides a frame for regression and the development of a cohesive transference, which represents the central area of pathology. Group treatment, by the nature of its format, provides a more limited regressive experience, and the presence of others allows for different opportunities for examining unconscious process.

Change is not only effected through regressive processes but can be achieved by other "therapeutic factors" as well. We categorize these as follows:

- Supportive
- Self-revelation

- Learning
- Psychological work

The oft-stated advantage of group therapy has been the opportunity for feedback as a source of learning. That is far from a simple process, and effective feedback generally takes place in a setting of positive relationships. These elements are discussed in the next chapter as mechanisms and processes of change.

FIVE

Mechanisms and Processes of Change

> Any change, even a change for the better, is always
> accompanied by drawbacks and discomforts.
> —ARNOLD BENNETT, *The Arnold Bennett Calendar*

In the preceding chapter we examined factors salient to change in group psychotherapy. In this chapter we explore several additional factors which we term mechanisms and processes. Mechanisms refer to ways in which the *person*, consciously and unconsciously, may use the therapeutic factors in the service of change. Herbert Kelman (1963) lists three such mechanisms: imitation, identification, and internalization. Processes refer to how the *treatment context* facilitates the mechanisms. Ralph R. Greenson (1967) lists four such processes confrontation, clarification, interpretation, and working through (these are discussed in detail below).

Individuals repeat behavioral and emotional patterns that were of value to them when they attempted to solve difficulties in the past. When these patterns cause problems in the present, they often appear as "symptoms," personality constrictions or distortions. Interactions in the interpersonal field of a group often evoke these patterns. These repetitious patterns are the essence of transference.

For example, people are influenced by the social setting, the culture, the presence of others and by their wish for acceptance and approval. These social influences are responded to uniquely by each individual. Internal processes of basic trust (not only of others, but of one's own emotional structural stability), of control and power, of reliability, and other variations on these dynamics may interfere with or enhance acceptance of social influences. In addition, a sense of genuinely being understood and being connected contributes to being influenced. Although this is partly conscious, unconscious elements are also present in the development of group standards and norms.

With this brief background, we now turn to examining the mechanisms of change. These mechanisms do not take place in isolation, but rather occur in interaction and processes. They are separated here for heuristic purposes.

THE MECHANISMS OF CHANGE

Imitation

In therapy groups members have the opportunity to observe many interactions, styles of relating, and problem-solving techniques. Much of the early learning in groups, as in life, is imitative. Elements of the therapeutic factor of learning, including vicarious learning and modeling, can be subsumed under imitation.

For example, patients who have difficulty tolerating and sharing strong emotions can first observe other members interacting intensely. In the group, as they learn that members are not harmed but rather are typically drawn closer by such exchanges, these patients see some hope for change and, as a consequence, can begin to share feelings by imitating those members who are more successful. Though primarily used in the beginning stages of group membership, imitation remains one of the ways in which members gain new behavioral options throughout their treatment. The patients' experience of success following imitative behavior makes the group more attractive, enhances a wish to belong, and increases cohesiveness. This furthers identifications among the members. Imitation is by no means limited to group therapy, but group therapy, by virtue of the multiple interactions and relationships, expands the opportunities for change through imitative learning.

Identification

Identification has been defined in a variety of ways. We are using it here, following the description by Loewald (1973), to mean an unconscious process in which the subject takes on parts or aspects of another. By taking on aspects of another, the individual changes by altering perceptions or affects. Identification carries with it elements of support. Although some elements of support are quite conscious, there are clearly unconscious elements—for instance, the general sense of well-being and relief many people experience after belonging and emotionally participating in a group for a few meetings. Identification may be used in the service of growth or resistance, and each instance must be understood separately.

Freud (1921) initially postulated that group formation takes place as group members identify with one another via their shared identification with the leader. Without these bonds there is no group. Peer identification also takes place as the members tell about their life experiences as well as their reactions to current events, both within and outside the group. Consciously these identifications may be expressed as feelings of attraction, belonging, and attachment to the members and the group. These are the building blocks from which group cohesiveness develops. Similarly, universalization, the sense that one is not alone in one's feelings, furthers group attraction and identifications among members. A reciprocal process begins that enhances these powerful influences which members have upon one another. The resultant identifications alter fundamental ways the members perceive and respond. The incremental building of identifications forms the base for lasting change.

Identification can be readily observed in group interactions. For example, identification can be seen in nonverbal behavior when two or more patients simultaneously shift body positions and then several more members unconsciously adopt the same body position. This usually reflects a similar affect or perception by these individuals regarding the individual or topic under discussion.

It is not uncommon for these identifications to become conscious during the group. Members will point out that individuals have changed in how they respond or interact. They seem to view situations differently than they had in the past. (Recently a member announced, "I am proud of myself. I was wrongly criticized at work, but I responded like Arnie—I knew it was my boss's problem, not mine.") These observations may startle the individuals who had been unaware of the changes, and yet upon reflection they easily agree that their inner responses are different, less conflicted, and more flexible.

Such identifications usually are temporary unless the sources can be analyzed and integrated by the individual. One such source can be identification with the therapist. Sometimes this identification takes on concrete forms such as dressing as the therapist does or purchasing automobiles like the therapist's. Patients often surprise one another with the observation, "You sound just like the doc!" or "You're playing doctor again!" (This behavior can sometimes be understood as imitation as well.)

Particularly important are the hoped-for patient identifications with the therapist and therapeutic attitudes: the tolerance of feelings, the introspective stance, and the effort to understand as well as react.

Identification with emerging group norms and values is an important element unique to groups. As members experience a sense of belonging, they are strongly influenced by and identify with norms of openness, examination of their own participation in the interaction, and consideration of the process elements of a particular series of interactions. These identifications arise within the group and are not readily attributable to a particular person.

Imitation and identification are two of the major mechanisms which facilitate change. Much change can be accomplished on the basis of these mechanisms alone. They form the underpinnings for group attraction and cohesion. By virtue of these mechanisms much of the data necessary for understanding the complex connections between the unconscious and the conscious, the past and the present, are made available. Imitation and identification may explain the changes that occur in those patients who grow and change even though they sit rather silently in their groups.

Internalization

Internalization is an advanced and durable mechanism of change. Internalized change is not the result of something taken in from the outside, but rather it is due to a shift in the psychic structure of the individual so that his/her experiences, both conscious and unconscious, are shifted to a more mature level of functioning. Internalization is the mechanism by which psychological change becomes an enduring and functioning part of the personality.

Healthy internalization results in greater flexibility in handling both internal and interpersonal states and is the consequence of working through conflicts or building new psychic structures to handle previously disruptive anxiety. The therapist and others can facilitate healthy internalization by detailed examination and reexamination of emotionally laden interactions. Through the processes of confrontation, clarification, interpretation, and working through, individuals integrate knowledge gained in the here-and-now transactions with its sources and prior assumptions. This results in an increased integration of affects and object relationships, as well as diminished inner conflict.

True integration can be observed when patients evidence new behaviors or responses. For example, the patient who entered therapy suffering from paranoid ideation was eventually able to state to the therapist: "This year when you announced your vacation I again felt that you were not going to meet this group because you needed to get away from me in particular. I fantasized you were going to continue to meet all your other groups. It's the same old fantasy I've had in previous years. But this year it's just a fantasy, and it doesn't even have much emotional power for me. It's the price I've paid all these years for being the only child in my family to be put up for adoption." This represented a significant change. The "symptom" did not totally disappear, but the fantasy was not acted upon. In many instances, internalization and shifts in personality structure are demonstrated by more rapid resolution of a problem (i.e., a conflict emerges and is resolved in much shorter order than had taken place at the beginning of treatment).

Internalization often arises directly from group membership. The network provided by group interaction helps shape a sense of personal identity (Pines, 1998). A sense of belonging to the group and being truly engaged at a deep subjective level in its interaction leads to internalization processes that may be profound.

Summary

In order to be effective, the mechanisms of imitation, identification, and internalization must take place in the context of appropriate support and group cohesion. In practice, these mechanisms are not completely distinct. Change can occur so subtly that it is often observable only after it has taken place.

The manner in which members come to value dreams might be used as an illustration of how these mechanisms occur in concert with one another. When a member first reports a dream, there is usually some interest shown by the others. The therapist, too, by his/her verbal and nonverbal communications, indicates his/her interest. It is not unusual for some members to begin reporting dreams by way of *imitation* of others who have done the same. They do so to please the therapist. Furthermore, other members initially imitate the therapist's investigative style of trying to understand the dreams. At the level of *identification*, the members may find that they have a new attitude about dreams. They may experience a sense of excitement and stimulation when a dream is being reported, and they may develop a sense of curiosity about not only the dreamer's associations to the dream but everyone's associations. These are not entirely conscious responses, but rather they arise as identifications with the therapist's interactions with the members. At the level of *internalization*, members may find themselves experiencing a fundamental shift in their thinking about dreams and dreaming. In successful groups, a norm develops to explore dreams as useful ways of self-learning or uncovering hidden aspects of the group interactions. The use of the dream for exhibitionistic needs or as a shield diminishes, and the members believe that dreams are valuable tools for learning. In other words, the patients internalize the therapist's value system regarding dreams.

TRANSFERENCE

We discuss transference here because it is an important aspect of the therapeutic processes. We have previously discussed transferences in psychoanalysis and group therapy from the perspective of depth and intensity (see Chapter 4). Transferences and the repetition compulsion (within the dynamics of the group) are the forces that give coherence to understanding a person's behavior and feelings.

The role of unconscious drives, wishes, affects, and defenses in interpersonal transactions and their specific function in the formation of transference neurosis have held center stage in analytic psychotherapy. The psychoanalytic situation was thought to be the optimal setting in which patients would reexperience their past relatively free from external stimuli and from the impact of the person of the analyst. Freud (1905), almost from his earliest theorizing, appreciated the omnipresence of transference: "Psychoanalytic treatment does not *create* transferences, it merely brings them to light like so many other hidden psychical factors" (p. 117). Within the analytic relationship, a relatively specific reenactment of the central (pathological) conflict emerges, and interpretation of the transference will be mutative (Strachey, 1934).

The early group therapy theoreticians transposed the dyadic situation into the group, and with it the therapist's efforts to maintain a blank screen attitude, which was thought to elicit a transference neurosis. In the extreme, this resulted in what Leo Stone (1961) referred to as the "cadaver model" of the therapist. In this framework, peers were representative of siblings or objects of displacement from the authority of the therapist (A. Wolf & Schwartz, 1962). The argument was considered valid for individuals who grew up with siblings and, as well, for the single child, who would inevitably have fantasies about brothers and sisters. In this model the impact of the therapist is thought to be minimal and the therapy setting would allow the transferences to emerge.

A more contemporary model emphasizes the contribution of the patient's perceptions of the analyst and the treatment situation, taking into account their reciprocal interactions. This approach searches for and focuses on the here-and-now transactions (Cooper, 1987; Greenberg & Mitchell, 1983; Summers, 1994). The interactional patterns in groups provide opportunities to explore differing aspects of transferences: the transactions with the therapist among the members and the members' image of the group-as-a-whole (Stone, 1988).

Some group-as-a-whole theorists have focused upon the parental nature of the transference (Bion, 1960; H. E. Durkin, 1964; Scheidlinger, 1974). The theory of individual development has been transposed to stages of group development; the patients' responses to the therapist were formulated as transferences at oral, anal, and oedipal instinctual levels (Savaray, 1978). Also, the image of the group-as-a-whole became a transference object and metaphorically has been described in terms of the bad and good maternal object (H. E. Durkin, 1964; Scheidlinger, 1974).

A great many group interactions can be understood as fragments of transference responses. H. E. Durkin (1964) puts the matter succinctly: "if the therapist regards the intercommunications as free associations and searches out their latent intent, he will have no difficulty in identifying transferences in the group" (p. 147).

This expanded perspective places transferences along a continuum in which the analyst, the peers, or the image of the group-as-a-whole can be objects of transferential feelings. Transference manifestations include an individual's habitual reaction patterns, which overlap with character formation. For example, each person's manner of entering the group, of greeting other members, of managing separations, or of nonverbally communicating (i.e., how he/she holds his/her body) can be explored both as character and as transference.

Authors who adhere to the theoretical position that a therapeutic cure is achieved only with the resolution of a transference neurosis argue that this cannot be achieved in the presence of others (since consensual validation would hinder the development of transference). However, they incorrectly equate genetic reconstruction with depth. Indeed, group therapy can both intensify and dilute transferences. Horwitz (1994) highlights elements that intensify transferences as mutual stimulation (including affect contagion and identification), frustrating inputs (including the need to share and stimulation of rivalry), and protection and support of shared group affects (including universalization and increased group cohesion). Factors that dilute transference include reality inputs (including diminished idealizations, pressures to conform, and reality orientation of the members), multiple transference targets, and opportunities for withdrawal. Horwitz asserts that whole-group interventions tend to intensify and individual interventions tend to dilute transferences.

Supportive elements (including cohesion) and transferences have been separated to provide some clarity. However, in practice many obstacles arise from the individual (transference resistances or character traits) and the interaction among members to the creation of a functioning group. Much of the early learning that individuals gain in their groups is the result of the examination and modification or dissolution of those obstacles (e.g., development of safety and basic trust). For some this may be the central element in all their therapeutic gains.

THE THERAPEUTIC PROCESSES

By the therapeutic processes we refer to *how* the therapeutic mechanisms are used in the treatment context. The therapeutic *mechanisms* are made more complete by linking them to the *processes* by which they occur with therapy groups. The processes that induce and promote imitation, identification, and internalization are intimately imbedded within the relationships that are established in the treatment and the understanding that members have gained from the group interactions. In the psychoanalytic situation Stern et al. (1998) state:

> Anecdotal evidence suggest that after most patients have completed a successful treatment they tend to remember two kinds of nodal events that they believe changed them. One concerns the key interpretation(s) that rearranged their intrapsychic landscape. The other concerns special "moments" of authentic person-to-person connection . . . with the therapist that altered the relationship with him or her and thereby the patient's sense of himself. (p. 904)

In group treatment sources for genuine connections occur with peers as well as with the therapist. As the process proceeds, member-to-member interactions seem to become the more important (Crouch et al., 1994).

Confrontation

Foulkes (1961) spoke of groups as "halls of mirrors." This phrase aptly connotes the potential effectiveness with which groups can confront individuals with aspects of themselves they had been unable to see. A particular advantage to group psychotherapy arises from the opportunity for members to observe others interacting and in those interactions to see aspects of their own behaviors. Conversely their interactions are open to observation by others. In dyadic treatment the therapist has to rely upon reports from the outside world or use the interactions in the two-person field as the source of data for confrontation.

Pines (1981) described a dynamic that precedes confrontation. He maintained that as an individual becomes a functioning member his/her neurotic inner problems become evident as a communications block. Such blocks, or blind spots, may be raised to a level of self-awareness through confrontation.

Recognition of the problem is necessary before there can be agreement about what work needs to be done. Earlier psychodynamic literature refers to this as making the ego-syntonic ego-dystonic. Confrontations in this context are efforts to point out to the patient his/her behavior, emotional state, or problems. They primarily address external aspects of behavior, and as such are observations or responses to interactions or comments about the affects aroused in the confronter.

Confrontations do not address inner motivations or unconscious assumptions. A comment such as "You are always interrupting others!" is a confrontation, whereas "You are always seeking attention!" is not. The latter attributes meaning and as such is an interpretation. Often, particularly early in group experience, when patients make comments to one another that assume or attribute meaning and motivation, they are met with denial and/or anger.

Confrontation is an attempt to indicate to a patient that a problem exists; it is not an effort to gain or impart understanding per se.

In dyadic therapy the therapist is the confronter and therefore judges the pace at which confrontation should occur. Group therapy provides more complex and varied opportunities for confrontation because there are a great many potential confronters in a group. Indeed, to the degree that the members heed the agreement to share their emotional reactions to one another honestly, there is continual confrontation and feedback. Because confrontation is considered such an integral part of group psychotherapy, a great deal of effort is spent in making the group safe for confrontation and in making sure the confrontations are useful. This is especially true because many patients enter group psychotherapy with explicit requests to have feedback about their behavior. Though consciously wishing for such information, patients discover that they also have considerable resistance to learning about themselves.

Confrontations may be constructive, destructive, or a mixture of the two. It is important to create a supportive atmosphere which enables members to give and receive important information through helpful confrontations.

Many members are quite limited in their ability to give feedback. Others can give feedback in only the most benign situations and become anxious and frozen the moment intense affects are mobilized. The therapeutic task is not only to train members to overcome these fears but to understand the dynamic underpinnings of them. Gaining the ability to give nonjudgmental feedback or confrontation signals an advance in ego functioning. Indeed, members often cite their newfound abilities to confront others as a major step in their therapeutic growth and one of the special advantages of group therapy.

Learning to confront others successfully includes acquisition of a sense of timing, the capacity to form an alliance, and empathy. Although these elements may not be consciously integrated, their absence can be readily discerned. Timing rests in part on an appreciation of another's inner state and on a judgment as to whether the information can be productively assimilated at the time. The state of the alliance also influences the usefulness of a confrontation. The same confrontational material that can be heard and used from one member may be disregarded if coming from another. It is not unusual for accurate feedback to go unheard because of conflict. In such circumstances the comment "I don't trust you, so why should I listen to you?" might be heard. Therapists have long been aware that negative transferences block learning. This is particularly so in dyadic treatment. One of the major advantages of groups is the opportunity to learn about oneself from peers, with whom less intense negative transferences may develop. Finally, for a member to momentarily put him/herself in another's shoes and learn about that person's inner world is essential not only for understanding the other's emotional state but for being able to anticipate the effect of receiving the information (Stone & Whitman, 1980).

Many, if not most, confrontations carry with them an implicit request to "stop doing" whatever is being done. This is particularly the case when there is intense emotion in the group. For example, a member might blurt out something about another member that has been unspoken, like "You always attack us!" or "You continually put down women!" The message is clear though not explicit: "Stop doing that!" A hostile attack may be revealed by the use of extreme expressions like "always" and "continually." These words most certainly will evoke defensiveness in the confronted member. This situation rarely results in increased curiosity but usually results in a struggle between the confronter and the confronted member. Such a struggle may be productive for all concerned, but it is different from the growth-promoting confrontation. Of course, therapists are not immune to making confrontations bearing the covert message "Stop doing that!" In these cases a struggle results between the therapist and the confronted patient.

How information is conveyed to the individual being confronted is a matter of central concern—is it offered insensitively or in anger, or compassionately and empathetically? Most patients are capable of finding ways of confronting one another that are helpful and therapeutic.

The group agreements (see Chapter 8) provide an opportunity to confront members with their self-defeating behaviors. Patients agree to a variety of constraints in order to maximize their therapy. As patients choose to keep or break their agreements, they have many opportunities to be confronted about their characteristic styles and values. On many occasions entire groups will collude to avoid confronting a specific patient over a breach of the agreement.

For example, a member's absence from a group changes the nature of the interaction, yet members often avoid confronting the absent person. This avoidance may have many roots: it may be because the members are too angry and fear that they will expose an unacceptable aspect of themselves or they will evoke a counterreaction; or it may be because they do not wish to express their *pleasure* that the particular member is not present; or perhaps because they wish to leave open the option of *their* not attending all meetings themselves. Therapists are not immune to avoiding such confrontations. At times members do not recognize the significance for the individual or the group of such absence (Counselman & Gans, 1999). In some instances, the failure to confront another member represents a group-as-a-whole resistance, and the therapist may then be in a position to help members gain new self-awareness through a confrontation.

Some authors have suggested confrontational techniques concerning a patient's uses and abuses of the agreements. Borriello (1979) has elaborated a radical technique of confrontation with regard to breaches of the agreements, which he believes is crucial in working with patients suffering from severe acting-out character disorders. Following any violation, he directly tells his group that the rationale of the contract (his term) is to help patients break self-destructive patterns and that members do themselves a disservice by continuing their therapy while being unwilling to do what is required to change. Ormont (1967) addressed a subtler violation of the contract. He differentiated between expressions of feelings and personal attacks, viewing the latter to be acting out and therefore antitherapeutic.

CLINICAL EXAMPLE

During a heated interchange Rebecca said to Morris, "That was stupid." Morris angrily responded, "You bitch!" The therapist deemed neither of these interchanges therapeutically productive. After the subsequent prolonged silence, the therapist chose to address Morris, asking him to describe what he felt when Rebecca had called him stupid. Morris was then able to say he had felt humiliated. He went on to say that he often worried about whether he was as smart as others in the group. The atmosphere in the group changed, and it became possible to address Rebecca's initial "confrontation."

*   *   *

Fortunately, even unsuccessful or erroneous confrontations, when properly handled, can provide an opportunity to study interpersonal modes of relating. Therapists contribute to the safety of the group and illustrate alternate ways of confronting others when they teach members to comment on their own responses to an interaction rather than criticize another member.

Most confrontations take place among members or between therapists and members. However, one form of confrontation in groups is distinct. Looking into the hall of mirrors, patients might observe others involving themselves in unproductive and pathological behavior and begin to be curious about the extent to which they too engage in identical or similar behaviors. This is a form of self-confrontation.

CLINICAL EXAMPLE

Jerry, a never-married man approaching midlife, often rambled in the group. Eventually, following a number of confrontations, he could interrupt himself from talking in his rambling style. In an individual session he talked about being enraged with his mother: she talked "through" him and he wanted to choke her. He added that he also identified with her, and then he began to wonder if the group members felt about him the way he felt about his mother. After a pause he enumerated three individuals whom he was quite certain had been enraged with his ramblings.

*   *   *

Jerry used his individual sessions to expand on the knowledge he had gained through the repeated confrontations to gain some insight into the source of his behavior and he was able to achieve insight on the impact of his ramblings on others. He was then able to bring that material back into his group.

In a therapy group no confrontation is given in isolation. Every member of the group hears it and is affected, even though the confrontation may have been directed primarily at another member. Thus, interventions must take into account more than an appreciation of the openness of a particular individual to hear them—they must include an awareness that the other members will have their own responses.

Clarification

Greenson (1967) stated, "Clarification refers to those activities that aim at placing the psychic phenomenon being analyzed in sharp focus. The significant details have to be dug out and carefully separated from extraneous matters." Groups provide special opportunities for clarification to take place. One aspect of the process is the richness of experiences in the group itself, which enable patients to see repeating patterns. Members are a well of information about one another's behavior. It is a common experience for members, after a confrontation, to remember similar interactions or behaviors that have occurred in previous meetings. Often incidents dating back months or years are recalled in vivid detail; in other instances members will recall important pieces of previously shared personal history and will relate them to the current confrontation. For example, a member might notice that another has become withdrawn in the group; a second person might observe that the withdrawal took place after an angry exchange; a third might recall that similar processes had happened 3 weeks before; and finally the confronted individual might recall that he often ran to his bedroom when his alcoholic father would become violent. The initial confrontation of the present behavior, followed by members' recollections of prior similar events in the group, led to the individual's recall of important early family experiences. This example illustrates how clarification serves to organize and highlight such data. Much affect-laden material, previously split off and disconnected, can now be brought to bear on a specific and related issue. It is the weight of these episodes being repeated over and over in the group that contributes to individuals questioning themselves. This increased curiosity represents an important aspect of the change process.

Clarification results in patients gaining new understandings about the place of a particular action, feeling, or interaction. The *why* awaits interpretation. Nonetheless, it is very therapeutic and freeing for individuals to begin to notice repetitive patterns to their behaviors or feelings. Clarification often flows from the interactions among group members and from interactions between members and others as related in the group. The process then deepens as the clarification evokes new (though connected) feelings and responses. In addition, more than mere recollection is occurring, since in the immediacy of the recall in the group new interactions are happening. If maladaptive patterns are continuing, they will emerge in the interaction.

In contrast to individual psychotherapy, the main thrust of the clarification in groups takes place in a public arena. In individual therapy, while some of the clarification necessarily occurs in the examination of outside events that are reported in the therapy, most clarifications emerge from the relationship between the patient and the therapist. In group therapy outside events are also used but the in-group relationships are sufficient to provide the necessary clarification. This expanded database is used by both patient and therapist in examining perceptions, feelings, and behaviors. When a patient complains about the behaviors of a spouse, for example, it is usually possible to understand that patient's contributions to the marital dilemma by an examination of his/her interactions with group members.

It has been maintained in some quarters that the intensity and extent of transference is limited in group psychotherapy, since groups focus more on the here-and-now interactions. But transference *is* a here-and-now experience. It is the eruption of previously acquired distortions into the present. Groups offer an even wider set of opportunities for the exploration of such distortions. From our perspective the development of a coherent transference response in groups is at least as intense as in individual therapy and indeed may even be amplified by the experience of multiple peer transferences.

Interpretation

In ordinary discourse we interpret and assign meaning to our interactions. For instance, the paranoid person assigns a highly idiosyncratic meaning to events, which in his/her world is an interpretation. The manner in which interpretations are presented to patients has substantially changed in the past several decades, as the role of the therapist has shifted from one who pronounces his/her understanding to one of a collaborator who presents interpretations as tentative hypotheses that will be open to correction or alteration by the patient. Rubovitz-Seitz (1998) distinguishes between "positivist" interpretative models, in which knowledge is defined as empirical, objective, and certain, and the "postpositive" model, in which knowledge is pluralistic, data driven, pattern seeking, context sensitive, and may arise from multiple methods (p. 25). The former is usually presented as certainty, whereas the latter is presented as tentative, asking the patient for elaboration or correction. In clinical practice an interpretation is an assignment of meaning. It is not a truth, but an effort to mutually gain understanding of an individual behavior or affect state.

An interpretation is distinct from a clarification in two important ways. First, an interpretation is aimed at the unconscious, whereas clarifications are directed to the conscious or preconscious of our patients. Second, clarification broadens the data base by citing similar examples and sharpening the focus on a particular behavioral constellation. An interpretation is designed to make unconscious phenomena conscious, to attach meaning to events, behaviors, or feelings. It attempts to help the patient gain an understanding of the hidden motivations and conflicts contributing to pathological behavior.

In dyadic psychotherapy, interpretations are classically interpretations of transferences, resistances, and defenses. In group therapy, interpretations of interpersonal *style*, with resultant implications about underlying character and defenses, are also available.

Two major components are intertwined in a successful interpretation: the emotional and the cognitive. Further, no interpretation will be effective unless the timing in which it is offered is correct. By definition, interpretations help patients become aware of something they have been unaware of previously. This is most effective if there is an optimal emotional element involved. Interpretations can be too intellectual or they can be delivered in the midst of an emotional storm. There is little likelihood that interpretations at either end of this continuum will be effective. Ideally, the patient is first given the opportunity to genuinely experience the affect. The here-and-now interaction of the group enables the therapist to make interpretations at points where they have considerable emotional relevance and impact.

As noted above, the timing of interpretations is critical. Interpretations can be offered a long time after the affect was most heated because the time lag provides sufficient distance for the individual to integrate what is being examined; as Pine (1985) has so eloquently stated, "Strike while the iron is cold" (p. 153). If there is too much affect, the interpretation cannot be integrated.

Unfortunately, there are many occasions when interpretations are offered solely (though unconsciously) to protect the therapist or the group members from the intensity of affect. In such cases the therapist prematurely offers *understanding* and thereby shuts down the affect.

Interpretations examine unconscious conflicts and wishes, as well as the subsequent defensive responses or adaptational shifts. Optimal interpretations should go even farther and include some speculation as to causality. This does not necessarily include a genetic reconstruction, but linkages with individual development are not excluded.

In groups the leader is confronted with a myriad of variables in attempting to frame an interpretation that will be most useful to the patients and the groups. For example, should the therapist focus his/her interpretation on specific individuals, the interactions between individuals, the interaction between specific individuals and the leader, subgroups of members and the leader, fantasies about the "outside world," or the group-as-a-whole? Each focus is an apt target for interpretation, and the art of being a group therapist is to know when to use which. As Foulkes (1973) states:

We can focus on the group-as-a-whole or on any one individual or individuals in their specific interaction. As that happens in meaningful form, any point of view and the different meanings dovetail. It is not the case that one viewpoint is right and the other wrong. It is rather as if we took photographs from various positions. One picture may be better for certain purposes and others less good, but all of them show what is true from the position from which they were taken. However, the total process must always have been defined from the total field. (p. 153)

The following subsections present guidelines to help group therapists decide when, how, and where to make interpretations.

Group-as-a-Whole Interpretations

The followers of Wilfred R. Bion have demonstrated that there are always group-as-a-whole processes at work. To dismiss interpretations at that level is to overlook a source of great learning for our patients. An examination of the process provides insight for the members by helping them understand their involvement in and contribution to groupwide phenomena.

There are two types of group-as-a-whole interpretation: those focused on the group's reaction to the leader and those focused on the group itself.

Leader-Directed Interpretations. Beginning with the formulations of Freud, emphasis on transference to the therapist has been one of the cornerstones upon which psychodynamic psychotherapy is based. Therapists are very important people to their groups by virtue of the powerful position they occupy. Group-as-a-whole therapists have always made good use of leader-directed transference interpretations. Indeed, therapists who assume the role of the relatively silent, nonintrusive psychoanalyst encourage feelings to be directed toward themselves by the very nature of that role. The task of interpretation is to bring these responses into the members' awareness. Nonetheless, as important as they are, there are limitations to the effectiveness of focusing exclusively on leader-related transferences. Such an exclusive focus unnecessarily diminishes the multiplicity of peer transferences and relationships that are uniquely the province of group psychoptherapy.

Group-Directed Interpretations. In addition to transferences to therapists, individuals have specific transferences to the whole group. Various patients experience the group itself as engulfing, destructive, warm, protective, or secure. H. E. Durkin (1964) and Scheidlinger (1974), for example, suggested that on occasion the transference to the therapist (irrespective of gender) is paternal while the transference to the group is maternal. Kernberg (1975) expanded that notion by suggesting that patients with preoedipal pathology are particularly prone to the development of whole-group transferences. He maintains that whole-group interpretations are important in helping such patients gain insight and understanding.

Whole-group phenomena are the most evident at predictable developmental points and during crises. Whenever a boundary is breached, for example, when a new member enters, the entire group responds. The precise reaction for each individual varies, of course, but the group has to integrate the newcomer. After all, as soon as a new member enters, it is from that point on a different group. It may be assumed that each member is either coping with or avoiding the groupwide task of assimilating or rejecting the new member. In self psychology terms, the group serves as a selfobject for what Kohut (1976) labeled the groupself. A variation of this emerges when there is disruption to the continuity of the meetings either by vacations, absences or new members. The result may be a sense of fragmentation of the group. Addressing this draws attention to the soothing and self-organizing (selfobject) function of the group.

Affect-laden interactions stir responses in all members, who in turn respond. Nothing happens that does not impact on the whole field. A member's prolonged silence may have as strong an impact as the revelation of a poignant or dramatic event.

Leader-directed and group-directed interpretations are too often viewed as competing, mutually exclusive foci. In fact, they are complementary. Group-directed interpretations tend to help individuals examine issues of universality and commonality and, from that involvement in a common cause, to learn of their uniqueness. Roller (1989) has observed the paradox: "You can discover individuality in a group setting" (p. 96). Leader-directed interpretations tend to focus upon individual differences and from that to a deeper understanding of the fact that beneath the differences is a similar yearning for love and affiliation in all people.

An important variation of whole-group interpretations are those aimed at subgroups. A therapist's comment on similar behaviors or feelings of specific members (a subgroup) addresses the others as outside the subgroup and thus is an intervention addressing the entire group (Stone, 1998). Agazarian (1997) asserts that addressing subgroups has the advantage of not creating isolated or deviant members.

CLINICAL EXAMPLE

A group had experienced erratic attendance stimulated by a series of interruptions in the regular meeting schedule. This resulted in one session in which only two members (Mr. A and Ms. B) attended. The session was productively spent discussing Mr. A's response to the possibility of his mother requiring a kidney transplant and his fears of her death. The following week all members were present. After several perfunctory explanations of the absences, a member inquired what had happened the preceding week. In response Mr. A and Ms. B began to intently discuss together what had happened to Mr. A's mother during the past week (the atmosphere was that of a replay of the preceding week).

The therapist intervened, stating that it was as if two subgroups were present: the two members from last week and those who were not present then. He inquired what was it like to be present or to be absent. This interpretation brought into consciousness how a split was being created, and it stimulated an active discussion of the meaning of missing meetings.

*   *   *

In this example the therapist recognized that by defining the subgroup of those present the preceding week he was also defining a subgroup of those who were absent—thus the entire group was involved.

Incorrect or poorly delivered interpretations in any mode may be injurious. When group-as-a-whole therapists err, it tends to be in the direction of offering interpretations in an oracular, mystical fashion, fostering regression and dependency. On occasion the interpretations are offered mechanically; the statement "The group is . . ." homogenizes the members. Such interventions almost always result in narcissistic injuries to some members. The individual feels hurt, diminished, or just plain ignored. Malan et al. (1976) have documented the clinical ineffectiveness of a therapist's exclusive adherence to interpretation of group-as-a-whole, leader-directed transferences. Fortunately, such extremes are no longer typical.

It is quite possible to blend a group-as-a-whole focus, which underlines the importance of group process and transference to the leader, with more interpersonally based foci, which take into account more of the humanity of individual members. One successful solution is to make individual interpretations around a common group conflict, and then, when sufficient work has been done, to make a group-as-a-whole interpretation to demonstrate certain commonalities or a primary theme (Horwitz, 1977).

Individual Interpretation

Interpretations in group therapy are often made to individuals. Therapists should not lose sight of the fact that groups did not come for therapy. Rather, individuals came for help and therapists chose to offer those persons assistance in a group setting. Nevertheless, as we have repeatedly stressed, any intervention, and particularly an interpretation provided by the therapist, will impact upon the group, potentially altering the entire atmosphere. Indeed, one essential consideration in addressing an individual member is that the person may be filling a role for the group (the spokesperson). Thus directing the interpretation to a single individual may be a preliminary step to making a whole-group interpretation. This approach could be considered a foreshortening of the process described by Horwitz (1977; see above) in which the theme is elaborated in several individuals prior to making linkages to the whole group.

One strategy available to the therapist is to make an interpretation to individuals about their behaviors or affects that resonate with a group theme prior to explication of that theme. This has the advantage of strengthening the alliance with the particular individuals, and their associations may significantly deepen the process. A follow-up group-as-a-whole interpretation generally engages all present. In some circumstances elucidation of the theme is unnecessary, as the members make the connections themselves.

A second strategy is for the therapist to make individual interpretations following a groupwide interpretation (the extreme of this method is that of Henry Ezriel, see Chapter 2). This approach may be used when several members contribute to an emerging theme, and their contributions are pointed out at the time of making the whole-group intervention. The therapist may then invite the others to contribute their responses.

Not all interactions are a primary product of group transactions. Some represent a specific pathological configuration that emerges in the group. One such example arises when one member dominates and controls meetings. The therapist then has the complex task of helping the other individuals understand their reactions and contributions to the process, as well as assisting the monopolizer in understanding the sources of the monopolization.

Some patterned individual behaviors become very apparent in the group. Interpretations of those behaviors are particularly powerful when they include specific reference to the process and emotional sequencing that occurred.

CLINICAL EXAMPLE

Sally, a woman with severe borderline personality disorder, rarely spoke in the group. When she did, she usually gave a religiously oriented "speech" about the sins of the world. After many months, the therapist noticed that Sally varied her behavior in one repetitive manner. Whenever another woman missed a meeting, and especially when a woman terminated the group, Sally became much more agitated and yet much easier to understand. When the therapist accumulated sufficient evidence of this behavior, he pointed out the behavior while also offering an interpretation. He said, "Sally, it seems that whenever a woman is not in her usual seat in this room, you feel just as you did when your mother was hospitalized." The comment was offered in a spirit of mutual curiosity, not as a dictum presented from "on high." The members immediately confirmed that they too had noticed that Sally's behavior was notably different in those specific instances. This was a beginning point in helping Sally gain increased insight into the effects on her adult personality of her psychotic mother's having been permanently psychiatrically hospitalized when Sally was 3 years old.

*   *   *

The fact that many people are present adds an important dimension to interpretations directed toward any particular individual. On the positive side, as other persons hear interpretations directed toward a specific member, they gain a deeper understanding of that person which they may subsequently apply in their dealings with him/her. Other members may also find specific interpretations relevant for themselves, even though the interpretation was directed to another. It is not uncommon for members to have an "Ah ha!" experience while sitting back and observing interactions between the therapist and other members. Finally, their observation of various resistances to hearing interpretations is often useful in members understanding the various ways they themselves resist hearing new information.

There are also drawbacks entailed in individuals hearing interpretations directed toward others. The most obvious and difficult problem is that some patients are ready to hear an in-depth interpretation before others are ready. The therapist is thus confronted with a dilemma: whether to withhold information and understanding from a member who is ready to hear and use it in order to protect another patient who might be overwhelmed by the interpretation even though it is not directed to that member. In such instances it is better to offer the interpretation. In cases where it is clear that another patient will find such an insight painful and alarming, the therapist can offer empathic understanding that this comment will likely be difficult for him/her to hear even though it is directed to another. For example, as a therapist prepared to interpret erotic transference from one female patient, he first said to a newer member with a history of brutal incestuous experiences with a stepfather, "I am aware that it may be difficult for you to hear what I am about to say to Joan, but it represents an opportunity for both of you to learn more about yourselves." A rule of thumb in such matters is to side with growth and not with pathology. Thus, to withhold the interpretation from the patient who is growing in order to protect the more fragile patient usually does no good for either member.

What to Interpret

Interpretation is an art and is not conducive to learning by rote. Often the therapist "feels" rather than "knows" what is the proper target of an interpretation, since at any meeting there are probably several options for offering insight. Moreover, some interpretations arise from knowing the patients and the group and "spontaneously understanding" an aspect of the interactions. Such interventions have been labeled "disciplined spontaneous engagements" and represent the therapist's "generative intent" (Lichtenberg, Lachmann, & Fosshage, 1996). In the early days of psychodynamic group therapy, the mechanisms for change were viewed exclusively through transference and resistance, those mechanisms used in traditional analysis. As experience in the workings of groups has increased, therapists have understood that communications are responded to by all members, and their responses can serve as a reliable guide for making interpretations. An explication of the group process or individual responses that will enable patients to more fully understand what they are unconsciously or preconsciously communicating is usually the most successful interpretation. The therapist continues to help the patients see that various dysfunctional behaviors are in fact *solutions* to earlier, often unconscious or repressed problems.

An example of the process the therapist must go through in determining when and if to offer an interpretation is the following:

CLINICAL EXAMPLE

A relatively new group of recovering alcoholics was uncertain about how they might consider the emotional components of their drinking problems. One member began the meeting with a remark about feeling upset and anxious before going to church. Another continued, remembering that she had been upset by bad dreams and wondering whether she could do anything to stop them. Yet a third wondered if the second member was speaking about dreams or delirium tremens (DT's). And all this was followed by a discussion of the physical problems associated with alcoholism, most notably blackouts.

*　　*　　*

Here, the therapist was confronted with a dilemma. Should she offer an interpretation that would clarify the unconscious or preconscious communications in the group? She could, for instance, point out that the members seemed to have some anxiety about coming to the group (church) and that the anxiety seemed to relate to their concerns about whether psychological or emotional (e.g., bad dreams) issues might be addressed. Indeed, she could point out that in response to those topics the group shifted the focus to biology—bad dreams or DT's?, which led to a physiological state of no awareness (blackouts). By documenting the path of the group's associations, the therapist could offer an interpretation of the covert communication hidden beneath the overt content and thereby could help the group gain insight into what were the "real" concerns in the room. However, such interpretations require a state of therapeutic alliance and motivation. Interpretations offered prematurely serve only to stiffen the resistance and the commitment to not knowing.

In this immature group the therapist chose not to offer an interpretation of the defenses. She understood the dilemma as a questioning of her capacity as leader, as well as the group's ability to tolerate the affective components of their problems. The choice was made to provide a model for identification rather than an interpretation. Thus the therapist quietly turned to the patient who had been disturbed by her dreams and asked that she relate them to the group.

In this instance the therapist determined that the group would be best served by *demonstrating* that she and the group could tolerate emotions, rather than by interpreting the fears about that. Had there been greater group maturity, with demonstrated capacity to tolerate powerful affect and a history of strong therapeutic alliances, the therapist would have offered the interpretation. It likely would not have been an error to offer the interpretation even at this early date. This would have allowed the therapist the opportunity to test her hypothesis regarding the capacity of members by observing the group-wide response. The modeling response, however, represented a low-risk opportunity for the group to mature and members to risk more vulnerability at a later date.

This example not only indicates the complexities of a therapist's decision about whether and when to make an intervention, it also demonstrates the variety of useful responses available to the therapist. There is rarely one correct response. The therapist could instead have offered a model for identification by turning to the woman who was anxious before going to church and asking for more details about her anxiety. This would have served just as well as the revelation of the dream material. Or a confrontation aimed at focusing the affect could have been included—something like "Perhaps people are wondering just how much feeling can be shared in here."

The rationale for making one choice rather than another is aided by the therapist's capacity to predict the outcome of the interpretation. Interventions that lead to an elaboration of the material discussed, associations to new ideas, or exploration of affects are generally effective. Closing of the topic, repetitious descriptions of similar events, or constriction of affects are indicators of an unproductive therapist intervention. In the foregoing example, the therapist predicted that interpretation of unconscious material at this time would be met with resistance and instead chose to utilize the authority of her leadership to function as a model for identification. The primary goal at this time was to help set an important group norm: "Feelings can be expressed and explored in this group."

Recent advances in technique following the concepts of psychology of the self (Stone & Whitman, 1977, 1980; Kohut, 1971, 1977) have given new richness to our understanding of the functioning of interpretation. In this tradition interpretations are focused on the process of narcissistic injury. Group therapy provides fertile ground for narcissistic injuries. Members are continually feeling ignored, left out, insulted, or misunderstood. When interpretations by the therapist are directed to other individuals or to the group-as-a-whole, some members feel injured, as if they have received major blows to their self-esteem.

In groups many sequences are activated that result from natural, everyday varieties of narcissistic injury. Interpretations may be aimed at demonstrating to the member or the group the process of their interactions, pointing out the precise sequence as it emerged in the session. This is done so that the injured members can examine the sequence to learn more about their vulnerabilities and their responses to injury. For some individuals the interpretation can provide an experience of being understood, genuine insight, and increased capacity to contain their feelings of hurt. With increased ability to maintain their balance they are more able to see others as separate people with their own needs and wishes. The result is increased reality testing. Moreover, such an interpretation might help other members by making them aware of sadistic elements of their personalities that might have contributed to the injury received by the initial patient, just as they may have injured other important people in their lives.

Peer Interpretations

Most patients enter groups not knowing how to make interpretations, and the ability to make interpretations may represent an expansion of self-awareness or may precede it. The mechanisms of imitation, identification, and internalization may be instrumental in helping members gain increased interpretive skills as they observe and are influenced by the therapist and by more interpretative members.

Peer interpretations have unique power in groups since patients often have less resistance to learning about themselves from their peers than they do from authorities. For certain counterdependent patients, peer interpretations seem to be the *only* interpretations that are acceptable, at least early in treatment. The fact that peer interpretations have special influence makes it important for leaders to be willing to suffer the narcissistic assault of waiting until someone else offers an insight that the therapist had known for some weeks. The therapist will not get credit for having helped, though he actively deferred offering the insight in the hope that a peer would provide it. Of such occasions, as Foulkes and Anthony (1965) said, "There are times when the therapist must sit on his wisdom, must tolerate defective knowledge and wait for the group to arrive at solutions" (p. 153).

This is not to suggest that peer interpretations are routinely superior to those of the leaders. In fact, peer transferences within the group can considerably complicate the interpretations given and received. From a technical standpoint peer interpretations are often ill timed, too superficial or deep, or just plain wrong. In sum, peer interpretations are vulnerable to the same dangers as those of the therapist. However, such mistakes on the part of patients are not tragic, because they become grist for the therapeutic mill, setting in motion new interactions and opportunities for learning.

Working Through

For most patients psychotherapy requires an extended period of treatment to produce substantial and enduring change. Freud introduced the concept of "working through" in 1914 when attempting to answer the question, "What accounts for the fact that psychoanalysis takes so long?" (Brenner, 1988, p. 94). It should be remembered that this was at a time when analysis of 1 year was considered lengthy.

Working through is the final essential element in enabling patients to change. Confrontation, clarification, and interpretation help the patient to become aware of conscious and unconscious elements that create difficulties. Through these processes patients become familiar with the many facets of their fundamental psychological patterns and become aware of the habitual resistances to seeing or integrating those problems. However, these elements alone are insufficient to bring about deep and lasting change. In classical theory the emphasis in working through is on increasing patients' capacities to examine themselves, to understand conflicts and areas of vulnerability, to interpret their own behavior, and to help develop more varied and flexible defensive systems that protect them from undue anxieties while allowing more authentic intimacy with others and access to their own personal potentials. A self psychological formulation of working through posits the therapeutic task of assisting patients to understand their areas of vulnerability to an absence of or an insufficiently responsive other. The working through strengthens the self and allows for resumption of psychological growth (Kohut, 1971).

There is considerable diversity regarding what constitutes working through (Brenner, 1988). Is it something the patient does or something the clinician does? However one conceptualizes working through, it is a slow and incompletely understood process.

The working-through process consumes the major portion of time in psychodynamic psychotherapy. Pathological behavior, thoughts, feelings, and reactions appear, are worked on and understood, only to reappear in slightly different form. It often seems that in the process of working through we are essentially saying to our patients, "There it is again," "There it is again," and "There it is yet one more time!" The repeated opportunities for patients to examine the many facets of their problems are a major contributor to change.

It is one of the therapist's creative tasks to examine the multiple facets of a problem and find a way of presenting them to the patient or the group that will not be boring or repetitious. Sometimes obvious repetitions cannot be seen or heard until they are presented with a slight variation in meaning or phraseology. This does not mean that the initial understanding was incorrect, but individuals pick up and respond to interpretations or confrontations in their own idiosyncratic ways. The therapist must try to reach the individual on his/her own level and not ask that the therapist's words or precise manner of phrasing represent the final word. As more data are added, new material is also uncovered that adds to the richness of understanding and further helps the individual gain self-knowledge.

Therapy groups offer special advantages, along with some potential shortcomings, in facilitating the working-through process. In this setting, the group itself is an arena in which patients demonstrate their pathologies in great richness and subtlety. The opportunity to expose and explore many variations on a common theme results from these multiple relationships. The process is facilitated and inhibited by the presence of others. Sometimes feedback about behavior and character style can be received more easily from group colleagues than from the authority-figure therapist. The members of the group often pick up subtleties of behavior that the therapist misses. Further, members may use the group to try out new ways of coping or managing conflict and anxiety. Groups provide instant feedback on the success or failure of such new behaviors, at least in terms of their interpersonal consequences.

On the other hand, working through can be inhibited by the presence of others who vie for time. Sometimes the feedback and interpretations offered by group members is incorrect or a consequence of their own pathology, and this can complicate the working-through process. On occasion it may appear that a member's capacity to fully experience a transference reaction is inhibited by the consensual validation of the other members. Glatzer (1989) questions whether or not "the presence of fellow members makes therapeutic regression in analytic group psychotherapy different because of the quicker check with reality" (p. 293). She implies that working through even the most difficult issues is possible in group therapy. Though therapy groups are not the same as real life, they approximate life's interactions more obviously than does dyadic therapy.

In psychodynamic therapy it is the study of the resistance, the elaboration of the defenses, that is the point of the inquiry. Whatever latent conflict or emotion is hidden away will come to the surface of its own accord when the defensive structure is understood, appreciated, and made more flexible and appropriate. It is the working-through process that allows the patient to become accepting of his/her defensive structure, to recognize that it served a valid function in history even if it has become too burdensome in the present.

Membership in a therapy group exposes predictable patterns of interaction, and this in turn facilitates working through. Ongoing therapy groups provide repeated experiences with newcomers, departures, trust, autonomy, competitiveness, exposure and shame, and sexuality. Each reexperiencing of these issues and events offers a new opportunity to gain new understanding, attempt new behavior, and to work through chronic character styles. The relationship with the therapist and among the members as they learn to know, accept, and respect each other's subjective experiences is bound to be a part of the working-through process (E. S. Wolf, 1988, p. 153).

An example of working through as an analysis of resistance is the handling of acting out. Acting out has been a topic of much concern for therapists because the situation is rife with opportunities for patients to "do" rather than to "feel." This action could take place either in or out of the treatment setting. Psychodynamic group therapists, however, understand that such action is more than acting—it is also communication. Ackerman (1949) has pointed out that acting out need not be an impeding factor. Rather, patients have the opportunity to act out or demonstrate their transference reactions by their relationships with other members. In fact, acting out is used not only to avoid feelings or understanding but also as a covert means of communicating about and gratifying the impulse in question.

Exploration of acting-out behavior can be utilized as a vital element in helping patients understand the breadth and intensity of their feelings.

CLINICAL EXAMPLE

Ruth had experienced early losses in her life, and in the group talked extensively about loneliness and emptiness whenever a member would be absent or leave. As the transferences intensified, Ruth began to cope with her distress by establishing a liaison with another member outside the group meetings, a relationship that helped her experience continuity. She also began to miss sessions herself prior to and following any interruptions in weekly meetings. These actions were initially unconscious, then well rationalized. Gradually, Ruth, with the help of repeated interpretations, came to understand these behaviors as attempts to manage the deeper, painful feelings surrounding separations both inside and outside the treatment setting. At that point she began to experience great pain and despair, which were followed by a period of growth.

*   *   *

Friedman (1988) describes this process as follows: "When, because of personal involvement with his psychoanalyst, a patient is inclined to accept the analyst's view of his mind, then he begins to look for problems relevant to analysis, starts to see questions and answers of an analytic sort, and practices them in many examples (called working through)" (p. 239). When her group therapist first began linking Ruth's behavior to her feelings about loss she was nonaccepting. She could neither see nor experience any connection. With the repetitive enactment of the problem, Ruth began to experience the problem more consciously and she could then consider the therapist's view. This helped her make internal connections between her affect and the various behaviors which followed.

In contrast to individual therapy, where much more time might be spent in examining and understanding the patient's transferences, current life, and history, the group situation provides a breadth of experiences in the here and now. Working through is characterized not merely by having the same old memories reworked and reworked, or the same problem examined over and over; rather, group patients have ample opportunity to see and live out many manifestations of their current distortions and pathologies. Working through takes place as the patient connects in-group insights with real-world experiences and historical data (see the clinical example of Sarah in Chapter 9). However, complete insight and understanding is not the final arbiter of working through. Evidence that significant change has taken place can be appreciated when a previously well-defined conflict emerges and is experienced less intensively and for a shorter duration (Rubovitz-Seitz, 1998) or when a patient's interpersonal network is obviously enriched.

SUMMARY

In this chapter we have examined the elements that are essential in the process of helping patients change through psychotherapy. Fundamental to effective group psychotherapy is the conviction on the part of the members that focusing on the intragroup events represents a major opportunity to learn about themselves. The therapist's position is that of both an expert and an emotional participant. The therapist alternates between the stance of a separately functioning individual who observes the process and a person who is emotionally engaged with the group where his/her own affects can be used as information about the group interactions. The data collected from these vantage points are used to reflect to individuals that which might not otherwise be apparent to them. The clinician is also an object for the transference fantasies of the members. Within the safety of a supportive, cohesive group, bounded by the mutual agreements and protected by the presence of the leader, members are free to interact spontaneously, express strong emotions, talk about aspects of their lives felt to be shameful or terrifying, and step back and observe the effects of such sharing. Gradually they come to understand that interpersonal relating often represents consequences of intrapsychic conflict. Alonso and Swiller (1993) have summarized the following as the curative factors in group therapy: (1) vital enactment of the characterological dilemmas of the members; (2) exposure and the resolution of shameful secrets; (3) support around the universality of the members' wishes, fears, and distress; and (4) reintegration of split-off aspects of the self.

We conceptualize individual change as taking place via the mechanisms of imitation, identification, and internalization. Changes are facilitated by the multiple opportunities for relating and observing offered by groups.

Through the processes of confrontation, clarification, interpretation, and working through, members gain insight and self-understanding. These processes lead to shifts in the intrapsychic structures and capacities to manage stress and anxiety. Groups provide unique and potent opportunities for each of these mechanisms and processes to work effectively.

SIX

A Systems Approach to Forming a Group

Be prepared.
—LORD Baden-POWELL OF GILWELL

S uccessful psychotherapy groups require careful planning. The task is not simply to gather six to ten individuals together, set a time, and commence. Rather, the
enterprise requires a substantial foundation. In this chapter we examine the
contextual (milieu) elements which influence the formation and maintenance
of a successful therapy group. Then we focus on how to compose a group, including group agreements and principles of assessing patients to optimize the
"fit" with the group.

THE TREATMENT MILIEU

All too often new groups are formed in response to the enthusiasm of the
therapist without regard to the realities of either patient availability or an appropriate flow of referrals. Only in unusual circumstances are clinicians able
to form groups from their own caseloads. Thus, other sources of patient referrals are necessary. It is very disheartening to begin forming a group, recruit
only two or three members, and find no additional referrals in sight. At the
outset it is necessary to assess whether or not there is a reasonable expectation
that a flow of patients will be available. To ask, "Are there sufficient appropri-

ate patients available now to begin a group?" is not enough. There is a further important question: "Will there be sufficient referrals in the future to guarantee successful continuation?"

Patient Availability

Availability of patients can be influenced by broad social factors. For instance, the excitement about growth groups in the 1970s fueled an explosion of interest in group psychotherapy. Yet in the latter half of the 1970s and into the 1980s, public policy led to a sharp reduction in the number of long-term patients hospitalized in state facilities with large numbers of patients being referred into the community for continuing care. This seemed to create an opportunity for rapid expansion of group therapy; however, treatments for this population were generally slow to develop.

In the 1980s and 1990s succeeding cultural shifts attempted to provide broader health care coverage at lower cost. This shifted the primary treatment paradigm away from expensive long-term individual treatment and moved treatment planning away from the healer and toward insurance companies. In the arena of mental health care, considerable emotional heat has been generated by the intrusion into the privacy of the patient–therapist relationship and therapeutic decision making (Tuttman, 1997). Yet the environment has significantly changed, and clinicians now find it necessary to find ways of demonstrating the effectiveness of their treatment in terms of expense, time, and clinical outcome.

Surprisingly few health maintenance organizations (HMOs) have embraced group therapy as a viable less expensive treatment. Kaiser Permanente's Northwest Health Plan, according to the *Wall Street Journal,* offers coverage for 40 sessions yearly for group therapy compared to 20 sessions for individual therapy. Some 20% of the plan's current patients are in groups compared with practically none a decade ago (Jeffrey, 1999). However, not all HMOs have chosen this path, and in some there is an almost complete absence of group treatments. Public acceptance of HMO policies has resulted in an upsurge of time-limited, symptom-specific treatment at the expense of long-term psychodynamic groups. A report of the Group for the Advancement of Psychiatry (1992) predicted that in the future most psychotherapy would be brief and conducted in groups. (See Chapter 15 for an examination of psychodynamic time-limited groups.)

As evidenced by the response of the HMOs, considerable variation exists in the reception to group therapy. Historically, there was widespread acceptance of group treatment due to the support of highly visible and admired clinicians. It was not unusual for patients to request group treatment in locations where such clinicians practiced, since they might have known others in the community who had been successfully treated in that format. The opposite was true in other settings, where individual therapy was preeminent, and considerable resistance existed to sending patients to a group. Such devaluation highlights a primary task of the clinician—to educate his/her colleagues about the efficacy of group therapy. Similarly, if the social milieu emphasizes behavioral or pharmacological treatment approaches and is not attuned to psychodynamic/analytic modalities, the possibility of obtaining referrals will be limited unless the therapist demonstrates the potential of group therapy to help patients.

Even if the therapist determines that there are ample patients who need a group, that does not mean there will be a sufficient number of patients who will choose to join. A clinician must anticipate that a high percentage of suitable candidates (perhaps as high as 50%) will not choose to enter a group even when there is a good relationship with the therapist. Thus, it is reasonable to anticipate interviewing up to twice the number of patients that one hopes to have at the start of treatment. (See the research by Budman et al., 1988, and by R. H. Klein & Carroll, 1986.)

In most instances carefully prepared, determined clinicians can successfully overcome the systemic resistance to group therapy, the increased regulation of psychotherapy by third-party payers, and prospective patients' fears of joining a group. We now turn our attention to the tasks of optimizing the flow of referrals in clinic and private-practice settings.

Clinic Settings

In a clinic the therapist needs to understand and relate to the administrative and authority structures (McGee, 1969), and the institution must be prepared to support a group program. Only rarely do clinics support group programs and refer freely to group therapy. It is important to recognize administrative problems posed by therapy groups, such as the need for larger interviewing and waiting rooms, greater soundproofing, and clerical support. Subtle administrative resistance may emerge if an alliance with the administration is not firmly in place and these details are not openly discussed.

Clinics in which groups do not enjoy a ready-made acceptance will also benefit from an educational program for the staff. The program may be didactic presentations at staff meetings. It is preferable, however, if the therapist can have a small number of staff members actually observe a newly formed group in operation for a number of weeks. With patients' consent, it is possible to have observers without adversely affecting the treatment. The observers might be introduced as members of the clinic staff who wish to learn more about group therapy. Such direct involvement typically engages staff in an immediate and active interest in the program. It also offers an opportunity for those with no experience in group therapy to witness how effective group treatment can be. If that is not practical, the clinician should speak often with the referring therapists so that everyone continues to feel involved with the workings of the group.

It is particularly important to ensure that persons with the power of referral support the group program, since the flow of patients has an enormous impact upon the formation of groups (Johnson & Howenstein, 1982). The classic study by Yalom (1966a) on dropouts is a striking testimonial. At the outpatient clinic of Stanford University, Yalom was able to start nine new groups within a period of 8 weeks simply by administratively closing off the option of individual treatment and routing all new patients to group psychotherapy. The fact that nine groups could be started in such a short time is ample evidence of the effectiveness of administrative clout. (Furthermore, follow-up research indicated that patients reported equal satisfaction with their treatment as when they had been carefully triaged and referred.)

Experience has shown that even with careful attention to the administrative elements, forming a group requires considerable work. Although multiple sources exist for recruiting patients, they are not all equally effective. A hierarchy, beginning with the most optimal source, will help focus the clinician's efforts (Stone, 1996a):

- Therapist's own case load
- Colleagues' caseload
- Intake (clinic admissions)
- Patient review (staff) conferences
- Transfers from departing therapists
- Waiting list groups
- Continuing education seminars
- Posted notice

The impetus to begin a group may arise from the clinician or as an administrative request. In either circumstance, the optimal place to commence recruitment is from the therapist's own caseload. This has the advantage of the clinician knowing the patients and having an already established relationship, a situation that increases the likelihood that individuals will enter and remain in group therapy. A similar dynamic exists if the therapist spends time discussing group treatment with his/her close colleagues. Supportive associates are more often willing to make the required effort to help start a group than are persons with little emotional linkages to the therapist.

As noted above, it is important to track how referrals are made. Those who have responsibility for clinic intake or who lead staff conferences where patients are reviewed are valuable resources. They have the authority to direct the flow of patients to particular treatment modalities. Often these individuals need to be informed about the effectiveness of group therapy, since it may not be their own preferred form of treatment.

CLINICAL EXAMPLE

In a clinic where the program was floundering, a newly hired experienced clinician with particular interest in group therapy was placed in charge of the intake. After a brief period in which he gained appreciation of the "politics" of the situation, he was able to quickly gather optimal patients to form a new group for himself and act as a conduit to support other groups that were facing serious census problems.

*   *   *

Contact with departing therapists may encourage referrals; in training settings, contact with supervisors at the time of rotations may funnel individuals into a group.

A useful approach to creating greater visibility and increasing acceptance of group programs is availability of treatment at the "front door" of the clinic (i.e., waiting list or intake groups). Such groups may be used primarily for orientation, psychoeducation, or provision of immediate therapeutic services. Following participation in these time-limited groups, clients may be more attracted to entering ongoing dynamic group treatment (Stockman, 1997; Stone & Klein, in press).

Maintaining awareness of group treatment through the clinic is an additional approach to continuing the flow of referrals. Arranging for case presentations or continuing education seminars is useful for that purpose. Requests for referrals in flyers and posted notices in staff meeting places can serve as reminders of the presence of group treatment but seldom produce a flood of patients.

Private-Practice Settings

The private sector is not insulated from psychosocial forces nor from the need to educate and support a referral network. Insurance coverage has become limited. HMOs, preferred provider organizations (PPOs), and a variety of managed care systems increasingly monitor and limit the type, duration, and cost of treatment. The impact of these practices on actual therapy remains uncertain. Group therapists quickly find that they need to develop a sizable network of referral sources. Some communities do not value group therapy as much as others, and in those communities the flow of patients is negligible unless the therapist is willing to actively promote his/her group practice. In such a situation the clinician may occasionally feel pressured to select unsuitable patients in order to sustain a slim referral network or even keep a group alive. This usually results in a dysfunctional group.

The opposite situation is equally problematic. An established group therapist may be inundated with referrals and not have places to accept new patients. Continual rejection of patients referred to group therapy tends to stem the flow. Keeping the spigot flowing at an optimal rate is difficult. A therapist can often keep the referral network intact by locating an opening in some other group as a service to both the patients and professionals who make new referrals. The clinician who provides an ombudsman function keeps his/her referral network flourishing.

As we have emphasized, therapists should search their own caseloads as a primary but not exclusive source for group members. Clinicians should pay careful attention to their own affect as they begin considering specific individuals as candidates. For example, if one feels uncomfortable at the prospect of a particular individual joining a specific group, the roots of that discomfort should be fully explored before inviting that person to join the group. Beginning and running groups is a highly emotional experience for therapists as well as patients. It is exhilarating to interview a patient and have him/her agree to enter a group; conversely, it is discouraging when a series of prospective candidates either fail to appear for an initial interview, reject the idea at the time of screening and preparation, or accept and then fail to enter the group.

In the recruiting process clinicians may explore two paths: referring patients to the group and discontinuing individual treatment, or combining individual and group treatment. While there is debate in the field as to the advisability of seeing the same patient in both individual and group therapy, we are convinced this is both a viable and extremely powerful modality. Ironically, a therapist sometimes has difficulty shifting patients from individual to group treatment, even when he/she plans to continue the individual sessions. As noted previously, if clinicians are reluctant to refer a number of individuals to their own group, a countertransference reaction may well underlie the decisions. For example, sometimes a therapist feels protective and does not want to expose the patient to potential criticism in a group. Another possibility is that the therapist is unwilling to put an individual in the midst of powerful negative transference into a group lest that person cause the other members to have negative feelings toward the therapist. Consultation or discussion with coworkers can help resolve these countertransference problems. Occasionally the result of the clinician's heightened self-awareness is increased patient flow, as the therapist comes to recognize and alter subtle communications to colleagues that interfered with their making referrals.

One argument against seeing one's individual patients in group therapy is that it causes undue rivalry and competition among the members. In fact, there is *always* competition, rivalry, and great concern regarding the issue of which patient the therapist prefers. The addition of one's individual patients to a group does not *cause* this dynamic and in fact often facilitates exploration of envy.

There are also significant emotional considerations when another clinician refers a patient to a group. For instance, is the referring therapist a trusted colleague or a stranger? The quality of the relationship with the referring clinician is likely to have an emotional impact on the therapist, as he/she assesses the potential group candidate. The combination of group and individual therapy offers many opportunities for splitting, and therapists who know and respect one another can help the patient avoid this problem. Another element to be determined is whether the referring clinician has been actively treating the patient and, if so, whether that treatment will continue. It is important to assess as fully as possible the basis for either decision. For instance, is a decision to discontinue dyadic treatment a countertransference enactment by the therapist or the patient acting out against the therapist? If answers to these questions do not emerge in the interviews, then direct discussion of these issues with the referring clinician is in order. We have described some countertransference dynamics that may prevent referring patients to a group. Similarly, countertransferences may be activated that lead to individuals being referred to a group. An often-cited manifestation is dumping unattractive patients into groups. Many times when an individual therapist finds it impossible to treat a patient, he/she concludes, "This patient needs a group," when what he/she really means is "Perhaps other patients can say directly to this patient what I, as a professional caretaker, do not feel I have a right to say!" Ironically the patient who cannot even establish a viable relationship in dyadic therapy is typically *not* a very good candidate for a group. Further, such patients sense that they are being dumped. It is an experience in life about which they have some expertise. When the referral is an attempt to avoid dealing with unpleasant sides of the individual therapy, the patient often retaliates by quitting the group prematurely. In clinic settings, this dynamic is often enacted when patients are "dumped" into groups by a departing therapist.

Sometimes the individual therapist refers a patient to group in order to avoid unrecognized intimate *warm* and *loving* feelings that exist in the dyadic relationship. Since many patients are referred to the group principally because they have difficulty in establishing or maintaining tender relationships, a referral under these conditions represents an unconscious collusion by the individual therapist and the patient to avoid the intensity of their affect.

The reason for considering some of the less complimentary motives for group referrals is that these are very often either unconscious or not discussed, and knowledge of these problems will help both individual and group therapists in evaluating and preparing such referrals for successful engagement in subsequent treatment.

For a great many patients termination of the individual session is not indicated and a combination of group and individual therapy is the most useful treatment format. This combination is explored in depth in Chapter 11.

COMPOSING THE THERAPY GROUP

The composition of a group influences the individual just as the individual impacts upon the group. This leads to viewing group formation from two perspectives. First, the referring therapist needs to determine whether there is a group best suited for his/her patient. Second, the group therapist should determine which patient is best suited for a particular group. We next look at the issues of group composition from both perspectives.

Group Goals

We begin with an examination of the goals for the group as a fundamental consideration for matching patients and groups. Groups may be composed along a variety of continua. Time-limited groups are often formed on the basis of demography (e.g., women, men, adolescents, gays), crisis (e.g., divorced or bereaved individuals), or symptom (e.g., alcoholic or anorexic patients). In such groups there is an emphasis on patients' capacity to work in a reasonably focused manner (Budman, Simeone, Reilly, & Demby, 1994). Such an emphasis takes advantage of the group therapeutic factors of universality and acceptance. The fact that individuals begin with the knowledge that in some fundamental ways they are similar to others serves to hasten the initial, trust-building stage.

Other factors must be considered when forming groups for significantly impaired individuals (see Chapter 14). These patients may have major psychotic illnesses (e.g., schizophrenia or bipolar disorder) or personality characteristics that have severely limited emotional, cognitive, interpersonal, and adaptive capacities. For these patients with chronic impairments, groups, within a dynamic framework, include a focus on creating a supportive environment and assisting members to improve their interpersonal relationships and quality of life.

In the tradition of open-ended, long-term psychodynamic groups, a few authors (e.g., Bach, 1954) suggest that it is not helpful to place patients in groups according to some notion of which groups are best for which patients. According to this point of view, groups should model life, and therefore patients should be referred solely according to who comes along next. While the pragmatics of private practice sometimes make this more the rule than the exception, such a practice is nonetheless far from optimal. A primary consideration is an assessment of the level of functioning of the group: at what level is the group functioning, and what is the potential for change. Groups that may initially be composed in anticipation that members can examine their relationships may not evolve to that developmental level. The characteristics of specific members (i.e., severe trust issues or borderline personality disorder characteristics which are not initially discernible but emerge in the therapeutic process) may limit the rate at which all members achieve ego development.

In forming a new group a therapist can only make the best possible judgments about the potential level of group function based on the persons being screened and selected. In ongoing groups a review of the predominant themes over a period of time will assist the clinician in determining the level of group development. Some groups struggle with fundamental issues of trust for years, whereas others characteristically deal with anger, and still others are concerned with intimacy, individuation, or competitiveness. The presence of a patient working at a different level may even catalyze particularly painful but important sectors of pathological functioning that might otherwise go unexplored, but the therapist should not count on this happening.

Assessing Patients: Preliminary Formulations

The clinical interview is the primary basis for determining a patient's capacities to enter and participate in a psychodynamic group. In some settings, information from the referral source or clinic records replace careful personal evaluation by the clinician. We strongly discourage this practice. We believe that the clinical interview is fundamental. By attending to the presenting problems and listening to the interpersonal history of a potential group member, it is usually possible to generate several viable hypotheses as to the basis of the problems. These data can be discussed with the patient as a part of the presentation of the group agreements—the negotiation about choice of treatment modality. These formulations will also be useful to the therapist in predicting the patient's probable course in the group. For example, many patients unknowingly are unable to form relationships because they suffer from insufficiently mourned losses. It can be hypothesized that in the life of the group someone important to the patient will terminate and that this will offer the client an opportunity to relive such loss experiences.

In assessing an individual's "fit" for a particular group multiple aspects of ego functioning are to be explored. In evaluating ego functions, a broad view of the primary defenses utilized by different patients is gained. Healthier clients rely on reality-respecting defenses (like intellectualization, rationalization, or undoing), while less advanced clients rely on reality-distorting defenses (such as projection or reaction formation). Our least advanced patients, on the other hand, utilize reality-denying defenses (including denial and splitting). Again, mixing these patients will make the task of forming a group quite difficult.

Patients at various developmental levels are attempting to accomplish different tasks in their groups. The healthiest patients are typically working on issues of intimacy and authenticity, whereas the least advanced clients are working on resolving splitting, emotionally sitting in the room with other human beings, and developing even the most minimal connections to others.

In many cases the major source of data about the interpersonal life of a patient emerges from the relationship in the therapeutic or preparatory interviews. If therapists will pay special heed to their affective responses to the patient, they will gain access to a veritable gold mine of information. For example, if the therapist is bored or easily distracted and feels "alone" in the office or wishes the clock to speed up, the chances are that he or she is sitting with a schizoid, obsessional, or severely narcissistic patient (excluding the obvious alternative that the therapist is struggling with personal issues of his/her own that are not evoked by the patient at all).

Alternatively, a borderline patient is almost never boring. He/she may be frightening, stimulating, enraging, entertaining, or demanding, but rarely boring. In the first instance the individual therapy can flounder on the rock-hard defenses of intellectualization and isolation of affect, and with the borderline patient the therapist may be held at a distance by the aggressive, hyperactive self-presentation. For many of the former patients, eventual exposure of the underlying conflicts reveals that noninvolvement is a defense against perceived terrors and dangers of intimacy. A very important component of this is the fear of nonresponse by an unempathic significant person (Wogan, Getter, Anidur, Nichols, & Okman, 1977).

As already noted, when an individual's "fit" for a particular group is assessed, several areas of ego functioning should be explored; these are meant to be general guidelines and represent our approach to thinking about aspects of the prospective member's history and prior relationships:

- Acknowledging need for others
- Self-reflective capacity
- Role flexibility
- Ability to give and receive feedback
- Empathic capacity
- Frustration tolerance
- Preexisting relationships

Information about these areas is never complete, and a great deal of the information may be outside a patient's awareness. However, it is possible to generate several viable hypotheses about each of the above areas of functioning in preliminary screening evaluations by attending to the presenting problems, assessing one's emotional reaction to sitting with the patient, and listening to the developmental and interpersonal history of a potential member.

Acknowledging Need for Others

A primary consideration that reflects ego capacities is the patient's awareness of his/her need for others. Following the tenets of object relations theory, we believe that *everyone,* irrespective of pathology, wants and can profit from the experience of intimacy, of loving and being loved. One accurate means of diagnosing individuals may well be to assess how much they try to pretend that wish is not present.

Closely linked to acknowledging a need for others is the person's ability to trust. Individuals approach trust building from very different perspectives, depending on their psychological health. Healthier patients approach a new group with fundamental trust in others. Less healthy clients enter with clear ambivalence about trusting others. The most disturbed patients enter with an absolute conviction that others are not to be trusted. Patients may not be conscious of their level of trust and distrust, and full appreciation of this sector of the personality may only emerge over time. Individuals from these three separate perspectives would have great difficulty even understanding one another, much less arriving at some acceptable level of trust that would allow them to successfully benefit from a group.

Self-Reflective Capacity

A patient's ability to experience and reflect upon his/her interactions is an important indicator of ego capacity. Some patients become emotionally enmeshed in the group interactions and have a very limited ability to utilize their observing ego on the affect stirred in the therapy. Other clients are so intellectualized in their defensive structure that they never allow themselves to spontaneously "be" in the group. The goal for the first kind of patients is to help them develop the ability to move from experience to observation and intellectual understanding. The goal for the second type is to experience the impact of the interactions before using their intellect. The therapist should be wary of having too many patients representing either end of that continuum simultaneously in the same group.

Role Flexibility

As we discussed in Chapter 3, there are a variety of roles which can be assumed by group members. An optimal goal for patients would be achieving sufficient role flexibility so that they can successfully function as both leader and follower. The leader role is linked to an individual's relationship to authority and developmental experiences with parents. The follower role is linked to peer relationships in which collaboration, cooperation, and intimacy are associated and can be traced to early sibling or educational experiences. In addition, a series of other significant roles may be productively explored in the pregroup interviews. Benne and Sheats (1948) distinguish among roles that will facilitate group progress and problem-solving capacity, maintain or build the way the group is working together, or satisfy individual needs. The applicant's capacity to work effectively or ineffectively within organizations and social settings will provide clues as to potential group roles. Both leader and follower roles are available for all members. Taking a detailed history of the patient's functioning in his/her family of origin, on committees, teams, work groups, and other groups will provide predictive information regarding the role the patient will likely assume in a therapy group. More often than not, individuals seeking group therapy have histories of poor functioning as effective leaders and followers. Thus, we usually find individuals who have proclivities toward being harmonizers, compromisers, standard setters, opinion givers, moralizers, and so forth.

Using the data from the pregroup evaluation, the therapist can make inferences about the role a patient may assume in the group. By generating such hypotheses and observing the subsequent behaviors and feelings of the patient, formulations can be either validated or discarded. If major revisions are necessary, this may be the result of new information or faulty empathic connection between therapist and patient. At the same time the therapist can gain a historical vantage point that may be utilized in helping the patient understand the connections between in-group responses and those from the past (Rutan & Alonso, 1978).

CLINICAL EXAMPLE

Elaine came to group to work on her terror of intimacy with men. Successful individual therapy had given her insight into the roots of her difficulties, but she wanted to join a group in order to gain actual opportunities to meet and relate to men at an intense level. She knew from individual therapy that the women in her family were flawed, her mother being psychotic and usually mute and her sister being retarded. Elaine, though raised by a loving aunt, nonetheless had an image of herself as defective and inadequate. The therapist decided to place her in a particular group because he hypothesized that a woman in that group, Francine, would stir very important, though painful, feelings for Elaine. Francine was a seriously depressed and very silent member, often not speaking for months at a time. Within 3 weeks, Elaine stated that she was leaving because she found it was not helping and because she was getting more anxious. She stated that she was having difficulty sleeping the night before the group. In this case the therapist, having made a preliminary hypothesis, simply said, "A family with women who are silent when you need them to be helpful is a familiar problem, Elaine." Despite the fact that Elaine had never mentioned Francine, she instantly began weeping and yelling at Francine for being so "hostile."

*   *   *

This represents an example of a therapist carefully selecting a group for the patient based upon a hypothesis that under the regressive forces stimulated by entry into a group and coming face to face with a silent woman, Elaine would soon find herself in the role of the neglected child. The regression interfered with Elaine's capacity to recognize Francine as a person with her own difficulties, and the therapeutic efforts would be aimed at helping Elaine gain greater flexibility in addressing similar situations.

Ability to Give and Receive Feedback

Experiential training groups (T-groups) highlighted an additional criterion particularly relevant to group therapy: the ability to give and receive feedback appropriately. These twin abilities are a central part of the experience in a therapy group. Ormont (1967) places the task of giving feedback in a traditional psychodynamic frame. He succinctly states that patients may express how they feel but may not attack others. His emphasis is on educating members for an appropriate interpersonal role, although he realizes that the ineffectual interpersonal behavior is part of the problem for which a patient seeks help. By highlighting this ground rule, Ormont reinforces the norm of safety and sets the stage for analyzing the difficulty of remaining in role. We do not recommend making this a part of the group agreements because it is unfortunate but true that some patients need to experience their interpersonal style and begin to observe their behaviors as expressions of underlying issues of sadism and rage. Some seriously impaired, entitled individuals persist in believing that they have the right to express themselves in whatever way they wish, despite concerted efforts to both set limits and to interpret the behavior. On rare occasions this may lead to removal from the group (see Chapter 14 for additional discussion of removing group members).

Equally important is the patient's ability to listen in an open fashion, without defending or justifying a feeling or position, but being able to consider what has been said. Again, such behaviors are not typically part of the repertoire of most patients. Not uncommonly, patients with significant early developmental conflicts will respond to questions or interpretations almost instantaneously. If they are questioned, they may well acknowledge that they never "heard" the question, much less considered it. By their very nature, groups provide growth-producing experiences for patients to genuinely feel helpful to others or to have the capacity to listen nondefensively to other people.

Empathic Capacity

An important consideration in assessing a prospective patient's "fit" is the patient's empathic capacity, which is a corollary of the individual's capacity to shift roles (Abse, 1974; Stone & Whitman, 1980). The ability to empathize—that is, to temporarily put oneself emotionally in the shoes of another—implies that the individual has been able to reach a stage of development where others are experienced as separate, with needs and wishes of their own. Some prospective members only possess rudimentary empathic capacity, and their inclusion into group treatment mandates that this missing function be filled by others, a task that most frequently falls to the therapist. In groups, initial experiences of finding sameness and experiencing it with another may be precursors of empathy (Detrick, 1985; E. Shapiro, 1998). A prospective member who is unable to demonstrate a nascent capacity to acknowledge similarities with others or feels so alienated or different (and maintains that as how he/she is) is an unlikely candidate for group treatment.

Empathic capacity extends beyond the interpersonal relationships and includes the group situation. One aspect of empathy with the group is the requirement of maintaining confidentiality. Some individuals are either too gossipy or need to utilize group information as a base for power or to gain attention and thus cannot adequately respect the tenet of confidentiality. For such patients it is not a question of which group is best—no group is suitable, since their inclusion unduly risks harm to the other patients.

Frustration Tolerance

Entry into dynamic therapy carries with it inherent frustrations. The therapist may not directly answer questions, and gratification of needs is frequently frustrated. Action is discouraged or analyzed, and evidence for patients to have the perseverance and courage to stick with it is an important attribute. The individual who has a history of changing jobs or frequently quits projects in frustration is a likely candidate for premature termination. A corollary of this criterion is the individual who does not recover from emotional injury, that is, empathic failures (Harwood, 1996). Those persons stubbornly hang on to experiences of being hurt and hold grudges. They have the potential to become destructive to the group process with bitter diatribes against others (Nitsun, 1996).

Preexisting Relationships

A criterion of a different sort is that the applicant have no preexisting relationships with members that would inhibit the work of the group. It is important during the screening to learn enough about the patient's life and activities to be reasonably certain that a stranger is being introduced into the group.

Exploration of work or recreational activities may expose a situation where a prospective member has continuing and significant contact with someone already in the group. Usually awareness of the patient's home address and place of work alerts the therapist to the possibility. If there is reason to believe pre-existing relationships exist, then considerable tact is required to elicit sufficient data on which to base a decision to accept or not accept such an applicant. It is clear that certain relationships are of sufficient importance as to limit the freedom to share. This is especially true in work-related situations, where, for example, one member might have administrative responsibility over another member or where a minister might find himself in a group with a parishioner. Many variations of this problem exist, especially in smaller communities, and it is a part of the therapist's responsibility to take reasonable care in protecting the member's anonymity.

*   *   *

Despite precautions, sometimes acquaintances or friends will be placed together in a group, and then rapid but thoughtful decisions must be made regarding the nature of the group's composition. Once a new member has walked into the room and thereby breached the confidentiality of the others, the decision regarding the continuing membership is part of the group process, though the responsibility for such a decision usually rests with the therapist.

CLINICAL EXAMPLE

In one instance, following a careful evaluation a man joined a mature group only to be confronted at the end of the initial meeting by a woman saying that one of her best friends was the new member's steady girlfriend. The woman had realized this part way through the session, but had been uncomfortable and not revealed it until just prior to the time to end.

The new man then asked what to do, and the therapist stated that the task of the group would be to decide whether this unexpected complication would compromise the therapy of either the new patient or the woman in the group. In the remainder of that session and in the next the group actively discussed the pragmatic difficulties this situation posed as well as a myriad of feelings elicited by it. For example, the woman associated to the lack of privacy she experienced in her home. Ultimately the group decided this was not a tenable treatment situation and the new patient accepted the therapist's offer to join another of his groups.

*   *   *

Handling this delicate problem in the group setting modeled for the group that nothing is beyond the scope of the group. Further, the full exploration of the feelings evoked by this situation allowed the new member to leave without feeling injured or rejected, and he was able to join a new group quite successfully.

CLINICAL EXAMPLE

A different situation occurred when a new man entered a group only to discover that many years ago he had been engaged to marry a member of the group. (To add to this surrealistic meeting it happened that the electricity was out and the meeting was held by candlelight!) Not surprisingly, the two were very surprised to discover each other again after so many years. (This relationship had occurred in another state, and there was no way the therapist could have known of it.) That relationship had ended very painfully when the man simply disappeared without a word. The woman was in therapy to deal with her depression, and one significant stimulus for that depression was the failed engagement. She had never married. The man came to therapy because of his terror of intimacy and his lack of contact with his affective life. Ultimately they and the group decided it would be most productive for them to remain in the group. The woman wanted to learn more about what happened in their relationship. The man felt it would be useful to have a woman in the group who knew his family and history well. They remained in the group many years, and aside from a brief attempt at acting out and resuming their romance (they went out to dinner one evening), they both made excellent progress in their group therapy.

*   *   *

As the second example suggests, not every preexisting relationship precludes placing people in the same group. However, our experience indicates that putting persons with any degree of prior relationship in the same group usually results in havoc and should be avoided. In the event that it is determined that the therapy is untenable, the new patient is always the one that ought to leave.

Choosing the Optimal Group

These considerations will assist the group therapist in placing individuals together in the creation of an optimal therapeutic environment. The therapist has to be concerned with both the individuals and with the group itself. Ultimately, care should be taken to ensure that the maximum effectiveness of the whole group benefits each individual. Ideally, groups are finely tuned organisms, not conglomerates of randomly selected individuals.

Demographic Considerations

Widely diverse groups often find it harder to develop cohesiveness and an optimal working environment. An individual who is markedly different along a continuum of age, gender, race, culture, and/or ethnicity may have difficulty joining. Equally important are group dynamic phenomena, which include the tendency to isolate, stereotype, or scapegoat the "different" member.

Nevertheless, these differences in themselves are not reasons to exclude prospective members unless they represent extremes, say, evidence of significant ego weakness in the individual or inflexibility in the group. In ongoing treatment, the goal is to meld together individuals sufficiently alike that they can understand and empathize with one another but sufficiently different as to offer different perspectives and different strengths to each other. We now explore the following demographic elements:

- Age
- Gender
- Culture and ethnicity

Age. Newly formed groups should not span too wide an age range. Individuals in their 50s by and large have different life concerns than individuals in their 20s. While a wider range can be beneficial in more mature groups, it typically makes it more difficult for members of new groups to cohere and have a sense of belonging. For example, new groups of younger adults ideally should have an age range of approximately a decade. For older adults (in their mid-30s and older), a broader age range is workable. Further study is needed regarding the issues of adult development and life transitions in order to help us conceptualize age factors more precisely.

Gender. Research in differences in gender development have taught us that gender exerts a powerful influence on how individuals think and feel about themselves and one another, particularly as it impacts on social, economic, political, and cultural interactions (Lazerson & Zilbach, 1993; DeChant, 1996).

The gender of the therapist is one consideration in choosing a group for a particular person. Although patients may develop paternal or maternal transferences to a clinician of either gender, the person may prefer either a male or a female leader. This often represents an important clue to emerging transferences, either positive or negative. Stereotypical, cultural expectations of women leaders serving as the all-powerful, selfless, noncritical, and nurturing mother are particularly stressful for women in leadership roles (Rosenberg, 1996). Thus, exploration of the response to the gender of the therapist is a valuable element in anticipating the nature of the client's group participation. If the patient seems inflexible, there is little to be gained in insisting that the patient enter a group with antipathy directed to the therapist on the basis of gender. One alternative is to provide a group with coleaders of both genders. If a patient is currently in ongoing individual psychotherapy, it may be helpful if the group therapist is of the opposite sex.

Though single-gender women's and men's groups offer a great deal, in ongoing psychotherapy groups it is advisable that the groups be mixed in gender. (Why rule out half of the human population from the therapy experience?) Ongoing groups are concerned with helping their members learn as much as they can about living in the real world, and as such they should include men and women. It may be a reasonable alternative for individuals particularly frightened of the opposite sex to enter a single gender group preliminary to an open-ended, ongoing mixed group.

Many clinics find that their patient populations are notably skewed with regard to gender. The most usual situation is for clinics to have many more female patients. Under such circumstances, groups may form with all women, with the stated plan that men will be added later. The goal of equal gender distribution may not be attainable. But the situation where there is only one man (or woman) in the group is to be avoided. Indeed, it is preferable that the group makeup include at least three members of each gender. If one's referral network is such that this is difficult to accomplish, leave chairs open for men or women and wait until there is an appropriate patient. If the goal is eight members, then no more than five seats should be filled by one gender. Optimally, as just noted, a group should have at least three persons of each gender. This allows a person to individuate from a pair.

Culture and Ethnicity. As populations become more diverse, and with greater acceptance of psychotherapy, individuals from different cultures and with different ethnicity are applying for treatment. Specific and general psychosocial factors must be taken into account in helping not only the individual with a "different background" to benefit but also the entire group to gain from such a member's participation (Brook, Gordon, & Meadow, 1998). Hopper (1996) addresses the question of the "social unconscious" in clinical practice:

> Whereas we have come to accept the validity and utility of the concept "unconscious" for phenomena originating in the body, we need a concept like the "social unconscious" in order to discuss social, cultural, and communicational constraints. It is virtually impossible to learn about some aspects of such constraints, because inevitably we are caught up within them and formed by them. (p. 10)

In many large U.S. cities white Anglo-Saxon individuals are a minority group. Hispanics, Asians, and African Americans together compose the majority. Dalal (1997), examining the impact of color/race on the internal image, asserts, "It should be remembered that whilst colour is a trivial, superficial, difference—of no importance in itself, what is of importance is [*sic*] the significances and meanings attached to it, and the fact these are interiorized in profound ways" (p. 207). Language comprehension or use may represent important communication barriers for the patient and therapist. It is not always apparent when language difficulties are present, particularly when clients experience shame with their problems.

Less obvious cultural differences may emerge quite unexpectedly. For example, increasing emphasis on diet and food selection may be a source of stereotyping.

CLINICAL EXAMPLE

In an experiential group for therapists in training, Audrey introduced herself by expounding on her attitudes towards diet and mental health. She discussed at some length her views of the "dieting culture," which were moderately divergent from the mainstream. As she talked about how she fed her children and what restaurants she frequented there was a rise in tension in the group. A somewhat more sophisticated member commented that she often ate when she was anxious. That comment enabled the group to address more usual themes.

Considerable important therapeutic work was required for the leader to recognize and "metabolize" his own discomfort with Audrey. He then proceeded to assist members in addressing their emotional reactions to her. Audrey subsequently revealed that, although her diet was very important to her as a person, she used this aspect of her self to determine how the group would accept her, since she knew she was not "mainstream." It then became possible to link Audrey's initial disclosure as having a basis in common with the others, testing trust and safety in a new group.

*   *   *

This example illustrates a "cultural paranoia" and xenophobia which often requires clinicians to actively intervene to alter the process (Fenster & Fenster, 1998).

Interpersonal Style

We now turn our attention to an additional frame of reference in composing a group—that of interpersonal style.

Whatever the ego development, age, or gender, each patient also has an interpersonal style. For example, patients at any developmental level can be domineering or retiring, gregarious or shy. For the purposes of an optimally functioning group, a variety of styles is mandatory. It may well be that a good mix is the single most important aspect of group composition.

The variety of interpersonal styles has been condensed into four quadrants of the well-known circle conceived by Timothy F. Leary (1957): domineering versus submissive styles forming the vertical axis, and outgoing versus shy and withdrawing forming the horizontal axis. It is our contention that effective groups have members representing all four interpersonal styles. A group filled with shy and retiring individuals will not have the emotional electricity that one with greater variations presents. The presence of different styles is the external presentation of each person's psychic organization. As the underlying bases for the self-presentations are exposed, individuals have an opportunity to learn about aspects of themselves that have been hidden. We assume that much interpersonal conflict is based on members disowning aspects of themselves that are present in others. Inclusion of patients with diverse styles gives each member the opportunity to learn from the comparisons and contrasts that will inevitably take place.

The optimal composition for an ongoing psychodynamic group is for members to be similar in terms of ego development and different in terms of interpersonal style. Furthermore, it is important that each individual have aspects of at least one other person in the group with whom he/she can identify. This is not necessarily a surface identification. Rather, commonalities must be sufficiently near the surface so as not to isolate a member.

It should be underscored that we are discussing issues of composition for newly forming groups. Mature groups can tolerate and benefit from greater heterogeneity among members; indeed, different levels of ego development become assets. Specifically, the addition of patients with early developmental concerns allows the higher-level patients access into primary process, while the higher-level patients help the more disturbed patients translate their inner chaos into secondary process. In new groups major disparities in ego development simply frighten the members and make the development of cohesiveness very difficult.

SUMMARY

Composing a group is a complex task. Clinicians need to carefully and thoughtfully attend to the milieu in which they intend to conduct their groups. Multiple levels of social and cultural factors impinge upon being able to form and sustain group treatment. Familiarity with these elements will improve the likelihood of success.

No two groups are identical. As the classical Gestalt psychologists noted, the whole is greater than the sum of the parts, and this is certainly the case in an effective therapy group. The effectiveness depends upon the subtle interplay between the members. Therapists have long noted how dramatically the atmosphere in a group can change when just one member is changed. Thus therapists must be very sensitive to the twin issues of "Which group is best for each individual patient?" and "Which patient is best for any particular group?"

SEVEN

Patient Selection

Every man is under the natural duty of
contributing to the necessities of the society; and
this is all the laws should enforce on him.
—THOMAS JEFFERSON TO FRANCIS GILMER, 1816

In the preceding chapter we examined the treatment milieu, sources for referrals, and characteristics of both the group and the prospective members. We emphasized that clinicians must be clear about the nature, goals, and membership criteria of the group they wish to begin. In this chapter we focus on patient selection for open-ended, long-term psychodynamic groups.

Unfortunately there are very few research data to provide specific guidelines on how to most effectively select patients for groups (Piper, 1994). The clinician has to fall back upon accumulated experience that has focused mainly on *unsuitability* for group psychotherapy rather than on positive indicators.

Most who seek therapy do not initially consider entering a group. Indeed, if group therapy is suggested, it is not unusual for individuals to express doubts about the referral. Fortunately there is strong research support with which to address clients' concerns. Fuhriman and Burlingame (1994), while examining the question, "Does group psychotherapy work?" state, "The general conclusion to be drawn from some 700 studies that span the past two decades is that the group format consistently produced positive effects with diverse disorders and treatment models" (p. 15). Moreover, Piper (1993) found no appreciable differences between outcomes of individual and group therapy in a review of meta-analytic studies.

Therapists must deal sensitively with the doubts and concerns that patients have regarding the specific benefits of entering a group. This often includes providing some information about why group psychotherapy has been suggested, how it works, and how it may directly help with the issues these patients have brought with them. In addition, the prospect of joining a group typically raises more anxiety than does the prospect of beginning dyadic therapy.

Almost all patients are potential candidates for group psychotherapy. As we noted in Chapter 1, the pathologies of the modern era are primarily difficulties in gaining and tolerating authentic intimacy. Rutan and Alonso (1979) have stated, "Group therapy, by its very format, offers unique opportunities to experience and work on issues of intimacy and individualization. In...groups, the community is represented in the treatment room. It is usually impossible for individuals to view themselves as existing alone and affecting no one when in a group therapy situation over any significant period of time" (p. 612). This view recognizes that interpersonal interactions reflect the internal world of the individual, with all of the inner beliefs and feelings that have contributed to development of relationship problems.

We believe that a key element in assisting individuals to accept group treatment is providing specific reasons for such a recommendation. Through careful gathering of historical information and assessing the quality of the relationship in the interview, the clinician can link the patient's problematic behaviors and feelings to what he/she may anticipate experiencing in the group. For example, as we explore a patient's reluctance to join a group, we may find the patient experiencing precisely the issues and feelings for which he/she comes to therapy. This information then can serve as a segue into imagining with the patient how the problems will emerge in a group. The process orients prospective members in the direction of appreciating that the group will become a microcosm of their lives (Slater, 1966).

If most patients are good candidates for group therapy, we need to be clear about exclusionary criteria to ensure that we do not place individuals in a group when there is little reason to believe they would do well in that setting.

PATIENTS WHO SHOULD NOT BE
SEEN IN GROUPS

There are a number of situations and circumstances where individuals should not be accepted for group therapy. These diverse elements include the following:

- Patients who refuse to enter a group
- Persons unable or unwilling to keep the group agreements

- Instances when the therapist is too uncomfortable working with a particular individual
- Those for whom group is a poor risk

Patients Who Refuse to Enter a Group

An obvious but often overlooked element in the selection process is the prospective member's willingness to join a group. A significant proportion of patients who are referred to a group never enter. In a study comparing short-term individual and group treatments, Budman et al. (1988) reported a significant difference in rejection rates between group and individual therapy. In the study, individuals were referred to group or individual treatment through random assignment: 76 patients were assigned to groups, but 26 (34%) failed to join their groups. The reasons given included outright rejection of group treatment, time conflicts, moving out of the area, or loss of insurance due to a job change. In contrast, of 51 patients assigned to individual treatment, only 3 (6%) defected from the study. In another study Klein and Carroll (1986) retrospectively examined 716 referrals to an outpatient group treatment component of a large university hospital clinic. Astonishingly, 41% never entered a group. For the majority of these individuals, the following reasons were given: the patient canceled appointments or just did not show up for them, the patient was no longer interested in any treatment, or the patient was specifically not interested in group therapy. Approximately 8% of all patients agreeing to enter groups never attended a meeting. These studies, conducted in clinic and HMO settings, may not reflect the experience of the private practitioner. They do highlight the gap between the initial idea of referring an individual for group treatment and the actual entry into treatment.

These days more and more individuals come seeking group therapy with the proviso that the group must meet certain predetermined criteria. With gender consciousness raising, there are women and men who wish the group composition to be of one gender. Sexually abused individuals are another group of patients who request to meet with persons with similar histories. Further, with the advent of managed care, the press toward treating discrete diagnoses in time-limited diagnosis-specific groups has increased. The basis for these requests is useful to explore, but it would generally be unwise to use the persuasive position of the therapist to recruit people requesting specific types of groups for a "usual" psychodynamic group.

Forming a group is stressful for therapist and patient alike. Seldom are there too many prospective members. Given patients' general hesitance about joining therapy groups, therapists may spend considerable time exploring dynamic bases for such reluctance. The power of suggestion and covert "pressure" may overcome conscious resistance without truly altering a client's underlying uncertainty. The situation is ripe for countertransference enactments.

The potential for these individuals to prematurely terminate their group is substantial. If the therapist allows sufficient time, some of these patients may successfully join at a later date. No person should be forced, overtly or covertly, to join a group. If a patient does not willingly join, no matter how convinced the therapist is that group therapy is the treatment of choice, that patient is a poor candidate.

Persons Unable or Unwilling to Keep the Group Agreements

The group agreements (see Chapter 8) highlight certain additional exclusionary criteria. Patients who cannot realistically be expected to abide by their agreements owing to either pathology or life circumstances (e.g., a professional athlete, a nurse with varying shifts, or an airline pilot who cannot commit to a regular weekly meeting because of his/her work schedule) should not be included in group therapy. While these individuals may be ideal candidates on all other bases, it is helpful to neither the patient nor the group to allow an individual member into a group with a "special" set of agreements.

A more problematic situation arises for some individuals who may have planned an extended period away prior to their entry—for example, the school teacher who will be away for 2 months in the summer or an individual who anticipates elective surgery and an extended convalescent period. Sometimes leaders desirous of filling their groups will allow such members to join. Inevitably, however, these special cases prove difficult for all concerned. If at all possible, the entry of such patients should be deferred until a more continuous commitment can be made.

Therapists' Comfort Level with Certain Individuals

There can be little doubt that clinicians vary in their degrees of comfort while treating different patients and pathologies. A therapist's negative response is transmitted and impacts upon the group's capacity to help particular patients. Some therapists, for example, are uncomfortable with alcoholic, passive, or overaggressive patients. A clinician's response to patient's external characteristics should receive attention (e.g., obesity, or eccentric appearance or behavior). Such responses raise red flags, and the meaning of the clinician's response should be explored. If there is difficulty in resolving the countertransference, then excluding those patients from the groups of *those particular* therapists seems a reasonable decision.

Poor-Risk Patients

Poor risk is predicated on statistical probability, and yet prediction of outcome in psychotherapy has not been reliable (Luborsky et al., 1980). Nevertheless, clinical experience has shown that some individuals are unable to utilize the group experience, either dropping out, remaining stuck, or interacting in ways that are destructive to the group.

Historically, poor risk patients are identified as persons deemed likely to prematurely terminate their treatments. Not only does dropping out diminish the likelihood of therapeutic benefit (although not all dropouts are treatment failures), but these events are likely to negatively impact upon the remaining members and the group atmosphere. The most cited study is that of Yalom (1966a), who developed a list of nine categories that characterized early departers: (1) external factors, (2) group deviancy, (3) problems of intimacy, (4) fear of emotional contagion, (5) inability to share the doctor, (6) complications of concurrent individual and group therapy, (7) early provocateurs, (8) inadequate orientation to group therapy, and (9) complications arising from subgrouping.

Reexamination of Yalom's data suggests an alternative classification. As Yalom suggests, the categories do not clearly separate individuals, which diminishes the usefulness of the various categories. Using the tripartite perspective of (1) intrapsychic defense mechanisms, (2) interpersonal relatedness, and (3) group-related factors allows for a reassessment of the material. For instance, a patient who is fearful of intimacy might present with externalization, denial, or somatization; or such a person might engage in disruptive behavior when anxious. The same patient, depending on the perspective of the observer, could be seen as deviant, as an early provocateur, as having fears of emotional contagion, or as having difficulty sharing the clinician. Further, the individual character styles interact with group processes. Some groups can tolerate silent, withdrawn members for long periods, whereas others may welcome an individual who is provocative, outspoken, and occasionally acts out. A caveat: the data on dropouts should also be considered from the perspective of the treatment process, since dropouts generally occur in response to some interaction between the patient and other members, or in response to the emerging norms. It is sad but true that some patients drop out because the group *is working* for them—that is, the individuals find themselves overwhelmed by the very affects and difficulties for which they came to treatment.

Advances in theory and increased experience have diminished the categories of poor-risk patients. Today categorical exclusion is a waning phenomenon. Most exclusionary recommendations in the literature can be countered by other published recommendations that such patients are treatable in groups. For example, in the early years it was thought that homosexuals could not be successfully treated in groups with nongay members, but experience has proven this false (Stein, 1963; Stone, Schengber, & Seifried, 1966; Frost, 1990). The same scenario exists for persons with borderline and narcissistic character disorders (see Wong, 1979; Roth, 1979; Stone & Whitman, 1977; Kanas, Deri, Ketter, & Fein, 1990).

Nevertheless, in addition to the general exclusion criteria cited above, certain additional diagnostic exclusion criteria should be considered. These include persons in crisis, those who have problems with impulse control, and those with character defenses minimizing interpersonal relatedness. These are discussed in the following subsections.

Persons in Crisis

The most frequently stated reason for exclusion is that the patient is in an acute crisis. This can be a developmental crisis (such as marriage, divorce, or retirement), situational crisis (death of a loved one, or physical illness), or a crisis of pathology (eruption of a psychotic process or extraordinary anxiety). These patients require a great deal of attention, and they do not have the time or interest to meet and develop relationships with a number of strangers in a therapy group. Sometimes it is not obvious that the person is in crisis, and at other times the duration of the "crises" seems to mitigate the situation, only to emerge very quickly and lead to that person's abrupt disappearance from the group.

CLINICAL EXAMPLE

Valerie, a 46-year-old twice-married teacher with three adolescent children, had learned the year before that her second husband was having an affair and wanted to end their marriage. Brief marital counseling had not resolved their differences. Valerie then consulted a psychopharmacologist who prescribed antidepressants, which provided only partial relief. During this period the husband had remained with the family in their home.

It was Valerie who wondered about group therapy for additional help with her depression and interpersonal difficulties. Valerie reported "always feeling depressed," and although superficially popular, she had felt alone and lonely throughout her life. Her first husband was physically abusive, which she kept secret for several years. She left only after the abuse became obvious to her friends, who insisted she obtain a restraining order. She promptly returned to her hometown.

In her second marriage she was a "supermom," attending to all the children's needs. She dealt with her husband's financial overextension by working harder. She said that she never expressed her anger at her husband until he tried to bite her—at which point, 3 weeks prior to the consultation, she had asked him to leave home.

Though Valerie verbalized an intense desire to enter a group, in the preparatory interviews the therapist sensed that Valerie was very ambivalent: she worried about affording regular therapy; her insurance coverage was uncertain; she showed limited understanding when it was pointed out that both husbands had been abusive. After attending one meeting, Valerie canceled the two succeeding sessions and then called the therapist to announce that she was moving out of the city.

*   *   *

Although there were a number of elements in this example that mitigated against placing Valerie in a group without engaging her in a more extended period of evaluation and treatment, financial considerations and her insistence had tipped the scale. In retrospect she had not resolved the crisis of her marriage, and only through physical "flight" could she achieve emotional distance.

Just as the individual in crisis has little energy to devote to others, by the same token the group has little reason to devote great amounts of time to the crisis of a stranger. Naturally, patients who are already group members and undergo a crisis find their groups to be extraordinarily healing resources during these troubling times.

Persons with Poor Impulse Control

Other populations are routinely excluded from heterogeneous psychodynamic groups. These include individuals with insufficient impulse control (so that the physical safety of other members cannot be guaranteed), chronically psychotic patients, patients with organic brain syndromes, and sociopathic patients. Taken as a whole, these patients share a common trait. None can establish the minimal object relatedness that is required for a therapy group to work effectively. They are often the patients whom individual therapists find so difficult to treat that they refer them to groups.

Patients in those categories might be effectively treated in homogeneous groups. For example, Comstock and McDermott (1975) found that homogeneous groups of individuals who have recently attempted suicide held the most hope of any treatment modality for helping these patients. Similarly, groups of mentally disturbed offenders (e.g., sexual offenders, arsonists, shoplifters) or alcoholics, who are homogeneous as to symptoms but quite different in underlying psychodynamic configurations, can be very effective in diminishing pathological symptoms. It is not uncommon for these patients to require individual therapy to assist them in integrating the data generated in their groups. The practice of combining individual and group therapy is discussed in Chapter 11.

Persons with Certain Character Defenses

Character defenses may be considered a person's way of "being in the world." A fundamental premise of psychodynamic theory is that behavior and personality serve an adaptive function. People protect themselves to prevent retraumatization. Some difficulties become apparent in assessment interviews, whereas others may only emerge in an unfolding therapeutic process. Character defenses are among the most difficult to alter in psychotherapy because they are accepted as "givens" by the patient. Though group therapy is the ideal treatment for a person with troublesome character defenses, as the individual can hear from and experience from other members the effect of his/her "character" on them, some people with particular types of character defenses are high-risk additions to groups. In particular, these are individuals whose defenses minimize the importance of relationship and project responsibility exclusively onto others.

One example is the individual who is unable to hold a steady job and whose difficulty is invariably attributed to a personality conflict with a superior. No hint of personal responsibility can be elicited. From the patient's perspective, he/she has just been the victim of terrible luck in finding the right job fit. When the clinician gently speculates that because of this pattern, this person just might develop similar conflicts with the therapist or a group member of "high status," the response is one of incredulity. The absence of self-awareness and responsibility are warning signals of possible premature termination. Other scenarios are those persons who become very uncomfortable with strong affects, such as aggressive or loving feelings. They may be deeply offended with four-letter words, and they may attempt to impose similar rigidity on the group. If at least temporarily successful, they may well evoke considerable antipathy; if they fail, they are likely to drop out.

Although it is reasonable to speculate that these patients actually harbor the feelings they are refusing to entertain, their rock-solid defenses seldom provide a glimmer of what is underneath. If they are able to remain in the group, the clinician can anticipate periods of very difficult work. Some narcissistic and borderline patients may present with ordinary defenses and only under the sway of regressive group forces and deep seated vulnerability expose difficult, seemingly unyielding defenses. (See Chapter 14 for additional discussion of borderline and narcissistic disorders.)

Nitsun (1996) identifies a subgroup of individuals who are described as having problems with what he labels "group-object relation"; this term signifies the manner in which "individuals characteristically perceive and relate to groups" (p. 166). Exploring the prospective patient's role in prior life groups provides some prediction of the group role he/she will adopt. Bullying, victimization, or scapegoating behavior, if consistent or extreme, may be important signals for a potential misfit and dropout.

Our caveat regarding these persons is that we should recognize that we have not reached a stage of sophistication enabling us to predict a specific individual's success or failure in therapy. Piper (1994), reviewing the literature on client variables, reflects upon the usual state of affairs: "Clinicians may be unwilling to deny a 'high risk' patient an opportunity to have a valuable experience in a therapy group. Risky clients sometimes surprise us" (p. 107). We opt for an optimistic appraisal regarding the usefulness of groups for even those patients with major difficulties in interpersonal relatedness, and we are likely to put them into our groups. The interaction between character styles and group composition can either enable or frustrate the individual's participation.

PATIENTS FOR WHOM GROUP PSYCHOTHERAPY IS THE TREATMENT OF CHOICE: REVIEW OF THE LITERATURE

Stein (1963) approached the problem of selection primarily from a psychodynamic perspective. He suggested that group treatment would be appropriate for those patients who exhibited intense, sticky transference in individual treatment; for those with superego problems, particularly patients with overly strict superegos; for those with obsessive–compulsive features and guilt; and those who need ego support and reality testing through identification with others. As a corollary to the problem of intense transference, Stein noted that other members served as displacement objects, enabling an individual to work on problems without the disruptive intensity of an individual transference. Examined nearly four decades later, Stein's criteria are suggestive of patients diagnosed as having preoedipal psychopathology. Perhaps this schema served to direct the therapist to a position of understanding rather than categorizing, thus enabling the clinician to more comfortably include these patients into group treatment.

Guttmacher and Birk (1971) expanded Stein's list, emphasizing the therapeutic advantages of the here-and-now axis of group therapy. This axis can be used as a selection criterion by focusing on those patients who can learn from confrontation. Patients who fulfill this criterion do not view themselves as responsible for the conflicts they experience. Their pathology is ego-syntonic. Groups offer repeated opportunities for such patients to hear from members the effect of their behaviors upon others. Further, groups allow them gradually to make their pathology ego-dystonic and thus more amenable to change. The increased interaction and the development of multiple transferences are not necessarily equivalent to the dilution and diminution of transference reactions (see Ethan, 1978; Horwitz, 1994). Guttmacher and Birk (1971), for instance, emphasize that the frustration evoked by having to share the therapist can expose intense and important envies and rivalries.

Kadis, Krasner, Winick, and Foulkes (1963) proposed a slightly different schema for selecting patients, also on the basis of dynamic considerations. They suggested that patients be assessed across four dimensions: (1) ability to tolerate anxiety, including the potential for disruptive anxiety upon entering a group; (2) identification and empathy with others, including the background and similarity of experiences that would allow them to sit with others; (3) ego strength, including vulnerability to interpersonal stress and the potential to tolerate attacks, criticism, or closeness; and (4) interlocking of patients' defense systems. The initial three criteria are designed to predict the kinds of responses a patient might exhibit upon entering treatment. The fourth dimension is specifically a group-related criterion that is used to predict whether patients' characteristic defenses will meld or clash with those of other members.

Zimmerman (1976) also considered group-related dimensions in the selection process. He emphasized the prospective patient's ability to maintain a sense of self in the face of group processes that might be experienced as sucking the patient into an undifferentiated mass. Patients who might be vulnerable to that pull are described as adhering inflexibly to social, professional, political, or moral positions. They might present themselves as arrogant, pedantic, and extremely prideful. These characteristics are reminiscent of the deviant whom Yalom (1966a) pinpointed as a possible early group dropout. In pregroup interviews, Zimmerman (1976) evaluated an applicant's ability to change roles—for example, to move from listener to speaker to empathizer, and so on. He raised questions about the patient's ability to maintain confidentiality and secrets, and he suggested that persons in politically or socially prominent roles, or their relatives, be excluded.[1]

In contrast to the dynamic classifications are the behavioral/phenomenological approaches. Patients considered for groups are those having problems with intimacy or leading lonely, isolated, dreary lives. They avoid social situations or have a paucity of intimate personal relationships. Conversely, some patients might be overdependent or overdemanding and group therapy would be recommended in order to dilute these behaviors (Neumann & Geoni, 1974). Classifications such as these tend to emphasize problems in effective interpersonal functioning at both ends of a continuum (Grunebaum & Kates, 1977): at one end are the withdrawn, socially inept, uninvolved individuals; at the other are the demanding, self-centered, and controlling persons. Groups are expected to act as equalizers by activating the withdrawn and by socializing the more narcissistic, self-centered, or acting-out individuals.

Recommendations regarding the inclusion of patients with somatic complaints seem to follow the trends we have already noted. Some believe these are precisely the patients who can learn about themselves and their inner world. Others believe somatization is a poor prognostic sign, since such pa-

---

[1] Cultural difference could account for this suggestion, since Zimmerman (1976) reported on work conducted in Brazil. Grotjahn (1975), in a contrary opinion, described successful integration of famous people into his groups.

tients will not have the psychological mindedness necessary to utilize psycho-analytic group psychotherapy most effectively.

Interest has been growing regarding patients with alexithymia, a term coined by Sifneos (1972) to describe individuals who have no words for feelings. Initially, this deficit was thought to be characteristic of patients with psychosomatic illnesses. Difficulty identifying inner feelings exists in varying degrees, and subsequently the concept was seen as applicable to patients fitting many diagnostic categories. Characteristically these individuals are referred to treatment by a significant other or by a physician who has been unsuccessful in treating a variety of physical complaints. Such patients may complain of feeling isolated or misunderstood, even though there is an external facade of sociability. In dyadic treatment they are frustrated and frustrating, as sessions are often bland and affectless. Referrals to group therapy are sometimes made when therapists are discouraged because of little or no progress in the dyadic work, and thus these patients often come to group feeling they have failed. For some such patients, however, the group provides an opportunity to vicariously or directly participate in the affective experience of others, which assists in their identifying their own feelings.

Intimately associated with the problem of alexithymia is the patient's difficulty empathizing with others. Deficits in identifying others' feelings, linking behavior with affects, or understanding the emotional meaning of members' interactions are some manifestations of deficits in empathy (Kleinberg, 1991). Swiller (1988) recommends that these patients be treated in concurrent group and individual therapy.

Piper and McCallum (1994) add to the list of general selection criteria. They include patient characteristics of motivation for therapy and for changing behaviors, a positive expectation for change, a susceptibility to group influence, and a willingness to help others. Noting that persons with good interpersonal skills are those who may least need group treatment, these authors opt to select those with minimal levels of interpersonal skills. However, it is unlikely that a group will succeed if a majority of members have limited social skills, but choosing persons with varying skills along the interpersonal axis will lead to interactive groups with the potential for members to learn from each other.

DIAGNOSING AND EVALUATING PATIENTS FOR GROUP

Despite the need to carefully assess exclusionary criteria, it is our contention that group therapy should be considered as a viable option for most patients seeking treatment. Very often just raising the prospect of joining a group evokes a powerful reaction. To the degree that these reactions are relevant to their presenting problems, a group might well be a primary treatment modality. When patients see the connection between their presenting concerns and their interpersonal relations, they often willingly enter groups.

A great many patients who are potential group candidates devote considerable consultative time preoccupied with interpersonal difficulties. For instance, they might complain about their spouses, bosses, children, or friends, in a seemingly endless litany. However, no change takes place and troubles persist. Before group therapy can be effective, these patients need to accept some personal responsibility for their interpersonal difficulties. So long as they project all problems onto others, they remain uninsightful and resistant to change. When this ego-syntonic behavior is not quite so ingrained, groups can help such patients begin to see their contributions to the interpersonal impasses.

In all diagnostic evaluations, it is important to listen for and focus on a patient's interpersonal transactions. When it seems clear that this arena is central to the presenting concern of the patient, then group therapy should be actively considered as the primary treatment.

When patients become *too* involved with their therapists, the transference becomes unmanageably powerful. These patients previously were labeled "overly dependent"; more recent formulations emphasize some patients' needs for an idealizing transference in order to recommence an interrupted developmental process (Stone, 1992b; Kohut, 1971, 1977). By virtue of the presence of other members, groups provide a helpful distance from the therapist for such patients. This allows them space to examine their feelings about the therapist and to compare and contrast their responses with those of others. An exception to this is the patient for whom jealousy and possessiveness are so strong that the presence of other people in the therapeutic arena is simply overwhelming.

As we review criteria for selecting patients, we would also suggest that the psychopathology of the prospective group member is not the only consideration in the process. A therapist who rejects several successive group applicants might review the cases with a colleague to determine if the decisions are based, in part, on countertransference. Such responses might be reactions to common characteristics of the patients or to the referral source.

Clinicians also need to take into account systems issues impacting upon their decision making. In today's economy many therapists are pressured to begin groups and to keep them full in order to decrease waiting lists or increase productivity. Referrals from colleagues who have been frequent suppliers of members may be difficult to turn down, even though the therapist recognizes that the patient is a high-risk group referral.

Factors related to functioning of the group also require scrutiny. If the census is low and the therapist fears that morale will deteriorate or the group will disband, there is a greater tendency to accept new members, in part to reassure those already present. An opposite situation occurs, often in clinic settings with relatively inexperienced therapists, when clinicians reject suitable candidates because they fear the response of those already in the group. The common rationalization, based in part on more specific countertransference, is that the prospect is too ill and will disrupt the group.

Next, several examples illustrate the process of evaluation and selection for referral for group therapy.

CLINICAL EXAMPLE

Sister Annette was a 33-year-old nun who sought psychotherapy for her heightened anxiety. She felt her anxiety was rooted in her flagging dedication to the Catholic Church and to her religious beliefs. However, she could not gain any precision in describing what doubts she was having about her faith. As was the custom of the evaluating therapist, the prospect of group therapy was mentioned. Sister Annette immediately became very anxious and stated that she could "*never* be in a therapy group." When the therapist inquired why, she said, "There would be all those men there talking about sex. It would be no place for a nun." Using the projected data gained from her guesses about what a group would be like, Sister Annette was soon able to see that her anxiety was actually stemming from heightened sexual feelings and corresponding guilt about them. In light of this she decided to enter a therapy group to see what she could find out about her sexuality in the safety of a therapeutic setting. In the course of several years of group therapy this patient was able to own, explore, and become comfortable with her sexuality. Eventually, she decided to retain her vows of chastity and to remain in the convent, and she was able to continue her career without the anxiety that had brought her to treatment.

* * *

This case illustrates how the mere mention of a therapy group can evoke powerful and important affects that can assist the diagnostic and dispositional questions. When the specific affect aroused is closely connected to the presenting complaint, then group psychotherapy can be seriously considered. Even if not, sometimes the feelings stimulated are of sufficient importance that the patient and the therapist agree that group therapy might be very helpful.

CLINICAL EXAMPLE

Bill was a young man who seemed psychologically minded. He complained that he was a 28-year-old virgin in a social milieu in which dating leading to intercourse was the norm. Bill felt blocked in his understanding of why he could not date successfully. Individual therapy was fascinating and rewarding for the therapist, since Bill vividly described his inner world in a creative and captivating manner. The external focus was on Bill's continuing conflict with bosses at work. There was an absence of discussion of peer relationships and no mention of dating. When the therapist initially suggested that group therapy be added to Bill's individual treatment, Bill engagingly described how the suggestion had evoked feelings as powerful as an avalanche in his mind. The anxiety that he experienced was so intense that he declined the suggestion. Nevertheless, no change in his life was occurring, and several months later the therapist again suggested group treatment, explaining that Bill rarely spoke about troubles with dating and his social life, despite these being his initial reasons for seeking treatment. Again Bill refused, but with less anxiety and vehemence. Six months later, Bill himself raised the question of his entering a group, saying he felt his individual therapy was at an impasse. In the course of his group treatment Bill was able to examine his anxiety about sexuality, his competitiveness with men, and his seductiveness with women. After joining a group, Bill made important personal gains.

*   *   *

This example illustrates some dynamics of the process of adding group to individual therapy. Bill shifted from interpersonal to authority problems in the individual treatment, subsequently getting stuck in a transference impasse that seemed to preclude examination of the presenting peer and social problems. The referral to a group loosened that therapy impasse. Clearly, the referral did not occur quickly. The therapist's willingness to raise the issue, offer the suggestion, and accept Bill's refusal was ultimately rewarded when Bill himself was able to initiate the referral.

CLINICAL EXAMPLE

Carl was referred as a candidate for a group because of his anxiety and depression over his wife's threatening separation and divorce. Carl, though a very successful executive businessman, had almost no awareness of his inner world. Indeed, his history was so bereft of any close relationships that it was remarkable that he had managed to marry. Group had been suggested to him by a previous therapist because of the barrenness of his interpersonal world. However, the evaluating therapist did not accept Carl into a therapy group. Rather, it was determined that Carl was not well suited for group therapy on at least two counts. First, he was in an immediate crisis: he was reeling from the prospect of losing his only viable relationship, and he was quite desperate. He would not find it easy to put that desperation aside long enough to meet, trust, and negotiate some relationship with a series of strangers in a therapy group. Second, Carl's interpersonal skills appeared so impoverished that it was likely he would be overwhelmed by a group, not assisted by it. Carl was referred again for individual psychotherapy, where he began to gain insight into how disconnected from his feelings he had been and how that meant that he was dramatically short-changing his wife in their marriage.

* * *

This example highlights a case where the screening therapist decided group therapy was not the treatment of choice. The patient in this case quite willingly accepted the referral, but the group therapist, evaluating the patient's crisis around the divorce, recommended a period of individual therapy before exposing him to the more stimulating interaction in a therapy group.

CLINICAL EXAMPLE

Duane was referred for severe headaches that had forced him to take a leave of absence from work. He had consulted numerous physicians in an attempt to find a definitive diagnosis, all to no avail. Two psychiatrists were consulted, but both were unsuccessful in engaging Duane in self-exploration. The third psychiatrist he found was able to initiate a usable alliance, and Duane began looking into interpersonal stresses in his life. History revealed that just prior to the onset of his headaches, Duane learned that his supervisor would be changing jobs and that Duane was in line for a promotion. To Duane a promotion meant giving up his old relationships and joining the ranks of management. Even more important, during the same time period, Duane's wife had taken a full-time job outside the home and was no longer devoting herself exclusively to housework and the care for their 12-year-old son. Duane recognized that these were both important events, but he could see no connection between them and his headaches. Duane maintained his conviction that his was a biological problem, and he was referred to a pain clinic.

* * *

This example is cited to indicate the importance of negotiation in referring a patient to group. If any modality of psychotherapy is to work, it is almost mandatory that the patient have some understanding of and agreement with, the reasons for selecting the modality chosen. Duane could never accept the rationale for group therapy, and thus he was not referred to a group.

CLINICAL EXAMPLE

Ellie was an attractive, appealing, 35-year-old woman who had first contacted the group therapist 5 years earlier. At that time she expressed an interest in group therapy, but she never made an appointment. Two years later she again called, somewhat embarrassed, and again said she wanted to join a therapy group. Once again, however, she declined to make an appointment for an evaluation. She said, "Let me think about it. I'll get back to you."

She did get back to the therapist, again 2 years later. This time she made an appointment and came for the evaluation interview for group therapy. She was very clear about her reason for coming to group therapy: "I want to get married." She presented as a bright, inquisitive, and very motivated individual, despite her hesitancy in actually getting started in a group. She readily accepted the group agreements, and when she hesitated about setting a beginning date the therapist said, "You are clearly ambivalent about joining a group. This is not surprising since it is a frightening thing to do. Perhaps it would be best to set a date and just begin." She thanked the therapist profusely and said, "You *do* understand me."

She came to the group on the appointed day and was welcomed warmly by the group. They clearly perceived her as a good addition to the group. She was open, able to talk in her first meeting, and again in this setting commented on how the therapist understood her and pressed her to join quickly lest she wait another 5 years. She ended her first session by saying, "I'm so glad I came here. This feels like the right place for me at this time."

However, during the intervening week she called the therapist to say, "I'm going to quit the group. It just stirs up too many feelings for me." The therapist suggested that perhaps this was an indication that the group was going to be particularly helpful, especially if the troubling feelings she was experiencing were familiar feelings. Once again she commented on the therapist's wisdom. But she did not come to the next meeting.

Ellie did attend one more meeting. Prior to the meeting she had again called the therapist, saying she was definitely quitting but wanted to come to the group and tell them personally. However she arrived 10 minutes late and never managed to say anything about leaving. She never came to another session, and when the therapist contacted her she apologized but said it just was not a good time for her to be in group therapy.

*   *   *

In this case, the therapist had ample data to predict that flight might be Ellie's main defense. Her ambivalent approach to group therapy had lasted more than 5 years. In terms of the "exclusionary criteria" cited above, the patient was not in crisis, did not suffer from problems with impulse control, and seemed capable of honoring the group agreements. At first glance she appeared to have fine interpersonal abilities (she was appealing and "likable" to the therapist and to the group). However, had the therapist been more curious about the patient's long process of joining a group and related that to her stated lack of success in establishing viable intimate relationships, he would have seen that beneath a veneer of social competence Ellie was an extremely frightened and anxious woman. Clearly the therapist did not spend sufficient time exploring the depth of her fears about joining a group. The group that this patient joined had been meeting with four men and one woman for more than a year, and it is likely that the therapist's countertransferential need to add women to the group led to an inadequate screening. The result was that the patient suffered a "defeat" and the group endured the trauma of a group dropout.

SUMMARY

In this chapter we have examined guidelines for the evaluation and selection of applicants for group psychotherapy. Historically, economic considerations (lower group fees) were paramount in selecting patients for groups. More recently a great deal of attention has been devoted to exclusion criteria but much less to inclusion criteria. Diagnostic classification systems that could assist in inclusion criteria were reviewed here. These systems utilize both intrapsychic formulations and interpersonal behavioral criteria. No single current system fully accounts for the complex situation of an individual with strengths and weaknesses who is entering into a particular group with its own particular values, norms, history, and interacting individuals.

Once individuals have been selected as suitable for treatment in group therapy, three tasks remain for the therapist. The first is to prepare the patient for entrance into a therapy group. The second is to negotiate the group agreements with the patient. Those issues are explored in the next chapter. The third task concerns handling the details of the therapeutic frame (frequency, duration, size, and gender distribution), which are discussed in Chapter 10.

EIGHT

Patient Preparation and the Group Agreements

The best preparation for tomorrow is doing your best today.

—H. JACKSON BROWN, JR.

PATIENT PREPARATION

Controversy exists about the nature and goals of preparing patients for group therapy. No one method has been universally accepted. Kaul and Bednar (1994) state, "Almost all the cognitive, behavioral, and experiential components of pre-group preparation have been demonstrated to produce favorable effects, but none of them seem to be consistently superior to any other variable" (p. 174). Nonetheless, entering a group is a stressful process and informing patients about what to expect can provide some feeling of preparedness even though what will actually occur can never be fully known or predicted.

We believe the process should begin with one or more individual interviews. It is not possible to adequately assess a patient's suitability for group therapy in general or for a particular group without spending some individual time with the patient. The amount of time required to fully prepare a patient for a group depends on many factors, including the therapeutic sophistication of the patient, the amount of preliminary work that has gone into the decision to join a group, and the skill and experience of the therapist. If a patient has come seeking treatment and has not considered group therapy, it will take longer to prepare that patient for group therapy. There is a delicate balance between not bringing a patient into a group prematurely and not establishing a dyadic relationship that interferes with the patient using the group setting.

A clear set of group agreements is the necessary foundation for any successful group. The group agreements will be discussed later in this chapter, but for now it is important to state that each new member must receive, understand, and accept the agreements *prior* to entering a group.

Frequently patients' responses to the referral process and preparatory interview(s) reveal questions about their motivation for change. Motivation may be the least rigorously used word in our field, since it can be presumed that any patient who seeks therapy is motivated for change. The question is "What *kind* of change is desired?" Sometimes the wish is simply for symptomatic relief, to satisfy some external pressure, to return to some previously disturbed homeostasis in life, or sometimes for a magic solution to life's problems. Many times a patient will accept referral to a group out of a wish to please the referring therapist or to avoid some difficult therapeutic impasse in the individual treatment. When clinicians have one goal and patients have another, and where there is also a lack of clarity in the evaluation and preparation phase, problems in treatment and difficulty in termination are likely to ensue (Levinson & Astrachan, 1974).

As therapists discuss elements involved in joining a group and explain the group agreements to the applicant, careful attention must be paid to what the patient wants and how the desired goal is to be accomplished. This is the essence of motivation. Preparation for joining a group should accomplish the following:

1. Establish a preliminary alliance between patient and therapist.
2. Gain a clear consensus about the patient's therapeutic hopes.
3. Offer information and instruction about group psychotherapy.
4. Deal with the initial anxiety about joining a group.
5. Present and gain acceptance of the group agreements.

The time required to accomplish these tasks varies according to the therapist's personal preference and experience, the amount of decision making and working through regarding group therapy the patient has done prior to coming to the group therapist, and the capacity of the patient to relate meaningful emotional elements in his/her life. If the patient comes referred specifically for group therapy and some of the working through of the idea of group therapy has already been accomplished, experienced therapists can usually prepare a patient in one visit. Stone and Rutan (1984) found that the number of pregroup interviews does not correlate with patients remaining or terminating prematurely. Some patients need at least several weeks of preparation, whereas others can be prepared in one meeting (see Bader, Bader, Budman, & Clifford, 1981).

If a patient has not had prior psychotherapy, it is wise to have several individual interviews before the patient joins a group. For patients with no understanding of how psychotherapy works, groups often seem random and not relevant for the patient's concerns. Research suggests that patients referred to group therapy as their *first* and *only* psychotherapy are at unusually high risk of prematurely dropping out (Stone & Rutan, 1984).

Establishing Preliminary Alliances

The minimum task in the screening and evaluation process is for the therapist and patient to meet and establish an alliance that will serve the treatment. Treatment relationships are built on both conscious and unconscious processes which are described under a variety of terms including transference, working relationship (alliance), and real relationship. Sorting the threads of these various formulations is difficult. Patients sense intuitively (and partly unconsciously) the kind of people we are—the real qualities of our capacities to provide a safe environment (Adler, 1996). Meissner (1996) asserts that the working relationship (alliance) is based on the clinician in the therapist role, which differentiates between, yet overlaps, the *person* and the *role* of the therapist. Within the relationship to the *person* of the therapist, patients may try to bypass therapeutic work and turn the treatment encounter into a social relationship (Horowitz, 1979). These distinctions may be useful in alerting clinicians to the multiple meanings of their patient interactions.

No matter how good the patient feels about the therapist, he/she is entering into a situation in which others are present. This makes it more significant that he/she has an understanding of the procedures. Given the power of stranger anxiety, joining a group can be very stressful and stimulating. The process is eased if entering patients have at least a minimal alliance with the therapist. For less developed or frightened patients, this rudimentary alliance is a necessity if they are to get past the early anxiety.

Gain Consensus on Goals

Misalliance in therapy is often founded on a lack of agreement between therapist and patient as to what the patient really wants or needs. The example of Duane in Chapter 7 is typical. In many instances a therapist would have referred Duane to a group because the *therapist* was convinced of its efficacy despite Duane's unwillingness or inability to see its usefulness. If Duane had entered a group, it can be assumed that he would have become a "premature terminator."

Any good referral for treatment is the result of a negotiation with the patient (Lazare & Eisenthal, 1979; Lazare, Eisenthal, & Frank, 1979). In group therapy, where the immediate gratification of contact with and the undivided attention of an individual therapist is diminished, the therapist and patient's mutual understanding of treatment goals forms an alliance and helps the patient manage the rigor of the treatment format. A patient who feels forced or seduced into a group may find it very easy to forget the agreements and to look for more gratifying help. If the patient is a part of the negotiation and feels a willing and active participant in determining his/her treatment goals, the times of stress are less likely to result in revoking group agreements and abandoning treatment.

Imparting Information about Groups

While many patients have had previous experience with one or more individual therapists, not many have had group therapy experience. Moreover, since groups evoke intense affect quite rapidly, patients need to feel "grounded" by having specific information about how groups work and what they can expect from being a member.

Information can be transmitted in a variety of ways. In addition to describing the general structure and rationale of group therapy (Yalom, 1975), some authors suggest giving reading material to prospective members (Gauron & Rawlings, 1975) or didactically explaining the group process (Wogan et al., 1977). Others have suggested either observing a session behind a two-way mirror or actually participating in a session followed by discussion (Wogan et al., 1977). Truax and Wargo (1969) studied the effect of having applicants review excerpts of a tape recording of a "good patient" in group therapy. Those who participated in the pretraining materials showed greater improvement in the 3 months of study than those who had not.

Although good arguments can be made for all the procedures just cited, there is no evidence that any one format leads to fewer early dropouts or to greater or more rapid success during treatment. Yet the ideas embodied in the pretraining studies point the way to preparing patients for the special conditions existing in a psychotherapy group.

Typically, the information about group therapy includes the group agreements, specifics about how the group works, and answers to realistic questions that the patient might raise. For example, many patients ask, "How many men and how many woman are in the group?" or "How long do people typically stay in your groups?" or "Will I know any of the members?" Although questions can represent metaphorical statements about deeper concerns, patients have a right to know the specifics about the venture they are about to undertake. Bader et al. (1981) also note that the group therapist is more active in the evaluation sessions than in the group itself. Applicants should be forewarned that the therapist will be less active in the group and as a consequence may seem unavailable and distant.

Patients often inquire about how they will know when their treatment is completed and how they will leave the group. By carefully defining initial therapeutic goals, clinicians and patients can assess when these (or new goals emerging during treatment) are achieved and the patient may initiate the process of termination (see Chapter 16 for a specific discussion of the termination process). Linking the completion of goals with ending treatment empowers the patient and helps balance the playing field. It is also true, of course, that a great many patients do not have specific or easily definable goals for treatment—rather, they wish for "more intimacy" or "less anxiety." Others find that the goals they came for are not the goals they remain for. Nonetheless, the question "Do you feel you have gotten what you came for?" is useful in determining when it is appropriate to terminate. This also protects the patient from the therapist's wish to "cure everything!" when that may not be the patient's goal.

Although we believe that there is a potential core in each person that would like to be cared for, there exists the opposite, that of the person who is both self-reliant and independent. By addressing ending therapy, the clinician conveys that treatment is not forever.

How one determines *when* to leave should be distinguished from *how* one should leave. The process of leaving, emphasizing the significance of saying goodbye to important relationships that will be established in the therapeutic endeavor, is a very important aspect of the entire therapeutic endeavor.

Finally, physical and practical arrangements also should be explained. Patients need to know the day, time, and place of the meeting, along with the fact that these variables are not flexible. Inability to make the time commitment eliminates a patient from further consideration. The day and time of the meeting, as well as fee information, should be mentioned during the initial telephone contact in order to ensure that the applicant can conform to these basic requirements. It is best to provide the remaining orientation material during the presentation of the group agreements.

When members enter existing groups, the veterans quickly take on some information-giving functions, telling the newcomer by word and deed how the group works and what is expected. For example, within a few weeks a new member will likely learn that intense affect is permissible and valued, that dreams are relevant material, that honesty and self-curiosity are esteemed qualities. In a newly formed group, the treatment process and the evolving norms usually provide information at a pace that the members can use effectively.

Deal with Initial Anxiety about Joining a Group

Patients are typically quite anxious about joining groups. For those whose anxiety is conscious, the therapist should help them understand that anxiety about joining is universal, as well as help them explore the specifics about their anxiety. For patients whose anxiety is unconscious, the therapist should help raise their anxieties to awareness.

Exploration of dreams is one useful approach. If asked, a surprising number of patients will report having had bad dreams just before the initial screening session or between screening sessions. These dreams may be used to bring into focus some of the anxieties that the patient has about the forthcoming treatment.

CLINICAL EXAMPLE

Hedda, a nurse who was consciously very enthusiastic about entering a group, reported that after the initial screening interview she had developed a headache which she linked to her fear that the group would evoke more feelings than she could manage. This was part of the cause for her headache. She then related a dream she had the evening following the first screening session. "I was in intensive care. I said to the mother of a patient, go ahead and cry; your son has been through a lot, but don't be upset." Exploration of the dream revealed some of its meanings. The intensive care unit had yet another meaning. Since group therapy was being added to her individual sessions, this meant an intensification of her treatment, which further stimulated her fears. The end of the dream referred to two of her habitual defenses: support someone else ("a lot of people talk to me about their problems"), and minimize or deny anxiety. Further associations were elicited which indicated how physical complaints were used in her family to manipulate others, and during childhood her parents were particularly unavailable to the patient or her siblings because of illness. Ultimately the children had turned to one another for support, but Hedda was aware of how competitive they had been for parental attention. The dream brought all this material directly into her awareness as Hedda prepared to enter the group.

*   *   *

Often useful material about patients' anxieties may be gleaned by directly inquiring into their fantasies about the group or their feelings about joining. An applicant's history of entering social groups or organizations will further elaborate and focus on typical anxieties and defenses. Therapists need to be sensitive to any subtle communication from prospective members that might inform us about the nature of their anticipatory anxiety.

Present and Gain Acceptance
for the Group Agreements

If the individual members are the bricks that make a group, the group agreements are the mortar that binds those parts into a therapeutic whole. As early as 1920, McDougall indicated that the single most important means of harnessing the potent forces in groups was the establishment of an overt, mutually agreed upon set of goals and guidelines for rules of behavior.

Unfortunately, the word *contract* is often used by clinicians (and was the word used in the first edition of this book). This leads to the understanding by both patients and therapists that these preconditions to joining a group are a collection of hard and fast laws. We prefer the term "group *agreements.*" Patients are expected to be *responsible* for their agreements, not blindly adhere to them. It soon becomes clear that these agreements often conflict with other agreements (e.g., family or work). Patients are asked to cooperate with this arrangement; this is a conscious agreement that reflects the level of ego functioning and the therapeutic alliance. Both conscious and unconscious forces will result in patients altering or circumventing the agreements.

Though they are established by the leader, the group agreements are not only between the individuals and the leader; they are also between the individuals and the entire group. A breach of the agreements affects everyone. We now present a model set of group agreements that has worked well in our experience with all psychodynamic therapy groups. Except in the case of some time-limited, homogeneous groups that may not have pregroup sessions, these agreements should be presented to each potential member prior to joining a group. Furthermore, acceptance of these agreements should be a precondition of joining a group.

THE GROUP AGREEMENTS

1. Agree to be present each week, to be on time, and to remain throughout the entire meeting. We try not to make agreements that are impossible to keep or are inherently conflictual. The agreement places attendance very high on one's priority list. It also recognizes that there will be occasions when one cannot attend. Some therapists include the provision that a member who is planning to miss a meeting will tell the group in advance, and if that is not possible then the therapist is to be notified. If patients notify the therapist that they will miss a meeting, the therapist may simply announce the absence or may give the reasons cited for the cancellation. In either case the important norm is that absences should be discussed, and if possible the individual and/or groupwide meanings of the absence should be explored. When patients miss meetings without prior notification, a different dynamic ensues, and that too can be explored. Through repeated experiences in groups, members learn that absences have multiple levels of meanings.

CLINICAL EXAMPLE

In one meeting both a man and a woman were absent. Both members had a conflicting commitment to attend a Cub Scout meeting with their respective sons. In the following session the therapist reflected on the different meanings of the absences. In the man's case he considered the absence a healthy, adaptive choice. This man had come to group to deal with his distant relationship with his son, and taking time to be with him at one of his activities represented a visible sign of therapeutic growth. The woman's absence was understood very differently; it was seen as a resistance to therapy. Her presenting issue had been symbiotic overinvolvement with her son, and forfeiting commitments to the group represented another reenactment of the initial problem.

*   *   *

Patients also should understand that the therapist will not be present each and every week. Therapists take vacations, get sick, and go to professional meetings, but they too have a responsibility to notify members when they will be away. The amount of notice given by therapists for upcoming absences is directly tied to theory. The traditional psychodynamic therapist tries to balance interruptions in the ongoing process and still provide sufficient time to enable members to process a forthcoming absence. Generally such interruptions should be announced at least 2 or 3 weeks in advance, preferably at the beginning of a meeting. A therapist relying on object relations theory might notify the group as soon as he/she knows of the upcoming absence out of a conviction that the therapist is "altered" by the knowledge of the absence and that the patients deserve accurate information about that alteration. What is important is that the members are provided ample opportunity to fully respond and explore their reactions to the upcoming interruption. Moreover, group members soon learn to identify with the therapist and eventually discontinue the all-too-frequent last-minute announcements—"Oh, by the way, I won't be here next week" made at the end of a meeting. If members continue a pattern of announcing absences at the last moment, this subtle action then becomes easier to discuss when the therapist has initiated a more appropriate model.

The therapist's extended annual vacations ought to be announced 1 year in advance, and members should be reminded again 3 or 4 months prior to the interruption.

Some therapists expect patients to schedule vacations to coincide with their own. While this is the ideal arrangement because it results in the least disruption in continuity, it is unrealistic in most circumstances. This option is viable only when the therapist takes the same vacation time each year and when the members have sufficient flexibility in their work and personal lives that they can schedule vacations accordingly.

The essence of this portion of the agreement is to encourage as much continuity as possible. Each time a single member is not present, something is lost. Nonetheless, comings and goings are an important part of life, and there is much to be learned by how individuals manage the inevitable absences.

Different kinds of groups can modify these agreements for their specific needs. For example, in a time-limited group, this agreement can be changed to "You agree to attend each of the meetings."

2. Agree to work actively on the problems that brought you to the group. Ideally, people who join a therapy group do so in order to make substantial changes in their lives. This portion of the agreement specifically provides information on aspects of patients' behaviors leading to change. We suggest that people talk about the emotionally relevant elements in their lives, including dreams, which may be useful in helping them understand aspects of their interactions. We ask them to observe and share the internal reactions that they have during the meetings, including their feelings stimulated by the interactions with one another and the therapist, and by being a member of the group. In reinforcing this important element, which focuses on the here and now of the sessions, we often use the opportunity to comment on the group as a microcosm. Though the focus is on feelings, perceptions, and memories that are stimulated in the here and now, often the group interactions resurrect salient current and past elements in their life experiences, both problematic and joyful, and these are important to discuss because we are trying to know each person as fully as possible. Memories that are awakened during a meeting, as well as the associations to external events, all are relevant. The stimuli are presumed to be the group members, and they are expected to discuss openly as much of their inner world as possible.

This stipulation serves at least three valuable purposes. First, merely talking about one's inner responses may be therapeutic. Keeping old fantasies and feelings bottled up adds to the individual's isolation. Self-revelation can appreciably alter that state of affairs. Second, once feelings are shared publicly, they are open to exploration. Members also have the chance to confirm or deny the assumptions regarding what will happen if others know what they are really experiencing. Third, they also have an opportunity for consensual validation of affective responses. If an individual becomes angry at another member and expresses it, then he/she can discover whether or not he/she is the only one experiencing anger. If others are also angry, the member can presume that in this instance his/her emotional gyroscope is properly aligned. It is also true that in some situations several members in a group have a similar affective response, only to learn that they share a common defensive stand. For example, individuals may at times unconsciously provoke angry responses in order to keep others at a distance or to expiate guilt.

Finally, if the member is the sole individual experiencing a particular affect, most frequently anger, he/she can entertain at least three hypotheses. It is possible that person is the only one aptly responding to the situation. It is also possible that there have been group dynamic processes in which others "dumped" unacceptable feelings onto the person. Thirdly, the person could be responding to a cue from his/her own life and not to the "reality" of the current situation. If it is the latter, representing transference, the member has an opportunity to explore the specific and other parallel situations in order to see if he/she is routinely distorting.

3. *Agree to put feelings into words, not actions.* Patients agree that membership in a group means expressing feelings verbally, not behaviorally. Traditionally this agreement proscribes violent behavior such as striking others, throwing objects, or damaging property. But violence is masked in many ways, and verbal violence, as distinguished from an expression of anger, falls within this part of the agreement. Violence in the form of virulent verbal attacks by one member toward another is thus prohibited. Patients can learn to put even their angriest feelings into words which will not violate others.

A more problematic area for many therapists is the matter of affectionate or soothing physical contact among members. It is not unusual for one member to reach out and touch, or perhaps embrace, a weeping colleague. Since this is a socially acceptable way of expressing feelings, such actions are often unexamined or even congratulated. Some therapists may rationalize such contact as solely therapeutic, since they see no harm coming from warm touching in the group. However, ambivalence, terror, dislike, or even hate may be hidden behind the behavioral facade. There is a place in therapy groups for a gentle touch or hug as an authentic expression of communicating deeply felt emotions, but these acts should always be examined for their full meaning and impact.

CLINICAL EXAMPLE

Typically a box of tissues was placed outside the group circle. If there were tears, a caring member would get up and provide a supply of tissues. One evening a member, discussing the recent death of her brother, began to cry and was within a few minutes given some tissues. She stopped and then protested, saying that her grief had been interrupted. In further discussion the group began to realize that they were masking their own powerful feelings, triggered by this loss, behind the social act of caring. The group norm changed, and members who failed to bring a handkerchief learned to ask when they wanted to dry their eyes.

CLINICAL EXAMPLE

Ruth began to cry as she said that she felt she simply could not change. The members sat silently for a few minutes, and then Sylvia said that she would like to hug Ruth. Ruth became very angry, stating, "I could not tolerate that!" She expounded about the insincerity of social hugs and linked this to her narcissistic mother always telling her that she loved Ruth but behaving in very different ways. Sylvia felt responsible for Ruth's escalating discomfort, and she was confused because her attempt had genuinely been to soothe Ruth. Tom pointed out that they knew each other well enough to distinguish between what was genuine, unauthentic, deep, or superficial. He added that if he hugged Sylvia she would know whether it was a sexual advance or more platonic affection. Ursula said she felt just like Ruth but that she would have accepted Sylvia's hug and not said a word about her discomfort. Victor pointed out that it was a sign of Ruth's trust in the group that she could tell the group her feelings about the proposed hug. He pointed out that she was probably more trusting of the group than she let on.

*   *   *

A great deal of important data surfaced as the members talked about their feelings rather than using the shortcut of action. In the end, Ruth felt very comforted by Sylvia.

Some therapists specifically prohibit eating or drinking during groups (Ormont, 1967). (These days everyone prohibits smoking.) A common rationale for this stance is that such behaviors diminish useful anxiety and tension that could more profitably be experienced. Each therapist must decide how specific to be with regard to the behavioral prohibitions, since many actions can be handled through interpretations. The therapeutic management of some of the extreme instances of acting rather than verbalizing will be discussed in Chapter 14.

4. *Agree to use the relationships made in the group therapeutically, not socially.* How patients may utilize the relationships made in their groups is a matter of divergent opinion among therapists. Some therapists absolutely prohibit out-of-group contact; others openly support, reinforce, and all but require it.

The fundamental use of the group is for therapeutic, not social, purposes, and in the long run the two are mutually exclusive. As patients express their feelings for one another, including their yearnings to socialize, a considerable pressure to act emerges. The wish (on the part of both the therapist and patients) for patients to use the relationships gained in their groups outside of the groups is understandable. For many patients the contacts with their group colleagues represent their most viable and authentic relationships. Restricting their use and enjoyment of such contacts may feel unduly harsh and withholding. Nevertheless, it is more therapeutically profitable to discourage extragroup socializing, since doing so reduces the variables affecting group behavior and increases the likelihood of spontaneous revelation of affects in the group. Further, if the use of in-group relationships for social purposes is thwarted, patients tend to gain their own social networks outside the group more quickly. Of greater significance is that they feel less dependent and more autonomous when the social network utilized is really their own and not one provided by the group.

The language of this portion of the agreement contains room for creative debate. Members are left to discuss and decide what constitutes therapeutic as opposed to social interaction. All groups have relationships that extend beyond the actual meetings. Even the moments before and after the group session represent opportunities for important interactions. Group members can be told that any extragroup interactions may well represent important ways of managing feelings evoked in the therapy. Therefore members should discuss emotionally meaningful extragroup contacts in order to enhance learning. Within this framework of dynamic understanding, patients can be reminded that the primary use of all the interactions with group members is therapeutic.

5. Agree to remain in the group until the problems that brought you have been resolved. This agreement is often seen as problematic by applicants. It actually contains complex elements, because instructions on how to leave the group are implicit.

Patients are invariably anxious about entering a group, and they often attempt to master their anxiety by envisioning their early weeks as a trial period. Some therapists deal with this by asking that entering patients agree to remain for a specified period of time, generally 3 months. This practice presumably helps new patients remain through the early difficult period and long enough to develop a stronger therapeutic alliance.

The trial period is inadvisable for two reasons. First, any newcomer breaches group confidentiality, and if there is an agreed-upon trial period the group process likely will be skewed toward caution rather than openness until that trial period has expired and the patient has committed him/herself to joining. Second, some patients simply stay for the duration of the trial period and then leave. In this situation the therapist is left with little or no therapeutic leverage, since the patient has indeed fully adhered to the agreements.

Acceptance of this agreement does not prevent premature quitting, but it does remind the patients that they had agreed to remain until they had resolved their presenting problems. In addition, many patients experience the agreement to remain in the group as an initial source of hope and are comforted by the clear expectation that group therapy can help them resolve their problems.

This agreement also begins the norm setting about how appropriate terminations occur. As patients consider termination, it is very useful for them to make their decisions in light of their agreement: "Have I resolved the problems I came with?" The subsequent discussion of presenting problems is one element in the review process that is essential to successful termination. Establishing this as a norm opens the door for discussing how one should leave. Part of the initial orientation includes information that leaving a group is an important event and saying goodbye, though often painful, is not to be avoided. Patients learn that they should not abruptly stop therapy; rather, they should spend time examining the changes they have made and their feelings about ending treatment.

6. Agree to be responsible for your bill. In this day of diminished third-party payment for psychotherapy, group therapy often seems attractive because each session is less expensive. Some managed care companies, recognizing the value of groups, have developed ways of providing a greater number of sessions than they provide for dyadic treatment. When insurance is available, patients and clinicians should become familiar with the details of reimbursement and the company's requirement for reports and record review. (Record maintenance will be discussed below.) For some patients this diminished fiscal responsibility may be detrimental. They correlate expense with emotional commitment and may use the termination of their annual insurance payments as a reason to leave treatment.

At the very least patients should be responsible for their bills. If possible, patients should pay the therapist directly and then receive the insurance money themselves. If there is a problem in insurance payments, the patient, not the therapist, should negotiate with the company. Optimally, the therapist should fill out insurance forms only the first time. Thereafter, where possible, the patient should be responsible for completing the forms, using the same repetitive data (including diagnosis) and the proper dates and amounts, with the therapist simply checking for accuracy and then signing the form.

It is wise to stipulate that statements will be handed out during the first meeting of the month and that members are expected to pay in full before the next bill is distributed. There are certainly other ways of implementing these principles. What is important is that the fiscal elements of the agreement be spelled out in detail and patients understand that financial matters are also group business.

It is essential that therapists are clear and forthright with the members in how they charge for missed sessions. Some therapists have a clear understanding that patients will be charged for scheduled meetings whether or not they attend. In individual therapy, if a patient misses a meeting, the therapist can choose to fill that hour and therefore not suffer a financial loss because of the patient's absence. In groups we do not have the option of temporarily replacing an absent member. Thus, no matter the reason for absenteeism, members are charged for their seats. If this agreement is used, patients need to be reminded that third-party payers do not reimburse for missed meetings.

Other therapists prefer a less rigorous approach to fees and do not charge patients for vacations or unavoidable absences such as illnesses or required business trips. In these cases the therapist is placed in the position of having to work with the patient to determine which absences are "acting out" and which are unavoidable. For the therapist choosing this approach, the key variable is consistency, so that patients can gain the most from analysis of how they choose to attend meetings and handle payment of fees. An alternative is for the clinician to determine in advance a set number of sessions that the member may miss and not be charged. Under this arrangement any reason for an absence would be included. One guiding principle is that the therapist should not be put in the position of deciding what is a "good-enough" absence for which the patient does not have to pay. A clear policy regarding missed sessions allows the therapist to remain in the position of therapist, aiding the patient in learning about the meaning of absences and the feelings about the group and money.

Another important principle is the separation of the therapist's financial interests and the patient's therapeutic responsibility. In whatever manner therapists manage fees, part of the group agreements relate to their expectable earnings. Further, the agreements are a structure that patients might use for their own internal needs, as an opportunity to rebel or to deprive the therapist of real or imagined gratification. This enables the therapist to comfortably examine absences whether or not a fee is charged.

It often seems easier to discuss intimate sexual experiences than financial matters. Therapists face more than a strong social taboo when they bring up a member's overdue fee—extremely strong feelings of shame, embarrassment, narcissistic injury, and rage are mobilized. (It is quite usual for a group to react to a therapist raising the issue of unpaid fees by protesting, "That is private information and does not belong in group!") Yet, to avoid dealing directly with the meaning of money and the payment of fees runs the considerable risk of colluding with patients' resistances. Financial matters are not private matters because there are invariably groupwide meanings and reverberations when a patient falls behind in paying fees. Indeed, members learn that delays in payment have meaning, and with experience they identify with the therapist and learn to examine not only the question arising when a payment is delinquent but the more general meaning of money in their lives.

As a part of the continuing emphasis that everything can be discussed in the group, the therapist must deal forthrightly with fees. We prefer that statements be distributed and payment received during sessions. This simple practice invites candid discussion of financial matters in the group.

7. *Agree to protect the names and identities of your fellow group members.* This portion of the agreement is saved for last because there is usually an input overload when the group agreements are discussed and members often do not recall all the elements. Mentioning the requirement to protect other members' anonymity last gives it a deserved special emphasis.

Confidentiality is the cornerstone upon which group therapy relationships are built, and yet it is rarely completely maintained. Therapists often ask patients to agree to "keep in confidence all that is shared within the group." We believe this is a troublesome way of handling the issue for at least two reasons. First, it is an agreement not likely to be kept. As the group becomes important to people, they will talk about their experience with others. Sessions can be very stimulating, and talking about what happened is a reasonable way to begin to integrate strong emotions. Every therapist will recognize his/her propensity to seek out a colleague after an affect-laden meeting in order to "blow off steam" and further process what happened. Obviously, such discussions go on as a matter of course between cotherapists. It would be unreasonable not to expect the members to do the same. Second, to ask patients not to speak of their group experience is to place them in a double bind. On the one hand, by virtue of being treated in a group, they are told overtly and covertly that it is healthy and helps them to grow to share intimately with other human beings. On the other hand, they are told, "But don't tell anyone about this!"

In fact, we hope our group patients do talk with their significant others about their group experiences. If they are in concurrent individual therapy, it is therapeutically imperative that they discuss the meetings in their individual therapies. It is also enriching to share some of what is learned in a group with loved ones. The end point of group therapy, after all, is not that individuals merely become intimate and honest with other group members, but rather that they gain authenticity with others in the mainstreams of their lives.

The fundamental concern with the issue of confidentiality is that the anonymity of the members be protected, and the agreement to protect names and identities serves that purpose well.

THE THERAPIST'S AGREEMENT

Thus far we have emphasized the agreements as an initial structure for the conduct of treatment from the perspective of the patient. The clinician also enters into an agreement with the group and its members. In relation to the group, clinicians help define the boundaries of what information they will bring from outside into the meeting, thereby in part clarifying patients' responsibilities. The areas covered in this portion include the following:

- Information gathered in diagnostic or regularly scheduled individual or family sessions
- Chance meetings or observations about the patient (e.g., outside the group)
- Phone calls or contacts with other therapists
- Information provided to insurance companies
- How group material will be used by the therapist in lectures or writing

These elements all involve confidentiality and delineating responsibility for providing how information will be used therapeutically. Some clinicians draw very tight boundaries and indicate that any outside contacts with patients are confidential and that it is the patient's responsibility to bring relevant material to the treatment. Others indicate that they may use all information gathered from the patients in order to be as helpful as possible. Either position is defensible, but it is vital to have a clear policy which is set forth before patients enter a group.

The distinction between scheduled and chance meetings is worthy of note. At times members may be struggling to address their feelings about an accidental encounter, and the therapist's willingness to be open about the contact may provide permission for all to address leader-directed responses. It also reinforces the maxim that there are optimally *no* secrets in group. Variations in these positions abound, and clinical judgment is often needed.

Clinicians must have informed consent to contact others about the patient. Some therapists will not accept potential members without permission to contact the referral source or individual therapist. This might be limited to the initial evaluations or might be ongoing as part of collaborative work. If there are more or less regular contacts between the therapist and outside clinicians, under what circumstances will the member be informed? It is our opinion that therapy proceeds most effectively when all the mental health professionals involved are in contact with one another. This not only widens the perspective on our patients, it greatly reduces the possibility of splitting between therapists. Given that often group therapists, individual therapists, couples' therapists, psychopharmacologists, and other professionals involved may not even know one another, the opportunity for splitting is immense.

Patients need to be informed of the clinician's record-keeping practices. When anyone in the group uses insurance, the usual policy includes the company's right to review records. If members of a group have such insurance, it is important that the therapist keep separate notes regarding these patients so that the anonymity and confidentiality of other group members are not compromised when insurance companies review notes.

Describing how the therapist will interact within the sessions should be kept brief. Patients will soon learn about that. A general statement may be sufficient indicating that the therapist will try to understand the members and their interactions and convey that understanding in a manner that will be useful to them.

The group agreement, including responsibilities of patients and therapist, contains a great deal of information, and members integrate, recall, or distort relevant aspects of it. This then becomes information about their internal processes and can be utilized therapeutically.

SUMMARY

Entering a therapy group is a difficult task for anyone. Potential group members come to us because they have more than the usual amount of anxiety in interpersonal situations, and thus careful preparation for their entrance into groups is a necessity if successful therapeutic work is to follow.

An important ingredient in proper preparation of a patient is imparting and gaining acceptance of the treatment goals. If there appears to be a significant discrepancy between the patient's motivation or goals for therapy and those of the therapist, it is wise to delay the entrance into a group until those issues can be clarified. Often a therapist, anxious to have a new member, will avoid dealing with these conflicts in the hope that they can be resolved by the group. This inevitably leads to problems that are best resolved before the applicant joins the group.

The presentation of the agreements, along with examining the overall response of the patient to the idea of entering a group, offers an important opportunity for gaining information about the patient whether or not the applicant ultimately chooses to join. Patients exhibit a variety of responses such as compliance, acceptance, anxiety, rebellion, rejection, and so forth. These responses should be viewed as more than just overt responses to the agreements themselves; they should be seen as potential windows into the inner world of the patient.

The group agreements are not a formal, written document; rather, they are the verbal agreement between patient, therapist, and other members regarding the ground rules of the group's operation. The agreements are the foundation for a productive and safe therapeutic environment. The specific elements we have presented should be mutually agreed upon treatment guidelines.

A number of elements constitute the agreements for ongoing, open-ended therapy groups; the patients agree to the following[1]:

1. To be present each week, to be on time, and to remain throughout the meeting.
2. To work actively on the problems that brought them to the group.
3. To put feelings into words, not actions.
4. To use the relationships made in the group therapeutically, not socially.
5. To remain in the group until the problems that brought them to the group have been resolved.
6. To be responsible for their bills.
7. To protect the names and identities of fellow group members.

The therapist also informs members about his/her part in the agreement. Delineating information that will be brought into the group by the therapist, policies about fees, and the manner of participating in the sessions will indicate that all participants in the group have responsibilities in providing the best possible therapeutic experience.

We are convinced that any group needs a clear set of agreements in order to be effective. Furthermore, the agreements become a powerful tool in analysis of various resistances and character traits. Remember, these are *agreements*, not *law*. We expect our patients to be *responsible* for these agreements, not to always keep them. There will be times when other life responsibilities, such as to family, will perforce take priority over the agreements with the group. For group therapy to work well, however, the members need to give the group agreements a high priority and to be responsible for them even when they opt to honor other agreements (meaning that the member should discuss the reasons for breaching the group agreements and be willing to explore deeper potential meanings of those breaches).

---

[1]If the therapist has a procedure for dealing with the absence of the leader (such as making up the meeting or providing a substitute leader), this should be part of the original group agreements (see Chapter 11).

NINE

The Role of the Group Therapist

I have to follow them, I am their leader.
—ALEXANDRE-AUGUSTE LEDRU-ROLLIN, attributed

One of Freud's more famous remarks was his comparison of psychotherapy to chess. Of the latter he observed, "Anyone who hopes to learn the noble game of chess from books will soon discover that only the opening and end games admit of an exhaustive systematic presentation and that the infinite variety of moves that develop after the opening defy any such descriptions. The gap in instruction can only be filled by a diligent study of games fought out by masters" (Freud, 1913, p. 128). Similarly, the beginning and end of therapy can be taught—less so the middle. If the comparison with regard to the role of the individual therapist holds, it is even more pointedly true for the group therapist, who shifts among group, interpersonal, intrapsychic, and cultural perspectives. Group therapists are continually confronted with a richness of data, and great skill is required to sort through it in order to focus upon and use the most relevant and powerful material. It is this very complexity that contributes to the therapeutic potency of groups.

The literature offers little specific assistance to therapists in organizing and assigning priorities to group data (Rutan & Alonso, 1978). In this chapter we elucidate a number of principles that should provide assistance in determining when and how to intervene. For heuristic purposes we separate leader activity into role and focus, each composed of several continua (see Figure 9.1).

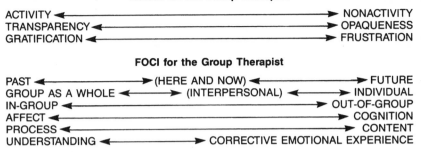

FIGURE 9.1. Leadership dimensions of the group therapist.

The three continua that represent the style dimension are considered in parallel. That is, each leader is continually and concurrently making decisions about how active, transparent, and gratifying to be. The six continua of the focus dimension may be considered a hierarchy. The therapist's attention should first be focused on the past–present continuum, then on the group-as-a-whole–individuals continuum, and so on. While the complexity of group interactions does not allow for hard-and-fast rules about how to attend to group data, considering the focus dimensions in the order presented in Figure 9.1 will often help clarify material.

Where any therapist operates on the style and focus dimensions is in part related to his/her theoretical persuasion (Christ, 1975; Kauff, 1979; Lieberman et al., 1973; Rutan, 1992; A. Wolf & Schwartz, 1975; Yalom, 1985). A therapist who adheres to group-as-a-whole processes generally will choose to focus on the in-group, affect, and process ends of the respective axes. A traditional psychoanalytic therapist may highlight transference aspects of interpersonal transactions, fantasy life (content), and the importance of the past. Of course, these same therapists may eschew transparency, gratification, and activity on the role dimension.

Although on some occasions it is most therapeutic to operate from an extreme pole of any continua, it is important for therapists to understand that there are consequences to these decisions.

THE LEADERSHIP ROLE DIMENSION

Members are very watchful of their leaders, heeding what they say, how they say it, what they reveal about themselves, and how they relate. The warmth in the voice, the eye contact, and the feelings exhibited nonverbally are elements to which patients pay close attention. Further, the leader serves as a model (through both imitation and identification) for observing and using group phenomena. Therefore, it is important that therapists thoughtfully assess the manner in which they relate in order to understand fully the implications of their style on the treatment process.

Activity versus Nonactivity

Groups, particularly in early phases of development or at times of high stress, are likely to be preoccupied with the therapist's activity. Members complain about the quantity or the quality of the therapist's participation, creating considerable pressure in the therapist to respond. The therapist is continually balancing the issues of silence versus verbal activity. Overactivity may result in infantilization of members, whereas underactivity or excessive withholding may result in narcissistic injury followed by withdrawal and rage.

In general, the most useful activities for leaders are internal ones—feeling, empathizing, and hypothesizing to further understanding. Overt activity for the leader is primarily verbal. How much does one speak? How cryptic or extensive should one's interventions be? How *much* speaking the therapist does is separate from the *content* of the activity (speaking). The therapist's role is essentially reactive rather than initiating. The dynamic therapist waits for the group process to occur and then comments on it.

It is unusual for a dynamic therapist to initiate discussion. Any agenda the therapist needs to bring to the group (e.g., the announcement of a vacation, or of an increase in fees, or the news that a member has notified the therapist that he/she will not be attending a meeting) should be announced at the beginning of a meeting. This procedure provides the members with the opportunity to respond with their own associations, secure in the knowledge that the leader has no additional significant agenda to introduce.

The patients' roles on this continuum are also primarily verbal. The therapist tries to establish the norm that change occurs most effectively when members feel, express, and talk rather than do. Therefore, expressing a yearning to physically embrace another member is considered more therapeutic and beneficial than actually embracing that person. This stance is obviously quite different from the more active therapeutic techniques, and it flows naturally from psychodynamic theory.

The place of touching and doing in therapy is a strongly contested issue in the literature. While no one can deny that human contact can be therapeutic, the tenets of psychodynamic theory stress the verbalization of affect rather than the acting on it. If we want to reassure our patients that the therapeutic arena is a safe place to experience and explore all affects in a psychodynamic manner, then it is imperative that they be assured that no physical action will follow. (It is one thing to sympathetically touch someone when one has warm feelings, but it is quite another if the affects being experienced are strongly sexual or aggressive.) When groups are allowed or encouraged to act on warm and affectionate feelings, a lingering question remains about what actions might follow when members are feeling angry, sadistic, or even homicidal.

Usually the therapist can set the norm for "talking, not doing" by flagging and commenting on even the most benign physical touching. If a member reaches to comfort another, the therapist can inquire, "What feelings were you expressing through the touch?" On those infrequent occasions when an actual threat of physical violence exists in a group, the therapist must not rely on interpretation alone but must clearly and promptly set limits on any potential action. Every effort must be made to avoid physical harm. It is reassuring to note that despite the affective power of groups, actual physical violence within them is extraordinarily rare.

Transparency versus Opaqueness

The transparency–opaqueness variable highlights the distinction between the members and the therapist. It is expected that members will allow themselves to be as transparent as possible, expressing their associations, emotions, secrets, histories, and thoughts. Therapists, however, should be transparent only in limited ways. It is usually helpful to reveal only that which is in the service of the treatment process. Even within the rather narrow confines of the dynamic tradition, however, there are differences in how therapists conceptualize their role on this axis. Strict traditionalists rarely give much hint about their own inner feelings, whereas practitioners with an object relations point of view often find it useful to share an emotional reaction to a patient or the group in order to facilitate exploration of projective identifications.

Therapists need to be particularly alert to avoid responses arising from their own inner needs or from pressures from the members. To the degree that patients are not burdened with the therapist's personal data, their task of transferring meaning and attributes is easier; conversely, the more members know about the therapist, the more difficult it is for them to fantasize.

No matter how strictly a particular therapist holds to the opaque pole of this continuum, after a time members come to know a great deal about the therapist. As an actively engaged participant in the group, albeit in a role different from that of a member, the therapist reveals a great deal in nonverbal ways. Patients learn to read body language and facial expression; they know when the therapist is pleased or displeased. It is not necessary, useful, or even *possible* for group therapists to be blank screens. Groups are intensely human encounters, and it is often impossible (or inhuman) for a therapist to avoid laughing at a funny moment or feeling tearful when a group is struggling with sadness. If therapists are empathically attuned to their groups, they are not immune to the affect that engulfs everyone. It is through the therapist's steadfastness to the task, through the concern, caring, and, thoughtfulness, and through the ability to be introspective, to tolerate affects, and to move forward in a therapeutic manner that the group members come to know a great deal about their therapist. The group process, complete with the consensual validation that this multiperson arena affords, means that the veil of secrecy of the therapeutic role is considerably lessened. Though patients will sometimes deny how much they know of us, they nonetheless know a great deal. For some therapists this reality is uncomfortable; for most, however, it is an enjoyable aspect of leading groups.

Much therapeutic benefit can accrue if the therapist is aware of this element of transparency and can respond if the members comment on it. Patients will occasionally pick up and comment on the affective state of the therapist, sensing sadness, boredom, or anger, for example. Moreover, a mistake or slip of the tongue can expose the therapist's unconscious just as surely and accurately as it can expose the patient's. Since one goal of psychotherapy is to help patients become more empathic, it is counterproductive for therapists to refuse to acknowledge patients' accurate therapist-directed empathy. To acknowledge that a patient has correctly sensed something is quite different from gratuitously offering personal information.

CLINICAL EXAMPLE

One evening the therapist prepared the group room for a group, carefully arranging the chairs and turning on the lights, etc. However, he failed to unlock the office door. He was perplexed when he entered the group room to find no members present.

Soon, however, he heard voices outside the door and went to check what was going on. At this point he discovered the locked door. He unlocked the door and the group paraded into the room, giggling and thoroughly enjoying the therapist's error.

The group leader had taken an unusual 2-week winter break, and the group had been angry and hurt by this abandonment. Indeed, two of the patients had been thrown into powerful and painful reactions, reliving the early abandonments by fathers. The leader was uncomfortable at the strength of the anger, but even more powerfully he felt guilty that he had contributed to such painful affects.

When the group sat down, one member immediately asked, "So . . . ?" The leader said simply, "I guess I have some feelings about sitting with the group right now." This honest acknowledgment that the therapist has an unconscious led to a very productive meeting in which the group explored the reactions they had been having toward the therapist.

*   *   *

Sometimes aspects of the therapist's personal life are public information and therefore come into the group. This can occur, for example, when the therapist gets married or divorced, a new car is in the office driveway, the therapist is injured, or something about the therapist's career is published in the newspaper. A therapist's pregnancy represents a particularly powerful and public piece of personal information that becomes known to the group. Furthermore, if one member discovers some personal information about the therapist, it is soon known by all. When patients comment about such aspects of the therapist's life, there is no reason not to indicate that such data is correct, although the precise timing of confirming the information will vary according to the situation and the theoretical orientation of the therapist.

There is one form of transparency which is always present for the therapist. With the shift in understanding the role of the therapist from "expert observer" to "participant observer," as evidenced in the intersubjective perspective of Stolorow, Atwood, and Brandchaft (1994), the therapist is always "present" in the therapeutic encounter. The intersubjective theorists suggest that there is a great deal of information gained through mutual empathy and that the therapist and patient are continuously involved at this level in an empathic and mutual interaction.

Despite the exceptions, patients do not come to hear about their therapist's successes and failures, joys and sorrows. Since groups so often achieve a family-like feeling, therapists are uniquely prone to the temptation to share irrelevant personal information with patients. Further, there may be some magical wish on the part of the members to hear how the therapist solves a problem or to know the therapist more personally in the hope that this will somehow solve their own problems. Requests by members for personal information should be explored to understand their roots, not gratified under the notion that for the therapist to be considered human personal information must be shared. Opaqueness should never be confused with emotional distance or lack of personal warmth.

Gratification versus Frustration

An artful balance should be made between gratification and frustration in therapy, whether it is group or individual treatment. Too much gratification results in insufficient anxiety to promote change. Too much frustration results in a relationship insufficient to promote the trust, caring, and safety necessary for personal revelation. In groups the therapist is freed to adopt an empathic observer role because the members can provide gratification when the leader does not. Thus, even more than in dyadic therapy, the group therapist can use the observational posture without unduly distressing a patient. Overgratification by the therapist may take the form of too much activity, self-exposure, or even too-frequent interpretations. Yet, too much frustration or too austere an environment can stifle group effectiveness. For example, some therapists inappropriately avoid eye contact when speaking to a specific member or when making group-as-a-whole interpretations. And yet, when members avoid eye contact, that behavior is usually a subject of exploration.

Therapists who enjoy working with groups doubtless satisfy some personal needs by choosing this modality. Many, for example, face an ever-present danger of falling prey to a countertransferential need to be central at all times. Through excessive gratification they may retain their centrality and make the group leader-dependent rather than balanced between leader-focused and member-focused tendencies. The goal in working on this axis is to allow the maximum usable amount of anxiety for each patient and for the group as a whole and not to interfere with the members' abilities to work with their feelings and relationships.

THE LEADERSHIP FOCUS DIMENSION

Leader activity involves not only a particular leadership role but also the leader's focus of attention. The continua on the role dimension are to be considered in parallel; that is, the therapist's role can be defined by all of them simultaneously. In the leadership focus dimension, leaders can vary their attention among the various axes. Indeed, the therapist may conceptually rank these axes in order to use them as aids in the task of understanding the multiplicity of data arising in a group. Though the elements are presented separately, there is obvious overlap and so no rigid hierarchy. Different therapists may choose to order the importance of the axes differently, but systematically considering each of them will often bring clarity to what otherwise seems chaotic.

There is no "right" place on these continua. The weight given a particular point on each of the continua reflects a therapeutic judgment about how best to help members change. We would suggest, however, that it is unduly limiting for therapists to restrict themselves to particular points on the axes. The art of being a group therapist is at least in part knowing when to focus on different points on these continua.

The Past–Present–Future Axis

All dynamic psychotherapies include consideration of an extended time dimension, one from the past, through the present, and into the future. A particular theoretical orientation may emphasize one point more than another, a fact exemplified by the particular importance existential therapists place on the end of life and our ultimate finitude. In psychodynamic therapy all points on this axis are important, but the initial focus of attention and exploration is on the here and now, that is, the present intragroup responses, interactions, and feelings. There is a mistaken notion that dynamic therapy focuses on history, the "there and then," but transference is a here-and-now phenomenon occurring between patient and therapist and between patients and patients (Michaels, 1981). The past is relevant to the extent that it informs or distorts the present.

Indeed, two important pasts develop in therapy: the treatment and the personal. In the treatment past are the events that have taken place in the therapy. Groups develop rich legacies, and members will often recall events or issues from the group's history that help clarify current events. One liability of the move toward more time-limited groups is the loss of the richness of the treatment history as a source of therapeutic data. The personal past brought by each member, including his/her social unconscious (Hopper, 1996), also becomes known to the group over time, and the exploration of each person's idiosyncratic reactions to current events takes on a new perspective when the uniqueness of each history is understood. As each member relives and re-members his/her past, new associations and memories are evoked in the other members.

Often what is happening in the present is unclear and can be understood only with reference to the past. For example, a member has an excessive emotional reaction to what appears to others to be a mild stimulus (what might be called a hundred-dollar reaction to a one-dollar event). This is often an indication that the member is responding to data from history, not the present. The precise timing of when to link the present with the past through interpretation depends on the clarity of the associations as metaphors and on the state of the therapeutic alliance (Katz, 1983). The personal past emerges in the stereotyped roles that patients adopt. These roles usually are ways of managing anxiety and conflict that have worked in the past. If members can become aware of patterned behavior and the meaning of that behavior, associations from the past will add to overall insight.

As with all elements in therapy, the past may be used defensively to avoid the present. The therapist is not immune to this tendency, and a common error is to prematurely shift the focus to the past in order to contain intense affects in the present. Patients also revert to the past as an intellectual or obsessional defense, and such flight should be considered in light of its use in maintaining both group and individual equilibrium.

Therapists can often use their own affect responses as indicators of the need to explore the past or stay with the current interactions. Feelings of boredom, lack of interest, or a sense of repetitiveness may suggest that the members have mobilized defensive patterns. These defenses might represent a response to an unattended group conflict, a product of individual character styles (roles), or newly emerging transferences. The past, either near or remote, may then shed light on the present conflicts. Often the therapist's anxiety is a reliable guide: If it feels more anxiety provoking to allow the current interactions to continue, then continuing them is probably the course where the most therapeutic value resides; conversely, if the therapist experiences anxiety over the prospect of linking current interactions to historical material, then making those links is likely the proper course.

Finally, the future is also always present. Patients come to therapy in order to make their futures better. They plan, think, and feel about what is in store for them. Many in-group behaviors can best be understood as predicting or trying out new responses. Fantasies about what someone will do or feel or how he/she may react in some outside situation are commonplace and are clearly future oriented. As patients near termination, they become more future oriented, wondering about their ability to be different from what they were before entering therapy. Furthermore, one of the goals of therapy is to help patients gain the ability to predict the outcomes of their behaviors.

Any debate about where to focus—past, present, or future—has been largely resolved: all three have an important place in treatment.

The Group-as-a-Whole–Interpersonal–Individual Axis

Leaders must move back and forth flexibly between observing the group as a whole, attending to the interpersonal interactions within it, and analyzing individuals. A primary focus on group-as-a-whole phenomena provides an opportunity for members to understand their shared, universal concerns and to gain understanding from their participation in the powerful conscious and unconscious group processes. A focus on interpersonal interactions assists in understanding communication blocks and distortions as well as the impact on others of one's personal style. A focus on the individuals within the group gives members the opportunity to examine their uniqueness and enhances a sense of potency in the world. To focus on one element to the exclusion of the others is to lose touch unnecessarily with powerful therapeutic forces.

Typically, one can give dominance to group-as-a-whole observations at those times when members are responding to the same stimuli, such as when the group's framework is affected—for example, when the group is forming, a new member is being introduced, a member is terminating, or the therapist's vacation is imminent. At these times when the group's boundary is altered or forming, attention to the groupwide reaction, and therefore to the individual contributions to that reaction, is most useful.

Groupwide reactions occur rather silently much of the time. Within the group there may be a subtle thrust for greater intimacy or increased expression of difficult feelings; in this process the members may be working to change old group norms toward greater spontaneity. Conversely, if the stress is too high, there may be movement toward restriction of feelings. When a group is feeling a powerful regressive pull, it is often best for the therapist to offer group-as-a-whole interventions. From this perspective, the notion of enabling or constricting solutions to group focal conflicts highlights the group-as-a-whole perspective (Whitaker & Lieberman, 1964); that is, generally it is not one individual who interferes with the expression of feelings or the discussion of a stressful topic but two or more individuals who are thus engaged, with the covert cooperation of the others.

Kernberg (1975) suggested that the group-as-a-whole–interpersonal–individual perspective might parallel developmental stages. He maintained that groups composed of individuals with preoedipal personality configurations can best use the group-as-a-whole focus, whereas members with oedipal personality configurations learn more from an interpersonal focus. However, this formulation overlooks the oedipal (and specifically sexual) attractions and rivalries that involve the whole group and that might be clarified for all members through group-as-a-whole interpretations. Furthermore, the less developed patients are often unable to profit from the lack of personal meaning in an exclusive group-as-a-whole approach.

The most productive interventions consider the varying involvement of the members in any meeting. For instance, an intervention directed to one member working on competitive feelings at an oedipal level in a group struggling with preoedipal issues of basic trust would miss the main focus of the group. The individual might gain from the intervention, but the group focus would rapidly shift away from competition and back to the central focus. Thus, the intervention would not lead to elaboration or working through. On the other hand, the same intervention in a group that was dealing with oedipal competitive issues may be powerful and therapeutically enabling not only to the particular individual but to the others as well, since the comment would likely stimulate relevant associations in several members. When a particular member is working at a significantly different level than that of the rest of the group, the therapist can often take note of it and refer to it at a later time when the group and that member are working at comparable levels.

There are occasions when one or several sessions might be devoted almost exclusively to a particular member's problems. This is appropriate in times of crisis, and the other members can learn from their inner reactions to the situation and responses to the distressed member. However, the therapist needs to maintain a broad perspective to ensure that the focus on one or two members does not become a pattern and thereby a detriment to free interaction. Indeed, sometimes when a particular individual is the focus of attention for a prolonged period of time, this represents a group-as-a-whole process in which that individual is speaking of feelings or concerns that are actually shared by the whole group.

There are staunch and avid practitioners of both the group-as-a-whole approach and the individual approach to group therapy. In fact, both aspects of group functioning are vitally important and work well in concert. The goal is not to select one or the other but to know how to use both effectively.

The In-Group–Out-of-Group Axis

The same principles hold for the in-group–out-of-group axis as for the past–present–future axis. It is certainly true that individuals sometimes associate to out-of-group events as an avoidance of powerful in-group affects. Even in these instances it is important that the therapist not imply that the out-of-group material is irrelevant. It is preferable for the therapist to tactfully link the out-of-group and in-group material. Here, again, the therapist's affect may provide a guide in determining where to ultimately bring the focus of attention.

Members have their in-group and out-of-group lives. Patients often talk about their relationships with group members, and they equally often speak of their relationships with important others outside the group (such as loved ones, parents, or bosses). The theory of group therapy assumes that individuals are always presenting the salient elements of their personalities and their conflicts in the group; thus, where possible, attention is focused on the in-group action, where the elements are more available for direct analysis. As with the here-and-now continuum, there may be many roadblocks in accomplishing this task. In the vast majority of situations, however, when patients use their interactions with one another or with the therapist or analyze their perceptions of the group, they gain important affective and cognitive appreciation of their problems.

Though the therapist should welcome and scrutinize all out-of-group material for its relevance to in-group matters, it is helpful to remember that not everything is a metaphor for some group transaction or feeling. The birth of a child, a wedding, a relative's divorce, a death—all are examples of important external events that probably have meanings that transcend whatever metaphorical analogue may be in the group relationships. Members can profit from the opportunity to talk and feel about such events in the company of valued others. Only a naive therapist slavishly adheres to the belief that such events are primarily transferences. It is not farfetched to believe that a neophyte therapist could interpret a story about a serious automobile accident involving a member's family as solely a metaphor for a damaging event within the group. Usually the introduction of powerful out-of-group stimuli does result in in-group associations that are profitably explored. The therapist needs to maintain a "both/and" rather than an "either/or" mentality in these situations. That is, even if the therapist relates external events to in-group matters, he/she should imply that both are important rather than reject the external material as pure resistance.

Clinical Example

Raphael returned to the group after recuperating from a heart attack. There was extensive discussion of the procedures and rehabilitation processes he had been through. Jenny arrived a few minutes late, in this middle of this discussion, and Rich commented on how nice her earrings looked. The members returned to talking about Raphael and expressed relief that he had recovered so nicely. At that point Will, a newcomer who had experienced considerable difficulty integrating into the group, spoke about how pleased he was that his hearing aids, which had been problematic, had been properly fitted and he was delighted with being able to hear.

The therapist heard both Raphael and Will's recitations of external events as personally important, but taken together with Rich's side comment regarding Jenny's earrings, the process suggested that these out-of-group events also carried a message about the emotions related to the group. It seemed the in-group process had to do with "looking and feeling better." For example, it was likely that Will's comments also were a communication about his relationships within the group and that he would be able to "hear" better now. The therapist expressed nonverbal interest in the discussion, but commented only about his pleasure in Raphael's return. His patience was rewarded when Will said, "I want to go back to last week. I felt hurt by a comment made then." If Will had not refocused on the in-group conflict, the therapist would have tried to find a way of relating the out-of-group content to the tension in the group.

*   *   *

The fundamental guideline is that most productive therapeutic work in the long run arises from the affective experience in the group itself. Some therapists attempt to mandate that groups will discuss nothing but their in-group relationships. Nonetheless, it is an oversimplification to see these as the exclusive focus, since individuals learn about themselves in their own ways and at their own rates. The therapist needs to monitor and reinforce the norm that examination of in-group transactions is the most productive but not the exclusive way of learning.

The Affect–Cognition Axis

Because psychodynamic theory began with the notion that understanding unconscious material would free individuals of their neuroses, conscious understanding was at first the mainstay of the curative effort. Rather quickly it became apparent that cognitive insight is an incomplete avenue to change, and therapists began including an emphasis on freeing affects and on "emotional knowing."

The exclusive attention to either extreme of this continuum is generally ineffective. What transpires in effective psychodynamic psychotherapy is a combination of feeling and understanding resulting in affective and cognitive integration. Emotional knowing arises from having deeply experienced a situation and fully felt the affects involved. The building blocks of psychological learning are affects, both felt and shared. To that degree, the first and most important focus of therapeutic attention is affect, not cognition. Often, cognitions are viewed as resistances to experiencing strong emotion. Nonetheless, therapeutic change is not a function of pure affect or pure catharsis. Once the affective data have been made available to the patient, a cognitive integration is very important. It is not enough that our patients feel; they must then understand as well. In research some data are "necessary but not sufficient"; the same is true for affect in psychotherapy. However, as with most principles, there are exceptions, and some patients change after gaining cognitive understanding that then forces them to experience affects.

Therapists have to balance their wish to provide cognitive closure with the need of patients to first explore, bear, and fully express their affective experiences. Typically, therapists err on the side of moving to cognition too quickly, presumably to reduce their own discomfort.

The Process–Content Axis

Communication in groups is simultaneously occurring verbally and nonverbally, consciously and unconsciously, and as a response to immediate and distant stimuli. Each meeting is fueled by each member's personal history, which evokes wishes, needs, transferences, distortions, and affective attribution of meaning. It is also fueled by the group history, by the relationships between members, and by those between each member and the leader. At all times members are negotiating their relationships with one another and with the leader.

The content (the overt meaning) of any given meeting cannot be divorced from the process (the covert meaning) because in almost every instance there is a connection between the two. The content might be a symbolic representation of a groupwide issue or an interpersonal transaction, or it might be a direct commentary upon the process within the group.

The therapist should keep an ear finely tuned to the process. Asking oneself, "Why is this association or series of interactions emerging at this time?" often provides perspective. Is the current discussion a direct result of what occurred a few moments ago, is it related to a general issue in the group, or is it idiosyncratic? The content of associations can be a metaphor of the group process. Through a judicious combination of both the content and the metaphorical references, the therapist can help members gain understanding of unconscious functioning. The unconscious is just that—out of awareness; furthermore, it is designed to remain that way to provide protection. Unless we steadfastly hear all content as potential process, unless we are aware of the interplay between process and content, we run the risk of missing important unconscious material.

CLINICAL EXAMPLE

During a meeting members found themselves involved in intense rivalry. Several began bragging about various personal exploits. The therapist initiated examination of the interaction by exploring the feelings of the members and by trying to understand the meaning of each exploit, thereby sharpening the sense of showing off or competing. The members understood that each story was an example of a personal triumph, and they could then recognize that they had become competitive with one another.

The therapist then noted that he began this meeting by announcing that a new member would be joining the group in 2 weeks. He pointed out that the initial response to his announcement had been muted, with a general tone of "Oh, good, the empty chair will be filled." However, the process then immediately shifted to the relating of exploits. While not specifically stating how he understood the meaning of the sharing of exploits but by simply indicating instead that he suspected there was a connection, the therapist enabled the members to emotionally connect the two processes. There followed an elaboration of the content as the members recognized that they had much more feeling about the prospect of a new member than they had been willing to acknowledge at first or even to know consciously. The members could then deal more directly with the competitiveness they experienced (process leading to new content), and in some cases they were able to make genetic reconstructions (understanding more fully the advent of rebellious behaviors as children during the time of mother's pregnancy).

*   *   *

Psychoanalytic theory suggests that nothing is random. Thus, a primary tool of psychoanalysis is free association. The assumption is that if analysands are able to reduce ego control and simply speak of whatever comes to mind, therapists can follow the unconscious connections between associations and help patients gain insight into their inner world. Group therapy expands this notion by asking that all patients speak freely of whatever comes to their minds or hearts. This is group process. One consequence of this theory is the assumption that groups rarely "change the subject." Rather, through conscious and unconscious associations the same subject is elaborated through the material that follows.

Self psychologists (Ornstein, 1978) use process in a particular way. In working with patients suffering from disorders of the self, the emphasis is placed on interpreting specific sequences—for example, a narcissistic injury and the subsequent response to that injury. The content of the response is used to highlight the process, including the precise empathic understanding of the injury (which is usually buried in the unconscious), as well as the details of how the patient (or group) tries to regain an inner equilibrium. Members may respond to a therapist's interpretation as a criticism, with associations suddenly turning to religious themes. The interpretation of this behavior might then highlight the experience of having felt criticized (and hurt) and then turning to a higher authority for more nurturance and protection. More typical is the sequence of individuals feeling hurt, repressing that feeling, and then quickly finding themselves enraged.

The Understanding–Corrective Emotional Experience Axis

The roles of understanding and corrective emotional experiences in the curative process have often been polarized and thought to be mutually exclusive. Does healing occur through insight and understanding or through the experiencing of life in different and more wholesome ways than before? In fact, both are necessary for effective psychotherapy. The notion of a corrective emotional experience is inherent in the nonjudgmental, empathic, supportive, investigative stance of the therapist. The benefits of such an experience in group psychotherapy have been emphasized by Yalom (1985), who stressed the therapeutic effect of group cohesion. The experience of belonging to a cohesive, functioning group, an environment in which wishes and needs are acknowledged and responded to positively, has a soothing, calming, and growth-producing impact. For almost everyone this is a corrective emotional experience. For some this is sufficient treatment; these individuals can stabilize themselves in the group setting and continue to grow on their own after terminating. For most patients, however, this fundamental building block needs to be supplemented by knowledge of unconscious inner conflicts or structural deficits.

Understanding and insight are useful in helping patients integrate and consolidate what they have experienced. A sense of knowing one's own sensitivities and vulnerabilities helps one master everyday stresses. Insight enables the patient to spot a troublesome area or behavior pattern and, one hopes, avoid what would previously have become a problem situation. Certainly, not all conflicts disappear, but many can be short-circuited through self-awareness.

Kris (1956) stated what most therapists have experienced—the realization that insight, either cognitive or emotional, is often insufficient to bring about real change in our patients. Fried (1982) suggested that "what matters clinically is that insight into most conflicts, be they preoedipal or oedipal, does not rectify deficits and malformations. They have to be corrected through the very repetitive experiences and challenges that groups offer in abundance" (p. 420).

Groups provide unique therapeutic opportunities to acquire both understanding (emotional and cognitive insight) and corrective emotional experiences. They provide opportunities to build new psychic structures through better, more authentic, and more nourishing relationships and to try out and practice new behavior patterns. Group leaders need not choose between the ends of this continuum. They need to ensure that both ends are operative and that patients are receiving both information and experiences.

A CLINICAL ILLUSTRATION OF THE LEADER ROLE AND FOCUS DIMENSIONS

In the following illustration the leader's role is examined across both role and focus dimensions. As usual, to best use these dimensions the therapist must have an awareness of the process that has been occurring in the group as well as of the presenting problems and personal histories of the members.

CLINICAL EXAMPLE

A mature group had been proceeding very nicely for a period of months. There had been a successful and moving termination of a patient the month before. Suddenly, in one meeting the members became moribund and depressed. After a prolonged period of silence, Sarah, who had experienced a long period of warm and affectionate feelings for the therapist (feelings the therapist also felt for her), exploded in a fury. She accused the therapist of not appreciating her gains, of not caring for her, and of giving all his attention to the other women members. Everyone present was confused by the unexpected depressed silence at the beginning of the meeting and by Sarah's surprising outburst, which seemed unwarranted to them.

The therapist, knowing the group process and Sarah's presenting problem and family history, was able to hypothesize about the seemingly strange responses. The process was initiated by the loss of the loved member, and the group was depressed because they had not sufficiently mourned that loss. Instead, with the leader colluding, they had focused on sad, warm, and loving feelings to the exclusion of envy and rage.

Sarah's initial presenting problem was her "insane jealousy" of other women, and her outburst toward the leader was a replay of her primary symptom. The etiology of her problem, in large measure, had to do with the loss of self-esteem she experienced at 6 years of age when a baby sister came into the family. As the group was saying its final goodbyes to the departing group member, Sarah inwardly turned her attention to the future and the expected "new baby" in the group who would come to fill the empty chair. Because of her history, she anticipated rejection from the leader and acted as if it had actually happened.

*　　*　　*

Here, the understanding of current group process seemed sufficient for understanding the depressed response of most of the members. However, Sarah's reaction did not fit and there was no overt stimulus. It was unclear what had precipitated her outburst until the therapist reviewed for himself the presenting problem and the significant historical events in Sarah's life. Indeed, the precipitant turned out to be a group event, but not the one that had been affectively important to the others. With this material raised to consciousness, the therapist could then make decisions about his interventions based on the dimensions shown earlier in Figure 9.1 as well as his clinical judgment. We now examine the therapist's handling of the situation first in terms of the role dimension and then in terms of the focus dimension.

Activity versus Nonactivity

The therapist chose to remain quiet to allow both the group depression and Sarah's attack to reach a crescendo before offering any overt responses. Had he not had some sense of what was transpiring, he might have felt compelled to intervene sooner in order to calm both the group and himself. Yet he was not inactive. He made a series of active choices: he did not interfere with the attack and the full expression of negative feelings; he did not offer a defense or a correction of Sarah's distortions about his warmth for her; he determined that all the members of the group could profitably bear the strong affect for at least 60 minutes before any closure was considered. Only then did he make a clarifying interpretation.

Transparency versus Opaqueness

The therapist chose to remain opaque, having determined that it would not serve Sarah to correct her distortion about his warmth for her. He felt Sarah would be better served if he helped her understand her distortion, and a full understanding required that she be allowed to experience it more fully. The therapist did not confuse the patient with contradictory data but, rather, kept a neutral position and accepted her attack.

Gratification versus Frustration

The leader was experienced by the group as somewhat frustrating early in the meeting when he simply accepted and encouraged the depressive feelings of the members. However, this was a mature group and there was sufficient alliance with the leader that the members were able to persevere, secure in the knowledge that he would sooner or later offer his observations. That is, they were secure in their conviction that his nonresponse, his failure to do anything to relieve the discomfort, was neither sadistic nor humiliating in intent.

The Past–Present–Future Axis

The therapist's full interpretation moved through the past–present–future axis and included references to the recent past (the termination), the distant past (Sarah's history), the present (the group's current reactions), and the future (the coming of the new member). To have focused exclusively on any single aspect of the time line would have been to miss important material.

The Group-as-a-Whole–Interpersonal–Individual Axis

When he did respond, the leader made both a group-as-a-whole and an individual response. He first responded to the whole group, commenting that Sarah's powerful response and the group's depressed silence had been linked, that both were indications of the members working through the termination of the lost member. He then helped Sarah understand her idiosyncratic reaction, how her reaction to him was a response to history and not to current reality. He helped her understand (through her own associations) how her sudden loss of self-esteem was connected to the forthcoming "baby" in the group family. Sarah readily accepted this interpretation and confirmed it by reporting a dream. In her dream the new member was female (as was the infant in her history), despite her rational conviction that a man would replace the man who had terminated.

In this situation the therapist chose to focus on the individual in order to help the group as a whole. This decision was predicated on the leader's observation that Sarah was filled with the most overt affect and on his conviction not only that she was experiencing a powerful replay from her history but also that in some important way she was probably a spokesperson for affects that were relevant to the group as a whole.

The In-Group–Out-of-Group Axis

In this illustration the members did not bring out-of-group material to the session. Interestingly, this time it was the therapist who ultimately introduced out-of-group material, linking the in-group affects to the now-departed member and to Sarah's family history. This process of first experiencing affects in the group and then placing them in relevant context outside the group is the ideal process.

The Affect–Cognition Axis

As usual in psychodynamic therapy, both the affective and cognitive aspects of insight were important in helping Sarah and the group learn from the exchanges in this meeting. Also, as is usual in psychodynamic therapy, the affective elements of learning precede the cognitive. That is, the therapist allowed a full expression of the feelings without prematurely bringing cognitive closure (i.e., linking the behavior to Sarah's past). It is a tenet of psychodynamic therapy that the most important learning occurs emotionally, though that is rarely sufficient for change without a cognitive component as well.

The Process–Content Axis

The axis of process and content is a particularly important one in this scenario. The leader both accepted the content as content and interpreted it as a coded communication about the group process. That is, Sarah was furious and convinced that he did not care about her. The leader did not deny that overt content, but he attempted to view it in the light of recent group process as well. Giving primacy to the process allowed the leader to help the members explore very important hidden feelings about the recent termination. Had the leader not looked at the process and linked the present content to the ongoing process, an important opportunity for learning would have been missed.

The Understanding–Corrective Emotional Experience Axis

Finally, understanding alone was considered important but insufficient to help Sarah and the group grow. It was necessary for Sarah, over the ensuing weeks, to put aside her intense rivalry with other women and try out new behaviors and perceptions of herself. Finally, when some months later a woman did join the group, Sarah responded very differently. She commented, "For the first time in my life I feel free to enjoy women rather than just experience them as competitors."

SUMMARY

The focus of the group therapist's attention should vary, not remain static. In each meeting there are allusions to current in-group issues, historical antecedents, emotionality and cognition, and so on. Therapists are often bewildered by the amount of information that confronts them, and in some cases they become paralyzed or simply focus on the most obvious or superficial data.

The two dimensions of leader activity and their component continua provide a way of ordering the plethora of data generated in every group. With this framework therapists are better prepared to make decisions about the use of self (the leadership-style dimension) and to organize their thinking and make appropriate interventions (the leadership-focus dimension). We suggest that therapists view the data in the order in which the leadership focus dimension continua have been presented here, beginning the sequence with examination of the here and now and continuing with the group-as-a-whole, in-group, affect, and process continua. One can move across the continua as needs dictate.

TEN

Beginning
the Group

A journey of a thousand miles begins with a
single step.

         —CONFUCIUS

I n this chapter we address several elements in beginning
the group. Preliminary decisions which establish the group
frame and composition are discussed. This is followed by
perspectives on the therapist's tasks and getting the group started.

Prior to the first meeting, the therapist has certain framing functions.
The degree to which these have been accomplished will help contain anxiety
and influence the patients' confidence in the enterprise.

Before the first meeting the therapist must clearly inform the patients of
the time, day, duration, and location of the group. Furthermore, each member
should assent to the group agreements prior to meeting the other members.

Ideally, a psychodynamic psychotherapy group would probably meet
once or twice weekly for 90 minutes and have eight members, four men and
four women. It is certainly within the tradition of practice for a group to meet
from 75 to 120 minutes and to have up to ten members. Some groups are homogeneous, for example, composed of members of one gender (see Chapter
15). These parameters must be carefully thought out and decided upon before
a new group is formed.

THE THERAPEUTIC FRAME

Frequency of Meetings

Though the usual frequency of group sessions is once a week, groups that meet twice weekly are not rare. Some therapists are beginning to experiment with even more frequent meetings. Birk (1974) reported that patients who failed in other extensive and intensive treatments demonstrated marked improvement when seen in a therapy group that met five times per week.

The optimal frequency of meetings depends upon the capacity of the patient population to hold a memory trace of the group from meeting to meeting. If the patients consistently "seal over," that is, lose contact with the affect from the previous meeting, the leader might consider increasing the frequency of the meetings. However, for most outpatient populations, once a week is sufficient. If meetings take place less frequently than once a week, the process seems to get lost and the therapeutic usefulness is diminished.

Some therapists increase the frequency of group meetings by utilizing the technique of alternate sessions, meaning that the group meets a second time each week without the therapist present (Kadis, 1956). The rationale proposed to support this practice is that by meeting without the therapist, members can learn to work without his/her presence, can begin discussions of their negative transferences about the therapist with diminished fears of retaliation, and can, in essence, become less dependent.

It is precisely the reasons put forward in support of alternate meetings that lead us to not recommend this approach. Members need to develop the capacity to feel secure in their affects and thoughts and need to develop independence from an authority figure. The therapist's task is to analyze resistances and difficulties along that path. If a patient needs to idealize a therapist, the basis for such a response is best worked through in the presence of the therapist. Testimonials by satisfied individuals indicate that there is value to the alternate session, but there has been no research into the processes, dynamics, or overall efficacy of this format.

Length of Meetings

As stated above, the range of clinically productive time for psychodynamic psychotherapy groups is between 75 and 120 minutes. Sessions shorter than 75 minutes usually do not provide sufficient time for the members. In sessions of more than 2 hours duration fatigue sets in, a condition that may harden or loosen defenses. Some therapists utilize marathon time formats specifically to invoke fatigue as a therapeutic element (Yalom, Bond, Bloch, Zimmerman, & Friedman, 1977). In psychodynamic groups, however, the object is not to defeat defensive structures but to examine and understand them. We find little use in extending the time frame to the point where undue fatigue, on the part of either the patients or the therapist, occurs.

The sole exception to this approach to the length of meetings is the option of using a "double-length" meeting after a week in which the group session has been canceled. This alternative is discussed in Chapter 11.

Time of Meeting

Given the logistical problems involved in gathering eight to ten individuals together weekly, most therapy groups meet before or after usual working hours. Arranging sessions when there is less likelihood of time conflict increases the potential for referrals. Therapists must continually weigh the disadvantages of sacrificing a time convenient for their personal lives against the advantages of offering a time that creates the best opportunity for the group to survive and flourish. In major metropolitan areas it is possible to run groups during the day. Even in such settings, however, the referral network is notably narrowed. Daytime groups typically draw from nonworking, self-employed, professional, student, or night-working populations. Early morning groups can avoid work conflicts but are a problem for parents of infants or school-age children. In the vast majority of instances, groups meet in the late afternoon or early evening.

GROUP SIZE AND GENDER DISTRIBUTION

The choice of group size should be predicated upon the number of patients with which a leader feels comfortable. The usual range is from six to ten members. For some therapists the dynamics that unfold with groups of ten feel comfortable and understandable, whereas for others ten in a room feels unmanageable. There is often a connection between the number of members and the length of each meeting, with larger groups meeting for somewhat longer periods.

Clinically, ten members seem to be the upper limit for productive work in a psychodynamic group. Beyond ten, less assertive members rarely have sufficient opportunity to discuss their issues. Fewer than six members creates difficulty in effectively utilizing the group process and diminishes the richness of interpersonal input. In smaller groups there is a great temptation for the therapist to focus on the four or five individuals and lose sight of groupwide processes. Further, certain members may feel overexposed or prematurely forced into a type of intimacy for which they are not prepared. Finally, there is some indication that for groups of four or less the group becomes so concerned with survival that other issues become submerged (Fulkerson, Hawkins, & Alden, 1981).

If at all possible, groups should begin with at least seven patients. Since research indicates that most new groups will suffer from one to three dropouts within the first few months, it is important to have sufficient membership so that there is a workable cadre remaining when dropouts occur. When groups begin with insufficient numbers, this is usually a reliable indication that appropriate referrals are in short supply and that the therapist will have continuing difficulties in maintaining a satisfactory census.

Some therapists, in anticipation of members dropping out, begin their groups with more patients than they consider optimal. This strategy, though protecting against the possibility of dropouts threatening the group's survival, ultimately forces some patients to leave. We believe therapists should never begin a group with more than the number with which they are comfortable, since they will remain uncomfortable until the group reaches optimum size and will be less able to make optimal therapeutic interventions.

Ongoing groups should have a balance of men and women. Often, women seeking treatment significantly outnumber men. In such instances it is possible to begin a group with a preponderance of women. For instance, if the therapist's goal is eight members, the group might begin with five women and whatever number of men are available. The remaining seats would be reserved for additional men.

GROUP SPACE

Group therapy differs markedly from dyadic therapy in space requirements. Too small or too large a room alters everyone's level of comfort and ability to work. Furthermore, the presence or absence of a waiting area affects where and how members assemble prior to the meeting time and has significant impact upon the range of choices they have in relating to one another. For example, in a clinic setting members may have to sit in a communal waiting area with other patients, an arrangement that diminishes pregroup exchanges.

Optimally, the group room itself can be made available at least 15 minutes prior to the beginning of a meeting so that the members may convene there. Some patients enjoy the socialization prior to the meeting, whereas others avoid it. These are not chance behaviors, and the subgrouping patterns and conversations that begin prior to the meeting are often important therapeutic material.

The seats themselves connote a great deal about how the group works and what is expected. How a therapist decides to set up the room with sofas and chairs is variable. (Sitting on pillows or on the floor is to be discouraged in adult groups.) Some therapists set a group size and leave a chair for the leader and for every potential member of the group. This arrangement emphasizes that members are absent and that there will be newcomers entering in the future. Furthermore, an empty chair looms large in a group after a significant member has terminated and is a powerful stimulus to the group's mourning process. An alternative procedure is to set up chairs only for those expected to attend a meeting; no chair is present for a terminated member, for someone on vacation, or for someone who called and announced an absence. In this case it is assumed that patients will remember the absent member. The general principle in either approach is consistency.

The seating arrangement should be comfortable enough so that individuals can easily sit for the duration of the meeting. Individuals select seating based on conscious and unconscious determinants. These choices are often connected to the patients' character styles or to dynamic processes taking place within the group. Observations about patterned choices help patients gain valuable insight. For example, who chooses the more comfortable-looking and the less-inviting seats? Who sits near other people, and who sits farther away? Who sits near the leader, and who sits far away? We learn not only from the type of seat chosen but also from its position. In some groups patients become rooted to particular chairs; in others the seating arrangement is flexible. It is best for the leader to sit in the same chair each week. This not only serves to underline consistency, but it provides the opportunity to glean meaning from the members' choices of seating vis-à-vis the leader. (For a more complete discussion of nonverbal communication, see Chapter 12.)

Some group rooms include a low table in the middle of the group. Indeed, this is standard practice for clinicians trained in the group analytic model. In the United States it is a less common practice. The main principle is that the group setting be such that members are not physically hidden from one another.

A particularly important aspect of the group space is the door, a boundary that must be regulated predictably. On occasion, patients and even inexperienced therapists will leave the door open after the session has begun with the expectation that a tardy member will soon enter. Obviously, an open door has considerable impact upon members' sense of freedom and privacy. Further, such an open door symbolizes an open acceptance of the tardiness. It is preferable that the door be closed at the time scheduled for the session to begin.

APPROACHING THE FIRST MEETING

At some point after all the preparatory work has been completed, the therapist and patients prepare for the meeting. Typically, everyone approaches this meeting with a great deal of apprehension and anxiety. Therapists wonder whether the patients who have been screened, selected, and prepared will actually arrive and mesh well together. Members worry about meeting strangers, but their anxiety is vastly increased when they remember that interacting will include sharing the most intimate details and secrets about their lives. All the usual concerns about trust and safety are, quite appropriately, central in the minds of the participants. This anxiety and apprehension regarding the initial meeting represents the first shared experience.

Everyone, including the therapist, approaches the unknown situation with his/her own particular fantasies, defenses, and coping mechanisms. Prior experience does not seem to matter—even senior therapists are filled with anticipatory anxiety. If therapists minimize the intensity of their anxieties, their capacities to use their own emotional lives as a barometer of the members' experiences are diminished. Both therapists and patients are concerned about how group members will work together, how members will respond to them, and how patients will respond to the group. The anticipatory anxiety patients experience may exaggerate coping patterns, but by that very exaggeration the anxiety is exposed all the more clearly.

The therapist's task is to create an atmosphere that provides the optimal opportunity for members to achieve their treatment goals of learning about themselves and their interpersonal and intrapsychic functioning. The ideal result would be a safe place for interaction and space for reflection.

In Chapter 9 we discussed six foci requiring the group therapist's attention. The following discussion puts these foci into operational tasks (these tasks overlap extensively, and they are separated only for heuristic purposes):

- Managing boundaries
- Bonding members
- Identifying themes
- Managing affect
- Handling metaphors
- Promoting insight

Managing Boundaries

Effective interpersonal boundaries are solid enough to provide distinction between individuals and yet permeable enough to allow exchange between individuals. We require boundaries in order to know who we are. Too tight a boundary restricts communication, leads to stagnation, and contains the potential for emotional death. Too loose a boundary leads to loss of self, panic, and a sense of psychic dissolution.

Groups as well as individuals require a boundary. In a well-prepared group, members are informed quite early in the process about the group's boundaries. These include the time that the group meets, the size of the group, how interruptions and extragroup contacts will be handled, fees (including charges for missed sessions), the responsibilities of the therapist to the members and group, and the fundamental responsibility of confidentiality. The potential group member needs this information in order to successfully cross the external boundary (frame) into the work space of the meeting.

Once a member of a group, individuals are confronted with yet more boundaries—"internal" boundaries that separate and define interactions and communications among individuals, subgroups, and the clinician.

These boundaries help define the "space" that is available for members to do their therapeutic work. The very nature of groups is such that members may withdraw and contemplate what has transpired; they are free to do that. Space may be thought of as allowing two modes of communication: *reactive* (the emerging of group norms, how people should behave) and *responsive* (an attunement, an emotional understanding of the other's inner world). Creating an atmosphere where both exist allows for personal, interpersonal, and contextual (i.e., the "we" of the group) discovery (Bacal, 1998).

Boundaries will be crossed and occasionally violated. The therapist has a fundamental monitoring (and decision-making) task which is necessary to preserve the functioning of the group. This task may be deferred but never ignored. A second and equally important task is assisting members in examining their own and others' relationship to the boundaries.

Bonding Members

Strangers meet for the first time in a circle. How do they begin to relate to one another? What does the clinician do to promote their interactions? Bonds are built at several levels. Presumably, the initial bond is to the therapist and some inner notion of "the group," derived from prior experiences of family, school, and community. For some, safety is *not* primarily in the relationship to the clinician but with linkages to peers. Others fear bonding, and they emotionally distance themselves, waiting to see what might be safe. Most persons have "social" ways of making contact: "What is your name?" "Where do you work?" "Are you married?" "Do you have children?" These are the socializing techniques and set the ground work for belonging to the larger enterprise.

The clinician's task is to convert these preliminary contacts into more substantial bonds and expand them into a sense of belonging to a functioning cohesive, coherent group. The therapist accomplishes this by attending to the whole group, subgroups, or individuals within the group. These comments can be focused on a theme or a common emotion, may refer to current or past experiences, in or out of the group. In the beginning phases of a group it is often useful for the therapist to promote a sense of belonging by focusing on the ways individuals are similar. It is common for some of this early bonding to take place outside the meeting time: in the waiting room, on the elevator, or on the way to the parking lot. These "casual" meetings can promote bonding or develop subgroups that interfere with the groupwide bonding process.

Clinical Example

In a relatively new group Flo had made it clear that she had major difficulty saying "no" to people in her condo complex who often asked her for favors or to run errands. She was isolated by the others who were uncomfortable with her passivity. In a subsequent session Pauline told about her wealthy sister's offer to give her an expensive present. Pauline said that she felt her sister would control her with this gift but that she found it hard to say she would prefer a less extravagant gift. Following some discussion of the pros and cons of Pauline's decision, the therapist linked Flo and Pauline in their efforts to say "no." Pauline was startled by the observation, and Flo was pleased by the linkage. Being aware that members are always attempting to bond when a new member arrives, the leader was able to highlight a similarity which led to Flo's more active participation in the group.

Identifying Themes

A postulate of psychodynamic group therapy is that groups rarely change the subject. It may *seem* as though the group material is diverse and unrelated, but usually there is an unconscious thread that ties all group material together. As members share their associations, a unifying theme usually emerges. One person picks up another's idea or emotion and elaborates or modifies it. Issues may start anew with an important stimulus in a session but then become derailed as important material from preceding sessions becomes more salient. This is an example of group process. Clinicians should attempt to follow the thread—a task often far easier to accomplish in retrospect than in the heat of the session.

Some themes are readily discerned, particularly when a boundary shift has occurred (i.e., a new member has joined, a member has terminated, or a therapist has been absent). Most of the time the essential "connectedness" of the group material is less obvious. Many times a conflict will emerge, remain incompletely examined (the norm), and continue to reverberate over a series of session. Shifts in themes provide access to discovering unconscious processes that have stimulated the change (Buchele, 1997). One measure of group maturity is the capacity of the group to look for and discover these underlying themes without assistance from the therapist.

The clinician infers themes. We can start with the working hypothesis that groups never change the subject (though often we are unable to discern the unconscious bridges between topics). If the therapist is able to identify a group theme and that theme becomes elaborated, then he/she will often come away with a sense of having had a "good" session. However, all hypotheses are just that; as more information emerges (either countering or supporting the original hypotheses), newer versions may emerge. This ideal sketch does injustice to the difficulty in discerning a main theme or determining the level of intervention that will be most useful (consciously or unconsciously) to the group. It is often believed that the therapist must pick up the theme immediately as it is occurring for it to have maximum impact. In fact, given the nature of group process, the themes from previous weeks linger on in the group for quite some time. Often therapists will "hear" the theme of a meeting while writing their process notes after the session. Groups can benefit from hearing about a theme even after the session in which the theme was dominant. The stance of the therapist is (ironically) often a lonely stance, and as Alonso and Rutan (1996) state, "the group leader must have the capacity to watch the group interplay with interest but also with the capacity to tolerate this activity without unnecessary interference or anxious hovering" (p. 156).

Managing Affect

Many therapists would rank managing affect as their most important task. Entering a group mobilizes a variety of emotions and defenses aimed at preventing psychic disequilibrium or disruption. This is true for the clinician as well as the members.

Emotions are expressed verbally, nonverbally, physiologically, and behaviorally; they are both in and outside of awareness; they can be labeled or unknown. Some may be expressed all too readily, whereas others are almost unavailable to their host. Groups are subject to emotional storms as the impact of affect contagion spreads—the spread may be to hyperactivity, or anger and rage, or into a downward spiral of lethargy, gloom, or hopelessness. Sudden projections and scapegoating may erupt. Clinicians face what appears to be a daunting task. Fortunately, in most situations patients protect themselves and initially make efforts not to expose raw and archaic emotional states. They test to determine what is safe to express. If too much feeling emerges, defenses are erected. This is true for most beginning groups, but not for all.

Mature groups have learned that powerful emotion is ultimately useful. However, powerful expressions of affect in new groups can be frightening. In the early going, rageful outbursts can disorganize a group. The therapist must find ways to intervene which do not diminish or discredit the feeling while retaining a sense of safety. Addressing the underlying sources of anger often effectively contains the outburst and reassures the members.

As the group evolves, members are more willing to learn about their emotional states and vulnerabilities. Therapists can be of considerable assistance in helping members overcome resistance to experiencing, expressing, and understanding their affects (S. L. Cohen, 1997). When no words exist, the therapist can label feelings. Clinicians serve as a container for groupwide projections and use their own feelings to identify hidden or projected emotions.

But these processes emerge gradually and the initial task is to be as certain as possible that no one is traumatized, either as the recipient of intense feelings or from marked isolation and aloneness by withdrawal. Nonetheless, there are some individuals who *will* be traumatized, just as they are traumatized by much of life.

CLINICAL EXAMPLE

Janine, a middle-aged married woman, was referred for group treatment prior to her discharge from partial hospitalization. She had a history of three hospitalizations for major depression in the prior 4 years, usually subsequent to stopping her medications.

Between hospitalizations Janine was a successful salesperson in an upscale women's apparel store. Her family was supportive of her seeking treatment, and Janine could articulate clear goals of wishing to become more assertive. She had learned this much about herself during her partial hospital stay and seemed eager to enter a group.

Janine joined a well-established group. She immediately found herself in conflict, protesting that members were irritable with one another and expressed angry feelings, whereas she had expected a "support" group. Efforts to help her tolerate the exchanges were to no avail, and she did not return following her fourth session. In retrospect, her departure seemed almost inevitable because of what had not been apparent in the preparatory interviews—Janine's inability to manage conflict, even as an observer.

* * *

The ultimate goal is not to avoid all trauma but to avoid trauma which threatens the life of the group or the capacity of an individual to remain in it.

Handling Metaphors

Communications, particularly of emotional states, are often expressed in metaphors. Discussions of authority (teachers, bosses, or the President) might be ways that members express themselves about the therapist; discussions of disappointed or mistreated children or abandoned animals may represent members' feelings about themselves; discussions of classmates, friends, or coworkers may represent feelings about fellow members; and those of organizations, countries, or communities may convey feelings about the group. The potential for such indirect communications is almost without bounds.

The use of metaphors can be seen as a compromise between direct expression and hiding of ideas or feelings. They serve a purpose: perhaps the hope is that they will go undetected and something can be conveyed "quietly." Alternatively, they may express the wish to be detected, to be brought to light so that they can be examined and their covert meanings exposed and integrated.

Therapists need to think metaphorically as they listen to the content, always keeping in mind the concrete and metaphorical levels of conveying information. It is all too easy to become lost in the mundane and surface discussion. Equally problematic are the too facile and prompt translations of metaphors into the here and now of the group. Patients do not need to be told what they are "*really*" feeling or talking about." A premature translation of metaphorical communication can be disruptive. It can be assumed that if the members were able to speak directly of the issues at hand, metaphors would not have been necessary. As Horwitz (1977) has emphasized, clinicians need to attend to the treatment alliance (best expressed in a sense of trust and safety) prior to examining the meanings of the metaphor. Additional technical elements in managing metaphors will be discussed in Chapter 12.

Promoting Insight

Insight, self-awareness, and self-understanding are key concepts in dynamic psychotherapy. What would we like to have patients know about themselves? In group psychotherapy, the emphasis has been on learning about oneself in the here and now of the meeting. What are one's feelings, thoughts, and physiological responses to situations? Do they represent a pattern (a character trait)? Does the pattern exist in the world outside the group? Did they emerge in childhood or at some traumatic event later in life?

Advances in the technique and theory of psychotherapy have increasingly focused on interactions in the present as the initial place for gaining insight. This may be judged "surface," but it may be very powerful and at times mutative. Certainly gaining knowledge of the sources of these difficulties and gaining a life view may add to the individual's conviction that an interaction represents a continuing and problematic pattern. The standard of insight has traditionally been knowledge into the sources of "pathology" emerging from childhood, but we have learned that for many patients this is an unreachable goal. Indeed, insight alone is insufficient for enduring change. Nonetheless, self-knowledge is powerful, and it provides a personal sense of control.

In the initial phases of treatment, building safety and defining roles and tasks are of greater salience, but insight into one's interactions may accrue along the way. Certainly there are many opportunities for such learning, as members individually and collectively demonstrate problem-solving and obstructive behaviors. One piece of insight that members may gain is that there is no prescribed time to gain insight and that it is never full and complete.

These tools represent a model for the clinician to use in thinking about what to address from the plethora of information that emerges in groups. There is no way for clinicians to organize the material in advance. Indeed, it is the unexpected, and learning how people are in groups, that can be both anxiety-evoking and stimulating for the clinician.

THE FIRST MEETING

The moments just before the start of the first meeting are a time of great excitement and anxiety, a common state of arousal shared by the therapist and patients. When the door is closed and the first meeting has begun, patients look around apprehensively and almost always fix their gaze on the therapist. Later in the life of the group the therapist will enter, sit down, and begin observing, but the first meeting represents an exception; in this meeting the therapist does have a responsibility for beginning the meeting.

The therapist starts by making it clear that he/she has met previously with each individual, that all have acceded to the same agreements, and that all have significant personal issues they wish to resolve. At this point the therapist should repeat the group agreements. In homogeneous groups, the therapist also makes it clear that the members share the common variable. Typically, he/she then suggests that people get to know one another, leaving the exact manner of that introduction to the members themselves. The leader should then sit silently (but not impassively) and observe the developing interactions.

From the moment the group begins, we have an opportunity to observe the approaches our patients utilize to cope with stress. The initial data available for observation and analysis are the various styles used by the members to cope with the groupwide anxiety. How the members handle that common anxiety depends on their personality structure, their historic defense mechanisms, and the specific interactions that actually occur in the group. Kauff (1993) states, "It is from the immediate behavioral data that we derive our explanatory notions of unconscious material and defensive operations. . . . *The more we can see of our patient in action, the more we can understand about our patient and the more he or she can understand about himself or herself and alter what is potentially alterable"* (p. 9; emphasis in the original). Therapists starting groups should be thoroughly acquainted with the formative phase of group development (which is explored in depth in Chapter 3).

The Therapist's Stance

When a group meets for the first time, there is an enormous pull on the therapist to reduce the initial anxiety by becoming active. The therapist wants the group to begin comfortably and certainly wishes to avoid such intense anxiety that members may never return. The members also want relief from the terrors of the unknown. The fantasy arises that the leader can reduce the anxiety. Nonetheless, therapists should resist the impulse to be overactive, because a style once established is difficult to break. In groups where the therapist is quite active in introductions and agenda setting, patients feel disappointed in subsequent sessions when he/she becomes less active and they, seemingly without the leader's protection, are faced with the unknown. Similarly, too austere a beginning may delay members' working. The clinician must monitor the state of the alliance because it is fundamental to shaping the group as an environment for change. Dies (1994), summarizing reports of patients' reasons for early departure from group therapy, states "leaders inactivity is a central factor in patients' decisions to forego treatment" (pp. 128–129). With this caveat, contrary to intuition, some therapists develop their own manner of conveying interest and concern and, even with new groups of less well developed patients, are successful in helping members survive and profit from a first session in which they have been left largely to their own devices.

After the initial comments, the therapist begins to show members how their fantasies and interactions in the here and now can be valuable in learning about themselves and the problems they have come to resolve. The main issue is that members should feel that they have learned something from their initial anxiety.

The Patients' Roles

The first meeting usually begins with rudimentary introductions. Names, ranks, and serial numbers are given, after which the members often fall silent. It is important that the therapist wait for the group to break the silence (it only seems as though it is going to last forever!). If the therapist indicates an early discomfort with silence by intervening too quickly, he/she may teach the group that they can get the therapist to respond by being silent.

If the therapist remains quiet, the members will begin to talk, sometimes about the problems that brought them, but often they will test the water by feeling out the others in an effort to access the safety and comfort they might expect from the group. There are rare exceptions when the therapist has misjudged the members' capacities to interact. Rather than sit in prolonged silence, the leader can intervene to protect members from the fears that silence can evoke.

Eventually, though by no means necessarily in the first meeting, someone in the group will offer the first group "gift," revealing information or feelings that make that individual truly vulnerable if the response is insensitive. Perhaps a member begins to weep or to tell in more detail why he/she is in the group. At this point the other members may or may not join the new level of sharing. If the gift-giving member has not revealed something entirely foreign or too personal, others will inevitably tell more of themselves. In the first meeting, what is shared is much less important than the fact that something is shared and that the response is not threatening. The group is beginning to test out what can be said in this room, and they are very watchful and wary of the reactions of the other members and especially of the therapist.

Ending the First Meeting

The ending of an initial group meeting should accomplish several objectives. First, if the agreements were not restated at the beginning of the session, such a restatement should be made at this time. Second, the group leader should make some contact with each member. In this first meeting it is especially important that all the members know they were noticed and attended to by the leader, who might say, for example, "We noticed a variety of ways in which people dealt with this common anxiety about beginning a group," and might then relate the responses he/she observed for each member.

Sometimes mere eye contact between the therapist and a member is sufficient to let the member know that some connection is being made. Beginning a group is difficult and, ironically, a very lonely experience for patients. It is unlike beginning individual therapy, where there is some cultural expectation that the therapist will listen attentively, will not be hurtful or vengeful, and will give undivided attention. In groups the patients must struggle for time and attention, and they have no assurances about how their fellow members will respond to personal exposures.

Despite the initial anxiety, almost all first sessions are judged a success by the therapist and the members. There is a feeling of exhilaration and pleasure that the enterprise has gotten off the ground. Before the first session members were so concerned with personal survival that the reality of the meeting is quite mild by comparison. Simply the recognition that others are "just as worried" is very helpful to each member and evokes a positive feeling.

There are few meetings in which the themes can be as accurately predicted as in the first one. For example, the therapist will be helpful and almost always on target if he/she closes the meeting by saying "The group has been testing to see how safe it is going to be to share what is most important in your lives with these people and with me" or "People have been saying 'hello' in a variety of ways."

THE EARLY WEEKS

After the initial meeting patients generally resurrect their defenses and characteristic patterns of interacting. Caution is an important dynamic, and an underlying behavior in the early weeks is testing to see whether the group and others can be trusted (Stone & Gustafson, 1982; Stone, 1996a). Members are experientially trying to establish group norms in order to institutionalize safety. Conflicts inevitably arise, however, since not everyone has the same safety requirements. The tensions between the differing needs fuel the interactions, but the pace is generally slow because dealing with these tensions directly involves many members' central pathological conflicts. Often patients become disheartened and disillusioned about the group during this time.

In this phase there is considerable testing of boundaries and norms. For a variety of reasons, members will come late or be absent. The therapist must draw attention to these violations of the group agreements in order to establish both the norm of exploring boundary violations for their potential deeper meanings and the norm of valuing the importance of the here and now. What complicates matters is the extensive use of denial at this stage. Members generally ignore or minimize the deeper meanings of others' behaviors. Therapists may feel they are swimming upstream. Members will create all sorts of pressures to keep the therapist from bringing boundary violations to their attention and especially to keep him/her from interpreting the meanings of these violations. Nevertheless, the therapist, with as much tact and therapeutic creativity as possible, must point out what is happening.

The boundaries within the group also require attention. Individuals erect barriers to giving and receiving information about one another. Usually no one person blocks development of trust and openness; instead, a collusion exists in which members avoid difficult affects, use anger as a defense against involvement, switch topics, and so on. While the content that is discussed might be quite revealing as to the hidden conflicts or fears of the speakers, the focus for the therapist at this stage is the process, that is, how members deal with anxieties and conflicts rather than the content of a particular conflict. The anxieties aroused in the early weeks tempt the therapist to close off affect prematurely with summarizing interpretations or to offer superficial reassurances that what members are feeling is not unusual. Instead, the therapeutic task is to help members tolerate and face the anxieties generated by the process.

During the early phases of a group, therapists sometimes become discouraged with the lack of progress and with the defensiveness and resistance of the members. It is well to remember that resistance is not a process designed to resist treatment; it is a defensive process designed to resist emotional pain. Typically, patients in group therapy have not had histories of sustaining, healing, and comforting relationships. It would be unnatural for them to assume that group relationships would be different. It would be much more pathological and aberrant if the patients suddenly adopted new behaviors in the group rather than relying upon the tried-and-true (albeit deficient) behaviors from the past.

In this opening period a number of interactive patterns emerge with regularity. In almost every group there is a period when advice giving is a common *modus operandi*. Members will present a problem or a conflict in their lives, and others will make direct suggestions about solutions. Analysis and understanding is not the goal; problem solving is. A number of dynamics may be covertly functioning in such advice-giving behaviors, such as a desire to remove problems that make people uncomfortable; to use tried-and-true remedies rather than recognize a sense of helplessness; to focus on external problems so that the more difficult task of dealing with the in-group interactions can be bypassed; to compete with the therapist for fantasied acclaim; or to demonstrate the members' ineffectiveness with one another. Only rarely does a suggestion have the potential to solve a problem inasmuch as patients have already received lots of advice and suggestions before they entered the group. When confronted with a period of advice giving, the therapist must help the members understand its function with regard to the group's development.

A similar situation occurs when a group focuses on one member as "sick." Overtly, all are altruistically working to help solve that individual's problems. However, by focusing on one member the pathologies of others are obscured. The parallel is evident with family interactions, in which a child may be labeled as "sick" and thus the scapegoat for all the family's difficulties. In a variation on this pattern members seem to be taking turns: "Last week we talked about Adam; now it's Betty's turn?" Seldom is this process explicit, but it subtly becomes established and serves to limit intragroup transactions.

These are but a few examples of the ways members and therapists attempt to manage the problems of developing group trust and cohesion. The analysis of resistances, character traits, and emergency defenses can all be used for therapeutic gain, but sometimes in these early weeks the therapist and members become discouraged because the group is not meeting their expectations. Under such circumstances the therapist's countertransference may result in scapegoating members who seem to be obstructionistic, or the therapist may become defensive and less open to hearing his/her patients. These problems affect the group atmosphere and promote dropping out, a problem we discuss in the next section.

The patients' discouragement often leads to depression, exacerbation of symptoms, or a futile attempt to arouse optimism about the group through reaction formation. The critical consideration for patients and the therapist during this time is to remember that the reawakening of primary defenses and pathologies is a sign that the group is in fact becoming effective; that is, as these behaviors are displayed, the members begin to experience their problems in the group itself.

DROPOUTS

Almost all new psychotherapy groups have one or more dropouts within the first few weeks. Such dropouts, while disconcerting and disappointing, should be considered an expectable part of beginning a group. A number of reports in the literature indicate that some 20–45% of charter members leave within the first year. The data seem valid for both clinic and private practice settings and for both inexperienced and seasoned group therapists (Stone & Rutan, 1984; Salvendy, 1993).

The reasons given for leaving are varied. Sometimes no reason is given at all. On occasion patients will suddenly find they have a time conflict, perhaps even pleading that the group time be changed to accommodate them. However, any change in the group structure is contraindicated. Many a well-meaning therapist has changed the time of a group to help a particular member avoid a time conflict only to find that the very member in question drops out anyway. Time conflicts, while certainly real in many instances, are nonetheless best understood dynamically, that is, as a communication about the patient's experience of his/her participation in the group.

The fact that the early life of groups involves people leaving prematurely dramatically reduces the members' optimism. It is not unusual for new groups to develop an atmosphere of hopelessness and discouragement and to begin questioning the efficacy of their treatment and the competence of the leader. The leader should encourage the open expression of these fears and doubts, thereby reassuring the members that all feelings can be honestly shared.

VERY SMALL GROUPS

For a variety of reasons there will be weeks when only one or two patients come to a meeting. Running a session with so few participants is a problem. Unfortunately, this is not unusual early in the life of a group, before cohesiveness has set in. Given the current climate, which stresses more time-limited, often biological treatments, ongoing psychotherapy groups often face times of low membership.

Inexperienced therapists often wonder whether they should reduce the amount of time or cancel the meeting if only one or two group members arrive. The press to cancel or shorten the time is the therapist's countertransferential attempt to avoid the affect (hurt, anger, disappointment, fear, and so on) stimulated by such a small group. However, to curtail or cancel the meeting would be to punish the very members who kept their group agreements and would certainly institute non-therapeutic norms. Furthermore, one is never certain that other members won't come strolling in late.

Leading the very small group is awkward for the inexperienced therapist. There is a temptation to revert to therapy techniques for individuals or couples. However, the group still exists in the minds of the members who did come, and the particular meeting occurs in the context of the failure of several members to honor their agreements. It is not unusual for these sessions of very small groups to have a significant impact on those who attend. The technical key for the therapist is to remember that this is still a group, albeit a very small and fragmented one. One of the major issues needing attention is the feeling on the part of those who came of being let down by their colleagues. Old feelings of separation, loss, abandonment, divorce, and family dissolution all may be awakened. On the other hand, for some patients the very small group means that they have more "air time." For others there is the increased and potentially terrifying demand for increased participation. How the attending members respond to the situation is potentially quite important.

The "small group" represents a subgroup, and when the others return, they represent a subgroup that was absent. The therapist is then in a position to explore the impact of the meeting on both subgroups—those who were present and those who were absent. By dealing with subgroups rather than individuals, no individual is singled out, and members are supported in examining the experience (Stone, 1998).

NEW MEMBERS

In ongoing groups the coming and going of members has great meaning. Each good-bye and hello means that the group itself changes. The therapist should encourage members to explore personal and groupwide meanings associated with the anticipation of newcomers prior to their introduction. Considerable pressure may arise within the group to avoid change, even at the cost of maintaining a lower census. Members will talk openly about their anxieties with the intent of coercing the therapist into delaying new additions. An alternative strategy occurs when they attack the therapist for making poor choices, hoping to influence him/her to reject some acceptable applicants. Finally, some may threaten to quit rather than face a newcomer, and on occasion a member actually leaves.

Various pressures may influence the therapist's decisions (see the example of Ellie in Chapter 7). It is not easy to decide when a group could benefit from more time to work on a loss or on the feelings surrounding the advent of new members. The repeated thought, "This is not a good time to add members" is often a manifestation of countertransference, and therefore acting on it may be an error. On the other hand, therapists can collude with the group to cover over patient feelings by prematurely filling an empty chair.

New members should never simply arrive at a meeting without warning. Old members need a period of preparation so that they may explore their reactions to the idea of a newcomer, but it is also important that they be able to come to each session without the concern that strangers might be present. The usual procedure is for the therapist, at the beginning of a meeting, to announce that a new person will be joining the group on a particular date. It is advisable to provide only that fact. Fantasies about the age, sex, marital status, and other details about the coming member all contain useful material from which the old members can learn. The length of time between the announcement and the actual arrival of the new member depends upon many variables. If a group has had an open chair for some time and has been awaiting a new member, 2 weeks can be sufficient lead time. If, on the other hand, the empty chair is the result of a particularly important or painful loss (a highly valued member who terminated or one who suddenly died), the time required to sort through feelings about another person joining should be longer. All other factors being equal, 2 weeks notice seems optimal. This provides members the opportunity to work on their reactions immediately and in the following week as well.

From a practical perspective a new person can be admitted whenever the appropriate preparation has been completed. There has been some support for the suggestion that new members be added in pairs, not singly, in order to protect them from being victimized by latent or overt hostility from the members. This practice is presumed to reduce the chances of newcomers dropping out prematurely. Stone and Rutan (1984) found that adding patients singly did not lead to unusual numbers prematurely stopping, and in fact the data suggest this approach diminishes the number of dropouts. By adding members individually, each new member has a time of separate introduction and the norm becomes established that empty chairs will be filled as they are vacated.

At times the therapist will be confronted by the situation of having two or more simultaneous openings and an equal number of applicants. The question at this time is "Should the new patients be added singly or together?" There are pros and cons to either answer. Ideally, each member has the opportunity to enter the group alone. This provides each new patient with a brief individual introduction, allowing for more individualization and affording a clearer view of the introductory dynamics of that person. On the other hand, if multiple openings are filled at the same time, there is the real advantage of closing the group boundary more quickly. Furthermore, the new members often experience a powerful and immediate alliance with those who join with them. The exception is when the new patients being considered outnumber the members already in the group. In that instance the entrances should be sequential so that there are never more new members than old. Naturally, on those occasions when groups have diminished to a membership of one or two, even that rule must be broken.

Each group develops initiation rites (Kaplan & Roman, 1961). The therapist sets the tone by restating the group agreements, which also reminds the existing members of those agreements. Frequently, the agreements are remembered incorrectly, and this habitual restating allows for corrections as well as explorations of the meanings of the distortion. Repetition of the group agreements puts everyone on an equal footing.

Some groups appear to greet newcomers warmly and enthusiastically, and only through closer scrutiny is ambivalence exposed. Retaining of the fantasy of "the good old group," which subtly excludes the newcomer, may be expressed by reminiscing or by cryptically referring to prior events. Another common initiation procedure is for groups to have dramatic and highly emotional meetings (see the example of Janine earlier in this chapter). In part such meetings can be understood as demonstrations of how much emotion, personal revelation, and confrontation can be tolerated. These dramatic meetings often have another unconscious element as well—an attempt to frighten off the newcomer or at least to test his/her mettle. Questioning new members about their histories and reasons for coming to group therapy is yet another initiation pattern. The questioning can vary widely in its form and intent, ranging from courteous inquiry of a new member, thereby offering him/her an opportunity to make connections with the other members, to grilling with no altruistic motivation (not unlike a fraternity or sorority initiation). Impressions at this time of change in group composition are valuable data and are available only briefly. Whatever initiation rites are used to greet newcomers, the therapist must help the group learn from them.

SUMMARY

Beginning a therapy group is an emotion-filled experience for therapist(s) and members alike. Despite the high anxiety that comes with the first meetings (stranger anxiety, fear of exposure, concerns about trust, etc.), these meetings are rather easy for the leader. The themes are clear—"How do we say 'hello'?" "Will I be acceptable to you, and you to me?" "Will this be a safe and productive place?"

Whatever concrete material the group produces, the themes that underlie that material *have* to concern the fact that this is the first meeting of strangers.

ELEVEN

Special Leadership Issues

As much as possible,
allow the group process to emerge naturally.
Resist any temptation to instigate issues
or elicit emotions which have not appeared
on their own.
                    —John Heider, *Tao of Leadership*

Therapists face a number of leadership issues with suffi-cient regularity to warrant special attention. In this chapter we will deal with a variety of these recurring and important issues: (1) shared leadership (cotherapy), (2) individual and group therapy combined, (3) leader absences, (4) transferring of groups, and (5) combining other treatments with group psychotherapy.

SHARED LEADERSHIP

In clinics and training settings, groups often have two leaders. When there are two leaders, the treatment dynamics are significantly altered. After addressing the arguments for and against shared leadership, we will subsequently discuss the dynamics related to therapists of equal or unequal experience, power, and status. For the sake of clarity we will use the term *cotherapy* to describe the shared leadership model, even though most shared leadership is not truly co-equal.

Why Shared Leadership?

Various advantages have been cited for a cotherapy model. These include:

- Dual leadership allows for a fuller and more complete view of the group and protects against blind spots in either therapist (Demarest & Teicher, 1954).
- Each therapist has the opportunity to move in and out of active and passive (or observational) modes (R. Gans, 1962).
- Watching a colleague at work allows a therapist to learn from that opportunity (Solomon, Loeffler, & Frank, 1953).
- Cotherapy offers the pragmatic advantages of providing ongoing coverage at times of sickness or vacation, increasing limit-setting capacities in working with certain patient populations (e.g., children, severely acting-out patients, geriatric patients), and making work with large groups easier. It also provides an opportunity for peer consultation and support (Getty & Shannon, 1969; Yalom, 1985).
- In private practice dual leadership has advantages of sharing work in what is ordinarily an isolated profession, and it also lessens the task of recruiting sufficient members since that responsibility is also shared (Concannon, 1995).
- The presence of a cotherapist lessens anxiety for the trainee (Yalom, 1985, p. 418), provides a sense of support, and allows for a shared responsibility.
- The treatment process of group psychotherapy may be enhanced by cotherapy inasmuch as this model theoretically offers a replication of a two-parent family. Even in cases where the therapists are of the same gender, it has been reported that patients respond transferentially as if to a male–female pair (Lundin & Aronov, 1952).
- Other authors stress the unique value of having a male–female cotherapy team that stimulates parental transference (Demarest & Teicher, 1954) and also offers each patient a same-gender therapist with whom to identify (Mintz, 1965).
- Another advantage of cotherapy stems from the manner in which cotherapists relate to each other, handle conflict, and communicate acceptance. Their relationship (if it is a healthy one) provides a model that patients may use for imitation or identification (Getty & Shannon, 1969, p. 769; Yalom, 1975, pp. 421–422).

We would add:

- Having two therapists, especially when their leadership tenures do not coincide, softens the impact of loss on group members when student therapists terminate their leadership as they leave training.

- There is also the reality that most training programs do not have sufficient groups to allow each of their trainees to lead a group individually.

Why Not Shared Leadership?

Despite the aforementioned advantages, cotherapy is not the preferred leadership model in most situations. In fact, many of the arguments for cotherapy turn out to be arguments against it. For example, is it really advisable to reduce the therapist's anxiety? Should not the therapist confront anxieties about entering the group alone that are similar to those our patients must face? Middleman (1980) agrees that dulling therapist anxiety does not advance either training or good clinical care. Likewise, the argument that cotherapy allows the therapist to drift in and out of focus, relying on the cotherapist to remain attentive, is flawed because at times of highest stress both therapists simultaneously would likely want to back away. In the treatment process the therapist is stimulated by the variety of passionate affects in the group. Optimally, the therapist can bear this affect and use it diagnostically and to guide technique. For example, if a therapist is feeling rageful, it is useful to determine if the feeling represents the containing of a projective identification, the reasonable human response to outrageous behavior, the empathic attunement to a rageful patient, or pure and simple countertransference. However, in cotherapy situations these passionate affects often become part of the cotherapy relationship, reflecting the truism that children can encourage parents to fight or love each other. Finally, in an era when mental health delivery costs are under close scrutiny, it seems hard to justify doubling the cost of group therapy by doubling the number of therapists.

Cotherapy is more difficult than solo leadership because it entails having to maintain the cotherapy relationship itself. Working in the intimate arena of a therapy group, cotherapists are exposed to highly stimulating situations and affects. As a result, cotherapists can become rivals—or lovers. Cotherapy is like a marriage, and the cotherapists who may have been courting before the cotherapy began are placed in a marriage-like relationship once it does. The ordinary adjustment period is stressed by an immediate task, namely, the equivalent of raising needy and (hopefully) outspoken children. No cotherapy teams automatically work smoothly. What makes cotherapy succeed is the maturity and willingness of the two leaders to continually work on and attend to their relationship so that tensions in it do not filter into the group. Cotherapists must be willing to devote considerable time to this responsibility. They must achieve a degree of comfort in disagreeing with each other, and they must determine the extent and nature of the disagreements they wish to air in the group (Lang & Halperin, 1989). When it goes well, cotherapy can be effective, but when it goes badly it is disadvantageous to everyone.

MacLennon (1965) noted that transferences arise between cotherapists and add to the complexity of sorting out the members' "real" and transferential relationships. The traditional boundaries between therapists and patients prohibit socialization, but there is no such prohibition for cotherapists. Indeed, since cotherapists are encouraged to use one another to unwind and to review the meetings, they have considerable informal, semisocial contact. The stimulation, or arousal of affect, in the therapist role requires that cotherapists be especially alert to the potential for acting rather than talking. We have seen significant therapeutic and social complications arising from cotherapists' acting on their feelings for one another, be they warm or hostile. Furthermore, the transferential relationship between cotherapists is often exaggerated by splitting defenses employed by the members (Greene, Rosenkrantz, & Muth, 1986).

CLINICAL EXAMPLE

Dr. X, a young psychiatrist, had worked for a year with Dr. Y, a psychiatrist many years his senior. After a year of working together Dr. Y left the community. Dr. X chose to work with a senior psychologist, Dr. Z, who had trained at another institution with a similar orientation to group therapy. Dr. X had often consulted with Dr. Z and found him pleasant, easy to work with, and very astute.

Once they began their cotherapy relationship, troubles emerged. Dr. Z seemed to have a highly individualistic approach to group therapy and described his work as "tracking" a patient. Dr. X, with more of a group-as-a-whole approach, was put off by this. After a number of sessions, Dr. X cautiously confronted the problem. Much to his surprise, Dr. Z said he believed that the only reason Dr. X had chosen to work with him was that he was a psychiatrist while Dr. Z was a psychologist (the implications of control and power were clear). Despite outside consultation the two therapists were unable to resolve their differences, and Dr. Z left the group.

*   *   *

This example illustrates an unfortunate and painful cotherapy experience. Dr. X was quite startled by what he sensed was a paranoid position on the part of Dr. Z. Dr. Z was equally surprised when he sensed control issues previously not visible in Dr. X. Clearly transference was at work in either or both therapists. That combined with the marked differences in theoretical approach and an inability to reach a comfortable solution to their differences led to Dr Z's departure. Not only was this a difficult experience for the two therapists, but the group suffered as well.

Patients may experience difficulty with a cotherapy format. Many patients find it harder to confront or disagree with two therapists presenting a united front. Others, rather than learning from differences between the therapists, are frightened by the cotherapists' inevitable conflicts. The notion that a cotherapy team represents an ideal mother–father pair is somewhat grandiose, since few cotherapy teams reach complete maturity or perfection in their relationship.

In the current cost-containment environment, there may be little justification for a cotherapy model. Controversy exists in how to charge patients when one of the therapists is absent. For some, the fee remains the same because patients are charged for the group; for others, the presence of both therapists is necessary to charge a full group fee (this argument, of course, is moot if the fee is set at a level for only a single clinician and the therapists agree to split the fees). For patients covered by insurance, which limits the total fee for a group session, cotherapy presents a problem. Further justification of cotherapy in terms of enhanced outcome is limited by the lack of research evidence that two therapists rather than one generally enhance the quality or efficacy of the therapeutic outcome (Dies, 1994, p. 141).

The Dynamics of Shared Leadership

The term *co*therapy implies that the leaders are of equal power, authority, and experience. In most circumstances, this is not the situation and the dynamics of leadership are changed when there is significant inequality of experience and/or administrative power between the two therapists.

There are fundamental principals of shared leadership that are important in all cases. Of utmost importance is the relationship between the two therapists. The leaders must have a fundamental respect for one another, even in the situation in which there is considerable difference in skill and experience. A second fundamental principal is that the leaders will allot the time necessary to explore the group process, the members' relationships (including transferences), and most importantly their own relationship. Conducting a therapy group is an emotionally important experience. When the treatment format changes from single to paired leadership, a new subgroup is established, and members respond differently and develop different fantasies about either each therapist or the pair. The clinicians need to spend time and effort to understand the nature of the complex relationships.

Dual Leadership

Dual leadership formats are those in which one therapist is much more experienced than the other, or one has more real power and authority than the other. Dual arrangements are common in clinics in which a staff person has a primary responsibility and assumes training responsibilities. In private practice a junior person may pair with a more experienced person, with the advantage of both being able to supply patients for the group, and the junior person learning from the experienced leader. Sometimes, the inexperienced person may be older, particularly in circumstances where the older clinician is learning a new skill. This reversal of the usual expectations of roles adds a dimension to how the leaders and members view the therapists (Dublin, 1995).

A primary reason for using dual leadership is to provide training for the junior therapist. While dual leadership is a superb training model, there are important drawbacks that require attention. For one thing, often the junior leader is being evaluated by the senior leader. This can be a disconcerting experience. The discomfort is only heightened when the group members add their evaluations of the effectiveness of the two leaders. The latter element follows from an almost inevitable sense that the more experienced leader may be providing "better leadership." Moreover, the senior clinician may modify his/her usual intervention style in response to the inexperienced leader's "errors" or misjudgments (Dies, 1994).

When the senior person has administrative (power) responsibilities, we believe that it is wise to make arrangements either for supervision or intermittent outside consultation for the dual therapy team. It can be very difficult for the members of the team to address their relationship without the assistance of someone who does not have direct responsibility for a student's progress or performance evaluation.

Coleadership (Cotherapy)

Cotherapy is defined as therapy by two leaders who are relatively similar in experience and power. There are many ways that leaders may differ. However, in clinics the similarities are usually on the basis of training status. Roller and Nelson (1994) maintain that "cotherapy is a commitment to a relationship with a peer in which significant therapeutic gains are possible for the patient and considerable collegial support and learning are possible for the therapists" (p. 304). Obviously, differences in ability to understand and to interact will emerge, but the fundamental criterion for successful working together is the willingness to devote time and effort to the cotherapy relationship. C. A. Rice (1995), in a survey of practicing clinicians enrolled in group therapy training programs, reported that almost three-quarters of respondents indicated that the cotherapy relationship was not a focus in supervision! Nevertheless, almost a third of those indicated that the supervision was helpful to their relationship.

Male–female coleadership, although appearing optimal in terms of "recreating the family," has the potential for evoking a number of important treatment considerations. Cultural expectations of men and women are assigned by patients, and if either leader deviates this may invite intense transference responses, which in turn may stress the pair's relationship. There is often considerable sexual curiosity (voyeurism) on the part of the group that can be uncomfortable and/or stimulating for the leaders. Moreover, there may be considerable rivalry and envy evoked in the members merely by the presence of the male–female leadership. The intensely intimate setting often results in powerful feelings arising between cotherapists.

CLINICAL EXAMPLE

Jane and John were psychology interns. As part of their training, they were to find partners to colead a therapy group. Jane and John had enjoyed a warm friendship during their first months of training and quickly selected one another as cotherapists. Each was married, and John was a new father.

As their group proceeded, their supervisor noted a sudden increase in acting out among group members, including two "couples" meeting outside the group boundaries. As the supervisor struggled to understand the meaning of this new group behavior, Jane and John "confessed" that they had begun an affair.

*   *   *

In this situation, the group had clearly sensed the special relationship that had developed between their new leaders. It was too dangerous to speak of it (or perhaps even to "know" it), but it was acted out in group behavior.

Coleadership, like any relationship, requires time and effort. It evolves over time, and with development of trust the experience can be gratifying and growth-promoting for the clinicians, who in turn experience their work as more effective and gratifying. On the other hand, this effort can at times distort the purpose of the treatment to a solipsistic exploration of the clinicians' relationship at the expense of the patients.

Overall, we feel that the disadvantages of cotherapy outweigh the gains. In training situations there may be no alternative if trainees are to gain experience as group leaders, but supervisors of these groups should be attentive to the increased problems cotherapy imposes on trainees. With certain patient populations, particularly the chronically mentally ill and children's groups, the disadvantages of cotherapy are outweighed by the necessity of having two therapists in the room if therapy is to proceed at all.

Rutan and Alonso (1980) have suggested an intriguing training alternative to the traditional model of cotherapy, an approach that incorporates the notion of a substitute. In this approach two leaders are employed, but each leads the group separately for a prescribed number of weeks while the nonleading cotherapist becomes a silent observer. This model offers some of the advantages suggested for cotherapy (such as binocular vision, peer consultation, sharing of responsibility, and covering at times of illness or vacation) while neutralizing some of the competitive features of traditional cotherapy. Cotherapy has particular advantages as a teaching tool, since the observer therapist can more easily lead a didactic session with trainees who have observed the group session.

COMBINING INDIVIDUAL AND GROUP THERAPY

There is growing interest in the advantages that may accrue when patients are seen in individual and group therapy concurrently (Alonso & Rutan, 1982, 1990; Battegay, 1972; J. S. Gans, 1990; Bernard & Drob, 1985; Wong, 1980). Each modality offers something that the other does not. In individual therapy there is the opportunity to focus precisely and in detail on the history, transferences, and associations of a single patient. In group therapy patients are seen in their interpersonal fields, and their characteristic relational and defensive styles are available for direct observation. Individual therapy invites a "vertical transference" (to authorities and parents), whereas group therapy promotes a "horizontal transference" (to siblings and peers). Therapists who have seen patients in both modalities are accustomed to finding new information in each setting. A morose, depressed patient in dyadic therapy might demonstrate a social aptitude in the group setting that the individual therapist could not have predicted, and a quiet, seemingly uninvolved group patient might relate a panorama of vivid reactions to and feelings about the group when in the safety of a dyadic therapy.

A variety of issues must be addressed when considering concurrent therapy (Rutan & Alonso, 1982). The major considerations are the following:

- When should group therapy be added to individual therapy, and when should individual therapy be added to group therapy?
- When should the patient see the same therapist in both individual and group therapy (combined therapy), and when should the patient see different therapists (conjoint therapy)?

Both combined and conjoint formats impact upon the relationship that patients establish in the group and with the dyadic therapist. These dynamics are explored below in conjunction with the discussion of the format.

Group Therapy Added to Individual Therapy

There are many situations in which it is advantageous to consider adding a therapy group to ongoing individual psychotherapy, among which are the following:

1. Patients in individual therapy sometimes experience difficulty generating sufficient associations, feelings, or memories to effectively fuel their indi-

vidual therapy. Groups evoke many feelings and memories for these patients, which in turn can then be used productively in both settings.

2. There are patients for whom the dyadic transference is insufficient to help them resolve their interpersonal problems. For such patients a group can assist them with relating to both sexes, different ages, and multiple personality styles. Borderline or narcissistic personalities are emotionally vulnerable to absences or separations. In groups, this dynamic is stimulated (if not overstimulated), and the combination of individual and group therapy may provide an optimal therapeutic format. Not only does a group provide patients with an opportunity to experience a much wider range of interpersonal options, but it also represents a situation that is more easily generalized to life.

3. Group therapy also benefits those patients who in the course of their individual work have made significant strides toward understanding the roots of their interpersonal problems and now need a laboratory in which to cement their gains or to further explore these issues.

4. In situations where a therapist becomes locked into a countertransference struggle with a patient, the addition of group therapy can often resolve the difficulty and thus save the individual therapy.

5. Entry into a group may also precipitate the end of individual therapy.

When group therapy is considered in addition to individual therapy, one should consider whether this might represent some acting out in the individual therapy. It is not unusual for a dyadic therapist to decide that group therapy might be a good addition to the treatment process because the patient has become burdensome, unrewarding, or frightening. There are also some patients who may not be good candidates for entering a group—for example, individuals who are unable to resolve splits or who are sufficiently masochistic that they offer themselves up as a scapegoat (Alonso & Rutan, 1990). As we noted earlier in discussing patient selection, severely schizoid persons, those who are unable to maintain confidentiality, or those who have not had a satisfactory relationship in their lives are poor candidates for group treatment.

Individual Therapy Added to Group Therapy

There are also many times when it may be helpful to add individual therapy to ongoing group therapy. Here are some examples:

1. The patient who is unable to express him/herself in the group is often assisted by individual therapy. This patient needs to be distinguished from the patient who refuses to relate to the group. Both can be helped to use the group more productively by supplemental dyadic therapy, but the latter type of patient should be helped to own the hostile aspects of his/her stubbornness as part of the referral.

2. The patient who in the course of group therapy has identified a specific area requiring more intensive exploration can use individual therapy to facilitate that. For instance, patients who hear about sexual abuse in group sessions and gradually become aware that they too were molested may need individual sessions to adequately explore their experiences. This situation generally is a result of effective work in group therapy; provided that individual therapy is understood as supplementing and not replacing the group, we do not view it as a resistance.

3. Some patients find the interpersonal setting of the group too frightening and need the presence of an individual therapist to help them remain in the group. Individual therapy can assist such patients by exploring the roots of their fears about group membership, thus allowing them to continue in the group.

4. When group members undergo an external crisis, such as a death in the family, short-term individual therapy is often a useful tool to help them through the time of crisis. A variation on this situation is the developmentally immature member who may react to a crisis, such as the simultaneous termination of several members or the expression of strong affect in the group, with a request for individual treatment. These members, who seem unable to directly address their tension within the group, usually attribute their difficulty to external sources, and seem temporarily unable to integrate the transferential implications of their external conflict, can be successfully managed with several individual sessions. They regain their balance through individual contact with the therapist and the opportunity to discuss their difficulties.

CLINICAL EXAMPLE

Lisa, a woman with a diagnosis of borderline personality disorder, had to terminate a group when her husband was transferred to a distant city by his company. In the new community Lisa interviewed several group therapists before deciding on a male therapist (her previous group leader had been female). In her new group Lisa spent much of the first year extolling the virtues of the old group and the relationships she had formed there. She insisted that everything about the new group, from the setting to the intelligence of the members, was flawed. She threatened to quit but agreed to meet individually with the group therapist. In the dyadic setting she was able to gradually work on the profound sense of loss she had about giving up her prior group. Moreover, several joint sessions were held with Lisa and her husband to address the marital conflict that resulted from the move.

*   *   *

Without the addition of dyadic treatment to her work in the group, Lisa most likely would have fled the group. The individual attention helped her maintain focus on her reactions to the separation. The individual therapy not only helped Lisa separate from her old group, it also served to strengthen the therapist's alliance with Lisa. This also illustrates how individual work can be used to supplement group work.

Once a determination has been made to combine group and dyadic treatment, the question arises whether or not the patient should be seen by the same or a different therapist in the two treatment settings.

Conjoint Therapy

Conjoint therapy, where the patient is seen in group therapy and individual therapy by two different therapists, is a common therapeutic arrangement. In many instances patients are referred for group treatment by a clinician who wishes to continue the individual therapy. If the patient is appropriate for group treatment, permission for the group therapist to communicate with the individual therapist must be granted by the patient. Conjoint therapy provides a fertile ground for splitting, and the antidote is for the two therapists to communicate regularly about the patient. It is not unusual for therapists who are strangers to one another to work with the same patient in this dual mode of treatment. It is important to gain the patient's agreement that there will be no secrets between the individual therapist and the group therapist. Even under circumstances when there has been an agreement to freely communicate, problems may emerge in which the patient may undermine the group treatment.

CLINICAL EXAMPLE:

A man in weekly individual psychotherapy requested group treatment. Following consultation with a group therapist, the patient entered a group in addition to his individual therapy. An agreement was reached that the two clinicians could discuss the salient dynamic issues. This arrangement worked well for the first year of conjoint treatment. However, one evening the patient announced that he had added a second individual therapy session and the only available hour would necessitate the patient coming to group 15 minutes late. Discussion between the two therapists revealed that the dyadic therapist had offered the second hour, not being aware that it would interfere with the group. Once the patient accepted the offer and revealed the overlap of times, the individual therapist worked, to no avail, at helping the patient understand the meaning of his behavior. In the group, the patient made it clear that he would not change his individual sessions. The fact that this conflict arose just after the group therapist had announced an extended summer vacation was dismissed by the patient, despite his previously acknowledged sensitivity to interruptions in the therapy. The patient ultimately terminated his group therapy prior to the summer vacation.

*   *   *

This example highlights the limits of what can be accomplished even with good communication between therapists. The dyadic clinician, having offered an additional hour and subsequently learned of its implications, was not in a position to rescind or insist on a change without altering the therapeutic relationship. The patient clearly was creating a provocative and difficult situation. Initially it appeared that there had been a collusion between the patient and the individual therapist to undermine the group treatment. This was not the case, and effective communication between the two therapists averted the patient enacting a split between the therapists that would have paralleled the split between the patient's parents.

When a patient refuses to allow the group and individual therapist to freely communicate, conjoint treatment is contraindicated. This patient has already indicated that there is a completely unshareable "secret" life and would be entering the group with a less stringent agreement regarding openness than others.

On the other hand, some individual therapists maintain that confidentiality of the dyadic treatment cannot be violated. This represents a different complication. While the complete commitment to confidentiality in the individual therapy relationship is understandable, it often implies that the individual therapist does not fully believe in the effectiveness of the group format. In this case the group therapist needs to assess the *patient's* willingness and ability to speak in group about what is important in the dyadic treatment. If the individual therapist considers an impermeable membrane between group and individual to be important but the patient does not, the patient may be accepted for group. This is not an easy decision, and some group therapists routinely refuse to accept patients when the individual therapist will not agree to mutual communication. The unwillingness by the individual therapist to share information creates the potential for a split, promotes secrets, and suggests that an antigroup bias may exist. We believe patients can be accepted in group under these conditions, though they are not ideal, *if* the individual therapist's position is based upon a theoretical conviction about the absolute privacy of communication in the individual hour rather than on a conscious or unconscious derogation of group therapy. In these cases the group therapist should tell the patient, "You will have a somewhat more difficult job than others who are in individual therapy. I will not be able to assist by collaboration with your individual therapist. Therefore, we will rely on you to ensure that the important material from your individual sessions comes to the group as well." It is also important that the group therapist not engage in splitting. The decision to completely protect the confidentially of individual sessions, while not one with which we agree, is nonetheless an honorable and defensible one.

Combined Therapy

Combined therapy refers to the practice of the same therapist seeing patients in both individual and group therapy. This format has the advantage of the clinician working in both settings and being able to work with the different transferential configurations. In the dyadic setting early developmental transferences may be the central focus, whereas in the group setting sibling rivalry, envy, and jealousy—triangular transferences—may be prominent. These latter configurations may assist patients in the process of separation and individuation (Praper, 1997).

Combined therapy is an extremely powerful therapeutic format (see Fried, 1954; Stein, 1964), but it requires that the patient and therapist reach agreement regarding the interface between the two therapies. Controversy exists as to the limits of confidentiality, with one side proposing a strict boundary between the two treatments (Wong, 1983; Alonso & Rutan, 1990) and the other maintaining that "the patient's contract should include explicit agreement that the therapies are not separated by a boundary of confidentiality" (Rutan & Alonso, 1982, p. 12). While either position is defensible, we opt for the latter since the former inevitably implies that there are some subjects that are just too powerful to be related in groups and runs the risk of the patient and the therapist having a "secret" from the group. Nonetheless, it is acceptable practice, if a therapist prefers, to maintain confidentiality between group therapy and individual therapy. It is most important that the therapist be consistent in whatever approach is taken.

Obviously, all of a patient's communications have relevance in both individual and group therapy. Nonetheless, some material clearly relates to one modality more than the other. Patients sometimes find it easier to speak in individual therapy of difficult material that belongs in group therapy, and vice versa. In such instances the therapist is faced with a delicate situation. On the one hand, the therapist wants to hear the material and help the patient understand it; on the other hand, the therapist does not want to collude with the patient in withholding material from the primary therapeutic modality. (In our experience, group therapy almost always becomes the "primary" modality for the patient.)

It is useful for therapists to remember that patients are free to talk about whatever they choose in either modality. Our role is not to punish them for choosing the "wrong" setting. However, it is certainly appropriate to explore with the patient why the particular setting was chosen.

CLINICAL EXAMPLE

In individual therapy John mentions that he is furious with Sally, a fellow group member. He also reports that he cannot tell Sally of his anger because he is fearful she will be devastated; nor is he convinced he can control his sadism toward her. Furthermore, he asks that the therapist not speak of this in the group.

The therapist is faced with a difficult problem. He does not want to forestall John's talking about his important feelings, and yet he does not want to enter into a collusion with John to keep secrets from the group. The therapist uses the individual time to explore John's powerful reaction to Sally, and says, "She must be very important to you." At the end of the session the therapist states, "You have some important things to discuss with Sally and the group."

In the following group session John does not mention his feelings toward Sally. In the ensuing individual session the therapist notes that John did not speak with Sally, and the focus of this individual session is on why John feels incapable of sharing these feelings in the group. Ultimately John links his feelings toward Sally to his ambivalent feelings toward his alcoholic mother. On the one hand, he is furious with his mother; on the other hand, he pities her and does not wish to cause her more pain. Historically, he would speak privately with his father about these difficult feelings. The therapy parallels that situation, and John's wish to speak with the therapist privately about his feelings toward Sally replicated his private conversations with his father.

Once John understood the etiology of his reactions, he was able to speak to Sally in the group. To his surprise, she was able to hear him and respond. He further learned how angry he had been with his father for colluding with him to make his mother the identified patient in the family.

* * *

Though it is less frequent, it is not unusual for patients to mention in group something they need to explore more completely in the individual therapy. Lipsius (1991) refers to this as "background use," where the patient sets the stage for further discussion of important material later.

Whether material is presented in either group or individual therapy with an intent to avoid it in the other modality, the therapist should neither force the patient to reveal the material nor collude to keep the material from the other modality. (This is true in conjoint as well as combined treatment.) Rather, the therapist should patiently work toward understanding why the patient feels the need for secrecy. Secrets are ultimately much less interesting than the reasons why the patient feels the need for secrecy, and it is usually much more productive to explore the fantasies about why material cannot be shared in the other modality. Nevertheless, occasionally the therapist will decide to bring material from one arena into the other. This must be done delicately and in full recognition of the fact that even if this is part of the therapeutic agreements, the patient may experience this as a breach of confidentiality.

It is not uncommon for patients in combined treatment to make references in the group session to material from their individual sessions. Many times such comments are meaningful to the current group interaction, and therapists must bear the burden of hearing their words or their meanings altered. Attention to the here and now of the communication assists therapists in maintaining narcissistic balance. In such circumstances therapists may compare the patient's perceptions with their own. The patient may be conveying information about a countertransference response of the clinician in the safety of the group. A premature confrontation of the patient's "distortion" may disrupt the treatment relationship. There are occasions in which the patient's distortion is grossly inaccurate, and the therapist may, following self-scrutiny, provide the correct information. To mention material from one therapeutic setting in the other is not breaking confidentiality, since the boundary of confidentiality surrounds both therapeutic venues.

For some primitive patients the dissonance raised by two different types of therapy may be more than they can integrate. This is less a factor of a particular diagnostic category and more a function of the individual's particular strengths and weaknesses. Some severely disturbed borderline patients can be greatly assisted by combined therapy (see the example of Lisa, above), whereas others inevitably use splitting and perceive one therapist or therapy as all good and the other as all bad. With the less advanced patients, careful attention must be paid to the benefits or liabilities of having the same therapist in both individual and group therapist roles. For some, the consistency of the therapist makes the divergent experiences tolerable, whereas for others, sharing their individual therapist with the group is more than they can tolerate. Again, in consultation with the patient, these decisions must be made on a case-by-case basis.

When individual and group therapy are used concurrently, it is important that neither be viewed as superior to the other. Rather, they should be seen as adjunctive to one another. There will be times during the therapy when the patient will give more weight to one or the other, and that is to be expected. In the usual course of events, patients gradually put more and more emphasis on their therapy group, and the individual treatment commonly ends before the group therapy.

When individual therapy and group therapy are viewed as cooperative by therapist and patient alike, they present a very powerful therapeutic modality for use with a wide variety of patients.

LEADER ABSENCES

Therapists take vacations, attend professional meetings, become ill, and occasionally have competing priorities that mandate not being present to lead their groups. Absences should be rare, and the decision to miss a group session is not one to make lightly. Nonetheless, even the most conscientious group therapist cannot be present every week.

Given the paramount importance of continuity and cohesion, any breaches in the schedule threaten the effectiveness of the group. Any absence of the leader is an important event, and the members' feelings concerning this event must be fully explored and used to enhance learning. There should be no attempt to blur the affects connected to the leader's missing one or more meetings.

The question then becomes "How is the group best served in this situation?" There are several options available, including the following:

1. Canceling the meeting
2. Providing a makeup meeting
3. Holding a double session before or after the leader's absence
4. Inviting the group to meet without the leader
5. Providing a substitute leader

As Rutan, Alonso, and Molin (1984) have pointed out, there is a theoretically valid rationale for each of these options.

Canceling the Meeting

Advantages

Time lost is lost forever. The cancellation of a meeting forces the members to fully face the absence of the leader and all the implications of that loss. One ramification of the leader's absence is that not only the leader but also the group is lost to the members for that period of time. Canceling the meeting is an option that does not offer false restitution. The search for painless solutions to life's dilemmas is one source of pathology for many patients. Thus, for most members simply canceling a meeting when the leader must be absent is potentially an opportunity for learning.

Liabilities

Patients do not always learn best by reexperiencing the full deprivation that may have led to developmental arrests. Some patients need a time of idealizing their group therapist (Rutan & Rice, 1981), and the treatment may be adversely affected by premature de-idealization of the leader, which could result if a meeting is canceled. The reexperiencing of painful affect, resulting from canceling the meeting, may simply reactivate the repetition compulsion without any working through. Also, especially when faced with a rather long absence of the leader, there are some groups or specific members who may not survive the loss of continuity. It is not unusual for vulnerable members to drop out of a group in anticipation of a disruption in continuity.

Providing a Makeup Meeting

Advantages

If leaders provide an opportunity to make up the lost meeting or meetings, this can demonstrate a commitment to the group and can heighten awareness of the mutual responsibilities involved in relationships. This option allows the members to avail themselves of the healing power of the group even though the regularly scheduled weekly meeting will not occur. It is unusual for a leader to offer a makeup meeting if only one session is missed. However, there are circumstances when there may be several sessions missed in a particular time period and the therapist decides to suggest an alternate meeting during that period. The most common situation is that of the Christmas and New Year period when two successive sessions will be missed. But there are other situations where vacation, holidays, and personal and professional obligations may all coincide. The therapist might then explain the situation and offer the possibility of an alternate day for the group to meet.

If this option is used, the time should be negotiated with the group rather than imposed by the leader. However, this negotiation should be based on a limited number of times (no more than three) offered by the leader. This period of negotiation often highlights character styles and issues of motivation for the members. (By the way, unless a makeup meeting policy was part of the original group agreements, the therapist should not charge members who do not attend the atypical meeting.)

Liabilities

One major problem with the makeup option is that it may suppress angry feelings. How can one be angry at an abandoning therapist who goes out of his/her way to make up the meeting? Indeed, therapists may invoke this option out of a need to please or avoid anger rather than out of a more thoughtful consideration of the pros and cons. If the makeup meeting option is used, the therapist needs to listen carefully for the members' negative affects about the original cancellation (and to the inconvenience that the makeup meeting may entail). Patients should not end up feeling grateful to the exclusion of other feelings about the lack of agreed-upon consistency.

A second problem with this option is the difficulty in finding a suitable alternate time. Anyone who has tried to arrange a meeting for six to ten people knows how complex and frustrating this can be. Indeed, if there is rapid agreement about an alternate meeting time, the clinician should be alert to the potential for a negative reaction to occur.

Almost invariably someone is unable or unwilling to meet at the time or day agreed to by the majority. To meet and exclude one or more individuals creates another array of problems and affects (specifically, feelings of exclusion, competition, and favoritism). If the makeup option is used, the therapist must decide in advance what to do if all the members cannot agree on an alternate meeting time. To meet without some members causes problems, but to allow a deviant member to force everyone else to do without is also a problem. The leader should also retain final decision power over when the meeting will be scheduled, since to open this to a democratic process raises more issues than it solves.

Holding a Double Session

Advantages

If one meeting is canceled, it is sometimes useful to meet for twice as long the week after the absence. Such an extended session should occur after the missed meeting rather than before it, since double sessions often stir up considerable affect and the members should not have to wait a prolonged period before meeting again. Furthermore, a double session after a missed session does not interfere as much with the experience of the missed week. Holding a double session is similar to holding an alternate session, since it indicates the therapist's willingness to be responsible to the agreements even while altering them; while not meeting at the agreed-upon time, at least the therapist is offering to meet for the allotted amount of time.

A particular advantage of this option is that the extended time frame allows for more sharing from some members. Other theoretical modalities (notably those that use marathon formats) have demonstrated the power of extended sessions. While we do not propose to defeat patients' defenses through sheer fatigue, the extension of time permits greater self-exposure. The danger of overwhelming defenses is minimized by the fact that the double session occurs in the context of an ongoing group.

Liabilities

The problems with the double-session option again include the possibility that the patients may not experience or express their feelings about the leader's unavailability or lack of dependability. Further, there is the danger that more fragile patients may be endangered by the expanded time. There is also the possibility that members may infer that twice as long is twice as good, which would then lead the group to wonder why all sessions are not of the extended format. As with the makeup meeting option, there is the thorny question of whether there is to be a double session for every missed meeting or just for some, as well as the issue of what to do if not all members can stay for the extended period. Finally, the therapist should alert members to the fee for the session. This is important because most insurance companies do not pay for two sessions in one day. The clinician may be unable to charge for his/her time if there is a limitation in the contract with the insurance company.

Inviting the Group to Meet without the Leader

Advantages

Some therapists use the format of the leaderless meeting as a routine part of the therapeutic agreement (the alternate meeting). Even in groups where the alternate meeting is not used, members frequently express the wish to meet during the leader's absence. Usually such a proposal dies during subsequent discussion. The response may be different if the therapist initiates the idea. A host of dynamics related to authority, power, and safety are mobilized, and marked emotionality generally results as members vehemently support or oppose the idea. An especially difficult situation arises if one or more members choose not to attend an alternate meeting: the leader will not be present to hear what may be said about the absent members. If this option is used, the therapist must make the usual group room available and discourage the group from meeting anywhere else. It should further be stipulated that the group begin and end at the usual time. This structure enhances continuity, discourages using the alternate meeting as a social encounter, and provides symbolic support. The alternate meeting also supports independence and implies that the leader has confidence that the group can function without him/her.

Liabilities

Of all the options available to deal with a leader's absence, we view the leaderless format as the least helpful and the most likely to result in problems. For one thing, there is really no such thing as a leaderless group. Indeed, the "ghost" of the therapist is strongly present even in his/her absence. A common "solution" to this dynamic is for the members to elevate one person to the leadership role. This has complicating implications for subsequent meetings. Moreover, many of the transferences in a mature group are between the members and, without the leader, patients may find it even more difficult to address their conflicts. Members give themselves permission to freely and spontaneously express forbidden affects as a consequence of their conviction that the therapist will provide safety.

Providing a Substitute Leader

Advantages

An unusual and yet viable response to a therapist's absence is to provide a substitute leader. Where possible, a consistent substitute leader should be available to be called upon whenever a primary therapist is absent. A substitute leader allows for continuity and predictability for the boundaries of therapy groups without implying that the group leader is all-giving or idealized. In the course of time, groups begin integrating the substitute leader as an important transferential figure. This model offers the following unique opportunities:

1. The group can actively explore the meaning and effect of the leader's absence without having to endure the loss of a session. The substitute leader can be facilitative in helping the group explore their reactions to the leader's absence.

2. The group not only gains from the different perspective of the substitute therapist but also has the opportunity to explore the different transferences that leader may evoke. Ideally, the substitute leader should be of the opposite gender from the ongoing leader in order to enhance these effects.

3. A group is able to continue functioning in those rare instances when a leader must be absent for a prolonged period of time, such as when illness, injury, or pregnancy occurs.

4. Peer consultation between the therapists is especially valuable. Since the substitute leader has the opportunity to meet with the group on different occasions, he/she has the overview perspective of seeing the patients periodically and can therefore help the ongoing therapist assess the progress of the members and of the group itself. Further, the substitute therapist might view particular members or group dynamics quite differently from the ongoing therapist, thus broadening the latter's perspective.

Liabilities

Providing a substitute leader also has its disadvantages. The introduction of a second leader occasionally invites splitting and other regressive defenses resistant to interpretation. In addition, the introduction of a second therapist means that a form of cotherapy has been initiated, along with all the complications of cotherapy mentioned earlier in this chapter. Moreover, as is the case when a patient sees one therapist in individual therapy and another in group therapy, the substitute leader and the ongoing leader do not see the patients together. This adds a level of complication and requires that the therapists communicate actively in the service of the treatment. The substitute therapist option becomes even more complicated if the substitute therapist is not available when the primary therapist cannot meet with the group. The group is now faced with a double disappointment. Finally, to the degree that one believes that *relationship* is a primary healing factor, the relationship to the therapist cannot be simply transferred to a different leader.

Conclusion

If there is any plan to deal with leader absence other than the usual exploration of feelings and memories evoked, this must be made clear to the group members from the beginning, preferably as part of the original group agreements. Generally, groups can tolerate leader absences very well, and unless there are extenuating circumstances we prefer not to hold a meeting or make up the time, thereby allowing the group to experience and learn from the therapist's absence just as they do from the absence of individual members.

TRANSFERRING LEADERSHIP
OF A THERAPY GROUP

Though therapists move, get ill, die, or retire, most commonly groups change therapists when a leader (or set of coleaders) finishes a period of training. Since beginning a new group is an arduous and often lengthy process, training programs, which are dependent upon there being groups for students to run, attempt to maintain ongoing groups that change therapists. Whatever the reason, loss of the group leader is a difficult challenge for the group (Chiang & Beck, 1988; Long, Pendleton, & Winter, 1988; McGee, 1974).

Changes in leadership can be divided into those that are planned and those that are unplanned, the latter being cases of illness and death. Sharpe (1991) suggests that the degree of difficulty in the transition period can be correlated with the length of the group's association with the previous therapist, the similarity in theoretical orientation of the two therapists, and the new therapist's potential for ensuring the group's survival. To this we would add that each clinician's personal characteristics and style set the stage for patients to compare and contrast the therapists. Whether the new leader is revered or severely criticized, it is important that he/she recognize that these are rarely completely accurate assessments. Rather, they represent part of the working through of this important change.

A change of therapists is never easy. Often, a planned transition becomes a crisis so filled with affect that the group suffers rather than learns from the experience. The model of grieving (an entirely expectable reaction to loss) is helpful in orienting therapists to the patients' reactions to transitions. The stages of grief include a stage of guilt, shock, denial, reemergence of somatic symptoms, or increased irritability or rage; self-reproach (members wonder if they might have been difficult in some fashion and thereby responsible for the therapist's departure); a yearning for the lost therapist (which may be problematic for the new therapist); and finally resolution. When the therapist is departing, anticipatory grief may be prominent. When the therapist dies, the grief can be intense. It is not unusual for one or more members to drop out instead of making the transition. Occasionally, a whole group is destroyed in this process. A number of strategies are available to make this crisis an opportunity for learning rather than a trauma. Each clinical situation requires close examination because each model has its strengths and liabilities.

Models of Transition of Leaders

How the new leader(s) is introduced to the group is a major concern. Several options available to accomplish this transition are discussed below.

No Overlap

In one model a departing therapist leads the group until the announced termination date and the succeeding therapist does not meet with the group until the following week. (There should never be a gap between sessions led by an outgoing and incoming therapist! Losing a therapist is a crisis for a group, and it is often difficult for the group members to contemplate "beginning all over" with a new therapist. If a gap occurs between losing the old therapist and beginning with the new one, the result is a disproportionate number of dropouts and groups often do not survive the transition.) This rigorous model focuses on the issues of the loss of the old and the impact of the new and maximizes the affective response. It offers the maximum focus on the feelings regarding the loss of the leader and is the option of choice when the ego strength of the members' or the group's developmental level is judged adequate to manage the intense affects aroused. This model promotes fantasies about the incoming therapist, since no concrete data exist about him/her (other than perhaps a name, which usually implies gender). Patients face the unknown collectively, but they each have fantasies about the benevolence or destructiveness of the new therapist. Sometimes these fantasies can be terrifying and not uncommonly lead to periods of emotional contagion in which all members, under the sway of the intense feelings, adopt a similar attitude or propose a behavioral solution, say, "Let's all have a goodbye party the last session." Clinicians are hard pressed to maintain their equanimity under the pressure of such groupwide emotions. Even when this approach is handled well, some patients may be overwhelmed and flee treatment.

Minimal Overlap

In the minimal overlap model the incoming therapist is simply introduced to the group 2 or 3 weeks prior to the outgoing leader's termination. Typically, the group is notified that the new therapist will be present for a few moments in the next group meeting. At that meeting the incoming therapist simply introduces him/herself and says something like, "I am looking forward to working with you." He/she also specifically mentions the date the new leadership will begin (the new leader should avoid engaging in a question-and-answer period). The new therapist then leaves, and the group continues. This model provides a bridge so that the group actually sees and meets the new therapist, but it does not unduly interfere with the group's saying good-bye to their exiting leader.

Observation

In the observation model (used primarily in training centers) incoming therapists begin by silently observing the groups they are to lead (Stone, 1975). This model promotes continuity and bridging of leadership, and members can begin to develop a relationship with the new therapist. Although there may have been only minimal or nonverbal exchanges, the members have an opportunity to assess the new leader, who in turn gains valuable information about the group and therefore comes to the task of leadership with knowledge. This also provides an important training opportunity for the incoming therapist, for whom leading a group may be a new adventure. The opportunity to watch a group in action without having responsibility for leadership is a fine way to gain experience. In training programs the observer also participates in postgroup meetings with the retiring leader and attends supervisory sessions on the group, thereby increasing his/her knowledge of the group history and functioning. An optimal observation period is from 3 months to 1 year (Stone, 1975).

This model also has problems. Pragmatically, an extensive time commitment on the part of the observer is required. Further, the observer must eventually move from the role of student to therapist in the eyes of the group, and this has powerful transference and countertransference implications.

Stage Phasing

In the stage-phasing model the incoming therapist becomes known to the group in stages prior to becoming the leader, appearing first as a silent observer and then functioning as a cotherapist during the final weeks of the outgoing therapist's tenure. The advantages of this approach are that it smoothes the transition, decreases stranger anxiety, allows for overt, experiential comparisons between the two leaders, and provides leadership opportunity for the new therapist. The main problem of this model is that it blurs the good-bye to the old therapist with the hello to the new one, often leaving both tasks only partially complete.

Conclusion

How the transition of leaders is handled is a complex and important consideration. Each model suggested has assets and liabilities, and each has implications for the treatment. Some models emphasize comfort, both to the group members and the incoming therapist, thereby maximizing the chances that the group will survive the transition while minimizing the options for affect and complete learning. Whichever model is chosen, it is strongly suggested that the incoming therapist routinely attend supervision of the group for some months prior to becoming the group therapist.

The central issue in transferring leadership remains how to maximize learning while minimizing unproductive anxiety and stress. As we discuss in Chapter 16, terminations reactivate feelings associated with all previous losses, deaths, and new beginnings. Members' responses to individual absences or group interruptions might prove useful predictors of the feelings and behaviors evoked by the therapist's departure. However, the change of therapists can awaken significant and unexpected unconscious material, perhaps stemming from the separation–individuation stage of development or from specific traumatic events such as a parent's remarriage or a parent who is only sporadically available.

Throughout the transition process it is useful to remember that one must say good-bye before one can fully say hello. The group is best helped in this difficult transition by ensuring that the members explore as fully as possible the feelings evoked by the loss of their therapist. In addition to transference, there are the realistic and conscious feelings of loss that must also be managed. Not everything is transference, and members experience a genuine loss when a therapist leaves. The incoming therapist should continue the group focus on the loss, even while the members are beginning to establish a relationship with him/her. Incoming group therapists must suffer through the realization that it will be many months before the group is really theirs.

Another aspect of the problem of transferring leadership is that of maintaining a healthy working alliance (Zetzel, 1956). Due to their public nature, groups provide more opportunity than does individual therapy for establishing good working alliances (Glatzer, 1978). Members can compare their perceptions and experiences to those of their colleagues and can use consensual validation as one means of discriminating valid from distorted perceptions. This is not to suggest that affects are suppressed by reality or that consensual validation can defeat transference, but members are able to use their trusting relationships with each other to explore and assess affects as they arise. Group therapy might be more successful than individual therapy in retaining working alliances even when therapists change because the important relationships among the members are retained.

Our experience in training centers suggests that a minimum 2-year tenure as group therapist is preferable for both the student and the group. Members usually spend considerable time preparing for the departure of a therapist, dealing with the departure, and building an alliance with the new therapist. At a minimum, it takes 3 or 4 months for an incoming therapist to truly become the leader of a group. When feelings are especially intense, it may easily require twice that time period. The time consumed by too-frequent leadership shifts diminishes the opportunity for undisturbed work on areas other than separation and loss. In training centers where trainees routinely leave in June or July, veteran group members usually begin inquiring in January if their leaders will be leaving in the summer (see comparable behavior in time-limited groups when the halfway point is reached—Chapter 15). These considerations should be viewed in light of the fact that the usual length of time for a patient to finish a substantial piece of therapeutic work can be 2 to 3 years even in an ongoing, leader-constant group (Stone & Rutan, 1984).

Guidelines for Transferring Leadership of a Therapy Group

Whatever strategy is chosen, using the following guidelines will facilitate the therapeutic transferring of group leadership:

1. The departing leader needs to examine thoroughly his/her own feelings regarding the leaving. Frequently, departing therapists experience significant guilt about abandoning their group in order to go on to the greener pastures that a posttraining life predicts. The patients have given a great deal to the therapist, have contributed to his/her training, and their reward is to be abandoned and left in the hands of a neophyte whom they must train. Not infrequently, the outgoing therapist also experiences feelings of competition with the incoming therapist. In training settings, where the new leaders are almost always less experienced, outgoing leaders might gain perspective by recalling how little they knew when they took over a group.

2. One may usefully consider the change of leaders, as noted above, using John Bowlby's (1973) continuum of grief: protest, despair, and detachment. These reactions, which Bowlby observed in infants suddenly separated from their mothers, aptly describe the reactions that members experience when faced with a forcible separation from their therapist. We must help the members avoid detachment by giving them the opportunity to rage and weep over this act of abandonment and to connect it to all the similar acts in their histories. This will enable the patients to say an effective good-bye, to own the gains and loves as well as the rages and disappointments with the outgoing therapist. Such work allows the members to test reality and demythologize the departing therapist, thus allowing them to reconnect to someone new. Even if this is not possible for each individual, the natural differences among members will call forth a broad spectrum of responses to the loss, verbalization of which will help the group as a whole tentatively move forward. It is often difficult for the outgoing therapist to hear and bear all the discomforting affects aroused by the departure. This might lead the therapist to prematurely accept a diminution of negative affect as a sign that the loss has been worked through. Typically, the outgoing therapist will need to continually invite expression of the rageful and disappointed affect.

3. The incoming therapist must work on his/her anxiety about becoming a group therapist. Typically, therapists have been trained in dyadic therapy first. There, the therapist is protected by the therapeutic role and the therapy is couched in privacy. It is often unnerving and uncomfortable for the therapist to "go public" and begin working in the open arena of a group. To complicate this matter, incoming therapists are often neophytes and worry that they will do the group harm (patients, sensing this anxiety, may inquire, "How many groups have you run before this one?"). One part of incoming therapists' anxieties typically includes feelings about the therapist they replace. It is important for new therapists to use supervision to work on the uncertainty and anxiety that accompanies becoming a group therapist; the same is true for experienced therapists who are taking on a new group. Transference looms large, and new therapists often lose sight of the fact that the beloved outgoing therapist knew just as little about groups when he/she began. Further, it is important to know that groups, no matter how abusive they might appear, want the new leader to succeed. Finally, the affects that fill the therapist are shared by the patients; they, too, wonder and worry if the new therapist will prove inept. And they worry that they will appear inept and unlovable to the new therapist.

4. Both the outgoing and incoming therapists need to examine their narcissistic vulnerabilities and their competitive strivings so that they will be able to tolerate the patients favoring one over the other. No matter how experienced they are or how clearly they understand the transferential basis of members' angry and diminishing feelings, therapists are vulnerable to feeling

hurt and defensive under continuing attacks and criticism. Therapists can re-mind themselves that such attacks may represent a positive sign: the patients feel comfortable enough to forgo politeness, and they have somehow deter-mined that the therapist is tough enough to withstand their attacks. Further-more, a common defense against the sadness of saying good-bye is to go away mad rather than sad. For a time, incoming therapists will have the role of step-parent, while the members continue the work with their "natural" parent who has left. The feelings of being ignored or belittled are never easy, and new therapists have trouble maintaining their therapeutic balance under such conditions. It may be helpful for incoming therapists to project into the future and realize that in a short period of time the members will likely be struggling over losing them and that a new incoming therapist will be bearing the brunt of those feelings.

5. The incoming therapist must receive a great deal of information not only about the lives and pathologies of the patients but also about the history of the group itself. The transition is facilitated if the incoming therapist can participate in the group supervision for some weeks or months prior to assum-ing leadership. Furthermore, the incoming leader should receive quite specific information about how the group works, such as where the group meets, how members assemble (in the waiting room or in the group room) or if the thera-pist goes to get them, where the leader traditionally sits, which patients sit reg-ularly in which seats, and so forth. The incoming therapist is not bound by these traditions, but it is important to know them.

6. In training settings, supervision should bridge all changes in leader-ship. When leaders change, if at all possible the old supervisor should con-tinue during the transition. This is especially important in groups with a single leader. In this way continuity can be borne by the supervisor.

7. The incoming therapist should make individual appointments with all the group members. The individual history for each patient that is provided by an outgoing therapist is an insufficient substitute for reviewing such data directly with the patient. These appointments also provide opportunities to accelerate the alliance between new therapist and members; they can also give members a chance to review their progress and to clarify goals they have for the future. If particular members refuse to accept the invitation to meet with the incoming therapist individually, they need not be pressed to do so. Rather, this behavior can be a source of curiosity and exploration within the group.

Summary

It has been our experience that more mature groups (those that have been in existence for several years and have experienced previous changes in leader-ship) are likely to gain from a no-overlap or minimal overlap model. Indeed, for those groups the transition is often a time of accelerated growth. In newer groups, the baton of leadership must be handed over more cautiously, probably invoking one of the bridging techniques. In groups with the most damaged patients, the primary goal is to transfer the leadership, not to enhance affect in the members; for these patients issues of basic trust (or distrust) are so powerful that they can profit from extensive contact with the incoming therapist prior to the actual change in leadership.

COMBINING OTHER TREATMENTS WITH GROUP PSYCHOTHERAPY

Quite often patients seen in group therapy are seen in other treatment settings. We have examined the issues involved when group and individual therapy are combined. Patients are often in additional *types* of treatment along with their group—for example, couples' therapy, biological treatments, or supplemental treatment from an entirely different theoretical perspective (cognitive behavioral, hypnotherapy, etc.). These situations, while potentially very useful to the patient, offer their own unique technical issues.

Combining psychotropic medications and psychodynamic group therapy may be the most widespread example of this issue; so we will use that situation to highlight issues that arise in combining different types of treatment. A survey of 148 experienced group therapists found that more than two-thirds of the respondents included patients taking medications in their "typical" outpatient groups (Stone, Rodenhauser, & Markert, 1991). The survey showed only slight variation in this percentage among physicians, psychologists, and social workers. Patients with anxiety states and mood and personality disorders were the most frequently included diagnostic categories. Schizophrenic (1%) and manic patients (2%), respectively, comprised only a small portion of all patients.

Theory assisting the clinician in conceptualizing the indications, goals, and dynamics of such a combination is incomplete. As observed by the Group for the Advancement of Psychiatry (1975):

> The determinants of the type of treatment offered are hardly ever very clear. To a considerable extent they depend upon the training and ideology of the manpower available for treatment. Those without licenses to use drugs, and who therefore can not prescribe them, frequently oppose their use. (p. 271)

> Even among those who are reasonably well-trained in both pharmacotherapy and psychotherapy, and who feel comfortable using them, there is a conspicuous lack of reasoned comprehension for their joint use and especially their interaction. (p. 272)

This should not surprise us since psychopharmacology and psychodynamic therapy are grounded in differing philosophies: from the psychopharmacological point of view, feelings spring from biological sources and can be modified chemically; from the dynamic point of view, feelings result from psychological sources. Medically, unusually intense affect represents a "symptom" to be relieved, while psychodynamically intense affect represents a psychological communication and an opportunity for learning.

Karasu (1982) attempts to both distinguish and relate these discrepancies by offering two target goals: the patient's state—the symptom picture—which is treated with pharmacotherapy, and the trait—the longstanding personality structure—which is treated with psychotherapy. Questions concerning the proper timing for introduction of one or the other form of therapy and the dynamics surrounding their combined or sequential use have not been fully delineated.[1]

Some therapists are uncomfortable with patients receiving psychotropic medications because of the therapists' belief that dynamic considerations take precedence. These therapists often hold that the underlying conflicts or personality deficits that result in symptom formation are interfered with by the use of medications. They further believe that removing symptoms lessens anxiety and decreases motivation for self-exploration. An additional argument is that "learning" under the influence of medications is not transferable to the nonmedicated state. Others further maintain that reliance on medications damages self-esteem since patients cannot take credit for their gains. Still other therapists tend to wall off discussion of medication as outside the arena of the interpersonal/intrapsychic investigations.

On the opposite side of the controversy are therapists who believe that excessive anxiety or mood fluctuations interfere with participation in the interactions of the group and that members can learn only when these symptoms are under control. Furthermore, the dynamics arising from discussing taking medication can be effectively explored. It is our belief that patients taking psychopharmacological agents can be successfully treated in groups if the therapist is alert to the impact of a member's pharmacotherapy on the group dynamics, transferences, and countertransferences that accompany a multimodal approach.

Rodenhauser (1989) has categorized the positive and negative effects of taking medication for the treated individual and for the group across dimensions of self-control, emotional connectedness, and technical/strategic as-

---

[1]There is controversy regarding the differentiation of state and trait elements of a number of psychiatric disorders, and indeed whether this is a valid distinction at all. The varying clinical responsiveness of certain longstanding depressive syndromes—diagnosed as dysthymia—to antidepressant medications and the exploration of including "depressive personality" as an Axis II diagnosis contributes to the blurring of these elements.

pects. The positive category of self-control includes an increased sense of responsibility, self-confidence, energy, reduction of internal stimuli, and reduction of stigma from disturbing behaviors. On the negative side are disavowal of responsibility, "sick role" reminder, impaired cognition, affect dulling, and stigma from taking medication. The dynamics of increased emotional connectedness include validation of the self, evidence of caring, rapid symptom reduction, and instillation of hope and trust. But these elements can be inverted and produce negative effects, such as loss of personal potency and/or decreased motivation.

Attitudes about medicine may have considerable impact on the group dynamics. In groups containing highly disturbed individuals, there is the potential for emotional contagion in which fears of overidentification with the medicated member evoke self-protective responses, such as withdrawal, scorn, or hostility. Concern about taking drugs may turn to oversolicitousness covering negative attitudes. Regression may occur when members identify with wishes for magical (drug) cure and thereby create a "dependent" group. There may also be subgrouping and splitting into "OK" and "not OK" camps.

The following example illustrates a confluence of individual and group dynamics in which a patient's reluctance to explore the meaning of taking an antianxiety medication parallels the patient's resistance within the group.

CLINICAL EXAMPLE

Quietly, at the end of a session, a patient asked his therapist to refill the medication he took before making presentations at work. The patient's shame in not being able to contain his anxiety emerged in his softly spoken request. The timing of the request effectively prevented immediate discussion of the topic. The patient, who was generally passive and quiet in the group, reenacted his problem of speaking before a crowd by requesting his medication in an unobtrusive fashion. In the following meeting, the members did not mention the medication until it was addressed by the therapist, who noted the possible dynamic meaning of the manner in which the prescription had been requested. At that time a variety of uncomfortable affects emerged around the medicated patient's request, and the members' own attitudes and passivity in exploring the problem, thereby highlighting the group participation in avoiding exploration in this facet of the patient's personality.

* * *

In sum, when considering whether or not a patient should use medication, we return to a point made earlier regarding the place of affect in psychotherapy. The goal in dynamic therapy is to stimulate and encourage as much *useful* affect as possible. When patients experience such high degrees of affect that their day-to-day lives and their therapy are compromised, medication might be considered.

METAPHORS AND TRANSFERENCES

As with any other discussion, patients may use talking about their other treatments as either a reality issue or a metaphor for their experience in the group (Zaslav & Kalb, 1989). Clues to their use of metaphors are apparent in the responses of the others. A preoccupation within the group with problems of medication side effects—namely, sleepiness and fatigue with an antidepressant, or dry mouth as an anticholinergic effect with a variety of medications— may represent anxiety about the power of the therapist (who may not necessarily be a physician) or feelings about the group-as-a-whole. Discussions about medications often become major preoccupations with members with early developmental conflicts as a way of testing the safety of the group atmosphere and, at an unconscious level, the limits of what can be discussed. Similar discussions appear on occasion during boundary changes such as vacations or other interruptions. The meaning of the discussion then becomes linked with the harm that is being done to the members. Conversely, the discussion may contain a covert request for medications to replace the group, and in this way serve as a transitional object.

Discussion of medications may also symbolize patients' hopes about the efficacy of the treatment or of their own selves. It may convey messages about authority and control, which is implied in the term "compliance" (Zaslav & Kalb, 1989).

Clinicians often are hard pressed to maintain their therapeutic stances and may be inclined to prematurely cut short discussions of medications. One indicator of a countertransference would be a comparison of the therapist's reaction to a discussion of medication for a medical illness (such as types of insulin for diabetes) to a discussion of psychotropic medications. In most instances, a therapist would listen for the feelings or the metaphor embedded in the former, but might have a certain dysphoria in response to the latter. Certainly, any illness may be a communication about the therapy, but there often seems to be a differential response to discussions of psychotropic and "medical" drugs. In this instance psychiatrists and nonprescribing clinicians may have different countertransference problems. The physician may feel compelled to attend purely to the content of this "medical" issue and feel unprofessional if he/she interprets process meaning to the discussion. Nonprescribing clinicians may feel ignorant or helpless when their patients discuss medications, and in response they may either feign knowledge they do not in fact have or adopt a position hostile to the taking of medication.

The response of members to an individual's discussing medications may also be a clue to countertransferences. Is the therapist pleased when the others do not respond, thereby suppressing the discussion? Conversely, does encouragement or participation in the discussion of others become annoying? Such reactions on the part of the therapist may provide important information about group-wide affects as well as countertransference.

It behooves all clinicians to be aware of the usual side effects of medications and to appreciate that some comments may be a patient's realistic effort to obtain information about therapeutic impact or side effects of the drug. Nevertheless, clues to other meanings can be obtained from the context in which the discussion arises. When the therapist is not a physician, metaphorical communication is more likely, but the possibility still exists that the patient is seeking information from others in the group who may be taking the same medication either currently or in the past.

Too little attention has been given to the impact of a member or members in a group being on psychotropic medication. As with all other group issues, exploration of the meaning of the medication for the individual(s) and for the group can provide information about ways patients communicate and protect themselves from uncomfortable affects. We have found no salient reason to exclude individuals using medication, if they are group appropriate, except for the therapist's personal preference.

As we addressed in an earlier portion of this chapter, the group therapist must attend to the relationship with any other treating professional. The psychopharmacologist's understanding of the causes of psychopathology differ from ours, and they may make treatment decisions that we view as counterproductive. Often medication changes are implemented without consulting or informing the group therapist. Psychopharmacologists may judge that the group clinician has not recognized the intensity or "seriousness" of a symptom and believe that a medication would be appropriate, useful, and/or necessary. Here, as in all such cases of collaborative treatment, patients need to give explicit permission for their caretakers to communicate. If they choose not to do so, there may be important transference elements that need attention. Some physicians may wish to have more formal arrangements with psychotherapists and spell out their wishes in writing. Meyer and Simon (1999) have published a draft of such a letter that balances the responsibilities of both clinicians. Certainly the practice of combining different types of treatment with group therapy can be valuable for patients, but not without an additional layer of collaborative work. We believe that the benefit for the patient justifies the necessary work. Perhaps the single most important asset of good communication between caretakers is to protect against splitting.

CLINICAL EXAMPLE

Willard was an explosively angry young man who had been fired from his last three jobs because of outbursts toward male bosses. His father had been a physically abusive alcoholic, and Willard had clearly identified with his father's bullying style. His relationship with the male leader of the group was contentious, to say the least. At one point in the treatment Willard's internist prescribed psychotropic medication. Willard reported that the physician had stated that the problem was "clearly biological in origin" and that the doctor had further questioned the effectiveness of group therapy.

The therapist was outraged at this seeming interference into the treatment. However, he controlled the anger, knowing that Willard may not have reported the conversations with his internist fully. He said, "Willard, I hope the medication is useful to you. Since your internist and I are both interested in your well-being, would you give me permission to consult with him so that we can coordinate our work for you?" Willard agreed and signed a release of information form.

When the therapist called the internist, he was surprised to find a quite concerned and caring physician who had been worried that the medication might complicate the psychotherapy. Indeed, he added, "I was in group therapy myself and found it very helpful." He went on to add that Willard had requested the medication and that it was Willard who had suggested he might be dealing with a biological issue.

*   *   *

With this input from the internist, the therapist was able to understand that Willard was using splitting as a defense and was "inviting" the therapist to react to him in a familiar, angry manner.

SUMMARY

Sharing leadership establishes a subgroup (the leadership pair) that requires care and nurturing. In this chapter we have examined a number of situations in which the boundary between an individual clinician treating a group is altered. Potentially this is a growth-producing relationship, but there are significant pitfalls. Combining group therapy with individual treatment or collaborating with a caretaker who operates from an entirely different perspective requires communication between providers and explicit permission from patients to do so. Collaboration is the key to unlocking the benefits of all forms of combined treatment.

We have also examined issues related to leader absences or leadership changes. Various models are examined to explore possible responses to a leader's absences, either short or long term. The more permanent loss of a therapist (when the therapist departs) is an important emotional experience of the therapist and patients alike. Clinicians have to work in a focused manner in order to make the most therapeutic use of these changes.

TWELVE

Expressions of Affect in Group Psychotherapy

Sometimes the heart sees what is invisible to the eye.
—H. JACKSON BROWN, JR.

In this chapter we address a number of ways in which affects are influenced by and expressed in groups. After an overview of affects in groups we will examine (1) contagion of affect, (2) projective mechanisms and scapegoating, (3) nonverbal communication, (4) dreams, (5) the therapist's needs, and (6) the group therapist's affect.

Infant research has demonstrated that from birth human infants sense conscious and unconscious feelings of another person via nonverbal cues (Stern, 1985). The mother (caregiver) who is affectively attuned to the infant provides the necessary emotional environment for the infant. Pine (1985) states, "Language arises against a background of well established ways of shared meaning between mother and child. . . . Before the child has acquired the concept of verbal language, she will interpret and respond to the child's gestures, vocalizations and babblings by attribution of meaning" (p. 33). These experiences are the basis for affective communication. Bowlby (1991) argues that the primary vehicle of therapy is communication. He further states that his research suggests that a primary obstacle to effective communication occurs when an individual's emotional "signaling" as an infant was not responded to properly. The human being appears to seek out relationships that will be emotionally satisfying. Experiences in infancy and childhood in which the other has failed results in defenses against additional trauma and lead to developmental arrests and distortions in relatedness.

T. Shapiro and Emde (1992) state, "A current overall perspective has it that affects are organized and organizing aspects of mental functioning. From an adaptive standpoint, affects need to be viewed in context, taking into account patterns that are biological, social and developmental. From a clinical standpoint, we also need to view affects in context, taking into account current defenses, signal affects, emotional communication with the analyst, and various regulatory influences (pp. x–xi).

Psychotherapists pay considerable attention to how patients expose, activate, or contain affects. Clinicians generally are concerned with repressed or suppressed emotions on one end of a continuum and with volatile, angry, and rageful feelings on the other (Stone, 1990). However, positive emotions such as pleasure, joy, and love are also an important part of psychotherapy. Lane and Schwartz (1987) assert that "much of psychotherapy consists of helping patients to clarify what they are feeling, understand the origins of their feelings, and tolerate their intense emotional states better while minimizing the tendency to exclude these states from conscious awareness" (p. 133).

AN OVERVIEW OF AFFECTS IN GROUPS

Individuals entering a group bring with them their search for emotional contact. They also bring with them their self-protective armor. Their entry into a group is suffused with anxiety, and group development is characterized by efforts to determine which emotions can be safely expressed. Emotions are omnipresent in therapy groups, and the members' experiences of sharing feelings, of universalization, and of acceptance and understanding rather than anticipated rejection and other aversive responses all are an important aspect of the therapy. Group development may be characterized by increased tolerance for affect diversity and expression. In contrast to the caution characteristic of the beginning group, emotional expression in the mature group is more spontaneous and is not prematurely interrupted or derailed by others. Closely tied to group development are member roles, which can also be viewed as behavior that titrates feelings (see Chapter 3).

Group-as-a-whole theories address how members in a group "work together" to manage and contain feelings. Wilfred R. Bion's basic assumptions can be understood as responses to disappointment with the leader (whether or not there has been a "real" disappointment or failure, the disappointment is based on archaic fantasies of the leader as savior). Group focal conflict theory (Whitaker & Lieberman, 1964) formulates the "solution" as a way to covertly satisfy emotional needs without directly addressing conscious or unconscious fear. A great deal of therapeutic work is aimed at removing barriers (resistances or defenses) to member's awareness, tolerance, and/or expression of emotions (S. L. Cohen, 1997).

Cultural elements (see Chapter 4) are also present and influence the expression of emotions. For example, the stereotype of men as suppressing emotions is one instance of such sociocultural influence. Clinicians serve as containers for feelings and provide space for members to experience emotions without premature interference. Properly timed and "dosed" interventions assist members' learning from deeply felt emotional experiences. Indeed, the clinician's effectiveness may be linked to that capacity.

Affective communication is also evident in nonverbal communications, projective mechanisms, and dreams. Nonverbal communications, which often express preconscious or unconscious feelings, provide opportunities for members to learn more about the manner in which they communicate their emotions. Projective mechanisms evoke feelings in others, and they are also modes of communication. Affects are thought to be the least disguised elements in dreams and often are the path by which the dreamer and the other group members can gain access to unexpressed feelings that may be stirring within the setting.

With this brief introduction, we now turn to various aspects of emotions in group psychotherapy.

EMOTIONAL CONTAGION

Anyone working with groups will soon observe the phenomenon of rapid, almost instantaneous spread of emotions. If one member becomes sad or angry, others will likely begin to experience the same affect. It is as if a wildfire has spread through the group. Certainly this dynamic contributed to Gustav LeBon's concern with the loss of individuality and responsibility that affects individuals when in a group, and in part he attributed this process to emotional contagion that sweeps through a crowd or a group (see Chapter 2).

Emotional contagion is not only a mechanism by which affect spreads through a group; it is also a way of communicating. (For example, it is against the law to falsely shout "Fire!" in a theater, since the ensuing panic can be disastrous; fear becomes amplified as patrons in the crowded theater almost instantly share in the feeling of panic.) The precise dynamic enabling the wildfire spread of affective states in emotional contagion is unknown. According to Freud (1921), "There is no doubt that something exists in us which, when we become aware of signs of an emotion in someone else, tends to make us fall into the same emotion; but how often do we not successfully oppose it, resist the emotion, and react in quite an opposite way" (p. 89). Freud posited suggestibility as the basis for contagion but considered this phenomenon as "an irreducible, primitive phenomenon, a fundamental fact in the mental life of man" (p. 89). Infant research lends support to Freud's hypothesis, as observations have demonstrated that the newborn infant is exquisitely responsive to emotional communication (Stern, 1985). It appears that these responses are genetically predetermined and are evidence of subcortical rather than cortical functions.

Emotional contagion can lead to scapegoating or so-called manic behavior. In the latter circumstance affective shifts are sudden and intense.

CLINICAL EXAMPLES

In a mature group, members tentatively began to explore sexual attractions that had been present for some time but had previously been too frightening to approach. Serena, an ex-nun, had remained silent. Suddenly Alex turned to her and asked if she had sexual feelings. She quietly shook her head. The members quickly began criticizing Serena as disapproving and critical. There was a sense of excitement in this attack. The group ignored Serena's prior recounting of her relationship that had ended with the death of her lover in a car accident.

The members responded to a therapist's announcement of a forthcoming vacation with an initial sense of loss and dread. The mood shifted dramatically to one of excitement and pleasure following the suggestion that the members get together for a picnic during the doctor's absence. The detailed planning of food, games, and whom to include in the outing took up much of the meeting. The therapist's efforts at examining the meaning of the discussion fell upon deaf ears, as the patients enthusiastically pursued their planning.

*   *   *

These examples highlight how emotion can suddenly spread throughout a group.

Although patients with developmental arrests are more prone to such responses, all individuals are susceptible to the forces of contagion. Yalom (1985) has observed that some individuals reject membership in a group because they fear that they will be affected by the illness of others. Some patients prematurely terminate from their group as a result of intensely affective meetings and their fear of overstimulation.

Therapists are not immune to the communication of affects. Indeed, countertransferences generally are the consequence of affect communication. In the classic conceptualization, countertransference is described as the therapist acting on feelings from the past that are reactivated by the patient in the present. A simple and commonplace illustration of the potency of affect communication is the therapist's experience of smiling or laughing during a group interaction and later realizing that he/she would probably not have had such a response if the same type of exchange had occurred in a dyadic setting.

SCAPEGOATING

The term "scapegoat" comes from the biblical story of Aaron confessing all the sins of the children of Israel over the head of a goat, which was then sent into the wilderness symbolically bearing those sins (Leviticus 16: 5–10). Thus, the origin of the term indicates the function—to protect the tribe, family, or group. Allport (1965) hypothesized that prejudice, at root, is societal scapegoating to provide a sense of solidarity among the majority. In group therapy scapegoating refers to the focusing of hostile, sadistic, and hurtful attention on one particular individual. Scapegoating serves a symbolic value similar to that in the biblical story; that is, an individual is scapegoated in order to protect the group. Toker (1972) has suggested that "the scapegoat is frequently essential for the adequate functioning of a group (whatever the nature of the group) in that he provides an area into which aggressions can be channeled and focused without presenting a threat to the psychic integrity of the individual or a threat to the stability and unity of the group itself" (p. 232). Bion (1960) also noted that fight–flight groups are prepared to sacrifice individual members in order to protect the group. Scapegoating encompasses intrapsychic, interpersonal, and group-as-a-whole mechanisms (Scheidlinger, 1982a).

Therapists must be able to distinguish between scapegoating and strong confrontations. Most confrontations are not manifestations of scapegoating. Some of the most important growth experiences are forged in strong, painful, and difficult interactions between members. Groups offer unique opportunities for receiving feedback about the less desirable aspects of one's personality. The key is to determine if the challenged patient is being hurt rather than helped and if the motivation of the confrontation is to inflict pain rather than to provide information. Since scapegoats often "volunteer" for that job, there is often a countertransference feeling in the therapist that the scapegoat "deserves" the attack. Scapegoating, if left unanalyzed, can be hurtful to the individual and the group.

Central to understanding scapegoating is the concept of *projective identification* (Fairbairn, 1952b; Guntrip, 1969; M. Klein, 1946). Projective identification is both an act of communication and a defensive maneuver in which individuals project onto others those traits or aspects of self-representations, and their associated affects, that are unacceptable as one's own. At the same time they retain a connection with the other through identification. Implicit in this process is the notion that the projector no longer has full access to the feelings as his/her own. Both a splitting of good and bad selfobject representations and a blurring of ego boundaries are consistent with the developmental level or the regressive state of the projector. The notion of projective identification has been used by some authors (Grotstein, 1981) to include the projection of object representations (and superego), which does not involve blurring of boundaries and is a more mature defense utilized by higher-functioning individuals. The regressive interpersonal and intrapsychic pressures of joining and belonging to a group account for the splitting and projection that take place for these latter patients (Scheidlinger, 1974).

The projection is not random but, rather, is directed to a willing recipient, an individual who in some substantial way demonstrates a willingness to accept the unacceptable qualities. The projector, in attempting to "change" the other, also maintains contact with the hated and dreaded parts of the self, which require continued projection. This ongoing involvement with the other is the essential clue to the process of projective identification (Guntrip, 1969). Thus, projective identification refers to a two-party phenomenon that involves both projection and an acceptance of the projected traits and therefore represents both intrapsychic and interpersonal processes.

CLINICAL EXAMPLE

In the process of working through a therapist's departure from the group at the end of training, the members expressed considerable sorrow but not anger. Jane, who had always been outspoken, created a scene at one of the hospital clinics, which included a shouting match between herself and a technician and ended with Jane's bursting into tears. Following the incident, she was called by a representative of the hospital patient relations unit in an attempt to mollify her. Jane angrily reported the entire event to the group, having erroneously interpreted the phone call as a threat that she would be banished from the hospital. Jane's tirade went on for some time. The members remained silent, waiting for the therapist to respond. It appeared that Jane had become the carrier of the group anger, even in the displacement. The underlying fears of retaliation for expression of their anger was apparent in Jane's tears. In this instance, Jane could have served as a potential scapegoat if the therapist had not understood the displacement and the members' anxieties. Jane could have been chastised as the "angry one."

*   *   *

At times members may use "the group" as the object of projective identification. The group becomes reified in the minds of the individuals and is experienced as a destructive force (Nitsun, 1996). In such circumstances the result may be emotional flight or termination from the group.

CLINICAL EXAMPLE

A woman referred by a private practitioner to a public clinic group soon began to complain about the ambience of the room. The identical seats felt like an institution—cold and uninviting. The blackboard made it seem like a schoolroom, rather than a warm group setting compatible to work. She was joined in her complaints by another member, who had been in the group for several years but who had not previously commented on the atmosphere of the group, which was so different than the group she had attended in another city. The therapist's and members' efforts to address these feelings as a response to the change, a displacement from the therapist, or feelings stimulated in the interactions were discounted, and the ambience of the room became a recurrent focus at times of apparent stress, which only slowly faded but was not "worked through."

*   *   *

Pure projection should be differentiated from projective identification. In pure projection the subject takes an unacceptable quality and disowns it by attributing it to another person. Simple projection is a one-person system in which the other person is an unknowing and unwilling party to the projections. An example of projection occurred when Sally, a member of the therapy group discussed in the previous clinical example, recognized that Jane was angry but chose not to comment. Later Sally said that she thought Jane would be disorganized by her anger just as she (Sally) was when she became angry. Sally was projecting onto Jane her belief that anger leads to disorganization.

Scapegoating may at times feel like pure projection, since it often appears that the scapegoat is an unwilling victim. However, closer examination will indicate that scapegoats indeed play a part in their fates. In fact, as Jane's behavior illustrates, they "volunteer" for the role by engaging in behaviors that draw the group's fury, thereby setting in motion familiar patterns. Scapegoats often played similar roles in their original families.

Therapists are not immune to becoming the objects of projective identification and scapegoats. Levine (1979) suggests that group therapists are particularly subject to scapegoating when they defensively refuse to understand the members' attempts to wrest power and control. More often, therapists are not scapegoats per se but, rather, containers for negative transferences (Tuttman, 1994). Patients usually are the targets of scapegoating.

Garland and Kolodny (1973) suggest four fundamental forms of scapegoating in groups: (1) ostracism, (2) institutionalization, (3) encapsulation, and (4) inclusion through introspection.

Ostracism is the most immediately malevolent form of scapegoating, since it often results in the scapegoat leaving the group. In ostracism the scapegoat is placed in an accustomed role as the "different" one, the "troublesome" one, the "group buffoon," and so on. This is commonly the experience of border-line individuals, who demonstrate object hunger, neediness, and difficulty in sharing. The recognition of these universal wishes are defended against by higher-functioning individuals, whose defenses against these unacceptable feelings are threatened by the borderline patient. (The scapegoat role and the divergent role have considerable overlap; see Chapter 3). As a consequence, the others attempt to rid themselves of these affects and drives by projecting them onto the scapegoat. The result is that the scapegoat not only feels the wishes more intensely but also feels more isolated. Under such circumstances the scapegoat may have the feeling of being in an all-too-familiar position and may drop out.

The *institutionalized* scapegoat is one who is so firmly entrenched in the role that neither the patient nor the group can gain any objectivity on how that role is serving a groupwide function.

The *encapsulated* scapegoat is allowed only limited participation in the group. An example of this is the member who becomes tearful and very emotional in the first group meeting. Group members generally are not prepared to tolerate or explore intense feelings so quickly, and they find ways of isolating the tearful person in order to contain their own affects. The members act as if the "offending" member should be punished.

The fourth form of scapegoating consists of involving the scapegoat in active, intrusive *introspection,* a hostile dedication to finding out what makes a particular member "tick." In the case of the aforementioned tearful member, others may grill the individual, inquiring, "What is wrong? Why are you so upset? Why can't you manage things differently?" Such questioning further isolates the scapegoat.

The analysis of scapegoating entails helping the entire group understand that the scapegoat role is unconsciously crucial to the emotional survival of the group. One of the characteristics of scapegoating is emotional contagion (Stone, 1990). Affects are no longer used as signals but are stimuli to action or other defensive responses (Krystal, 1974). Since the scapegoated individual often suffers great pain, it is advisable for the therapist to proceed as quickly as possible in understanding the function of the scapegoating and its role in protecting the group.

Scapegoating is a difficult problem for therapists. It represents a group-as-a-whole process. If the therapist moves to protect the scapegoated patient, the other members of the group may perceive this as favoritism or interference with their justified criticism, thus making the plight of the scapegoat even worse.

The therapist, understanding the projective processes, attempts to help the attacking members look at their own insecurities, which are triggered by the visage or behavior of the scapegoat. The scapegoat is often a singleton. When one or more others are found who have similar feelings, a subgroup is formed which protects the "isolated individual" (Agazarian, 1997). It is useful to recall that the role of deviant member is a relatively short step from the scapegoat role. Eventually, by helping the attackers realize that it is not the behavior of the scapegoat that is so troubling but their own feelings aroused by the scapegoat, the therapist is often able to help members modify their behavior. Scapegoating ends when the members own their projections and more clearly see their feelings in the scapegoat. Sometimes a comment by the therapist such as "The group is making John work very hard tonight" or "John seems to be voicing a difficult feeling that others may feel" can begin the process of stopping the scapegoat phenomenon.

While projective identification is involved in the scapegoating phenomenon, it is by no means found *only* in scapegoating. Later in this chapter we will discuss projective identification in more depth.

NONVERBAL COMMUNICATION

A great deal of highly significant emotional communication takes place nonverbally. Some is conscious and obvious, and some is unconscious and subtle. Nonverbal communication is not exclusively emotional. "Gestures may instruct, ask questions, or answer them: a finger pointing up or down, a nod of assent—or, for that matter the whole matter of signing" (Knapp, 1992, p. 242) Every therapist is familiar with the communication of the depressed individual who enters the therapy room very slowly, with head down and eyes averted, sits slouched in a chair, and remains silent. Facial expressions demonstrate basic emotions, including fear, anger, sadness, and pleasure. Silence itself can be experienced by others as control and power as well as more commonly as an expression of anxiety or fear. The manner of speaking, the rate, intonation, and prosody—the metrical structure—all convey important affective meanings. Other seemingly ordinary behaviors, such as crossing the legs, nodding the head, or selecting a particular seat in the group circle, have both conscious and unconscious determinants.

Birdwhistle (1970) demonstrated that body motion is a powerful cultural tool for communication. Through nonverbal channels individuals find out who they are relative to others. They make contacts and convey and receive messages through these channels. Signals are given that regulate the flow of information and the intensity of affects. Berger (1969), in discussing nonverbal communications, noted that they function in "the establishment, maintenance, and regulation of interpersonal relationships" (p. 30). We now examine two important modes of nonverbal communication in group psychotherapy—seating arrangements and body language—and then consider the therapeutic use of the data they generate.

Seating Arrangement

There are no stereotypical meanings to seat selection. The label "therapist's helper" is often signaled by a member's selection of the seat immediately to the therapist's right (the "right-hand man—or woman"), but that seat may also be selected by a patient attempting to avoid eye contact with the therapist or a patient needing to be in physical proximity to the therapist. A member in conflict with the therapist might select a seat directly opposite him, but the same seat might be selected by a patient desiring to get the best possible view of the therapist. A rebellious or competitive member might sit in a chair that members have accepted as belonging to the therapist. What is important is for the members to become curious about the particular meaning that might underlie the choice of particular seats. Understanding the nonverbal communications is facilitated by the therapist's sitting in the same chair each session. If the therapist sits in a different chair each week it becomes more difficult to ascertain the meaning of seating patterns relative to him/her. The members choose seats for conscious and unconscious reasons, and many choices are made primarily in relation to the therapist.

Members also indicate their feelings about one another in their seating choices. Sexual attraction may be communicated by "couples" sitting beside each other each week. Groups working on male–female competition may arrange themselves with the men on one side of the circle and the women on the other. Unspoken racial issues are frequently expressed when black and white patients sit on opposite sides of the circle.

The chairs themselves can be utilized in nonverbal communication. Members sometimes move their chairs subtly (or not so subtly) outside the circle when they are frightened, anxious, or angry. Conversely, members will move their chairs slightly forward when they desire attention or experience closeness.

There seems to be no diagnostic predictive value in how rigidly members remain in the same seats week after week. Rather, this seems to be a function of group norms and personal character style. Some groups have a norm that each chair is designated for a specific group member, whereas other groups change chairs regularly. These differences in style do not correlate with pathology.

Body Language

There is no doubt that body language communicates a great deal about affective experience. Blushing, sweating, knuckles whitening on a chair—all are clear messages of physiological and physical responses to affect. Because our culture places considerable emphasis on eye contact, persons who do not maintain eye contact while talking are often evidencing the presence of considerable affect. Head nodding not only signals agreement but also encourages the other person to continue.

In some instances body language communicates something quite different from the conscious experience or feeling of the individual. A member may complain that another has taken up too much time only to be confronted by the observation that he/she had been nodding in agreement all the while the monopolizer had been talking.

Scheflen (1964) examined nonverbal communication via careful study of videotapes. He found that body positions may be open or closed to include or exclude others. He also pointed out that body language itself can convey mixed messages, as when the upper body is open (arms at sides) and the lower body is closed (legs crossed). Scheflen further described how subtle head nods or body shifts signal a wish to end a conversation.

In another study Scheflen (1965) observed unconscious communication of quasi-courting behavior in psychotherapy sessions. He noted preening behaviors, such as hair stroking, rearranging clothes, or adjusting makeup, as standard courting behaviors in women; other characteristic body motions include prolonging a gaze, exposing a thigh, placing a hand on a hip, or protruding a breast. Men may adjust their ties, pull up their socks, or smooth their hair. Scheflen states that in most cases disqualifiers, such as not completing the messages or verbally noting that others are present, accompany such courting behaviors in groups. The timing and patterns of such behaviors are valuable data in understanding the groupwide or individual conflicts. If messages are given in an ambiguous fashion or out of the initiator's awareness, the potential for interpersonal difficulty is considerable.

Therapeutic Management
of Nonverbal Communication

Upon observing emotionally important nonverbal communication, the therapist faces several conceptual and technical choices. First, the therapist should try, if possible, to link the observation to the here-and-now transactions in the group. Second, the therapist needs to remember that most nonverbal communications are unconscious and must be treated respectfully. If too abrupt or direct a confrontation is made, the confronted individual may react with denial, upset, anger, embarrassment, or hurt. This response is related not only to the content of the material but also to the therapist's having observed and made public that which was out of the patient's awareness and control. Such a move by the therapist is often experienced as a narcissistic injury, may generate iatrogenic resistance, and does little to advance the work of the group. However, tactful identification of nonverbal behavior in the context of a positive therapeutic alliance can bring into focus certain identifiable personality traits.

CLINICAL EXAMPLE

During one meeting, a woman explained that she had been much more open with her friends recently, a change she attributed to things she had learned in group therapy. One friend had told her that she often led with her chin, which was a gentle way of telling her about her aggressive communicative style. The patient told of this encounter with pleasure and warmth, indicating considerable growth from her prior habitual defensive and provocative style. Later in the session she began to confront one of the other members, while simultaneously fiddling with her sweater and pulling it over her chin. When the therapist pointed out that she was covering her chin, she laughed and was able to explore her inner sense that she was acting very aggressively and was expecting retaliation. The nonverbal behavior had communicated her anxiety.

*   *   *

Therapists also communicate a great deal nonverbally. For example, they are not immune to affect contagion and can smile, laugh, or cry in response to spread of emotion through the group. Clinicians also reveal their feelings through their facial expressions or body movements, often unknowingly.

CLINICAL EXAMPLE

When Ariel terminated her successful therapy, the therapist was well aware that he would miss her. She had grown from a rather withdrawn, silent person to a genuine leader in the group. Moreover, she had entered into a second marriage that seemed solid and satisfying. In her workplace she had formed several close friendships, which was a marked change from her isolate position when she had entered the group.

Two years later when another long-term member was saying his goodbye and the members were mourning in anticipation of his loss, the theme of favoritism arose. At that point a member turned to the therapist and commented, "You really had a reaction when Ariel left. She was your favorite—it showed on your face; you really looked sad." The therapist was well aware of his response when Ariel had left, but he had not realized that it was so evident.

*   *   *

As patients gain experience with the examination of nonverbal clues, they will imitate and identify with the therapist, widening the scope of the group analytic process. It is not unusual in a group that has been functioning for a number of months for patients to comment to one another about a facial expression, a clenched fist, the tapping of feet or fingers, or a look in someone's eye. They also learn to recognize that shifts in body position are important communications. Even when the behaviors are conscious gestures, members may not appreciate the force of their message and the extent of the underlying feelings until the behaviors are pointed out.

DREAMS IN GROUP PSYCHOTHERAPY

Freud was not the first to consider dreams as important communications. The Talmud states, "A dream that has not been interpreted is like a letter that has not been opened." Freud's genius was that he was the first to interpret dreams rigorously, scientifically, and systematically. As with much of his work on unconscious material, Freud gained a foothold in working with dreams by postulating that they are a valid psychic communication that can be understood. His major contributions were developing a way of understanding the covert meaning from the manifest content and recognizing that dreams often represent wish fulfillment. Dreams, therefore, became a valuable window into the unconscious of Freud's analytic patients. Group therapists, following this lead, expanded the intrapsychic focus to include interpersonal and group-as-a-whole processes. Just as Freud began with the hypothesis that dreams depict something about the analytic situation, group therapists begin with the hypothesis that dreams reported in group sessions often depict something about the group itself.

Any groupwide conflict or shared anxiety may be vividly portrayed in the manifest dream or exposed through the members' associations (Klein-Lipschutz, 1953; Whitman, 1973). Dreams may also illustrate aspects of group development (Kieffer, 1996). Problems of joining and trust may be themes of dreams graphically presented in the first stage of group formation, whereas rebellion, power, and autonomy may be portrayed at later stages (Battegay, 1977). Some conflicts may have been dimly recognized or consciously avoided only to reappear directly or thinly disguised in the manifest dream content (Edwards, 1977; A. Wolf & Schwartz, 1962). Transferences or attitudes toward the therapist also may be brought to light via dreams. Conversely, the dreamer may be informing the therapist about a countertransference affecting the whole group. Dreams also convey valuable information about the relationships among members; there are often direct references to the group or to specific members (although not necessarily those with whom there is conflict).

It is also true that dreams reported in groups can provide access to an individual member's resistances, wishes, transferences, and conflicts. The dreamer is presenting specific aspects of his/her self. In this respect the dream is a "gift" revealing personal, historical, fantasy, or relational information about the dreamer (Neri, 1998). In examining a dream the individual, interpersonal, and whole-group elements should all be taken into account.

Clinical Examples

The New Member

A chronically depressed man, in the middle of a lengthy and painful divorce, entered an ongoing therapy group in order to learn more about himself and his troubled relationships with women. The night following his first group session, he dreamed that he was in line waiting to be seated in a restaurant. As he was waiting, a group of people pushed by him and were seated by the maître d'. He turned around and left the restaurant, reversing a sign on the front door to indicate the restaurant was closed.

*   *   *

Here, from the perspective of group development, the oral imagery of the restaurant is consistent with the dreamer's position as a new member and reflects one of the emotional themes of initial participation in the group: "Will I get enough?" Such imagery is typical of early group participation and does not automatically indicate major personal conflicts at an oral dependent level of development.

From the group-as-a-whole perspective, the dream represents the newcomer's perception that the old members are favored by the therapist, as depicted by the maître d'. The dream indicates the newcomer's concern that he will not be able to join the group fully. From the interpersonal perspective, the dream reveals a chronic defensive pattern—withdrawal and retaliation—that this patient invoked to manage rejection and pain. Finally, from the intrapsychic perspective, there are suggestions of a transference to the therapist and of ego distortions, which are represented in the maladaptive manner in which an ambivalence about being nurtured and dependent is handled.

Sequential Dreams

A woman entered a group in which continuing and vociferous conflict among several members dominated her first meeting. At her second meeting she reported a fragment from a dream she had the night of the first meeting: "I was driving a truck. Instead of going forward, it went backward into a very tight place."

The old members quickly recognized the dream's group-level meaning: the new member had felt stymied by the group conflict, unable to move forward on her own issues and backed into a corner. The therapist wondered whether the heated conflicts had been exaggerated in order to frighten off the new member, and he was concerned that perhaps he had brought in the member at an inopportune time.

In her third meeting the woman presented two additional dream fragments from the intervening week: "I was in a crowd of friendly people, and all of a sudden I gave birth to a baby!" She immediately associated to the group and to her new perception that the group seemed much friendlier in her second meeting. She said, "The baby is me. The group is a new beginning?" She then moved to her next dream, beginning, "Now for the one in which I die!" She dreamed that she was in a group of people, some of whom she recognized from work. Suddenly a man got up and shot her in the head. She associated to a man she had felt angry with and said that this dream had nothing to do with the group. Later in the session, however, she added an omitted detail: in the dream, immediately before she had been shot, one of the bystanders had said, "It's what you deserve!" This was the same phrase she herself had used earlier in the meeting. The repetition of the phrase helped her overcome an initial resistance to connecting the dreams to the feelings evoked in the treatment and helped her recognize her fears in the here-and-now group interaction.

* * *

This woman's dreams, reported in two successive meetings, illustrate a common pattern for new members: at first she felt somewhat overwhelmed by the group; when she felt safer, she could conceive of attaining her wishes, and only then could she expose her underlying fear of being attacked and wounded by one of the veteran members.

Related Dreams

Often various members of a group will have dreams that, when taken together, provide important information about a common group stress. Related dreams reflect members' responses to a common theme or tension and usually are presented in an atmosphere in which dreams and their understanding have become valued by the members.

A woman reported a recent dream: "I was looking for the therapist at his university office, but he was busy with other students and did not have time for me." She reported feeling "stunned and devastated." In the associations that followed, a man reported a recent dream: "I was taking a test in mathematics and an English professor, who was trying to help me, suddenly disappeared and was unavailable." Then he spontaneously remembered a recurrent dream from his early childhood: "I was riding in a streetcar and my mother was waiting for me at the end of the line. Just as I arrived she flew off and someone said she was a witch." Finally, a second woman reported a dream, which she termed a nightmare: "My daughter was inhabited by the devil, and I was trying to exorcise it but I couldn't do it." She awoke in a highly anxious and frightened state.

*   *   *

This fascinating sequence of dreams was reported in the first meeting following a series of canceled sessions due to the therapist's absence. It illustrates the interconnectedness of dreams by different members, each portraying the dreamer's response to the common stimulus of the therapist's absence and the canceled sessions. The representation of the unavailable therapist as a too-busy professor in the first dream is echoed in the second as a disappearing professor and in the third as the disappearing mother/witch. The last reference reminded the second woman of her dream involving exorcism, and it was through that association that she could begin to identify herself with the child who needed the devil removed.

The dream content also shows the reverberating theme of the therapist's other interests taking precedence over his interest in the members: one member's dream portrays the therapist as too busy with others; another's dream depicts the therapist as not qualified to teach a course (an English professor in a mathematics course) as well as being unavailable; and the third dream portrays the therapist as a mother who turns into a witch.

A Group Resistance

Many times, dreams reported in groups represent information about resistance to the group treatment.

A woman reported a dream "about the group": "I was in some sort of bus. Every time the bus came to a dangerous area, we would skirt it or avoid it. This occurred several times in the dream. I thought the bus had passed my stop, but a man who was a cooking expert and teacher got on the bus, and it seemed to head back to the right destination."

*   *   *

The dreamer initially spoke of how she habitually avoided all conflict, often by not knowing what she felt. But she implied others had joined her, since she directly identified the dream as being about the group. Her interpretation of the dream was that the "cooking expert" was the group therapist. Analysis of the dream elements by the group highlighted and confirmed the manifest content that the bus was in fact controlled by the passengers, and the teacher was not the driver. Through this the members were able to begin to acknowledge how they had all been contributing to the avoidance of the "dangerous" sexual feelings in the room.

The Grave Digger

Despite the emphasis on group process, it should be remembered that dreams are also communications about the inner states of individuals.

A longtime group member had spent most of his therapy minimizing the impact of his self-righteous intellectualizing on others. His interpersonal life was characterized by a great deal of acrimonious arguing, which his group interactions paralleled. During one session in which the therapist again pointed out to this man that members were trying to tell him how painful they felt his comments to be, he suddenly reported a dream: "I was digging around uncovering corpses. They were all in brown bags so that you didn't smell them or see them, but it was still pretty disgusting. I came across one corpse, and for no apparent reason I just cut off its head." He reported awakening both shaken and disgusted.

*   *   *

Here, the patient's understanding was that the head belonged to a particularly obnoxious, pompous, self-righteous colleague. The therapist, after eliciting the associations of others, suggested that this dream might represent the patient's efforts to get rid of a particularly distasteful part of himself. He immediately agreed, saying that as he was reporting the dream he realized that he was talking about how the group must perceive him and how he always anticipated criticism as he spoke. His dream clearly conveyed this patient's dawning awareness of something wrong within himself as well as with the interpersonal impact he made.

Techniques of Dream Interpretation in Group Therapy

Some groups avidly report and analyze dreams, whereas other groups seem never to relate dream material. More often that not, this is a function of the therapist's interest in dreams. Group therapists can dramatically affect the reporting and analyzing of dreams simply by showing interest. Ignoring dreams results in extinguishing their presentations.

Freud understood dreams to be a coded representation of important affect or inner conflict. To the degree that dreams reflect important unconscious material they are always coded. Thus, the manifest meaning of the dream is not the most significant meaning. Indeed, the most obvious parts of dreams are quite often distractions from more unsettling material. The classic tool for breaking the dream code is free association. Ideally, it becomes a group norm for all members to associate to a dream, since the collective associations may constitute a multidimensional report on the state of the group as well as of the individuals within it. Thus, the therapist should subtly discourage members from trying to understand or interpret the dream of a colleague and should, instead, encourage them to associate to it as if it had been their own. As illustrated in the foregoing examples, some of the associations may be other dreams or even interpretations of them. While the interpretations may be either accurate or inaccurate, they represent data about the contributor's personal conflicts. The therapist should not rush to make an interpretation but should, instead, wait to elicit associations from the dreamer and from the other members.

Since feelings are usually the least disguised elements of dreams, the therapist helps the members learn to explore the affect in dreams. Members frequently assist one another in overcoming resistance to full exploration of dreams by sharing openly their own feeling responses.

Usually the affects can be linked to shared feelings, and in this manner the therapeutic value of the dream is enhanced.

We do not recommend a rote practice of asking each member to respond to a dream. Rather, the flow of group associations helps clarify the dream's unconscious components. Thus, abrupt changes in topic that may appear to avoid material are usually an associative path that further elaborates or clarifies the latent meanings in the dream.

CLINICAL EXAMPLE

As a group was busily discussing their feelings about one another and about group interactions, one woman protested that she had not felt what others had been feeling. She angrily said that she experienced the therapist as pressuring the members to express feelings and that she was unable to do so. She then reported a dream which she presented as an afterthought and which to her had no obvious connection to the conversation that had gone before: "I dreamed there was an old black lady working on a man's head. I was behind a screen and couldn't see very well. Someone asked me to move something to the other side of the screen, but I wasn't able to do it." The dreamer immediately associated the black lady in the dream to the group therapist (a white male), "who works on heads." Then she felt confused and said, "I can't see what this dream is about, and most of the time I can't see what this group is about."

The associative process seemed to abruptly shift as a man began to talk to the dreamer about their accidental meeting outside the group sessions. He said that he was frightened by her, since she had seemed seductive at that meeting and thereafter. A raging argument ensued regarding who was trying to seduce whom. As the discussion continued and the feelings subsided, the therapist asked about the man's initial comment that he was frightened. The woman was startled and then acknowledged that she had never heard him say he was afraid, saying, "I didn't know he was afraid. I just knew I was afraid and had to protect myself by attacking him."

*   *   *

This particular dream, reported during a discussion of the member's difficulty in feeling connected to the group, provides an initial lead to its possible meanings. "Associations" often precede the report of a dream. The ensuing process added more data to a growing awareness on the part of the dreamer that she could not hear others' anxieties and fears. And her associations revealed much more. For example, the dreamer identified the therapist as a black woman, but other data suggest that the patient herself was also represented by the black woman. She worked on the man's head with her seductiveness, but she did not know what she was doing because she could not see. On the basis of data from prior group meetings, the following interpretation is likely. Although this patient controlled others (mainly men) through seductiveness, she was unable to recognize others' anxious responses, and when confronted about her blindness she reacted with anger and started a fight. Further analysis of the dream might also have produced results for the male patient, since he exhibited similar characteristics, having demonstrated seductive behavior when he felt insecure about himself in previous sessions.

Dreams can serve a great many needs and might contain important dependent, competitive, exhibitionistic, or narcissistic wishes on the part of the dreamer. Other members might respond to a dream by ignoring it and the dreamer or by presenting dreams in a competitive fashion. A plethora of dreams can be presented in order to avoid or resist other, more powerful feelings. This is often the case when the therapist finds that the group is flooded with dream material and great blocks of time are devoted to hearing and analyzing dreams. Dreams are so filled with potential meaning that therapists have the difficult job of deciding how much time can profitably be spent analyzing dreams without losing sight of the ongoing in-group process.

THE THERAPIST'S NEEDS

Clinicians enter the field with their own ambitions and ideals. Part of their education and training imbues them with a sense of professionalism and adds to their sense of themselves as individuals and their well-being. Friedman (1988) suggests that there are three needs in the therapist that are activated in every treatment and must be balanced by the him/her. According to Friedman, understanding the following needs, which are separate from the more traditional concept of countertransference, serves to sustain the clinician in the face of difficult therapuetic challenges:

1. *To act like a therapist.* Therapists need to hear the material from patients in the context of their treatment plan. For example, if patients only tell outside stories, this might frustrate the clinician's treatment plan to use data provided by the in-group transactions. Or, if patients do not relate dreams, some therapists may be frustrated that part of his/her skill is not being used.

2. *To satisfy curiosity.* Therapists are trained to be curious. They wonder about the members' internal worlds, their interactions, and their impact on the group forces. When groups seem stuck or members seldom have different or new associations, curiosity may be squashed and the process becomes routine and stultifying. Clinicians may inadvertently contribute to the suppression of their own curiosity by asking questions in routine fashion, like "What is everyone feeling?" or "Do others have thoughts about what Joe said?"

Curiosity may be limited to satisfying the therapist's theory; perhaps how material fits with his/her notion of psychogenesis. Friedman (1988) asserts, "But genuine curiosity is not as common as we like to think. One reason that genuine curiosity is so scarce is that it may conflict with the first decision-principle, which is to act like a therapist" (p. 105).

3. *To elicit something desirable.* In contrast to the first two balance problems, which are intellectually stimulating, this problem emphasizes the therapist's "urge to ignite a satisfying interaction with the patient" (Friedman, 1988, p. 108). This is an unconscious search for a relationship with the patient that is essentially an emotional interchange.

Patients are labeled difficult, in part, because of the repetitious way they engage and because "nothing seems to happen" in their treatment. A member expressed her feelings about a difficult absent member in the following manner: "He talks to the air." This woman's wish for some personal contact with the difficult patient was frustrated, and similar feelings are activated in the therapist. Meaningful interactions are limited by such patients' pathologies, and as the transactions with these patients become repetitious and stereotyped, the clinician's curiosity decreases and little is available to help him/her feel like a therapist.

A common experience for clinicians is to find themselves having difficulty following the group process as members seem to be talking about seemingly unrelated topics or overtly ignoring one another. A member may introduce a topic that suddenly "clicks," inciting curiosity and fitting with treatment goals. At that point the therapist likely regains a sense of engagement and becomes energized in organizing prior discussion into a coherent framework or internally tries out various interventions that may be used to further the treatment. In concert with Friedman, we see this as fulfillment of therapists' needs and potent contributors to the therapeutic atmosphere.

Illustrative of some of these elements motivating the therapist is the experience many clinicians have when presenting their process notes in supervision. When a supervisor clarifies a particular dynamic and the therapist has a solid grasp of the process, he/she is delighted to understand subsequent process, without any additional input from the supervisor. The material now makes sense, curiosity is satisfied, and even as the therapist might be reviewing written process notes, he/she has a sense of connection to the patients and the process.

Appreciation of our general motivations as therapists, as presented by Friedman, helps us maintain our balance and work with difficult individuals and the associated distortions produced in the group.

THE GROUP THERAPIST'S AFFECT

The emotional responses of the therapist are valuable, if not fundamental, elements in the conduct of psychodynamic therapy. Clinicians' feelings offer very important clues to what is happening in a therapy group. Freud (1910, 1915) recognized that patients, with their intense transferences, evoked unconscious responses in the therapist. Classically these inner reactions have been labeled "countertransference." This narrow definition brought precision but overlooked the obvious reality that therapists are filled with affect while sitting with patients. Under Freud's traditional formulation, therapists were often left feeling that their affective responses represented something harmful in the therapy.

More recently, the concept of countertransference has been expanded to include all the therapist's emotional reactions, both conscious and unconscious, which are evoked by the patient (Roth, 1980). The broader modern definition frees therapists to use their inner responses in the service of understanding. It also places the therapist under the mandate to carefully assess personal feelings for traces of traditional Freudian countertransference.

There are multiple sources for therapist affect. What is most productive in the therapy are those feelings in the therapist which are evoked by the patient. We suggest using the criteria presented in Figure 12.1 in order to assess

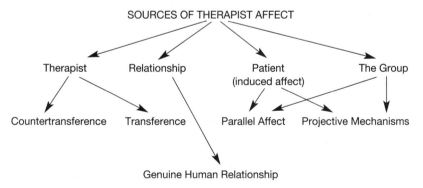

FIGURE 12.1. Criteria for assessing sources of therapist affect.

the sources of the affects that therapists experience. We believe that the modern definition of countertransference provides the clinician with the broadest therapeutic value of his/her affect. However, we are careful not to neglect the classical formulation, and see the two as complementary.

As Figure 12.1 shows, there are four potential sources of therapist affect: (1) the therapist, (2) the relationship between the therapist and a group member, (3) the patient, and (4) responses to the group-as-a-whole. As with the leadership dimensions presented earlier (see Chapter 9), these distinctions are heuristic. In fact, human relationships are far too complex to be so neatly compartmentalized. However, it is helpful to conceptualize the sources of therapist affect in this manner in order to assist therapists in gaining the most information from those feelings.

Sources of Therapist Affect

The Therapist

The goal of therapy is to facilitate the exploration of the patient's inner life. When we are filled with feelings, stirred by our own history and countertransference feelings, the therapy is not facilitated; indeed, our ability to understand and hear our patients is almost always clouded.

If therapists find themselves preoccupied with powerful feelings, including love, hate, or envy, because a patient is reminiscent of an important and ambivalently held figure from their past, it is their responsibility to work through that feeling. In extreme cases this would be cause for reentering therapy or even referring the patient to another therapist.

All feelings generated from the therapist are not countertransference. Therapists experience affects in response to the patient's transference or character style. These feelings are not classical countertransference because they are preconscious or conscious. Moreover, therapists typically tolerate certain transferences more easily than others. For some therapists the experience of being adored is difficult whereas being hated is easy; for other therapists the opposite is true. Therapists need to assess their inner reactions to ensure that they are not acting on such induced feelings. We do not want to communicate to our patients that certain transferences or character traits are acceptable while others are not.

CLINICAL EXAMPLE

Will, a single man with extensive guilt over his sexual impulses, often evoked attack and criticism with his character style of telling repetitious and rambling stories about his friends or family. He seldom dated, and when he did the relationships were short-lived because he seemed to antagonize his date.

In the group, as discussion of romantic attractions among members emerged, Will began to tell a bawdy story that contained images of woman wearing dildos. The therapist interrupted him and inquired what he was trying to communicate. As the process continued, the therapist realized that his intervention had been primarily an effort to prevent another attack on Will. There was little reason to believe that such an attack would have been destructive. In this case the therapist felt it would be useful to expose his countertransference to the group, and he commented directly that he had reconsidered his question to Will and believed that he had been trying to protect him from criticism.

*   *   *

Here, the therapist had not only responded to Will's style but had responded in part to his own discomfort with repeated enactments of masochism, and possibly to the explicit sexual content. This illustrates both modern and classical countertransference elements. He believed that in this instance the group could benefit from his acknowledging some meaning in the here and now of his intervention.

The first place to look when a therapist experiences powerful affect is to the self. This is in order to protect patients from the untoward effects of therapist countertransference in the treatment. A common example of a classical countertransference response arises when patients characterize their therapists as omniscient or omnipotent. Clinicians are frequently uncomfortable with such idealizations, and they may prematurely "introduce reality." Groups that have come to know their therapists and the typical ways they respond to patients will know that something is "out of character." Members are then in a position, either directly or through a metaphor, to offer consultation to the therapist.

The Genuine Human Relationship

Over the course of time in therapy we develop genuine human relationships with our patients. This does not imply that we act on them, of course. But it does mean that sometimes we are filled with feelings triggered by the relationship itself. When a patient suffers a serious loss, we feel sad. When a patient enjoys a monumental triumph, we feel pride and pleasure.

Another of the clinician's emotional responses considered in this section, yet one that has overlap with induced affect, is the ordinary response we experience with patients who are controlling, boring, self-absorbed, obsequious, or overly intellectual (i.e., difficult patients; see Chapter 14). We are referring here to what would be considered a typical response to the presentation of the patient. A monopolizing member induces a variety of affects, including feelings of irritation, annoyance, or boredom. The clinician's internal work of using these feelings may generate a series of ideas as to the source of the patient's monopolization (e.g., it might be a character trait or it might be a self-protective controlling response to a prior aversive group response). Alternatively, the patient may be a spokesperson for groupwide affective states.

Induced Affect

The most intriguing source of therapist affect is the patient. The processes here are often unconscious. It is difficult to distinguish between therapist's feelings induced by the patient's transference and those induced by the patient's character style.

The first is parallel affect. That is, sometimes therapists will identify a strong affect in themselves and will come to realize that they are experiencing what the patient is experiencing. This is most powerful when the affect has not been verbalized by the patient.

Clinical Example

The therapist was trying to attend to the complaints of a group member. The member was speaking of her dissatisfaction with her life, her sense that she has not accomplished what she had expected by this time in her life. However, the therapist was overcome with a feeling of fatigue. The therapist noticed that she was drifting into a fantasy that she was a surgeon. Rather than immediately cutting off the fantasy in order to attend to the group, the therapist recognized that she was indeed attending to the group and that her fantasy might inform her more about the group process. She continued the fantasy and found herself enjoying the life of a very successful surgeon, one whose successes were immediately and obviously apparent.

The therapist then understood that while the patient had not been successful at verbally communicating her despair and dissatisfaction, she had quite successfully communicated it at a metacommunicative level. The therapist was experiencing affect parallel to that of the patient—a sense that she was not successful enough, that she had followed the wrong career path, that somehow she had missed the essence of life. One important clue for the therapist in understanding that these affects related to her patient was the fact that these feelings did not have any conscious place in her own life. At a conscious level the therapist was very happy in her field and rather awed by the professional status she had attained. The therapist could understand that her fantasy about becoming a surgeon was her own defense against the projected despair. Using her own emotion as a guide the therapist responded to the patient, "It is as if you have missed the boat and life is passing you by?" The patient immediately burst into tears. At the same moment, the other group members, who until this point had been somber and rather disconnected, came alive and began actively interacting with the woman.

*   *   *

There were two levels of communication from this patient. On the one hand, she had developed a characteristic style of relating that seemed not inviting of interest or participation by others; it was typical that when she spoke others appeared bored. On the other hand, she was somehow communicating her despair and unhappiness. Eventually she came to understand that her character style was related to the punishment she received as a child whenever she voiced her needs.

A second patient-induced source of therapist affect is projective identification (Klein, 1946). In this very important defensive operation, the patient projects the undesirable and unacceptable affects about the self onto the therapist. (As discussed earlier in this chapter in the section on scapegoating, projective identification can also impact members.) The therapist contains and experiences these affects. If projection identification were at work in the foregoing example, the therapist might have experienced *different* feelings than the despair the patient was feeling. The therapist might experience the affect the patient cannot tolerate. Further, in projective identification the therapist is induced to respond in ways that are familiar to the patient from the past, thereby completing a life script that the patient expects to occur. Were projective identification at work in the earlier example, the patient might have rejected unacceptable feelings of self-doubt, holding instead to a counterphobic sense of confidence. This, in turn, would have protected the patient from identifying with a parent who was viewed as inept and defeated. The patient would view herself as superior to this parent and thus to much of the world. In the therapy the identical relationship is established as the therapist begins to feel incapable when with this particular patient.

CLINICAL EXAMPLE

Sam was a quarrelsome and critical patient. He accused the therapist of charging exorbitant fees, of not paying close enough attention, of having poor taste in office furniture. Not surprisingly, the therapist soon became filled with rageful feelings toward Sam. The other group members also found Sam problematic. He was critical of them as well and never seemed to be satisfied with any of their efforts on his behalf. The therapist allowed the rageful feelings to build and paid them heed. He recognized a wish to slap Sam across the face and tell him, "You should be grateful for all I have given you." The therapist was shocked at that atypical response to a patient but then associated to the patient's history. Sam had been placed for adoption on counsel of the state, who had taken him from parents deemed to be unfit. He had been adopted by a cool, passionless family, very different from Sam's biological family. Further, the only affect Sam reports his mother having displayed was anger. The therapist hypothesized that Sam was disowning the rageful parts of himself which wished to strike the therapist and before that his adoptive parents. How could he be rageful at those who had saved his life? Thus, those unacceptable feelings were repressed and found expression only in projective identification.

The therapist finally commented to Sam, "How awful it must have felt to have wanted to strike those who had given you a home." This was a shocking comment to the entire group since Sam had never alluded to such feelings. The data for the intervention came solely from the therapist's assessment of his affective reaction to Sam. Sam immediately accepted the comment, probably the first time he had uncritically accepted anything the therapist had to offer. The group was instantly more empathic to Sam and began to understand why he had developed a personal style which kept people at such a distance.

*   *   *

A third process in which patients' defenses induce affect in the therapist follows from patients' efforts to unconsciously learn more about their problems by turning passive into active (Weiss, 1993). In these circumstances, patients "plan" to learn other, more effective ways of managing difficult situations that generally had arisen in childhood. They induce confusing and disturbing symptoms in others, including the therapist.

CLINICAL EXAMPLE

Stone (1996a) reports a patient who described at great length his experience of being with his family at an Easter dinner. The description seemed endless and the therapist became aware of feeling very angry. He then reviewed the patient's history, recalling the many incidents the patient had described feeling tyrannized at family meals. The therapist commented that the patient seemed to wish for everyone present to experience and understand what he (the patient) had endured in the past.

*   *   *

The unconscious communication in this example was to induce in the therapist (and others) the experience of the patient, and possibly to determine if alternative ways of managing a difficult situation could be found. The therapist's intervention, although spoken to the patient, was also useful to the entire group, as it provided the others with additional understanding of a "difficult" member.

Affect Arising from the Group

A fourth source for therapist affect is his/her relationship to the entire group. Clinicians emotionally invest in their group as a group. We have previously mentioned the potential for the clinician being swept up in emotional contagion. Powerful group forces may tend to inhibit or pressure clinicians to act. Only on reflection may therapists wonder why they responded as they did (Yalom, 1966b).

Therapists, discussing their work, often refer to the Tuesday or the Wednesday group, and not to individuals. They react to the group as a living entity: when a difficult impasse exists, therapists may despair; when there are a series of terminations and no replacements in sight, fears for the survival of the group are stirred; similarly, when members seem unempathic or rejecting of someone in distress, feelings of compassion for the ignored person may be stimulated as well as irritation or anger with those who seem insensitive. With the limitations of participation dictated by their role, therapists may find themselves envying members' freedom to interact and express themselves; similarly, senior clinicians who had been group members at an early stage in their careers and seen advances in theory or shortcomings in their own group experience, may experience envy in the treatment they provide to their groups (Whitman & Bloch, 1990; Stone, 1992a).

In the conduct of combined therapy (see Chapter 11), considerable feelings may arise in the clinician related to working in this format. One source of feelings emerges in response to a particular series of patient associations. The clinician may have a great deal of relevant personal information that was obtained in the individual sessions and is distorted or ignored by the patient in the group setting. The therapist is concerned about the impact of revealing or withholding the information, particularly when it seems highly relevant to what is happening in the process. Clinicians who prefer an agreement that all data from one venue is applicable to the other must guard against holding secrets, on the one hand, and revealing data before the patient is prepared to deal with it, on the other. Those without such an agreement must find ways of managing their dysphoric responses. A second source of affect arises when a therapist who sees a patient in combined therapy feels that he/she may either offer preferential treatment to that patient or, conversely, may focus *less* on that patient out of a wish to not offer favoritism.

These are emotions that reflect the clinician's involvement with the group and are not specific to an individual. Rather, they reflect the response to feelings about group development or group dynamics.

Clinical Management of Therapist's Affect

It is exceedingly difficult for therapists to sort out the origins of their very strong feelings while leading a group. One way we have found that may help is to consider the following steps. First, try to determine if the feelings are modern countertransference or responsive to the patient's transference. If that does not yield an answer, then question whether the feelings flow from the human relationship with the patient (or the group). Next, ask if the feelings are invoked by the patient through parallel affect, projective identification, or turning passive into active. We find the latter two responses to be the usual unrecognized sources of disturbing and confusing therapist affect.

Considerable difference of opinion exists as to the wisdom and value of therapists disclosing their emotional states. The controversy was in part stimulated by the ideology of the sensitivity training movement in the 1960s, which espoused therapist self-disclosure as a model for patient learning. This position sharply conflicted with the overdrawn metaphor of the therapist as a blank screen. Research findings into therapist self-disclosure have been limited and equivocal. Some evidence exists suggesting that with group development it may be useful for therapists to be more self-revealing (Dies, 1977). Self-revelation should be restricted to the service of helping patients through an impasse or illuminating an aspect of the interaction in the here and now (see the example of Will earlier in this chapter). It should not be a routine aspect of the clinician's armamentarium but, rather, should be reserved to help in specific situations.

There are occasions when clinicians inadvertently reveal feelings. This is not surprising because even if the therapist has not said anything, there are many avenues for non-verbal communication. Patients may then comment about the therapist's affect: "You seem sad" or "You are angry."

CLINICAL EXAMPLE

One therapist was informed shortly before a group that a very close friend of his had been killed. Almost immediately upon entering the group room, a patient directly said that he appeared upset. In this situation the therapist directly revealed what had happened. The members then went on to process their responses to their peer who had made the observation and their responses to the clinician's self-revelation.

*   *   *

Difficult patients often evoke considerable anger in their therapists. This may be evident in facial expressions or in the tone of an intervention. Considerable clinical tact is necessary if patients confront the clinician with their observations that he/she is angry. This almost always throws the therapist off balance. A denial may reenact situations in which parents had denied the obvious, and such a response also undermines the treatment alliance. Under these trying circumstances, the therapist should attempt to determine the optimal amount of information to reveal, a very difficult assignment.

Being human, at times the therapist spontaneously expresses his/her anger. Patients are likely to be startled and outraged. Yet, as Tuttman (1994) asserts:

There are at least two ways of looking at this: if one feels strongly and passionately and one is deeply involved, the spontaneity of the reaction may reflect a healthy confidence in oneself, in one's emotions, in one's patients and one's group. . . . On the other hand a certain amount of control and restraint on the group leader's part is necessary so as to leave space for patients to manifest their ventilations. Clearly, some balance is therapeutically indicated. (p. 195)

Patients may be initially intrigued with their therapist revealing feelings, but they soon become disinterested if the clinician persists in sharing personal information, since they are in treatment for themselves.

Traditional countertransference responses are much more difficult to detect because they are unconscious. Often they can only be detected in retrospect in terms of a behavioral deviation from the clinician's usual way of conducting treatment. Coming late or excessively extending a session are clues that unconscious processes may be at play, as are a slip of the tongue (parapraxis) or forgetting a patient's name. A therapist's dreams, particularly those that immediately precede or follow a session, may provide yet more data. Sometimes reviewing the group roster and considering which patients one would most like to retain and which patients one would most like to discard can give clues to previously unrecognized favoritism or rejection. Of course, the traditional way of detecting countertransference is through consultation or supervision. Therapists who find themselves stuck or at an impasse and unable to sort out the basis for this state might seek consultation to try to determine if an unrecognized countertransference has contributed to the problem.

SUMMARY

In this chapter we have emphasized the manner in which feelings are communicated in therapy groups and the impact of emotions on the therapist. We have emphasized unconscious communications. Nonverbal communications contain both conscious and unconscious elements, and therapists "expose" themselves through this form of communication just as do members. Therapists' dreams provide still another road into their unconscious affects and often provide useful information about their groups.

We have addressed some of the technical problems that therapists face as they experience their own unconscious processes stimulated by their group interactions. This is no simple matter, and clinicians have a responsibility to scrutinize themselves, keeping in mind their behaviors that might be clues to their unconscious functioning.

Powerful feelings are evoked in all who sit in group psychotherapy, including the therapist. Classic notions of countertransference alert therapists to the possibility that unresolved issues in their own lives might keep them from hearing and understanding their patients or groups properly. However, that concept is too restrictive and threatens to close therapists off from a potentially valuable source of data. Modern practitioners of dynamic theory are very cognizant of their inner responses to patients. A major pathway to change has been seen as a two-step process: evocation of powerful feelings in the present, followed by cognitive integration, generally via interpretation.

THIRTEEN

The Therapeutic Process: A Clinical Illustration

A picture is worth a thousand words.

T he therapeutic process is so diverse and practiced so differently, even by psychodynamic clinicians, that some believe it is more art than science. Although art is involved, we are convinced there is a sound theoretical foundation for understanding how the process works. Given the intensely human nature of therapy, it should not surprise us that its practice is intimately linked to the therapist's personality and style. No two clinicians are precisely alike, and therefore no two clinicians should practice precisely alike.

The group therapist is confronted with a wealth of information. In the group each individual exhibits his/her interpersonal and intrapsychic strengths and weaknesses, transferences, and character styles. With these data therapists respond in ways that they believe will help patients change.

A considerable portion of our therapeutic work occurs in recognizing patients' associations as communications about the therapist, members, or the group-as-a-whole. Responses to therapists, other members, or the whole group may well represent transferences. Our primary task is to listen and attempt to understand. Borbely (1998) states, "We try to listen to the patient's productions with an ear to (consciously) *unintended* [*sic*] metaphors. . . . We frequently observe verbalizations that point towards a hidden metaphor, which as yet cannot be understood by the analysand or analyst" (p. 932; emphasis in the original). Through the ongoing interaction certain events may begin to carry particularly significant meaning for an entire group. These events are carried in memory and are referred to by either the therapist or the members as ways of highlighting or linking more immediate discussions to a meaningful occurrence in the past. Thus they serve as metaphors and have been labeled "model scenes" (Lichtenberg, Lachman, & Fosshage, 1992; Correale & Celli, 1998). They are useful in the working-through process, as they provide an organizing "structure" which can be modified as additional associations and memories are elaborated.

An observer watching a mature group may wonder about the seemingly idiosyncratic transactions and communications. With continued observation, it becomes apparent that what seemed strange to an outsider is thoroughly understandable to the members. Groups develop their own language, traditions, and metaphors.

The following clinical vignette illustrates how the present authors might respond to an actual group meeting. We hope this will provide a perspective on our thoughts and responses and that it will exemplify the differences in how each of us respond.

This group is led by Walter N. Stone, who has a great deal of knowledge about the individuals, their histories, and their manner of relating, as well as the group history. His comments on the process were made as he watched the videotape of the session and included notes he had made after the session. J. Scott Rutan was provided the brief description of the patients and the group given in the next section, along with the transcript of the session presented below. He did not have access to the historical material of either the group or the members, nor did he have access to the therapist's commentary until after having offered his own. (There are a few instances where Rutan contrasts or compares styles, and these comments were made after having seen Stone's comments.) Despite the limitations of this exercise, much can be learned about how clinicians might understand and intervene in a clinical situation.

Stone's comments are presented *in italics;* Rutan's comments are presented in **bold**.

GROUP HISTORY AND PATIENT DESCRIPTION

Group History

This group, originally composed of seven members, has been in existence about 6 months. One original female member had dropped out shortly after the group began. Her replacement, Joan, had been added about 2 months prior to this meeting. Joan had come to two sessions and then had missed all subsequent meetings. There was reasonable stability for six of the seven members. Nevertheless, in part because of the degree of their psychopathology, the members are still engaged in early developmental phase issues of basic trust, fears of loss of self, and fear of expressions of hostility. Thus they were reticent but not totally resistant to examining in-group interactions and conflicts

The therapist's approach is psychodynamic, *with* attention to group-as-a whole processes. Patients are expected to take the lead in choosing whatever they wish to discuss. The therapist's approach to leadership is to understand and then convey that understanding in a fashion that is useful to the members. In his interventions he may address whole group, subgroup, or individual issues. He tries to address individual problems in the context of the group process.

The Members

1. Bruce: A single man struggling in his first serious relationship, which is going badly. The couple has separated often. He seldom speaks in group, but at the time of the meeting was going through another separation, information he had withheld from the group. He was also planning a separation from the group, stating that a scheduling conflict in his graduate school class would require him to miss a semester of group. He was in combined treatment with the therapist.

2. Bob: A young man who was preoccupied with women. He would talk at length about meeting new women and had begun to explore his difficulty in maintaining a relationship, rather than continuing to focus on finding more women.

3. Melissa: Involved in a long-term relationship in which she was a caretaker, she struggled with unexpressed feelings of anger and resentment. She is the oldest child in a large family and had been given responsibility for her younger siblings. She was particularly resentful of her mother.

4. Norm: A bright man, he had held several high-level jobs but had become depressed, which lead to his losing his job. His recovery from depression was minimal despite several hospitalizations, electroconvulsive therapy (ECT), and multiple medicine trials. He had a positive relationship with a woman, whom he felt was very supportive, but he did not have any strong sexual desire; rather, he was pleased with the involvement that did not place many demands on him. He strongly resented anyone who accused him of not trying hard enough to return to work.

5. Ralph: A passive–dependent man, very closely tied to his mother, he was in conflict with his father over his relative lack of achievement in his life. He continued living at home.

6. Orin: An older retired man, he was suffering from diabetes, which had left him visually impaired and impotent. He was struggling with these illnesses as well as with the loss of his role as a wage earner.

7. Aileen: A rather quiet woman in midlife who had a long-term relationship with a man, she was struggling to determine if she should marry him. She was particularly influenced by her rather domineering father.

8. Joan: This member was added to the group recently, but she had not been attending.

THE CONTEXT

Several members had endured distressing events which for the most part had not been mentioned in the group, and a conflict among members had arisen. Intermittently, Orin had been talking about his mother's cancer, which sounded likely to be quite serious. Bruce had not mentioned his most recent breakup with his girl friend, nor had he mentioned that he was planning a leave of absence from the group because of a class scheduling conflict. Two weeks prior to the current session Bruce and Norm had been in conflict, and Norm left that session feeling that Bruce had criticized him for not seeking work. Norm did not attend the following session.

THE MEETING

Joan did not attend the meeting, and for the first time did not call to say that she would not be present. All the others, except for Bob, were present at the beginning of the session. Bob arrived several minutes late. There was an opening pause:

STONE: What's been happening?

RUTAN: It is of note that the therapist decides to initiate discussion. Certainly another option would have been to simply wait until one of the patients speaks.

ORIN: My mom's not feeling too good. Today she is going to the doctor to have her cancer measured to see if it's grown. Then Mary [his wife] is going to have surgery on her thumb; she has a big cyst.

STONE: That's a lot.

ORIN: She's had surgery on both arms and now she has to do it on her thumb.

AILEEN: Is that really unusual?

ORIN: She asked me to feel it, and I said, "It feels like a cyst under your skin," and she went to the doctor and that's what he said she had. (*pause*)

RALPH: I found out at church that one of the men I knew had cancer. It's pretty far advanced, and we talked a lot. I'm going to miss him.

NORM: (*looking at Bob*) You are smiling.

MELISSA: You have a new girlfriend?

BOB: Yes. We got together, and we are now dating. This is something she wanted to do. She lives about 50 miles away.

ORIN: Wow, that's a drive.

The discussion proceeds as Bob describes in some length how he met his new girlfriend at a social club, that he finds her nice although she lives a distance away, and that she is coming in to town this weekend.

MELISSA: When are you going to hang on to one of these girls?

BOB: I think she might be one I'm going to hang on to. She's real nice.

AILEEN: Where does she work?

BOB: She has a nice job, working in the office at X corporation. Which is near her home. But I was thinking about what Dr. Stone was talking about—how to figure out signals. It was difficult. I didn't expect anything to happen. But it all happened, so we decided to keep going to see how far it would go.

BRUCE: I was wondering with the other girlfriends you have—does it hurt, or how do you feel when it happens?

BOB: Sure it hurts. There is always a little pain there, but you get a little bit stronger each time, and maybe a bit better. That's how it is.

RUTAN: These individuals have suffered enormous pain in their early interpersonal contact. It would be unreasonable to expect them to warmly welcome new contact—in life or in the group. The role of the therapy is to help them understand how their past experiences have preordained that they would *not* expect to be loved and appreciated, and how this, in turn, leads to interpersonal styles that lead to painful but safe interpersonal distance. The in-group–out-of-group axis is important here. The therapist could refer all these concerns about losing people (Orin's concern with the physical well-being of his mother and wife; Ralph's concern about his church colleague; the group concern with

Bob's "losing" yet another girlfriend) to the group experience, where a female member has already left, Joan is seemingly on the way out, and Bruce will be missing a bulk of group time. On the other hand, the therapist could use the out-of-group data to explore feelings about rejection and abandonment and relate that to the group experience later.

Potential response: "Everyone seems to approach closeness quite gingerly. If you are to let others become important, either in this group or in life outside the group, you run the risk that they will die or reject you."

STONE: *Until this point about 10 minutes into the session, I have been quiet, with the exception of my opening comment and the one to Orin. I was feeling a bit of sadness for a moment as Orin began with a rather bland statement about his mother, because I had been feeling that she really seemed to be going downhill. Yet he switched very quickly to his wife, and I became aware that a theme of loss and separation had developed. I felt Orin was not ready yet to address his mother's illness any further, but I might explore it. Hearing the discussion as a metaphor about the meeting, I wonder how to enhance the group atmosphere to facilitate members exploring their relationships. Melissa has made an intervention that asks Bob to think about himself, and Bob has indicated that he uses the treatment to think about what he is doing (i.e., his reflection on my remarks). Bruce's question about separations is meaningful to him with regard to his girlfriend and his forthcoming absence. In addition, the missing member's unannounced absence has not been addressed. I felt it unlikely that Bruce would pursue his comment about separations by discussing his own current separation, because his style is to seal things over and present positive aspects of his conflicts.*

I considered my therapeutic aim as helping members explore their feelings within the group as a model for understanding themselves. I assumed that both Bruce and Melissa needed to talk about their external life experiences, but they also conveyed how they are experiencing relationships within the group. The two prominent relationship issues of which they are aware are the absence of Joan, the newest member, and the return of Norm after what all perceived to have been a tension-filled session 2 weeks before. A direct confrontation of what they are not addressing will most likely be experienced as their displeasing me and making it more difficult to explore their feelings.

I chose to label and thereby focus on affects that seem to be present in all of the major elements in the discussion. This provides therapeutic space for the members to address any of the issues, and it provides me with an opportunity to follow the process, assessing each individual's capacity to explore difficult feelings.

STONE: Everyone has been talking about breaking up a relationship. Orin has concerns about his mother becoming sicker and Ralph has concerns about someone at church having cancer. And so there is a lot of pain in relationships that happen and then break up. It is not easy. (*pause; about 1–2 minutes*)

BRUCE: Dr. Stone, I was curious about Joan. You said she was on vacation for 2 weeks. Is she still on vacation?

RUTAN: **As a result of the previous intervention, the group is able to contemplate their investment with in-group relationships (i.e., the missing Joan).**

   Potential response: None necessary, other than perhaps to report that Joan has not made contact (though that would be obvious from the fact that no initial announcement had been made).

STONE: I didn't hear from her today. So that's another relationship—here in the group. (*pause*)

BOB: (*Apparently uncertain about who Joan was*) Whatever happened to that other woman who was in the group? She came and left quickly. She used to sit over there.

BRUCE: That was Joan who sat there.

BOB: She was very nice.

Bruce: I miss her not being here.

RUTAN: **This is an interesting sentence. Does Bruce really mean he misses her not being here? A dynamic therapist is always listening for odd sentence structure, words that can have double meanings, etc. No response is necessary, but I would be listening to hear more of what Bruce feels about Joan's absence.**

MELISSA: Maybe we weren't so much of a challenge (*laughs*).

STONE: How do you mean, Melissa?

MELISSA: Our problems weren't hard enough for her to figure out I guess.

BRUCE: She went on to bigger and better things.

MELISSA: Yeah.

RUTAN: **When rejection comes, the narcissistic "little child" always assumes it has to do with something that is "wrong with me." Melissa's hurt (and anger) is evident in her comment. Bruce speaks to the rejection the members are feeling.**

Potential response: Joan's absence seems to have stirred quite a lot of feelings from "What did we do wrong?" to "We must not have been good enough."

STONE: *I felt very pleased with Bruce's response to my prior intervention. He brought the discussion into the group and one of the potential losses the entire membership had experienced. This includes me, and highlights the interactive (intersubjective) experiences of everyone in the group. My attempt to help Melissa elaborate on her fantasies about the disappearance had been followed by rather general statements, and I decided that the others might be able to either expand on what had been said or add their own reactions. I was concerned that the intervention might have seemed premature, but I was responding out of my knowledge of how members interacted and my hope was that this would keep the members focused.*

STONE: Perhaps you all have a reaction to her not returning. I don't know what's going to happen. She hasn't been here for a number of weeks now.

BRUCE: I'm concerned about her. She seemed . . . pretty . . . not unstable, but fragile. I'm concerned about that. Also, she was a good person to have in the group. *(pause)*

STONE: Any other reactions or thoughts about this?

NORM: Joan seemed like a nice person. She told us about how she baked things for her church, and it really helped in their sale. She seemed to care about people.

RALPH: She seemed nice.

MELISSA: Would you give her a call?

RUTAN: The members demonstrate some of their character styles in their responses to Joan's absence. Bruce is worried. The others mourn and miss Joan's "nice-ness." None seem to have access to any anger at the breach of agreements. Furthermore, Melissa's question (in addition to testing the group boundaries) clearly implies that she is concerned about Joan. From an object relations point of view, this direct expression of concern between members is very significant and should be highlighted.

Technically, the therapist is faced with a direct question. Whether to answer the question (content) or not is less important than to make certain that the affect and deeper meanings of the question (process) are explored. What does it mean to Melissa that the therapist would or would not attempt to make contact with a missing member?

Potential comment: "You care about Joan. What would be your hope, Melissa? Would you hope I would or would not call Joan?"

STONE: *I am a little startled by the question and momentarily pause trying to get my bearings; I am faced with a choice of whether or not to answer the question or explore the meaning of it. Of course, answering does not preclude exploration, but it might be experienced as gratifying the members and decreasing anxiety. Alternatively, answering might be an indicator that I am willing to interact in a responsive fashion that potentially could enhance members' willingness to further their psychological work. It is possible to consider this as an enactment: my countertransference triggered by feelings of loss may have led me to respond in a fashion that would reassure myself that I hadn't experienced the loss of a member?*

STONE: I will give her a call. *(pause) (to Melissa)* It sounds like you also had a reaction to her.

MELISSA: She . . .

NORM: *(interrupting)* Seemed like she had a lot of problems too.

RUTAN: **When a comment is experienced as an "interruption," it usually represents a continuation of a prior dialogue where the association is unconscious.**

MELISSA: I only met her once. Bill [her boyfriend] and I were on vacation after that. Bill was having trouble after losing his job, and it seems as though he has the possibility of a new one. He has had several interviews, so it looks promising. Many people don't make it to the second interview.

RUTAN: **"Making it to the second interview" may be an unconscious reference to Joan's trouble in making it back to the group.**
      Potential comment: "So Bill made it farther than Joan did with her 'interviews' for *this* job."

STONE: Excellent.

MELISSA: I hope they hurry up and decide. I am dying to get my money back, so we can go out and have some fun. We have been living very close to the line.

NORM: You are faithful to him.

STONE: *In retrospect, faithful is an interesting word, because Joan has been unfaithful! Is there an aspect of Norm's assuring himself that Melissa won't leave?*

MELISSA: I helped him out.

AILEEN: What started his troubles?

MELISSA: A long time ago, about 1981 or 1982 . I don't know the story, but some of the stuff, some of it . . .

AILEEN: I meant recently.

MELISSA: Oh, recently. (*pause*)

AILEEN: What happened when he left work?

MELISSA: I don't know. He couldn't handle the work any more. They were pushing too much work on him and he was the only one doing the job, and they kept pushing it. Pushing him. Bill is a hard worker. If you want something done, Bill gets it done.

AILEEN: Uh huh.

MELISSA: So they kept . . . He didn't have any time for a break. You know how guys around the office get coffee and talk to one another and stuff. They wouldn't give him any time for that. They kept saying, "We want this done" and "We want that done." There is a guy who threatened him. The boss threatened Bill and another guy. They were going to take him to . . . I don't know.

BRUCE: What did they threaten him with? Firing him?

MELISSA: They said if you don't get back in the room, and you know . . .

AILEEN: Get back to work.

MELISSA: He just kept threatening him. He threatened this other guy too—if he didn't get back to work he would be in trouble.

RUTAN: Through the metaphor of Bill, the group is struggling to find out why Joan has not returned. Was she pushed too hard? Did she feel threatened? What is it like when people are not "faithful?"

Potential response: "So as people try to understand what has happened to Joan, the associations go to Bill's troubles at work. Perhaps there is some sentiment that Joan was pushed too hard or threatened here in the group. There may also be some feelings about whether or not she was faithful to this group."

STONE: This discussion had gone on for some time. I felt that Melissa was under pressure as she was talking, and she was describing what was happening to her boyfriend rather than how it might be affecting her. The sequence had started out as a response to my efforts to explore the responses to the most recent member's failure to return. Did my agreement to call close the discussion, or did Melissa use it as a segue to talk about Bill's troubles and how she has been helpful? I wondered if Melissa might be experiencing some guilt. In addition, was the discussion about insensitive and threatening authority about me? It certainly was an issue for them, but it did not seem sufficiently focused nor involving others (although the possibility existed that Melissa was serving as spokesperson). Nevertheless, I had to make what seemed an uneasy choice between addressing authority issues or the reactions to the of loss of a member. I felt I should temporize. Perhaps then it would become clearer which was most salient.

STONE: So there was a lot of stress—in getting work done, and then there were the threats too.

MELISSA: I know. They were the owners, so I guess they were saying he had to get the work done.

AILEEN: If they had a deadline or something.

MELISSA: They didn't have any really important deadlines. Bill had them ahead so many millions of dollars. They just wanted to see how they could make him squirm. You know, that's what they were doing.

AILEEN: Did they know he had colitis?

MELISSA: I don't know if he told them. I thought he told them. Toward the end, when he entered the hospital and stuff, they said, "You didn't tell us you had this problem."

AILEEN: The same kind of thing happened to me.

MELISSA: Bill may be afraid of the guy, but I'm not afraid of him. I don't have a job there so he doesn't threaten me. I went and had a long talk with him, and he said, "Melissa, I shouldn't be talking with you about this, should I?" I said, "I guess you shouldn't, but you should do something about it."

RUTAN: **Beneath the "content" the members seem to be struggling with whether or not people ought to get "special attention" because they are *ill*. In addition, this represents yet another "boundary" issue for Melissa, which is likely related to her role in her family as the one who had to take care of her siblings.**

STONE: *I heard this "story" as a metaphor. It is material that fits with what I perceive to be an emerging group theme: "Who will speak up when others become passive and withdrawn?" I was feeling reasonably pleased with how the group was going and what I felt was my sorting out of a cogent theme.*

STONE: So you really spoke up for yourself and for him.

MELISSA: And for Bill.

STONE: And for Bill, yes.

MELISSA: He said if there's a problem, Bill should be bringing that to the office. I said you are right. That should be said . . . talk about it in the office. I knew that it was to the point, so no matter what I did . . . Bill kinda wanted me to.

RUTAN: **There seems to be a wish that someone had championed Joan's cause—and perhaps that someone had been their champion during tough times.**

Potential response: "I wonder if people feel Joan needed someone to be her ally here in the group. I also wonder how many of you feel you had allies who would stand up for you in difficult times."

STONE: *Here is another opportunity to address how one person is used by another and determine if the group can be mobilized to address the conflicts. I considered a possible response to directly explore the analogous situation in the group—that is, I had brought in a member who didn't stick to the job. I thought Melissa is not quite there yet (i.e., Bill was abused and possibly not taking excessive coffee breaks or goofing off). I chose to frame what Melissa had described in a positive manner, but as an intermediary step.*

STONE: You know, I think you are bringing in something very important, Melissa—that is, how difficult it is at times for people to directly deal with conflict and sometimes an intermediary helps, as you did.

RUTAN: **Here is a good example of how two therapists might take different aspects of group data and move with it. I "heard" the yearning for an ally, whereas my coauthor followed the equally viable theme of intragroup conflict.**

MELISSA: I don't know if I helped or made it worse, but he did want me to talk to the guy. Bill was having a problem with something in his lower abdomen, and they tried to say he was lying. The doctor said that it was so important that Bill go home and lay down and not get up. He did that and he had me call those people at work and he wanted me to tell them what was wrong. So I did, and they said, "I guess he should stay home and rest." (*pause*) They said he had to take care of himself. It was a long time ago.

RUTAN: **The group is questioning, "Should our liabilities result in our**

getting special treatment?" I would not feel a therapist response is needed, but I would continue to listen for this theme.

STONE: Melissa continues to talk, and although she pauses several times, the others don't respond. I really had hoped they would. Nevertheless, I felt my understanding of the process was OK, and that considerable tension was continuing over dealing with the feelings around the absences or the conflict between Bruce and Norm. Thus I make another effort to bring things into focus.

STONE: I think you are bringing things into focus, and I think it involves a lot of people. I don't think it is unique: how hard it is when somebody is stressed, is pushed to deal with somebody directly, and how sometimes it is helpful to have an intermediary like you, and sometimes it may not be helpful. I think it's often an issue we try to get clarified and see how people handle it.

MELISSA: *(with little pause)* Well, I wasn't there every day, and maybe Bill was trying to goof off. Maybe he was goofing off and he shouldn't have been. . . . No matter what, he was showing signs he couldn't handle it. Whatever happened it was time for him to move and get a new job.

RUTAN: The group is struggling with an important issue. Should the world accommodate to our problems? When faced with our limitations should we run away (look for another job)? Or should we face the limitations and seek to improve upon them? Furthermore, Melissa has brought up the thorny issue that perhaps Bill's reports to her were not entirely accurate. Again, I would await more data before responding verbally.

STONE: Good! Melissa has shown a bit of progress. She has moved from a position about what they were doing to Bill to a place where he may have had some responsibility in what had happened to him. Yet, Melissa continues to dominate the group (or they let her) and I find that worrisome, feeling that I need to find a way to get the others involved. I chose to use the difficulty Bill had in being direct as a jumping-off place to involve the group more. This choice fits with my way of providing the group to address dealing with direct feelings, and then, if that is successful, I might be able to bring it into the group and wonder if they have something they wish to say directly to me.

STONE: I think what is embedded in this is the idea that Bill would have felt better about himself if he had been able to say directly that he was having trouble and it was time to move on.

MELISSA: Yah . . . I guess years ago . . . nowadays people speak up for themselves, and I think Bill still is in the era when people didn't speak up for themselves.

STONE: Has this happened to others?

NORM: No. (*sighs*) I'm real bad about that.

STONE: That's a difficulty you have.

BRUCE: You are what, Norm?

NORM: I'm bad at it.

BRUCE: Do you. . . . Maybe you are bad at it until it gets beyond control, and you explode a little bit.

NORM: I don't explode any more. I used to, but not anymore. I'm on medication. It keeps me pretty calm. (*smiles*) I think I exploded too quickly and too easily. Just little things would set me off.

RUTAN: The age-old dilemma—is it my personality or my biology that is at fault?

BRUCE: Yah.

NORM: That still sometimes happens. I don't get violent or have crazy thoughts like I used to.

STONE: You do or you don't?

NORM: I don't like getting vengeance on that person or getting all involved or something.

BRUCE: That's a lot of progress.

NORM: Yeah, now I feel like I'm kinda a wimp. (*several members chuckled*) I do. You learn by the kind of raising I had. I had no raising. Where I was, I had no mother or father. You had to be tough. Now I feel like a marshmallow.

RUTAN: Norm is taking the important developmental view—"Who I am is at least in part the result of how I was raised?"

Potential comment: "So the feelings you have about yourself do not necessarily represent an accurate picture of your worth, rather, they reflect the feelings you have about yourself due to the way you were raised."

BRUCE: So you have to adjust to that now.

MELISSA: I go through phases like that. I was calm and easygoing and nothing could bother me, and then . . . People abused me, and I started feeling real abused, but then I wanted to be abusive, angry, and violent. I thought this is what I've turned into because it is how people took advantage of me.

NORM: Are you talking about now?

MELISSA: Yes. Now I'm trying to practice being . . . the way I was—easygoing—and not let people bother me any more. I can be sitting somewhere and wishing that they would shut up or I would like to smack them, (*laughs*) and that's not a good feeling—like you are violent.

RUTAN: The group continues to process their missing member. Now some of the angry feelings seem to be surfacing, along with the concern that anger is lethal.

Potential comment: "When one is left, abandoned or rejected, anger is one natural response. It is as if people are fearful that their anger is so powerful it can damage relationships."

STONE: I am still concerned with how to engage members, with less than half the group participating. However, in this sequence some of the concerns about expressing feelings seems to be emerging, which I am pleased to see as progress. This is familiar, and I can readily understand the others' silence. Thus I have an opportunity to make a group-wide intervention again.

STONE: Let me ask, and this may be something that is happening here—that is, you all were beginning to try to take a look at some feelings you might have about Joan's [the absent member] coming and then disappearing. One way people feel abused is to share things about themselves and then somebody just disappears. Now you are talking, and Melissa is making clear and Norm too at times, that in the past you felt that your feelings would get out of control. So you would pull back completely. So, I thought that people pulled back from any angry feelings they might have about Joan leaving or about my bringing somebody into the group who did not stick very long, because you are afraid you might get too angry or too upset. That is one way I was thinking about what you all were talking about. Does that seem right?

RUTAN: This therapist response is probably longer and more cognitive than necessary. Further, it may inhibit the members' expressions of anger at him for bringing in a "hit-and-run" member. Perhaps a simple remark like "There seem to be some feelings about my having brought into the group a member who was so disruptive" might have been more helpful.

NORM: It doesn't seem right to me, but I did like her. She seemed to be a real nice person and I actually did look forward to seeing her again.

STONE: *As we move along in the session, the members' difficulties in addressing feelings very directly emerge clearly. The sequence provides me another opportunity to inquire again about affective responses.*

RUTAN: Perhaps, given the less developed nature of this group, this might be a time for a thoughtful declarative statement: "You sound disappointed and/or angry."

STONE: Were you disappointed or angry in any way?

Norm: I wasn't angry. I was disappointed, and I think, too, that she might have a good reason for not coming. The way she was talking, not concerning the group, but herself. That way she was talking, she seemed she was having a hard time. She seemed nice, but she seemed to be having a hard time, so I don't say she should be or she shouldn't . . .

MELISSA: Maybe opening up to other people . . . She didn't, maybe she gave it some thought. Maybe it embarrassed her.

STONE: Possibly.

Ralph: Why would we be angry at you because of her not sticking. That's why I couldn't understand what you meant.

STONE: *Here Ralph seems to serve as a spokesperson for the perplexity they may all be experiencing in response to my previous comment. I uneasily wondered if I had overwhelmed them. Ralph, who seems to be the most alive member, may be the one to voice this concern. One possibility would be to ask others if they understood. I was aware that this woman had been in a prior group which had folded, and she had mentioned that in the meeting. But that piece of information had been "forgotten." Nevertheless, Ralph's naïveté provided an opportunity to make an "educational"-type intervention and simultaneously try to be open to critique.*

RUTAN: Group-as-a-whole comments, while often powerful and extremely helpful, can also be narcissistically injurious because individuals are "lumped together." In this instance, the group seems not ready to follow the leader's comment. One could simply sit quietly and let them proceed, or one could attempt to call into question the missing anger.

> **Potential comment: "There seems to be a sentiment that it is not reasonable or acceptable to feel angry when someone lets you down?"**

STONE: Because I bring somebody in and you sort of get to know them a little bit and like them, and then they leave. So people wonder what kind of choices I make to bring somebody into the group who wouldn't stay.

NORM: We had another person who didn't even come. [This was a reference the therapist had forgotten about, having announced that a person had agreed to join the group and then changed her mind.]

BRUCE: And one who left shortly—remember Anne. She left after a short time. . . uh uh . . . nothing . . .

STONE: What did you start to say, Bruce?

BRUCE: Just that I'm concerned about Joan. I have no anger, and I think a lot of us are kinda marginal when we come into the group, and you can't sort out all of them that are gonna make it or not make it. Any one of us could have dropped out a while ago. I don't feel at all upset that you picked some and they didn't stay.

RUTAN: Bruce raises a fascinating topic. He recognizes that he himself was a "risk adventure" in group, and he is grateful that the therapist gave him the opportunity. From that perspective, how could he be angry that the therapist tried someone else who was not able to make it?

MELISSA: I just wondered if it is anything to do with us, if she doesn't come. . . .

STONE: You are nodding Aileen.

AILEEN: Yes, I always think it's me. I'm the reason . . .

BRUCE: You always think it's you! She stopped coming to the group because of you?

AILEEN: Sort of. (*pause*)

STONE: With the pause, I decided to intervene, acknowledging the work that has been done is in order as a way of encouraging her to continue.

STONE: That's hard to talk about . . . those kind of feelings. (*pause*)

BRUCE: Talking of leaving the group, it's a good time to bring this up. I'm going to be going back to school in 6 weeks and I'll be out of the group for at least a quarter. So I have 5 or 6 more groups till I'll be going back to school. I'm sure going to miss the group a lot. It's one of the highlights of my week . . . the highlight of my week. (*pause*) You have to do what you have to do. There's no way I can come to group and go to school at the same time.

RUTAN: Now the group is confronted with a real dilemma. It has been hard enough for them to begin to allow a full range of feelings about an absent member. Now they have the situation of dealing face to face with a member who is threatening the same behavior.

STONE: *I was pleased. I thought wonderful—that's out on the table.*

NORM: Are you going to go to any therapy at all?

BRUCE: Pardon me.

NORM: Are you going to go to any therapy?

BRUCE: I'll still be seeing Dr. Stone once every 2 weeks.

NORM: You might need some before . . .

BRUCE: Yes, I won't be leaving therapy altogether. Just group.

NORM: Well, you are the big guy in the group.

BRUCE: I don't know. The fact is that I'm very uncomfortable with that. I try to do what I can. We are all in here to get as well as we can.

NORM: How do you feel about leaving?

BRUCE: I'm going to miss it a lot. I especially liked the past 5 or 6 weeks. I've felt much better, and I've seen people get better and grow. I see that from time to time. I like seeing that, and very importantly, I felt I've been growing and it's done so much for me. And just like you were talking about before. You used to be angry and explode.

RUTAN: It is fascinating to see how Bruce tries to avoid *really* telling people (including himself?) how important they are to him. First, he refers to the group as "it" ("I'm going to miss *it* a lot."). Then he speaks of watching people improve. It is typical for members to speak positively of "the group" as a way of avoiding direct expressions of affect toward specific members.

NORM: I break down for days and days.

BRUCE: You've calmed down a lot. That's the kind of work I want to do eventually. It's good for me to see these sorts of things happen.

NORM: You have always had a kinda ability to see things that other people didn't.

BRUCE: Thanks very much and that's a gift, and I had to learn how to control it. I'm still learning.

RALPH: How to control your anger?

BRUCE: How to control myself . . . my life.

RALPH: Correct me if I'm wrong.

BRUCE: You are right. Anger, too, that's for sure. Just everything.

NORM: Well, you've been good.

BRUCE: Well, I just didn't want to let this go by. The conflict we had two weeks ago. (*to Norm*) I didn't think you were so wrong at all.

NORM: Oh, really?

BRUCE: Really.

NORM: You didn't get mad over what I did?

BRUCE: No, I think the criticism you have of me was true . . . I tried to set myself as an example for other people and telling them what to do. That's a bad thing to do, I think. I thought you handled it well.

RUTAN: A very important moment in the group—anger is deemed potentially useful rather than always cataclysmic. It may also represent a "going-away gift" from Bruce to Norm.

NORM: Thanks.

BRUCE: And I'm sure you were upset about it for a while.

NORM: I was upset about it for 2 weeks. I thought about nothing else for 2 weeks.

BRUCE: I know, because I've felt that way in the past. You did well to do as well as you did.

NORM: I appreciate that. (*pause*) I really expected to come in here and have everybody jump on me, but I appreciate that. (*pause*)

STONE: Well, I am pleased, this session is going very well. They bring out the conflict within the group, and I conceptualize that is an indicator that the atmosphere feels better. The two men certainly have tried to be positive and helpful to one another. Norm's last comment "I appreciate that," makes me a little anxious, because I fear it will close off this potentially fruitful discussion, and I move to invite him to say more.

STONE: What would they have jumped on you about, Norm?

NORM: Same things we were talking about then. I don't want to bring up specifics.

BRUCE: I think you have to fight for your beliefs but not to get carried away with it, and he didn't.

NORM: I appreciate that. There was a time when I wouldn't have come back.

BRUCE: I know. I was concerned. I believe I know how hard it was. It wasn't a big explosion, but after a conflict like that to regroup yourself and come back . . .

NORM: I don't even know what I did or what I said. I kinda think about it. I went off.

BRUCE: I hope that helped you.

NORM: It helped me that you said that. What you just said. That means a lot to me.

RUTAN: From an object relations point of view, the fact that Norm was angered by Bruce signals that Bruce is an important person to Norm.

   Potential comment: "Norm, it sounds like Bruce is important to you." (Ultimately, discussing their intimacy with one another is much more frightening, even, than sharing their anger.)

STONE: I hope they don't seal it over. I will give it another try. It has been mentioned and the two men have agreed that talking about it has been useful, but Norm's notion about being jumped on has been bypassed. I might be able to keep it going.

RUTAN: Here we view the interaction quite differently. I see the potential for acknowledging affection and relationship as supremely important, whereas my colleague focuses on the avoidance of anger.

STONE: So the idea that you came in with, that everyone would jump on you, actually didn't happen.

NORM: No. And what's neat about it, it's an unusual thing for me to have. Growing up I just expected everybody to get me and they did.

BRUCE: Do you feel automatically in the wrong?

NORM: No. I got blamed for things I didn't do, and if problems happened, it was my fault. The other kids, they didn't want to hurt anybody but me. I even had kids circle round me and throw rocks at me. I always bring up things from the past. It still affects the way I'm dealing with things, but it used to be that nobody had mercy on me. Like one incident when I...it's hard to explain being alone. You have nobody to tell or defend you or anything, and when people keep hurting you and hurt you, you just expect it. I would come. . . Am I making myself clear?

BRUCE: A reflex almost.

NORM: You don't even give a person much of a chance to talk. Really. So many times when I was younger, I was mistreated and I felt that, if anything, I was always afraid like that.

BRUCE: The group is to experiment with too, as far as I'm concerned. Take chances. I don't know who said that one of the phases of recovery is to stand up for yourself, show your power.

NORM: Oh, really? Oh, power, that's what it's all about.

BRUCE: So I guess we all . . . most of us have to go through that before we can move on. We keep adjusting.

NORM: Well, it helped me what you said though.

STONE: Nice! Some good analytic work. Norm provided an important piece of personal history, and he recognizes that the past is still exerting a significant influence over him. Bruce, however, seems to be prematurely practicing his social work skills, and he has a tendency to close off discussions with cognitive framing. Maybe I can keep things going by broadening the scope of this discussion to include others.

STONE: I wonder, Norm, if there is a linkage between what you have been talking about and what Aileen said a few minutes ago—that is, that somehow Joan's not returning was linked to you; that you had done something wrong or bad; just like Norm had felt, like everybody would jump on his case for something bad. I think that people come with an expectation of what others will feel, but that may not be the case.

AILEEN: When Jerry [her boyfriend] is not making me happy all of the time, I tend to always fall back on being depressed.

RUTAN: Aileen is also indicating a rudimentary understanding that her depression serves a purpose. That is, when she is faced with unhappy feelings in the relationship she "falls back" on her depression.

STONE: Aileen has responded by addressing the issue of emotional separation when her boyfriend is not available as she percieves it by not smiling—this has echoes of a very early relationship between infant and mother. However, the focus was on the cause of difficulties, and perhaps I could move the process forward if that aspect could be addressed.

STONE: It's as if it's your fault that he's not making you happy. Is that it?

AILEEN: Sort of.

NORM: Do you feel that there is something else that makes you happy besides Jerry?

AILEEN: Oh, yes. Well, you know, my mother does. My mother's nice. My sister's nice too.

NORM: I mean hobbies and things like...people and everything.

AILEEN: I do sew. (*pause*)

NORM: Do you enjoy sewing?.

AILEEN: I enjoy sewing. I pick up some needlepoint. I have some I'm working on. I'm going to make a velveteen pillow out of it. . . . I'm going through a difficult phase. I'm not obsessing like I used to. Yet, I still am pretty anxious and wander around the apartment.

STONE: This sounds like some good news for her. Aileen's association to her mother and then to less animate objects supports the notion that she is regressed (or stuck) at an archaic level and work will be slow with her. Rather than an interpretation of the hopes she has for universal responsiveness, I choose to acknowledge the change she has experienced in order to help with the alliance.

STONE: That sounds like a real relief.

AILEEN: It is a relief. The trouble is that I still keep running around. It's kind of a weird position to be in.

NORM: I do that sometimes too. Sometimes, I just start talking out loud.

AILEEN: I don't feel for myself that this is anything particularly awful. It's just kinda goofy.

BRUCE: Well, it may be goofy, but there is nothing sick about it.

NORM: You can distinguish between the fact that you didn't do anything and your feelings? Can you? The feeling that . . .

AILEEN: Well, no. I kinda think things are my fault a lot.

NORM: They are not.

AILEEN: OK. That's good to know. Sometimes in my relationship with Jerry we go out and about and I kinda think that people don't talk to us very much; that it's my fault. I worry about that in church.

BRUCE: We have now had a couple of people leave the group, and I thought that they have left because of me. That's a lot the same way, I think.

STONE: Aileen seemed to overcome Norm's efforts to close down the discussion by bringing up her feelings of responsibility (her grandiosity? paranoia? masochism?). She is con-

veying the message that she wants to address these feelings. Bruce joins in. I offer some acknowledgment of the work they are doing.

STONE: Those aren't comfortable feelings.

NORM: I don't have them.

STONE: Not everyone does.

NORM: It seems like it would be a real hard thing to deal with. Either way if that's the way you feel. Whether it's true or not. I know in the past I had problems distinguishing from what was real and what wasn't. I would think that somebody didn't like me, and there was no reason for it.

AILEEN: I get a feeling like that in McDonald's.

NORM: It scares me.

BRUCE: When you do have it, it makes you feel even worse—there's another one who doesn't like you.

NORM: Yes. It was bad. I had it for about 10 years, and then I had a medication change and that helped and I forgot about it. The medication change helped me. Allowed me to heal.

RUTAN: Perhaps this is an attempt to short-circuit ownership of psychological aspects of the problems.

Potential comment: "People have been courageously exploring the deep feelings between people right in this room. These are important relationships, and by examining the feelings here we can learn a great deal about relationships outside this room as well."

STONE: The session is nearing the end, and there has been a great deal covered, considerable self-revelation, some dealing with intragroup conflict, but a modicum of self-protection persists. In addition, Norm has just introduced the positive effect of medication, and I would want to shift away from that focus to one in which psychological elements are central to the discussion. An intervention designed to acknowledge what has been accomplished and to provide a clear focus for them might help the members gain some continuity and continue the work in the next session. There is a danger in too extensive a summary, in that patients may wait for that and not be motivated to use their abilities to think about themselves, but the trade-off seems reasonable, since this is not a usual procedure for me.

STONE: I think we have covered a lot today. Old feelings about loss. And I do think they are somewhat linked because I think there was concern here in the group about the conflict in here that you (*to Norm*) had with Bruce.

Whether you would return and the fact that it got talked about openly, I think was very important.

NORM: I'm going to miss Bruce. I am!

RALPH: Me too.

BRUCE: I'll be here 5 or 6 more weeks. I'll let you know the exact date next week. It's about the 21st.

STONE: This turn in the discussion provides me with an opportunity to reinforce one of the elements in the group agreement regarding terminations, and also keep in focus the issues related to loss and separations.

STONE: It isn't often we get a chance to really say good-bye to somebody. This is an assumption, but Joan may or may not return. If she doesn't, there won't be a chance to say good-bye. At least here now there is a chance to say good-bye to Bruce and look at the feelings that are involved. Because I think Bob said earlier, and I think this was involved with what Ralph and Aileen said, that losing a relationship is not easy; and I think that there was concern that a relationship would be broken up with a conflict, and you are at fault.

RUTAN: The therapist has a difficult task—of trying to explore possible aspects of flight and resistance in Bruce's "school conflict" while not shaming or humiliating him.

BRUCE: That's good.

NORM: This is going to be a major victory for me. (*pause*) Not over you. Over myself.

MELISSA: (*to Bruce*) You should stop in when you get a chance.

STONE: Let's stop here, and we'll go on next week.

RUTAN: In my view, the therapist's comment, "Let's stop," is actually a minor error. It implies that we have a decision about when to stop. The ending of a group session is determined by the clock, not by the whim of the therapist.

COMMENTARY

This session began with a series of members' associations that could be understood not only as real experiences but as metaphors for losses within the group. Stone's initial decision revolved around helping the members elaborate their stories with a focus on affect or translating the metaphors into the group setting. Such decisions are based on knowledge of the patients and their capacities to explore in-group feelings. Certainly, not all progress is linked to examination of members examining emotionally laden experiences within the group. However, within-group interactions are the optimal source of data for patients who have the capacity to use them to reflect upon themselves, their interactions, and their prior experiences as a pathway to change.

This session illustrates the varying capacity of the members to examine their in-group processes. Several times they would use the therapist's focusing their discussion on the displacement metaphor to spontaneously address loss within the group. However, they also become uncomfortable, for example, when members expose their feelings of "responsibility" for Joan's departure. They attempt to manage their discomfort by requesting the therapist to act (e.g., Melissa's request of the therapist to call the missing member) or by a shift from in-group to outside issue (e.g., Melissa's shift to Bill and his prospective employment). However, there is always an echo of the primary group issue in the metaphors members use (e.g., "making it to the second interview").

The session also illustrates how different therapists can profitably use group data in different ways. For one of us the issue of in-group relationships assumed dominance, whereas for the other the issue of in-group anger was pursued. We are certain that each reader will find other aspects of the meeting to which they would have profitably responded.

The subtle weaving of in-group and out-of-group data is typical of patient interactions as they try to work within their own capacities to tolerate anxiety or other emotional discomfort (guilt, shame) and remain with the here-and-now process. If one person seems to change the topic, that may be an indicator of that person's particular vulnerability; in addition, that patient may be fulfilling a necessary role to protect the group. Most likely the "change of subject" just continues the topic but moves it to a "safer" arena. This is not an "either/or" situation; rather, it may represent "both/and." The clinician is in the position of assessing whether to address the resistance directly or allow the members to continue, anticipating that there will be future opportunities to revisit the focus. The decision not to intervene allows the clinician space to listen for additional echoes of the theme and gain additional understanding of the source of the resistance. Yet, such delay may be a missed opportunity. There is no "right way." Therapy is a journey without a clear map. One hopes that interventions point in the proper direction. Fortunately, our groups are excellent "supervisors" and tell us when we have taken an unhelpful route.

The group is designed to be of help to individuals. In the above session there is evidence of some members' capacities to work effectively with affect-laden issues, whereas others seem less inclined or able to do so. On the whole we would evaluate this as a successful meeting. We certainly can see where the therapist may have made alternative decisions about the interventions, and even some of the comments that seemed to interfere with the process by being "reassuring" (e.g., the comment "not everyone does" in response to Norm's comment about not having uncomfortable feelings).

No session can be "error-free." Patients can be forgiving if they feel that their therapist is genuinely interested and concerned. They will provide multiple opportunities to work on important conflicts if they are not accurately understood on any particular occasion. The therapist has the responsibility of self-scrutiny. The task is to listen, to the best of his/her ability, to patients' responses to interventions with an ear to listening (as well as using visual cues of non-verbal responses as indicators) for the possibility of having intervened in a detrimental manner. It is not the misunderstanding or the empathic failures that are destructive to treatment, but it is a consistent inability to recognize that one has misunderstood which will ultimately doom the therapy.

The therapist and the commentator each use several variations of psychodynamic theory to inform their work. In a highly condensed manner, we will attempt to summarize these thoughts.

Stone's primary theoretical base is that of group-as-a-whole processes grounded in the group focal conflict model (Whitaker & Lieberman, 1964) and of self psychology (Kohut, 1984; Stone, 1992b). Thus, he focuses on trying to create a group atmosphere in which the patients can slowly unfold their stories and expose their transferences in a setting where there is a respect for defenses ("enabling solutions"). The therapist's general focus is the traditional tripartite model (group focal conflict), in which comments about behavior or feelings usually contain a "because" ("You are angry because you felt ignored when you spoke a few minutes ago"—without often articulating "and you did not want to be ashamed of being passive"). These interventions primarily address here-and-now transactions in the session.

Part of Stone's style is illustrated by the phrasing of his interventions, which are not framed as merely soothing (which could be suppressive) but as a recognition of the difficult tasks that patients face in exploring their inner turmoil (empathic connections). Many interventions broaden one person's or a subgroup's comments to include the possibility of the entire group having similar feelings or responses. Interventions are often framed in a tentative fashion that facilitates the potential for patients to disagree or offer alternative formulations (attention to the alliance).

In addition to the traditional attention to patient's projections and defensive operations, the therapist is particularly alert to the development of selfobject transferences, which become evident primarily when there has been an empathic failure, either on his part, or by members or by the patient's experience of the whole group. Thus the therapist pays particular attention to "process." When the inevitable misunderstandings or injuries take place, he will try to elucidate the detailed process. In this group, composed of patients with significant personality constrictions and vulnerabilities, he sees his task as attempting to understand patients' caution (resistance to the transference) in the face of their histories, as well as their fears that they will be injured again. Although he does not eschew making individual "genetic" interpretations, he believes that if the setting is sufficiently safe patients will reveal important historical material that elucidates the sources of their vulnerable and fragile sense of self.

Rutan's primary orientation is object relations theory, and thus his focus is on the defenses employed to protect against intimacy and relationship. Whenever there is evidence of relationship, that is highlighted (see the exchange between Norm and Bruce). The theory is that the need for relationship is innate and always present no matter how much individuals protest. It is in the examination of in-group relationships that one has the most direct access to transference and defenses.

In addition, we both adhere to the psychodynamic principle that the group process is omnipresent. Whatever is being discussed, at some level it is a report on the most significant dynamic issues present in the group. Frequently, neither the therapist nor the members can decode the metaphors or they lose track of the process. Both come to recognize that through attentive listening and attending to their own inner responses they are usually able to regain the thread running through the discussion and regain their balance and understanding.

FOURTEEN

Difficult Groups and Difficult Patients

The greater the difficulty, the more the glory in
surmounting it.
—EPICURUS

C linicians are often confronted with groups that seem
stuck, confusing, or boring. They may even be frustrating, frightening, or rage inducing. Therapists may
describe the transactions in these groups as stilted, without affect, or unfocused, and they may label the content as banal. They are consistently unable
to find a central focus, or they find the discussions painfully repetitive. The entire group or particular individuals become the focus of the clinician's attention in these "difficult" situations.

Seasoned therapists are familiar with such situations and are often able
to gain perspective by providing sufficient "space" for the process to become
clear, by attending to their emotional responses, or by obtaining consultation.
Of course, we can never fully understand and are always seeking tentative understanding while leaving ourselves open to new information and modifying
our hypotheses. Nevertheless, groups and/or particular patients can be vexing
and discomfiting for the clinician and some situations may eventually end up
unworkable.

THE DIFFICULT GROUP

There are many ways to define a problematic group. Here is our working definition: a group for which any given therapist has trouble making and sustaining emotional contact with either the group or with specific members. This formulation leaves open the possibility that what might be difficult for one clinician may not be so for another. While the clinician's contribution to the difficult situation or the group must always be considered, our focus here is on groups or patients who would likely be difficult for any clinician.

Problems in Forming a Group

Many problematic groups are the result of either poor patient selection or the lack of a clear set of group agreements. Ideally, in the process of selecting candidates for dynamic group treatment, the therapist gains sufficient understanding of prospective members so that the group will mesh well and function smoothly. However, in many instances patients do not accurately report—or are unaware of—interpersonal aspects of their difficulties. The "problems" only emerge in the ongoing treatment process.

No selection process fully informs the therapist of what lies ahead for a new member. It is not unusual for individuals who appear to have serious psychopathology to integrate quite well into a group, whereas others who appear to have "ordinary" problems may end up contributing to serious problems of group formation and development. Therapy groups may be able to integrate and work with one or two such individuals, but a critical mass of severely impaired individuals may disrupt the process and lead to stalemates or, worse, disintegration of the group (Leszcz, 1989). At times, a well-functioning group that contains and appears to be working with several "difficult" members may be thrown into disarray with the addition of one more acting-out patient (Munzer, 1966).

Two quite different scenarios can lead to placing individuals with significant difficulties in a group. First, therapists often *deliberately* place such individuals in groups because there is a likelihood that these patients may benefit from group therapy. We believe that "taking a chance" is a worthwhile endeavor if clinicians are attuned to the potential difficulties for themselves, the group, and the individual. A second situation arises when the clinician *unwittingly* places unsuited or ill-prepared individuals into a group. Today, when insurance companies often do not reimburse for group therapy or managed care companies restrict the panel of providers, the general availability of patients may be diminished. This may unconsciously lead therapists to insufficiently prepare prospective members in order to save patients' insurance money for the group treatment. Further, when groups are reduced to a few members, in a rush to rebuild the census a clinician may not carefully evaluate a person's motivation or degree of interpersonal or intrapsychic disturbance (see Chapter 7). As a consequence of these factors, clinicians may place an unsuited or ill-prepared individual into a group.

The Role of Group Development in Problematic Groups

Understanding group development can be valuable in diagnosing a difficult group. Group development is a product of the interactions among members and with the therapist. Although norms and values are significantly influenced by the therapist, ultimately it is the members that create the treatment environment. Even with careful, well-chosen membership, patients' interactions emerge in the developing process that were not predicted or appreciated in the preparatory interviews. The dyadic relationship, no matter how carefully reviewed, cannot reveal all the interpersonal aspects of individuals that will appear when they join a group. As we have suggested earlier, the nature of pathology seen in modern clinical practice is relational, and transferring individuals from the safety of individual therapy to that of a group may evoke character defenses that were not obvious in the one-to-one format.

Nitsun (1996) lists the following characteristics of the group that elicit resistance and potentially inhibit group development: stranger anxiety, fears of exposure, lack of structure, insufficient leadership guidance, overstimulation by the presence of others, and interpersonal concerns. Either singly or in concert, these elements may create a "dependent" group that gets stuck searching for magical relief from the leader. At times it may seem that the entire group is resisting, whereas at other times the members may put forth one person as their representative. Leaders are likely to respond to such intense, unremitting demands with countertransference enactments that fail to help members gain perspective on their feelings or behavior. Under these circumstances, the potential is for groups to become mired in opening phase material, with repetitious themes expressing issues of basic trust or safety as well as dependency.

In other situations, a group may appear to make progress into the second phase of development only to find that there may be considerable resistance to expressions of anger, creating a group where only brief forays into the second phase of development are seen. The group may comply with an individual's vulnerability to angry interchange and regress to earlier developmental issues. In this situation, attempts to help members explore their underlying assumptions or reflect upon their interactions are rarely successful.

For example, the group focal conflict model (see Chapter 2) provides the clinician a way of identifying group responses as restrictive solutions, suggesting that members are bent more on self-protection than on managing change. They seem developmentally stuck. Wilfred R. Bion would probably have understood a failure to progress as members alternating among basic assumptions with only limited evidence of a work group (Hahn & Toman, 1997). When the clinician's self-esteem is linked to a time frame that predetermines the rate in which the group should traverse developmental stages, the therapist's countertransference frustration may further contribute to the therapeutic impasse.

Group Process

Group members have the dual tasks of understanding both interpersonal and internal processes. Therapists assume the major responsibility for monitoring both of these processes until the members become aware of these dimensions of their treatment.

Group process may be disrupted by the defenses employed by difficult patients. These individuals are often surprised or hurt by confrontations they receive or observe (see the example of Janine in Chapter 10). They manage their reactions by using defenses of projection, promise of behavior change, or intellectualization. Projection is conveyed by the expression "That's your problem"; by behavior—"I won't do that again"; and by intellectualization by—"Why do you think I act that way?" or "Maybe I did that because of something in my childhood." Frequently these responses occur rapidly, the patient thereby avoiding any time to reflect. They deflect the confrontation and protect the patient from the pain such confrontations evoke. This is further complicated by the interactive effect of this defensive behavior. That is, as these patients protect themselves they invoke additional responses from the others, turning what may have been a genuinely altruistic wish for the patient to gain self-awareness into anger or confusion.. The interactions can be frustrating when they deflect from the immediacy of the here and now.

Of course, these and many other responses to a confrontation of one's behavior are not unique to "difficult" patients. It is when they are habitual and/or not amenable to reflection that they become problematic and "difficult."

Another aspect of difficult interactions is one in which the group process is minimized or ignored. Sometimes patients seem unable to link their behaviors (verbal or physical) to processes in the group. These are people who are often considered habitual actors—that is, they come late, miss meetings, or withdraw, and when questioned they claim to be tired or merely thinking about something outside the session. It is as if they are walled off from others and the emotional links are denied.

Gans and Alonso (1998) have emphasized that difficult patients may be *created* by the group interactions. This process is similar to scapegoating, in which aspects of individuals become "fixed" in a single person or a subgroup. These are aspects of the others that are "unacceptable" and cannot be examined by the projecting members. Wright (1998) states, "These repetitious patterns or arrangements that people construct together help them develop a sense of familiarity, comfort, and order in their physical and social world. Once the structures are in place, they can become quite fixed and inviolate" (p. 341).

BORDERLINE AND NARCISSISTIC DISORDERS

A majority of patients who are viewed as "difficult" carry a borderline or narcissistic diagnosis. Increasingly, in the present climate of health care, patients with significant personal deficits which are primarily manifest in their relationships are referred to group treatment.

Fortunately, there is considerable evidence that difficult patients can benefit from psychodynamic groups. McCallum and Piper (1999) studied such a population and state, "the more patients were able to engage in psychodynamic work in the small psychodynamic group, the more useful the program was related. This finding supports the relevance of intensive dynamically oriented group therapy for treating patients with personality disorder" (p. 13). They conclude, "The outcome results cited in the present study are encouraging for clinicians who work with the challenging population in intensive group-oriented programs" (p. 13).

Borderline and narcissistic patients have received extensive attention in the current psychotherapeutic literature. They warrant special attention here because of the unique ways in which groups can help them and because of the technical considerations that therapists must take into account when treating them in groups. Since there is no unanimity in defining these patients, a more detailed description of their pathology is needed before presenting techniques for their group treatment. Due to their volatility and difficulty maintaining object constancy or self-cohesion, these individuals also are candidates for combined individual and group treatment. Moreover, due to their tendency to experience crises, medications are often useful to stabilize affective or cognitive disruptions. The concomitant use of medications for many patients in group treatment has become common practice, and this strategy was examined in Chapter 11.

The Borderline Patient

No integrated diagnostic schema exists for diagnosing borderline personality disorder, and efforts to categorize these individuals are based on descriptive, dynamic, or combined criteria. In general, patients with borderline personality disorder have, according to the fourth edition of the American Psychiatric Association's (1994) *Diagnostic and Statistical Manual of Mental Disorders* (DSM-IV), "a pervasive pattern of instability of interpersonal relationships, self-image, and affects, and marked impulsivity, beginning in early adulthood and present in a variety of contexts" (p. 280). Their interpersonal relations may be characterized as unstable, intense, or withdrawn. They may have outbursts of anger directed at others or the self. Their mood is equally unstable, though a chronic depressive element is frequently present. They have neither a consistent and clearly formed identity nor an ability to develop long-range goals or plans. At times of stress, often related to separations, these patients may develop brief psychotic episodes.

From an object relations point of view, borderline patients may be viewed as individuals for whom others are *too* important. They are insufficiently protected from interpersonal pain. (This is contrasted with the narcissistic patient, for whom the importance of others is unknown or underappreciated.)

Dynamic formulations about borderline conditions have focused on early developmental deficits in which internal object relations have not stabilized or separation–individuation tasks have not been mastered (Masterson, 1976, p. 3). Kernberg (1975) assumes that the fundamental defect is present in the ego capacity to integrate self and object representations. The internal objects remain split into all-good and all-bad entities. When equilibrium is disturbed, the aggressive drives overwhelm the "good" internal objects and anxiety becomes paramount. Projective mechanisms serve to protect the good internal object. With such developmental deficits, these patients have little or no capacity to maintain satisfactory and consistent internal objects (Adler & Buie, 1979). The immature ego development interferes with the capacity to tolerate or integrate ambivalent feelings, and as a result defensive splitting maintains perceptions of others as all good or all bad. It is no wonder that the variability of these patients' pathological configurations, differing ego capacities, and defenses create problems in making an accurate diagnosis and formulating a satisfactory treatment plan. As if that were not complicated enough, feminist theorists are raising questions about possible gender bias in this diagnosis, since the vast majority of patients diagnosed as borderline are female (whereas most patients diagnosed as narcissistic are male).

Individuals diagnosed with borderline personality disorder are difficult to engage in therapy, and the likelihood of their terminating prematurely is high. Yeomans et al. (1994) reviewed reports of dropouts from dyadic treatment. At 3 months the dropout rate may vary from 34% to 67%, and only 34%–57% of outpatients remain in treatment after 6 months. Careful selection of some higher-risk persons may decrease the dropout rate (Stevenson & Mears, 1992). The combination of difficulties in forming an alliance (impulsivity, affect intolerance, and resistance to change) are harbingers of poor treatment compliance.

The interpersonal difficulties of these patients are usually apparent from the moment they enter a group (Roth, 1979). They are particularly frightened by intimacy, closeness, and feelings of contamination or annihilation by others. In order to maintain their precarious inner balance, they consciously and unconsciously resist emotionally joining the group, and this resistance is often manifest through violations of the group agreements. Tardiness, absence, and a variety of self-protective responses are quickly apparent under the stress of entry into the group. Some borderline patients blame their referring therapist for their very presence, a solution that allows them to be present without being engaged. Under this condition—and there are many variations on this theme—they can observe and test the safety of the situation. Others, upon entering, soon conclude that they have nothing in common with their fellow members or complain that the discussions are irrelevant to their needs. They criticize the therapist for all sorts of shortcomings, sometimes very perceptively tuning in on the clinician's errors or empathic failures. In their criticisms, they may gather allies among other members, re-creating their world of all-good and all-bad objects.

Another subgroup of borderline individuals enters the group exhibiting domineering and overtly controlling behaviors. The familiar role of monopolizer or help-rejecting complainer place them at the center of attention, thereby partially gratifying exhibitionistic needs. The hostility they generate is quite familiar and serves to protect them from the greater dangers of intimacy. Such behaviors make these patients particularly prone to being scapegoated as other members project their own exhibitionistic wishes into these developmentally arrested individuals. The borderline members, for their part, are adept at using projective identification in order to protect themselves from recognizing their own affects (Ogden, 1979).

Despite these difficulties and confusions about borderline patients, there seems to be considerable agreement about the particular advantages of group therapy for them. Indeed, successful group treatment with this population was reported (by Shaskan) as early as 1957. Horwitz (1980) has suggested three elements of group membership that are advantageous for these patients: (1) transference diffusion, which especially diminishes the negative destructive feelings about the therapist; (2) social and emotional distancing, which allows the patient to withdraw and thereby regulate the intensity of affective involvement without immediate sanctions; and (3) social pressure, which helps regulate reality testing. Horwitz (1994) suggested that these advantages are relative, since transference in groups can be intensified as well as diffused and emotional distancing is often more difficult than in dyadic treatment.

There is some question as to whether technical modifications are necessary in the treatment of the borderline patient. In part the answer is related to group composition. One approach is to include one or two such patients in a group where others have reached higher developmental levels (Horwitz, 1977b). Under these conditions borderline patients seem to be able to learn from exploration or interpretation, and little modification in technique is necessary (Hulse, 1958). Another approach is to form homogeneous groups (Roth, 1980). There are certain advantages when all the patients are struggling with issues at the same developmental level. Diversity still remains, since individuals bring their own particular histories and interpersonal styles to bear on group interactions.

As mentioned earlier, borderline individuals utilize splitting of objects as a major defense. Kibel (1991) proposes that this characteristic defense can be used to therapeutic advantage by structuring the group so that the patient's image of the group as a whole is benign. This approach is based on outcome results with borderline patients treated at the Menninger Foundation in Topeka, Kansas (Horwitz, 1974), where the finding was that the development of the therapeutic relationship was of greater significance than the development of insight. Within this supportive frame, it is presumed that these patients expose their aggressively linked internal object relationships where they can be modified through partial identifications with others who have expressed similar aspects of themselves and have not been traumatized as a result. Moreover, borderline individuals, a significant proportion of whom have experienced physical or sexual abuse or have witnessed domestic violence, may alter or partially replace the images and experiences they harbor of their families (Herman, Perry, & von der Kolk, 1989).

When working with a borderline patient, it is important for the therapist to set realistic goals. Establishing a therapeutic alliance may be an appropriate intermediate, if not final, goal for some of these individuals. Attainment of that goal implies an ability of the patient to see both positive and negative aspects of other individuals and to experience them as separate, with their own wishes and needs. Further, it represents a significant advance in the ability of borderline patients to negotiate more mature object relatedness. Therapists must pay attention to the communications inherent in all their own behaviors with regard to these patients (Glatzer, 1978; Stone & Gustafson, 1982). Feldberg (1958) maintains that the therapist has to be more active with borderline patients than with neurotic patients. Interpretation may have to be supplemented by other technical measures, such as universalization, confrontation, and drawing attention to similarities among individuals (Roth, 1979). These technical strategies, in the context of a supportive group, allow for more gratifying interpersonal relationships, which proceed along the path of identification to internalization of more benign internal object relations (Kibel, 1991).

Several particular strategies aid this process. Because many borderline individuals do not recognize the impact of their behaviors on others, they are surprised, hurt, and defensive when feedback is given. By empathizing with their surprise and hurt, the therapist can make emotionally meaningful contact with confronted individuals. This strategy, which differs from the usual strategy of focusing on helping the patient hear the interpretation, thereby reinforces the benign safety of the group atmosphere.

A second strategy uses interpretation aimed at having the greatest impact on the other members, not the borderline patient. For instance, a therapist might normally draw attention to the fact that a member attacks others when he/she is anxious or frightened. However, if this interpretation were made to a borderline member, it would likely be met with denial. When the relevant interpretation can be offered to healthier members, the borderline patients can observe those members begin to appreciate the sequencing of anxiety and attack. This facilitates the borderline patient gaining perspective and becoming less likely to withdraw or counterattack. The result is not only a safer group environment for all the members but also a wonderful laboratory for the borderline individual, who has been able to observe the transactions with interest and safety.

Conversely, some direct interventions to the borderline patient may have much greater impact upon the other members. The clinician should appreciate that the intervention is heard by all. Thus an interpretation which offers an explanation of a particular process may not be readily heard by the patient (assuming that it is accurate, it might imply an emotional attachment which the patient is not ready to accept), but it may be more readily heard by the others. The others, with the understanding they accrue, may become more accepting and tolerant, thereby shifting a negative group atmosphere. They may also be in a position to observe and comment on similar sequences. If the peer transferences are not as intense as those directed to the therapist, the borderline person can "hear" and integrate such peer interpretations more successfully.

Borrowing from object relations theory, it is always helpful to keep in mind that even the most obstreperous patient is trying to be *in* relationship, not trying to avoid relationship. By the therapist continually pointing this out to the individual and the group, other members begin to gain empathy for the plight of the borderline patient.

In treating the borderline patient in a group with less disturbed patients, the therapist must balance the unique needs of the borderline person against the needs of the group-as-a-whole. For example, borderline patients often barrage therapists with questions, insisting that they get a direct answer. The basis for this behavior can be multidetermined: the behavior may be an enactment of the patient's sense of entitlement, fear of being ignored, low frustration tolerance, or wish for contact. Whatever the specific etiology of often obnoxious behavior by these patients, therapists are reminded that these individuals are trying to gain and sustain relationships. By answering their questions directly, the therapist may soothe the borderline patients temporarily but may set these patients up for the ire of the other members for having received this special attention. By the therapist not answering the question directly, borderline patients are protected from intense sibling rivalry but are left unprotected from the intense reactions to not having their needs met. Therapists must quickly assess the pros and cons of providing an answer when such patients begin to question them, since any choice includes assets and liabilities in the treatment.

Many of the ego deficits and problems in maintaining a sense of identity are evident as borderline patients join a group.

CLINICAL EXAMPLES

Despite having accepted the usual group agreements, George announced during his first group meeting that he would commit himself to remaining for only six sessions. At the end of his 6-week period, he extended his commitment for another 6 weeks. That was followed by yet another 6-week commitment. Only then could George feel safe enough to publicly commit himself to remaining in the group for as long as it took to work on his problems. Not only was this patient severely cautious, but his style was provocative and evoked criticism and resentment from the others. This only served to reinforce his reluctance to join fully because of his conviction that others would not like him. (This is yet another example of how projective identification serves to "train" the world to behave as expected.)

A borderline patient maintained her distance by angrily insisting that others reveal all the intimate details of their lives, all the while remaining resolutely mute about her own life. Her rationale was that she could feel safer and closer if others were willing to be vulnerable in her presence, but the actual effect was that others had no interest in being close to her. Nonetheless, the patient was able to persist in this stance for a number of years before consistently being able to examine her in-group behaviors.

* * *

The marked emotional volatility of borderline patients often startles the therapist and the other members.

CLINICAL EXAMPLES

A woman had seemed quite cooperative and insightful when the therapist focused an interpretation on her behavior. However, 30 minutes later she angrily screamed at him, "You're ignoring me!" when he was focusing on interactions between other members. The patient's difficulty in being able to share the therapist and maintain an inner representation of him as interested and concerned contributed to her outburst.

A borderline man was told by a fellow member, "You just interrupted someone again." He denied that he had done so and refused to even consider it a possibility, even though in the previous meeting he acknowledged that both inside and outside the group others had made that observation to him. His defiant stance enraged his group colleagues. Nonetheless, later in the meeting he turned to his original confronter and pleaded, "Let's be friends." He was unable to hear the response that friendship must be based on give and take and could not just be willed.

*   *   *

Here the fluctuation from an angry pout to a pleading request for friendship illustrates the borderline patient's emotional instability, need for contact, and lack of awareness of others' responses to the interaction. Borderline patients are particularly successful in gaining relationships; they are very difficult to ignore! Sustaining relationships is not among their strengths.

The therapist is often the focus of attention for the borderline patient, and the task of maintaining balance in the face of incessant demands or angry outbursts is difficult.

Clinical Example

One female borderline patient had the disconcerting habit of turning her chair so that she only talked to the therapist and only made contact with him; the therapist felt riveted to her and could not disengage himself from her. A male borderline patient unfalteringly insisted that the therapist follow up any clarification or interpretation with direct advice about how to change his behavior or how to make him feel his feelings.

*   *   *

The result of these and many other behaviors is that therapists find themselves on emotional roller coasters. They may be overstimulated or upset by the defensive maneuverings of these patients. This might be reflected in their dreams or in a feeling of dread before a session (Roth, 1980). A consultation with a colleague or an ongoing formal or informal opportunity for ventilation, processing, or supervision can be invaluable for the therapist trying to maintain his/her equilibrium in the face of these emotion-laden transactions.

The borderline patient's capacity to utilize group therapy most effectively is often enhanced by the concurrent use of individual therapy (Rutan & Alonso, 1982; Slavinska-Holy, 1983). The individual therapy format offers the opportunity for these patients to gain some perspective on the overstimulation that they often experience in the group, whereas the group offers them the protection of peers as they explore their powerful transferences to individual therapists.

So how should one treat borderline individuals in group therapy? Indeed, should they be treated in groups? If one holds to the fundamental psychodynamic principles, borderline patients are no different than any of the rest of us. They are trying to avoid pain and gain relationships. They have just developed a uniquely nettlesome defensive structure that works all too well. That is, like a skunk in the forest that "stinks up the place" when threatened, borderline patients have the capacity to make people not want to be around them, even as they yearn for nothing more than to be the center—and the exclusive center—of attention of those very others. And in their own unique way they do often gain a place of centrality in their relationships. Groups provide unparalleled opportunities for observing this defensive operation at work in the very interpersonal field in which it was most designed to function. For a therapist to generate special or unique treatment techniques for this population, while overtly caring and thoughtful, runs the risk of accepting the projective identifications of these patients and treating them as special.

The outcome of treatment of borderline individuals has not been sufficiently studied. Nevertheless, long-term follow-up reports of severely ill borderline patients treated with extended hospitalization and individual therapy provide hope that some of these patients can lead employed and self-supporting lives (Roller & Nelson, 1999). Yet, a significant proportion remain superficial and avoid intimacy (McGlashan, 1986). No parallel reports are available to assess the outcome of group treatment, but anecdotal reports of clinical experience have been promising.

Narcissistic Disorder

Throughout this book reference has been made to Kohut's (1971, 1977, 1984) contributions to the evolution of a psychoanalytic theory of the self and its applicability to the treatment of narcissistic patients. Kohut's theory emerged from an evolving concern in psychoanalytic theorizing in which, "an explanation was sought that was capable of addressing the indisputable psychological awareness of one's own being" (Socor, 1997 p.113). We will briefly summarize the central features of Kohut's self psychology, the controversies about and additions to the theory, and their applications to group psychotherapy.

Beginning with a focus on the consistent use of empathy and introspection as the primary tools in understanding inner emotional states, Kohut reformulated the theory of human development and placed the self at "the center of the individual's psychological universe" (Kohut, 1977, p. 311). The self, conceptually, is both a psychological structure that organizes experiences and an existential structure that is the center of independent initiative. The self is developed in the myriad interactions with "selfobjects," that is, objects (persons) available to empathically understand the self and fulfill certain psychological functions that the immature or traumatized self is unable to perform for itself. The archaic selfobject is experienced not as a person with separate needs and wishes but only as an object to fulfill functions. The need for the selfobject does not disappear but is necessary throughout the life cycle. However, the need is modified as the individual matures and the self assumes more of the self-soothing functions.

Self Psychology and Narcissistic Patients

Kohut (1971) initially formulated the presence of two developmental lines: the grandiose–exhibitionistic self, which requires phase-appropriate "mirroring" from the selfobject in order to develop ambitions and goals, and the idealizing self, which requires the opportunity to merge with an idealized other in order to develop values and ideals. These two "selfs" became the foundation of the bipolar self. In the 1984 posthumous monograph Kohut posited the need for an alter ego selfobject, which was conceived of as an intermediate area between the two poles. Kohut believes that the self's need for the sameness of the alter ego would aid in the development of skills and talents.

Psychopathology, within this framework, was conceptualized as a deficit in the development of a cohesive self, not the result of conflict among id, ego, superego, and reality. Symptoms of personality distortions are a consequence of failures of the self to mature and are formulated as the self's efforts to regain equilibrium or prevent further trauma (Kohut & Wolf, 1978). Destructive aggression and lust were formulated as responses to narcissistic injury or frustration and not as primary drives. The intensity and lack of resolution of conflicts reflect the underlying self pathology (P. H. Ornstein, 1991). This notion that psychopathology results from a deficit rather than a conflict is perhaps one of the major theoretical differences between self psychology and traditional psychoanalytic theory.

Significant revisions to self psychological theory have appeared in the past two decades (Shane & Shane, 1993; A. Goldberg, 1998). Goldberg suggests that Kohut's theory can be seen as developing along three streams: the traditional theory, intersubjectivity, and relational self psychology.

Within *traditional theory*, debate has emerged about the overuse of empathy and the forms and nature of the selfobjects. Ornstein and Ornstein (1995) acknowledge that other observational methods may be used; however, they are subordinated to empathy. Expansion of types of selfobject (e.g., "self-delineating" and "adversarial" [E. S. Wolf, 1988]) has raised questions regarding the nature of the selfobject: is it an inner experience or an actual entity? This raises the question of whether the therapist is an active participant shaping the therapeutic encounter or a functionary to be internalized into the structure of the self.

Intersubjectivity, which has been conceived as a field or system theory, posits that experience "brings into focus *both* the individual's world of inner experience *and* its embeddedness with other such worlds in a continual flow of reciprocal mutual influence" (Stolorow, 1995, p. 395; emphasis in original). In this system transferences are mutually activated and the focus is on the shared contributions and constructions of the therapist and the patient (A. Goldberg, 1998, p. 247). Intersubjectivity brings into focus the affective states of the participants.

Relational self psychology has addressed the issues of "optimal responsiveness" (Bacal, 1985) and thus the nature of the object as a separate individual. The focus on the actual (real) responses (a position buttressed by the work of Stern, 1985, on early infant–mother interactions), the role of the corrective emotional experience, and "the 'something more' than interpretation" (Stern et al., 1998) has increased interest in the relationship in effecting therapeutic change.

A further elaboration of the relational nature of the self is elaborated by Lichtenberg 1989) in his delineating "motivational systems"—the need for psychic regulation of physiological requirements, for attachment–affiliation, for exploration and assertion, for aversive reaction through antagonism or withdrawal, and for sensual enjoyment and sexual excitement.

The therapeutic process is presented in the following schema: Upon entering therapy a patient's symptoms may diminish or disappear as the symptomatic self is supported and sustained in the empathic therapeutic environment by the selfobject therapist. Self psychologists emphasize that empathy is not the same as agreement or sympathy, and the experience of being understood serves to stabilize the derailed self. Gradually, patients expose their developmental deficits and their concomitant needs for selfobjects. Inevitably, a break in the empathic connection (a narcissistic injury) occurs, and a patient may respond with his/her typical defenses (e.g., withdrawal or anger, somatization, or an "acting-out" behavior) in order to restore a sense of cohesion. The therapist, through introspection and empathy, attempts to understand and explain (interpret) the sequence of injury and the patient's efforts to regain internal balance and self-cohesion. In the optimal situation the patient responds with a restoration of self-coherence and, with repetition of the sequence, gradually acquires self-understanding and the capacity to soothe him/herself. This process has been labeled "transmuting internalization." This expansion and elaboration of self psychology has not always resulted in clarity, but instead represents the evolving nature of our theory building.

Many of the concepts of self psychology have been found applicable to group psychotherapy (Stone, 1992b; Harwood & Pines, 1998). Recently, particularly among group clinicians, interest in Kohut's concept of the *group self* (1976) has emerged; Kohut wrote, "we posit the existence of a certain psychological configuration with regard to the group—let us call it the 'group self'— which is analogous to the self of the individual" (pp. 420–421). Kohut is referring "to the self of a stable association of people" (p. 420). Boundaries between the personal self and the group self are not well defined and appear to overlap, but they are assumed to reach the deepest psychological levels

(Karterud, 1998). Ambitions and ideals are embedded in the core of the group self, and in group therapy these elements are represented by the clinician and the members (Karterud, 1998, p. 91). A letter written by a patient to her old group illustrates how the group selfobject can be idealized: "I'm helped when I recall how blessed I was to share the love and the kindness of my friends in the group and you [the therapist]. The memories of the intimacies we shared and the openness of our feelings helps keep me together" (Fried, 1973, p. 165). This letter illustrates the deep linkages between the personal and the group self, as the idealization of the process is conflated with those of the members and the therapist.

The power of the group as a whole to function as a selfobject for the group self that evokes a sense of well-being and power was observable during the height of the sensitivity movement in the 1960s, when many individuals behaved as if they were weekend T-group addicts. These group experiences provided a genuine emotional high derived from the impression of having merged with the idealized image of the group. The development of a stable and reliable transference to the group as a whole is extremely valuable in helping some individuals maintain a sense of inner cohesion (Meyers, 1978; Rutan & Rice, 1981; Stone & Whitman, 1977; Segalla, 1998).

Group psychotherapy does not provide the safety of the dyadic setting. The presence of others evokes fears of nonresponse from others and, as a consequence, presents a danger to the self. Almost universally, members fear the potential for narcissistic injury until some level of reliability and trust in the therapist and in the group interactions has been established. It is important, however, to distinguish between narcissistic needs present in all individuals and the emergence of coherent narcissistic transferences, which would indicate a significant disturbance of the self.

Within the group there are multiple opportunities for individuals to experience both enhancing and disruptive relations. The multiple transference potentials to the therapist and the other members may provide some safety when injury occurs at the hands of the therapist or a member, since there are others available as restorative or sustaining selfobjects (Harwood, 1992).

Many narcissistic patients exhibit considerable resistance to developing transferences. They anticipate that the selfobject will not be reliable and consequently resist acknowledging the importance of the soothing and satisfying merger with an idealized object or their inner need for an affirming or mirroring response. Among the many motives for resistance is shame. This painful affect arises from two sources: (1) narcissistic individuals may be consciously aware of their inner needs for selfobject responses and may be ashamed of such wishes; (2) shame may also be associated with failure to achieve the standards of the idealized self (Morrison, 1990). Some individuals with self disorders are unable to delineate or differentiate among affects. What may seem to be a resistance and what might be diagnosed as a depression may instead be a developmental deficit in which the patient complains of generalized dullness or loss of vitality (Stone, 1990).

Subtle tests regarding the group's reliability and safety are often conducted unconsciously by narcissistic patients prior to verbal acknowledgment of their transferential needs. Often the transference is established silently and becomes manifest only when there is a perceived failure on the part of the therapist or the group (Stone, 1996a).

CLINICAL EXAMPLE

Warren, a particularly articulate and gregarious member, spoke extensively of his difficulty in forming intimate relationships with women. He presented himself as a Don Juan, with many conquests and no loves. The narcissistic transference to the group emerged when he began to complain about absences by group members, which he felt ruined group cohesion. He could not verbalize precisely the inner upset he experienced, but he was vociferous in his declarations of discomfort. The transference reaction was particularly focused on one member, who often arrived late and who seldom spoke. It did not matter to Warren whether the member spoke, but his mere presence seemed very important indeed. The feelings of hurt and disorganization experienced by Warren when a member was absent were a consequence of his viewing the group as no longer being complete and therefore no longer being available as an idealized selfobject with which to merge. As Warren was gradually able to maintain his sense of inner stability, he could discuss his fears and wishes in more detail.

*   *   *

This example illustrates the confluence of the group self and the personal self. Warren's anguish had little to do with the particular person who was irregular in attendance, but rather reflected his archaic need for dependability. It is also an example of a transference to the "whole group."

Nonresponse from members may be followed by withdrawal or rage on the part of narcissistic patients, who often have some degree of awareness that their responses are out of proportion to the stimulus but who display or talk about their inner turmoil only after overcoming an initial resistance.

CLINICAL EXAMPLE

From time to time, Sylvia would report to the group how her relationship with her boyfriend was progressing. This was reported in a dispassionate manner, with no sense of urgency. One evening she began a meeting by announcing that her relationship had abruptly ended. As the discussion of that relationship continued, it became clear to Sylvia and the group that for months she had ignored the signals that serious troubles existed between her boyfriend and herself. Sylvia stated she needed him in order to feel that she was acceptable. As a consequence, she said, she had lived a fantasy of who her boyfriend was, refusing to recognize his particular realistic strengths and shortcomings. The group criticized Sylvia extensively for her failure to "face reality" with her boyfriend and for not discussing the relationship in more depth in the group. The therapist, however, suggested that Sylvia's needs to ignore the obvious flaws in the relationship were important and should be examined. He went on to state that it was understandable that Sylvia might have feared discussing her boyfriend in the group because it would have made her more aware of what she was avoiding. The therapist, who had a self psychology perspective, had to determine whether or not the group was functioning as a satisfactory selfobject and, if not, whether prior narcissistic injuries had significantly contributed to Sylvia's reticence. It is possible that the group represented a selfobject similar to her boyfriend, that is, a selfobject that was needed but feared and whose deficits consequently were denied or avoided.

*   *   *

Self psychology has placed the empathic connection between the individual and the selfobject in a central position. Failures in empathy are expected and, in fact, provide for growth, since the individual under optimal conditions will develop many of the functions formerly provided by the selfobject. But if the failures are too severe or too traumatic, deficits in the self develop. However, faulty empathy itself is not ultimately harmful; what *is* harmful is a lack of effort to be empathic. The therapist must maintain particular awareness of the vulnerability of the narcissistic individual to empathic failures and be alert to a host of subsequent responses (Stone, 1992b; Stone & Whitman, 1980). For instance, rage reactions are often a result of narcissistic injury, and interpretations of the empathic failure and the resultant hurt and rage will enable the injured individual to gain perspective and potentially to increase mastery over the vulnerability of the self. By continually considering that rage is potentially a reaction to narcissistic injury, the therapist reestablishes an empathic connection and creates an environment for renewed growth.

Several difficult problems encountered in group psychotherapy can be reassessed in the light of self psychology. The so-called help-rejecting complainer probably does not exist! That is, patients who have been given that pejorative label are probably exhibiting a fundamental inability to communicate what help they desire, demonstrating the presence of an empathic failure rather than a primary need to reject all help. These patients often gain a great amount of negative attention in groups, which may be preferable to being ignored or feeling isolated. They may also fear being understood (a variant of the contact-shunning personality), and they may feel elements of rage and revenge. Thus, multiple functions are conveyed in this behavioral configuration.

Another common problem patient in therapy groups is the monopolizer, who both wishes and fears the effect of recognition and admiration. The monopolizer therefore deals with the problem by remaining the center of attention and simultaneously fending off any real intimacy through verbal outpourings. This one-way dialogue also offers protection against hearing what others feel. At the same time, the monopolizer can maintain an idealized fantasy of the group and the therapist. Nonstop talking may keep him/her from hearing the members or leader speak and thus avoids shattering the fantasy. The empathic task is to recognize the manifestations of this patient's marked ambivalence.

Through focusing on empathic connection, the therapist can gain insight into those situations where members seem to erupt in rage or hurt for no apparent reason. In most instances these reactions follow a narcissistic injury that has gone unrecognized. One source of injury is a group-as-a-whole comment. The generalization inevitably inherent in such a comment cannot include detailed attention and understanding of each individual. This sets the stage for narcissistically vulnerable members to feel hurt and enraged. Another source is the inevitable intragroup conflict. Two individuals may demand attention and response at the same time, and a small slight or failure to fulfill the need of either may be experienced as a narcissistic injury.

Therapists should strive to create an atmosphere that enables the narcissistic transference to become manifest. This includes the difficult task of accepting patients' idealizing transference, rather than prematurely pushing them to correct their distortions (Rutan & Rice, 1981). The time will come soon enough when the therapist will be viewed as unempathic or uncaring, and this will result in sufficient hurt in our patients for us to observe their characteristic responses to narcissistic injury. When this happens, our narcissistic patients' responses to the group's or a specific member's failure to respond in accordance with their inner needs may be interpreted through an empathic understanding of their inner world and their characteristic interactions.

In sum, working successfully with narcissistic patients means gaining an empathic understanding of how these individuals' behavioral styles are attempts to shore up and protect their fragile sense of self. Self psychology's focus on maintaining an empathic connection to the narcissistic patient is an important ingredient in helping these patients.

REMOVAL OF PATIENTS FROM GROUP THERAPY

Members of groups are invited to speak the unspeakable and to present their least acceptable selves. Yet this at times leads to a situation where a member is perceived as damaging to the process of the group or as destructive to him/herself. More often than not, this situation can be handled through the power of interpretation, and the therapist should not move from feelings to action (i.e., banning the patient from the group). To remove a patient from a group is a serious matter; it may provide a sense of protection to the other members, but it also stirs in them the worry that they too might do something so awful that they will be thrown out. The decision about whether or not to remove a patient from a group must also be distinguished from the therapist's wish that the patient would leave or could be evicted. The latter is not at all unusual and represents an important opportunity for learning for the patient, since it is likely that the therapist is experiencing a common reaction to the interpersonal style of that patient.

At the risk of implying that the removal of a patient from a group is a more common experience than in fact it is, in practice it is rarely warranted. The present authors, whose combined experience in running multiple groups per week exceeds 60 years, have removed a total of two patients from groups.

There are two types of removal of a patient from a group: temporary (with the expectation that the member will return) and permanent.

Temporary Removal

A patient may be asked to leave a group session because of a temporary loss of self-control. This loss of control might result from an exacerbation of psychotic process (usually in the form of uncontrolled mania) or, less frequently, a relapse into an acute schizophrenic state. In most instances the deterioration is apparent over a number of sessions, during which the decompensation can be addressed and various approaches, such as individual appointments or hospitalization, can be explored. If at all possible, the individual should be allowed to remain for the duration of the meeting.

However, if the patient becomes so disruptive and out of control that removal during a meeting is required, the therapist is faced with the decision of whether or not to accompany the patient and make immediate arrangements for additional treatment or hospitalization. If the patient is so out of control that it is not safe for him/her to remain in the group, there is little reason to believe the patient is capable of suitable self-care. In such a situation the therapist must be the one to accompany the patient to whatever protective treatment might be available; this is too potent a situation in which to place a group member. If it occurs that the therapist must leave with such a patient, it is assumed that the group will continue the meeting until the usual time of completion even if the therapist does not return.

Another situation calling for temporary removal is a sudden display of dangerous acting out. In the face of violence, where there is a threat of physical harm to another, the initial response of the therapist is a forceful reminder that the group agreements call for talking, not acting. This should include a statement that inability to adhere to this agreement would be grounds for exclusion from the group meeting. In almost all circumstances, this reminder of the group agreements is sufficient to bring renewed self-control. Failing that, the therapist can attempt an interpretation, linking the present situation to some important aspect of the patient's history.

CLINICAL EXAMPLE

John had a history of criminal activity and violent acting out. His father had been a violent man who often beat John and all the members of his family. John hated his father and yet had modeled his life after him. He came to therapy when he found himself truly in love with a woman who would not tolerate his rageful outbursts.

In one meeting John became incensed at the criticisms he perceived coming from a female member. He stood menacingly and walked across the room to her, screaming at her. The therapist was alarmed and suggested that John return to his seat and talk about the feelings he was experiencing. He also reminded John that the group agreements were that he talk, not act. John, however, would have none of it. His rage escalated, and he raised his fist, clearly poised to strike the female member. The group leader, in a last desperate attempt to salvage the situation before he had to simply physically intervene and pay the consequences, said, "John, you are now behaving just like the father you profess to detest."

John looked stricken, dropped his fist, and sank to his knees weeping. He apologized to the female member, stating that he knew exactly how terrified she must have felt because he had experienced that fear during most of his youth.

*   *   *

In this instance reminders of the agreements were insufficient to intervene in destructive behavior, but the power of interpretation did work. These moments in group are exceedingly rare, probably rarer than in individual therapy because the holding environment of the group serves to contain acting-out behaviors. Had John struck the female member, he would have been banned from the group permanently. That breach of the group agreements would have been too egregious to allow continued membership. Furthermore, the other members would forever be fearful that the act might be repeated. If John had remained on the brink of control but had not actually acted, it would have been appropriate for the therapist to suggest that he leave the meeting and return the following week so that the incident and feelings could be explored without the danger of violence. Of course, one would hope that patients on the brink of losing control of violent impulses would leave of their own volition, thereby retaining some self-respect.

A situation that occurs with unfortunate regularity is when a patient attends a meeting while intoxicated. Some therapists routinely ban intoxicated individuals from group sessions, suggesting that they return when sober. This, however, is akin to barring depressed patients from attending when depressed or psychotic patients from attending when psychotic. If substance abuse is a presenting problem, it should not surprise us that it will occasionally enter the therapy. Nonetheless, the behavior of some individuals when intoxicated is so disruptive as to guarantee that no productive work in therapy can be accomplished during that session. Even in such an instance, it is suggested that the member be allowed to stay, the premise being that this is a communication to and about the group (Munzer, 1966). If, however, the behavior continues over several weeks, the therapist will have no choice but to ban the member until he/she demonstrates the ability to bear affect and attend the meetings sober.

Permanent Removal

Obviously, removing a group member on a permanent basis should be a last resort. One of three circumstances is usually the basis for deciding that a patient cannot return to the group: the first is a significant and continuing inability or unwillingness to comply with the group agreements; the second is an unrelieved lack of progress in the therapy; and the third, which is rare, is when a patient makes such progress that he/she outgrows a particular group and would benefit from a higher-functioning one. In all cases the situation is not acute and does not require immediate attention but, rather, is the result of careful deliberation over time.

Inability or Unwillingness to Comply with the Group Agreements

Sometimes patients' life circumstances are altered, and they can no longer attend group meetings on a regular basis. Naturally, alterations in attendance should be explored for resistance and unconscious operations, but there are real-life changes that are not resistance. The final decision in such cases rests with the therapist, and each case must be considered separately. A temporary change (e.g., an overseas assignment, a required class in school, or a new baby) that necessitates an individual's absence for 1–3 months is a dilemma. The time-limited nature of such an interruption generally should not necessitate removal from the group.

This situation does raise the thorny issue of the fee, however. Should patients be expected to pay for sessions they cannot attend for realistic and external reasons? On the other hand, should the therapist be expected to suffer a loss of income due to reasons quite beyond his/her control? Groups usually assume (or wish) that the therapist will not charge for extended absences of this sort. Clinicians have a range of acceptable solutions. Some therapists believe the group agreements apply and that members should be charged for all sessions in which they maintain their membership, even if they are unable to attend. These clinicians conceive of the fee as akin to college tuition—since the therapist cannot fill the seat of an absent member, the fee is due whether or not "classes" are attended. This serves many therapeutic purposes, including countering the wish that the therapist be the all-giving "good breast" that takes care of members in trouble. It also safeguards the therapist's income, which allows ultimately for more economical fees in groups. Further, it protects therapists from having to assume the Solomon-like role of deciding for which absences the patient should be charged and for which he/she should not be charged. Finally, this approach protects the patient from the anger of the therapist whose income is adversely affected by repeated absences.

Other therapists invoke a variety of responses to the issue of charging for a missed session. Some, for example, have a preset number of sessions from which a member can be absent without a fee being assessed. Others make judgments about fees for missed sessions and decide whether or not to charge based on the circumstances of the absence. Repeated "extended" absences can lead to a revision of such a policy, which, of course, should be discussed openly in the group. Certainly these are seldom uncomplicated decisions.

The decision to charge or not charge for missed sessions is ultimately a personal one for each therapist to make. There is no *right* way to handle this delicate situation. In many clinics and hospitals, missed sessions are not considered services rendered and it is illegal to charge for them. What is vital is that each therapist have a consistent approach and abide by it. Further, for the therapist to be able to deal with fees constructively, the therapist must be convinced whichever approach is taken is truly in the service of the patient.

More problematic is the dilemma created by a new life situation (e.g., a new job) that necessitates continuing intermittent absences or regular lateness. The rule of thumb is that members should be asked to leave the group when ongoing regular attendance is not possible. This should not be precipitous and can be discussed and learned from over many weeks. Also, the therapist needs to exercise common sense in invoking this action. If an individual has been a productive and active member of a group for a long time and gets a new job (perhaps as a result of work done in the group) which results in his/her coming to group 10 minutes late each week, the therapist must determine (1) if this lateness is really unavoidable or if it is an acting out of resistance and (2) if it (once it is clear that it is really unavoidable) interferes with the ability of the group to do productive work. While we would never accept into a group new members with an atypical agreement (e.g., that they will routinely come 10 minutes late), the situation is different when it occurs for an existing member. In any case, it is important that the issue be raised openly in the group and that the members be given ample opportunity to express their feelings about it.

Another type of situation that raises the question of permanent removal from a group occurs when a member is continually unable to manage his/her feelings without putting them into actions. For example, in some groups there are monopolizers, individuals who simply seem incapable of shutting up. They are clearly anxious and fearful of strong affect being evoked, and they are often narcissistic and have no sense that others might have needs, too. Another example of a patient whose behavior raises the possibility of eviction is the malicious or bullying member who continually intimidates other members; clearly, this type of patient makes the establishing of an atmosphere of safety harder to attain. Yet another example of a member who acts rather than talks is the patient who has relationships with group members outside the limits of the group sessions; this is in complete defiance of the group agreements. Often these are seriously character disordered individuals who are frightened of group intimacy and use pairing as a protection. In each of these cases the therapist may wish to evict the disturbing force, but that would put the therapist in exactly the same position as these troublesome patients; that is, the therapist would be acting rather than feeling and understanding.

In fact, all the behaviors mentioned in the preceding paragraph can be handled (with difficulty, it must be acknowledged) through the usual processes of confrontation, clarification, interpretation, and working through. For example, the monopolizer is almost never able to accomplish this role without the complete invitation and collusion of the group as a whole. In each of these cases the disruptive behavior can be interpreted to the benefit of all, so long as the therapist does not lose patience (and therefore patients). In very rare instances, after taking into account the meaning of the disruptive behaviors and attempting to help the member desist through understanding and/or limit setting, some patients must be removed from the group (Roberts, 1991).

One of the more serious problems with acting rather than feeling occurs when sexual intercourse occurs between two members. Sexual relations between members, whatever the specific meaning of the action to the couple, evoke in other members powerful feelings of envy, frustration, rejection, and distrust. If the involved couple is unable to discuss and explore their relationship openly in the group, one or both individuals might be asked to leave. This decision is essential if the couple refuses, even following discussion, to end their relationship.

Nonpayment of fees is yet another breach of the group agreements that can lead to eviction. Patients who do not pay their fees are usually communicating a powerful message. Their behavior can represent a statement about how much the therapy is worth, a wish to be special and treated for free, a means of dealing with anger toward the therapist, and so on. Whatever the specific meaning, it is a powerful and important dynamic that requires open exploration in the group. Typically, we therapists are reluctant to address issues of fees, since we seem to harbor some countertransferential feelings about charging for the work we do. This is a problem particularly for group therapists, who must deal with the affects about fees in a public setting. Money is a taboo subject but at the same time a royal road to unconscious material including primitive affect, aspects of personality, and dimensions of orality and anality—especially self-worth, greed, depletion, and withholding. Interpersonal transactions around money in group therapy highlight favoritism, sadism, masochism, secrecy, seduction, protection, and corruption. Lifting the taboo against discussing money unleashes material that may be potentially upsetting for the leader as well as group members. Issues previously condensed into the topic of money and then split off from other parts of the self are now re-owned and their relevance appreciated in sectors of life other than sole financial ones (J. S. Gans, 1992, p. 134).

Obviously, a member's failure to pay fees should first be broached as an important communication that patient, group, and therapist should attempt to understand. However, if the nonpayment continues, there remains no recourse other than to have the nonpaying member leave treatment. It should be noted that this is not really an instance of the therapist banning a member. Rather, this is an instance of the member putting in motion a dynamic that necessitates the eviction; that is, the member has chosen to leave.

CLINICAL EXAMPLE

Leonard consistently underpaid his bill so that his overdue balance slowly but surely mounted. The behavior seemed impervious to discussion and exploration. When the therapist questioned the meaning of the behavior, Leonard was "hurt" and professed to be doing the very best he could. The other members began experiencing rage at Leonard, in part because of his behavior with his bill and in part because the same behavior was replicated in his group interactions, where he did not really give what he owed to the others. When all dynamic techniques failed, the therapist ultimately had to indicate firmly that unless Leonard paid his bill in full within the next month, he would have to leave the group. Leonard was clearly startled and humiliated by this unexpected and unusual statement from the therapist. However, the ensuing week Leonard walked into the group and threw a check for the full amount at the leader. He was then sullen for several weeks in the group, and he occasionally fell slightly behind on his bill again. His sense of embarrassment and hurt over the confrontation continued for many, many months, but the limit setting was clearly useful to him and helped the group move past an impasse. It took

Leonard 2 years before he was able to gain insight about the etiology of his withholding money.

Too Little Progress in Therapy

In some cases it gradually becomes clear to the therapist, and usually to the group and the particular patient as well, that the group is simply not working. For whatever reasons, sometimes an individual simply cannot or will not use the group for therapeutic purposes. This may be the result of improper diagnosis or assignment to an inappropriate group, or it may be the result of character style and resistance. Whatever the reason, it becomes apparent that the patient is wasting his/her time and money by continuing in the group. In this case it is appropriate for the therapist to note this reality and to suggest the possibility of the patient terminating the group and moving to a different mode of treatment. The decision to stop the treatment should represent a joint decision and should come as a result of dialogue between the patient, the therapist, and the group. In many cases this is sufficient to jolt the patient into a new period of productive use of the group; however, in other cases the patient terminates and the group is left to mourn a failure.

It is an error to assume that a silent member is a member making no progress. Individuals use groups in many different ways, and for some the opportunity to sit silently is a therapeutic one. Pines (1991) has noted that some long-term members of groups, defined as those who remain in treatment from 5 or more years, are experienced as permanent group residents. Therapists may rely on these patients or may wish that they would terminate, but Pines suggests that these patients often use the group to sustain themselves.

Too Much Progress in Therapy

Sometimes an individual makes such substantial progress that he/she no longer fits in the group. This applies only to groups of highly disturbed patients. When one member has clearly progressed beyond the developmental level of the other group members, this should be noted and discussed in and with the group. This is not a situation where a member is barred from a group; rather, it is a graduation. The departure of a member, especially one who is exceedingly helpful and insightful, is difficult for the group. However, the process can be therapeutic if it is openly discussed and negotiated in the group.

The decision to remove a member from a group is a very serious one. It is recommended that the group therapist seek consultation from a trusted colleague prior to such an action in order to ensure that the therapist is not acting out.

COUNTERTRANSFERENCE CONSIDERATIONS

Clinicians inevitably encounter difficulties in working with therapy groups. These problems may arise from the group composition, the interactions among members, or from the particular pathological personality organization of one or more members which result in individual or group destructive transactions. Missing from this equation are the therapists' contributions. Leaders are subjected to periods of boredom or excitement and are recipients of intense erotic, aggressive, or hateful feelings. The process may feel fragmented, and therapists' emerging notions of themes soon seem irrelevant as topics get switched and linkages are hard to discern. Patients threaten self-destructive or other dangerous acts and the clinician begins to feel overly responsible, not only for the individual but for the entire membership as well. Many patients diagnosed as borderline, narcissistic, anxious, or depressed receive medications or require periods of hospitalization (Stone, Rodenhauser, & Markert, 1991). This adds an additional task of effective collaboration between caregivers. These elements alone or in combination may create considerable difficulty, and therapists often find themselves on an emotional roller coaster. It is no wonder, then, that countertransferences are difficult to manage and enactments take place. On the other hand, as Simone Weil (1997) said, "Difficult as it is really to listen to someone in affliction, it is just as difficult for him to know that compassion is listening to him" (p. 332). If the clinician is unaware of these feelings, he/she may contribute to a dysfunctional group by focusing on a single individual or a subgroup as containers of unacceptable affects.

Gabbard (1993) provides a list of several countertransference responses to borderline individuals that are applicable to working with difficult groups and patients:

1. Guilt feelings
2. Rescue fantasies
3. Transgression of professional boundaries
4. Rage and hatred
5. Helplessness and worthlessness
6. Anxiety and terror

One group of patients, particularly those in the borderline spectrum, present themselves as demanding, self-absorbed, self-centered, and emotionally labile. They often evoke feelings of frustration, dislike, even hate and rejection in their therapists. Clinicians communicate their emotional responses often paraverbally or nonverbally. These communications are sensitively "heard" by the patient, who may then confront the therapist. Clinicians are often caught by surprise when members confront them with an observation or interpretation based on the nonverbal message. In these circumstances it is not uncommon for clinicians to deny their feelings or to unconsciously "punish" the confronting member, thereby further undermining the treatment alliance.

The therapeutic task is to try to appreciate the patient's underlying vulnerability and the self-protective nature of these self presentations. The wish for and fear of genuine involvement is paramount and only slowly is amenable to change. The clinician may be fooled by what seems to be genuine progress one week, only to be followed by the usual defensive postures the next week. The erratic behavior evokes countertransferences which are not easily managed.

A second general category of difficult patients is the vulnerable fragile patient. . . . Individuals manifesting fragile characteristics seem on the verge of tears, emotional storms, or remain verbally silent and withdrawn. Silent patients evoke rescue fantasies and may induce clinicians to extraordinary acts to help them increase their participation. Alternatively, the therapist may withdraw from the patient, leaving the responsibility for interacting to the group.

CLINICAL EXAMPLE

A married woman in midlife entered a group to work on her social isolation. Suffering from recurrent major depression only moderately responsive to antidepressant medication, she soon made it evident that she was going to remain in the group for life, somehow basking in the interactions of others, but seldom speaking. She was forthright in stating this position. She spoke of how she had been repeatedly rejected and shunned when she told others about her depression and seemed content to sit through sessions in silence. However, she reliably attended the sessions and generally seemed accepted by the others.

The therapist wondered about his judgment in putting her in the group, made efforts to engage her with minimal and only temporary success, and struggled with feelings of just wishing to ignore her presence. Such behaviors evoke responses of overprotection, rescue, or withdrawal on the part of the clinician or the members. At times, he found himself aware that his preoccupation with her silence interfered with his attending to group process. Not until one of the members began to focus on the power of her silence did the therapist gain appreciation of aspects of his countertransference. Slowly, using this understanding, he was then able to help the patient and others explore her sense of helplessness and powerlessness.

*   *   *

This illustrates the power of silence, and fortuitously a member's complaint about this patient's power alerted the therapist to his unrecognized countertransference reaction.

A third group of patients are those who have limited capacity to put feelings into words. They respond as if they are emotionally hearing impaired, or they communicate through actions.

Therapists often will overestimate patients' capacities to put feelings into words, and they can become frustrated when patients are unable do so. However, groups offer unique ways to help even those who are unable to verbalize their affect.

CLINICAL EXAMPLE

Clarice, a single depressed woman in her late 50s on disability for a physical condition, struggled to free herself from a highly dependent relationship with her domineering and well-to-do older widowed sister. At this point in time, Clarice was severely limiting all contact with her sister. However, she did visit her sister recently and left a coat at her house. The coat was lost. The dilemma for Clarice was that she needed a coat and her sister has offered to buy her a new coat. However, Clarice feared she would fall back into a total dependency on sister if she accepted this offer. She plaintively entreated the group to tell her what she should do. However, she could only present this as a difficult *decision*. She had no access to the deep feelings that were part of this seemingly minor interaction with her sister. The group became frustrated with her continued requests for advice, since she could neither hear any suggestions nor examine her feelings beyond the simple statement that she didn't want to become dependent again.

Following a period of silence, Fred told about his concern for his brother who was suffering from terminal cancer, and he would feel very bad if he didn't visit him regularly. Cathy said that it was different in her family, and for many years she had fought with her sociopath sister. "But," Cathy went on, "when my sister was put in jail, I felt good . . . not bad . . . for trying to help her."

Though Clarice's view of her dilemma with her sister was simplistic and one-sided, the group associations that followed offered a different and more complex view of family interactions. Both Fred and Cathy associated to conflicted relationships with siblings, and in both cases they emphasized the *attachment* aspects of those relationships. Claire's "solution" of just staying away from her sister denied how important the relationship is. The therapist suggested that Cathy and Fred's associations might help Clarice consider more fully the relationship with her sister.

This intervention suggesting the positive contributions of the members to the process helped alleviate the groupwide frustration (which the therapist shared) with Clarice's demanding behavior and her inability to look more deeply at her own feelings. It also helped Clarice by illustrating how others, even unknowingly, were trying to be helpful.

*   *   *

In this illustration, the therapist was aware of his frustration with Clarice's recurrent "helpless dependency" on the group. He had become silently angry with her, yet maintained sufficient awareness of the process to "recover" and offer a potentially useful intervention. Although not the case in this example, clinicians experience considerable shame when they realize that they have "acted" on a countertransference, and they may react by trying to undo their behavior with overly solicitous caring.

An important overlooked element in the interactions that invariably take place with a difficult group or patient is the subtle violation of the agreements. Members act upon their feelings and are reluctant to verbalize them. They withdraw from, ignore, or only speak banalities to the offending member, or they may express their frustration and rage directly rather than examine their own experience in being in the group with this difficult member. The therapist can begin to make inroads into the destructive processes by helping the members examine these responses, which run counter to their agreements.

Nonetheless, there is great resistance to altering the groupwide response. Roth (1990) points out that the archaic ego of narcissistic individuals is protected by the group's use of concrete action and emotional discharge rather than examined through reflective activity. He emphasizes that there is an absence of ideas about what is happening among the members and a propensity to externalize conflict. Members of a seemingly average therapeutic group under the influence of the intense affects generated by a difficult patient resort to earlier defensive modes and affective states, and they are no longer able to observe their responses. Instead of learning, there is merely repetition, which leads members in a further downward spiral of decreasing trust in the group and its processes. No new ideas emerge.

Understandably clinicians sometimes find their responses altered in the presence of these difficulties. Indeed, awareness of our own violation of the agreements or of a departure from our usual mode of operating can sometimes alert us to the presence of countertransference enactments. Clues such as coming late, ending the session early, blocking on a patient's name in the middle of a session, or having difficulty recalling the central dynamic issues of the preceding sessions are useful indicators of the therapist's emotional state. At these times it is important for the therapist to carefully examine his/her own emotional position with the difficult group. The clinician's anxieties, sometimes expressed in dreams, can give clues to countertransferences. Recognition by therapists of countertransference prepares them to alter their interventions and potentially avoid therapeutic stalemates, thereby freeing the group to become more therapeutic.

Difficult groups and patients are difficult, in part, because they upset the therapist's balance. A member expressed her feelings about a difficult absent member: "He talks to the air." This woman's wish for some personal contact with the difficult patient was frustrated, and similar feelings may be activated in the therapist. Meaningful interactions are limited by such patients' pathology, and as the transactions with these patients or with the group become repetitious and stereotyped, the clinician's curiosity decreases and little is available to help him/her feel like a therapist. Appreciation of our general motivations as therapists, as sketched by Friedman (1988), helps us maintain our balance and work with these difficult individuals and the associated distortions produced in the group.

FIFTEEN

Time-Limited Psychodynamic Groups

Time is the wisest of all counselors.
—PLUTARCH

Time goes, you say? Ah, no!
Alas, Time stays, *we* go.
—AUSTIN DOBSON, *The Paradox of Time.*

I n this chapter we examine the value of psychodynamic
approaches to time-limited groups. *Psychodynamic* refers to
a way of thinking about people and psychotherapy and is
not constrained by time. Indeed, Freud's analyses, rarely lasting more than 6
months, would be considered "time-limited" treatment these days. For example, Freud analyzed Sándor Ferenczi three times—once in 1914 and twice in
1916—comprising a total of less than 9 weeks. But his record was probably
Max Eitington, whom he analyzed in 2 weeks (Kanzer, 1993). Ironically, as
classical psychoanalysis got longer and longer, Ferenczi became a voice for a
more active, shorter form of psychoanalysis (Ferenczi & Rank, 1925).

When Freud began his clinical work he practiced hypnotherapy, and the
goal of the treatment was to remove symptoms. With the discovery of transference, and as free association and dream analysis became the hallmarks of
psychotherapeutic technique, the ending of treatment became more vague.
The goal of psychotherapy was no longer the removal of the symptoms but,

rather, an understanding of their function. The result was that therapy took longer and longer—so much longer that Freud (in 1937) wrote "Analysis Terminable and Interminable." As the divergence between long-term and short-term therapy widened, certain characteristics began to dominate each. Long-term therapy became less focused, depended on the meandering of free association, and attended to underlying character style. Short-term therapy became more focused, with a concern for continually monitoring progress.

Recently there have been several factors that have pressed for shorter, more cost-effective treatments. For one thing, over the past three decades the cost of health care has escalated out of control, so much so that by 1993 health care accounted for nearly 14% of the gross domestic product in the United States (B. Weiss, 1995). Psychodynamic treatment contributed to its falling out of favor by never really defining when it was completed. The publication in 1980 of DSM-III, with its dramatic shift from a dynamic basis to an "atheoretical" descriptive nomenclature, altered the understanding of the psychotherapeutic process. Thereafter the presence or absence of specific symptoms would determine if an illness was present. One concrete result has been the move to more cost-efficient, shorter term psychotherapies (Sharfstein & Goldman, 1989).

HISTORY OF TIME-LIMITED THERAPY

Psychodynamic clinicians have practiced time-limited therapy for years, beginning with Sándor Ferenczi and Otto Rank. These early practitioners assumed the presence of unconscious data and that current problems have roots in history. Their focus was not on symptoms but on the problems underlying these symptoms.

World War II, with the sudden emergence of thousands of soldiers and civilians with emotional crises, created the fertile ground from which flourished many therapeutic modalities, including group therapy and short-term therapy. The great need, combined with the shortage of trained professionals, led to the examination of ways in which to make the therapeutic process more effective. Particularly in the military, the focus was on brief symptomatic treatment and getting soldiers back into the field as promptly as possible.

In more modern times Sifneos (1971) and Mann (1973) in Boston, Malan (1976) in London, and Davanloo (1979, 1980) in Montréal were probably the first to systematically apply psychodynamic principles to time-limited individual therapy. Each of these practitioners suggested that time-limited formats held more promise only for healthier patients.

Sifneos (1971) contrasts anxiety-suppressive and anxiety-provoking therapies. In anxiety-suppressive therapy, where treatment is restricted to 4–10 meetings, the goal of treatment is to impart better coping skills, reduce anxiety, and diminish symptoms. Sifneos advocates the use of anxiety-suppressive therapy with more disturbed patients. In an anxiety-provoking time-limited model Sifneos maintains that transference is "forced" and that anxiety is used as a curative lever. In this model the dynamic goals of self-understanding and character change apply. The number of sessions may be anywhere from 12 to 20. Sifneos believes that only the healthiest 2–10% of patients can use the anxiety-provoking model. With both therapies he recommends that the focus of the work be quite narrow, with the therapist acting in the role of "teacher."

Mann (1973) relies on an immutable termination date to promote affect. Furthermore, he has an inflexible number of 12 meetings for all patients. No time-limited model requires more of the therapist than Mann's, since he attempts to widen the scope of the therapeutic venture as much as possible. For Mann, the goal of time-limited therapy is to help patients identify the central issue that lies beneath their symptoms. Mann is also the clearest about using time as the agent of change. He essentially allows patients to believe that their problems can be resolved in the 12 weeks allotted, and then analyzes their reactions as it becomes clear that this hope will not be met. The range of diagnostic categories from which Mann is willing to accept patients is broader than that for any of the other time-limited therapists. The therapist's role in this model may be described as that of "empathic helper" (see Table 15.1).

Malan (1976), like Mann, sets a firm termination date (allowing between 20 and 30 meetings) in order to arouse anxiety and promote regression and dependency. Using object relations theory, he aims interpretations at patients' interpersonal styles, not their defenses. Malan suggests that his model, in which the therapist acts as "doctor," works best with relatively healthy or mildly character-disordered individuals.

Davanloo (1979, 1980) uses a much more aggressive approach, vigorously attacking the patient's defenses in a calculated effort to elicit anger. Here the therapist plays the role of "critic." Whereas Sifneos uses anxiety as a therapeutic agent of change and Malan uses dependency, Davanloo relies on anger. He suggests between 1 and 40 sessions as an acceptable treatment duration, and he believes that only the healthiest 30–35% of our patient population can respond to his techniques. Patients accepted into treatment with Davanloo must respond positively in their first meeting in order to continue with this format.

These pioneers in time-limited psychodynamic work did not apply their findings to group therapy.

TIME-LIMITED GROUP PSYCHOTHERAPY

"Time-limited" is not the same as "short-term." In fact, terminology has remained quite murky. Budman (1994) used the term "time-effective" treat-

TABLE 15.1. Dynamic Theories of Time-Limited Therapy

Therapist	Number of sessions	Focus of therapy	Role of therapist	Therapist behaviors	Patient selection guidelines
Sifneos (1971): Anxiety-suppressive therapy	4–10	Narrow; on crisis, coping; conscious	Teacher	Clarifies supports; decreases transference	Less healthy but able to recognize psychological origin of problem
Sifneos (1971): Anxiety-provoking therapy	12–20	Very narrow oedipal conflicts; unconscious grief; transference	Teacher	Interprets transference and resistance; idealizing transference becomes ambivalent	Very rigid standards; top 2–10% of clinical population
Malan (1976)	20–30 (with a fixed termination date)	Narrow; implicit (therapist finds it); unconscious	Doctor	Promotes "insight"	Relatively healthy; mild character pathology
Davanloo (1979, 1980)	1–40 (ca. 25)	Broader; resistance; use of aggression	Critic	Confronts resistance especially anger	Top 30–35%; must respond in first trial
Mann (1973)	Exactly 12	Broadest; "central issue"; time itself; termination	Empathic helper	Focuses on separation and stage where parent failed	Broader selection

Note. Adapted from Groves (1992, pp. 38–39). Copyright 1992 by The Guilford Press. Adapted by permission.

ment, whereas MacKenzie (1997b) coined the phrase "time-managed" group psychotherapy. Whatever the label, usually time-limited groups do not exist for more than a year, and the more usual time frame is from 12 to 30 sessions.

Time-limited group treatments initially lagged behind that of individual treatment, but the impact of short-term groups began to be observed in relationship to the impact of brief experiential training. Scattered reports of brief therapy groups began to emerge in the 1960s, and during the next two decades more reports and reviews appeared (Waxer, 1977; Imber, Lewis, & Loiselle, 1979; Budman, Bennet, & Wisneski, 1981; D. A. Goldberg, Schuyler,

Bransfield, & Savino, 1983; Poey, 1985). These reports describe a variety of approaches, including behavioral, educational, and psychodynamic formats. The groups were used for treatment of patients in crises, for problem solving, or for special populations or diagnoses (R. H. Klein, 1985).

Budman and Gurman (1988), who applied time-limited theories to work with groups, propose an "IDE focus," which refers to the *interpersonal, developmental, and existential* vantage points. Because these authors maintain that most change in group therapy occurs at the beginning, they attempt to provide a powerful model for change to occur in a few weeks. Unlike some time-limited therapists, Budman and Gurman do not prohibit patients from returning for several courses of time-limited treatment.

More recently Budman and his associates (Budman, Cooley, Demby, et al., 1996; Budman, Demby, Soldz, & Merry, 1996) have extended their work to patients with personality disorders. These groups, designed to balance this populations' need for more extensive treatment with the constraints of managed care, were time-limited but not short-term, lasting 18 months. Patients were generally at the higher end of personality disorder functioning, but premature terminations were substantial (51%). This proportion did not differ with reports on treating borderline patients in individual therapy or from dropouts of participants in long-term groups (see Chapters 9 and 14).

Likewise, MacKenzie (1988, 1990, 1993, 1997b) developed specialized techniques for employing group psychotherapy in a time-limited mode. For MacKenzie time-limited groups can accomplish a variety of goals: "psychoeducation, crisis management, or support and groups that are designed for active intrusive interpersonal work" (1993, p. 425). However, careful selection of patients is necessary and is dependent on the group goals. MacKenzie's approach is quite structured, with the leader assuming an active role.

Budman and Gurman (1988) and MacKenzie (1988, 1990, 1993, 1997b) combine psychodynamic principles with educational and behavioral interventions in their time-limited groups. The work of Piper, McCallum, and Azim (1992) with individuals suffering loss is in the tradition of psychodynamic therapy. They emphasize working through transferences in the resolution of grief.

Goals in Time-Limited Groups

We begin with a caveat: if a therapist sets group goals that are too narrow, there may be insufficient patients available to form a viable group; if the goals are too broad, there may be sufficient patients but group formation will be delayed and little will be accomplished in the available time.

In Chapter 8 we discussed the importance of setting goals in order to maximize success. Goals in open-ended groups may be quite broad but often involve an agreement to work on underlying personality problems. Initial goals often change, becoming more precise over the course of time. In contrast, in order to maximize the potential of the therapeutic benefit in time-limited groups, goals must be as clear and precise as possible. Although the emphasis is on precision, sufficient flexibility must remain to allow for individual variation. For example, a group might be formed to work on unresolved grief. Inclusion criteria might be reasonably broad with individuals working on delayed grief or a more contemporary loss (Piper, et al., 1992). However, the goals may be more specific, and only persons with specific loses might be candidates (e.g., death of a spouse or a child).

Time-limited formats have particular advantages in working with grief. Grief, in particular, is an affect that is aroused in a group that ends according to the calendar rather than when "the work is finished," since grief is a response to an ending that comes "too soon." Moreover, the forced ending promotes work on such issues as individuation and unfulfilled hopes.

Other groups may be formed around broader goals in which members are to examine their difficulties in relationships. Choosing members for groups of this type requires careful evaluation, because such groups often begin to examine transferences in the here-and-now interactions. Patients should have sufficient ego strength to be able to deeply engage and also process their experiences.

Lack of agreement on the goals of the work can lead to a significant misalliance in the therapy, and in a time-limited group there is no time to readjust that misalliance.

Composition of Time-Limited Groups

Due to the press of time, there are several differences in how one conceives of and composes a time-limited group.

Three features characterize the composition of most time-limited groups. The first is that the membership is limited either to only those who begin when the group is formed or to those who join within a limited time period. The second feature is that the composition is homogeneous according to demography, diagnosis, or crisis. Third, the developmental level of the participants should not be so diverse that, in the time allotted, the members cannot identify with one another.

In time-limited groups, members must be able to find something in common with other members rather quickly. In this regard time-limited groups are not so different from *beginning* open-ended groups. This like-mindedness can come from a variety of sources. One frequent model is demographics. These would include women's groups, men's groups, gay groups, adolescent groups, etc. Another homogeneous way of forming groups is by crisis. These would include grief groups, victims of violence groups, bereavement groups, etc. Finally, groups may be formed by diagnosis. These would include groups for eating disorders, for depression, for bipolar illness, etc. This last category is becoming increasingly popular in this era of discrete treatments for discrete diagnoses.

In each case, immediately upon entering a group, members have the potential for feeling a kinship with one another. They rely heavily on the curative factor of universalization.

Many individuals do not fit the usual criteria for time-limited treatment (group *or* individual), and yet managed-care and insurance companies, with their cost containment policies, have limited the extent of their insurance coverage. This press to reduce the cost of care often results in patients being referred to time-limited groups. Groups can be formed with limited goals, such as crises intervention or for posthospital adjustment. Patients who do not fit the ordinary selection criteria can often benefit from a supportive group focusing on symptomatic relief. These groups are noninterpretative, supportive, and include a modicum of advice giving and recommendations for alternative behaviors (R. H. Klein, 1985).

One model that may apply to such individuals has been described by Hardy and Lewis (1992). Working with patients, many of whom were recently discharged from a psychiatric hospital, these authors formed groups with limited goals that could be attained in 12 weeks. Following this 12-week group experience, the patients met with the group therapist individually to determine if they had reached their goals. If they had not, they could reenlist for another group. If patients felt they had attained their goals, they were given the option of selecting a new goal and joining another 12-session group. Some patients were reported to have enlisted in more than six successive time-limited groups. This is but one of a number of models of "intermittent" treatment that are emerging to meet the needs of our changing treatment environment.

Patient Selection and Preparation

If anything, careful patient selection and preparation is even more meaningful in time-limited groups. This is not always an easy matter because one of the motivations for a short-term group is cost savings, which leads to organizational resistance to conducting proper screening and preparation.

The group goal and composition are primary determinants of patient selection. In assessing patients' capacity to work toward a goal, the ideal candidates would have the ability to engage in interactions and to observe their own behavior, as well as have some capacity to experience and verbalize their feelings. Most candidates fall short in one or more areas yet can profit from their membership. An individual who might be considered significantly different on one or more dimensions (such as education, ethnicity, or ego strength) will have a difficult task identifying with others, even if there are other commonalities.

Patients need to be clearly informed of the time-limited nature of the group. Often there is an underlying fantasy that if more treatment is needed, the group will be extended. Obviously any indication of such a possibility on the clinician's part would undermine one of the particular advantages of time-limited groups—that of a specified ending.

Patients should also be presented with a clear agreement, modified as necessary from the one presented in Chapter 8. One modification might be that patients agree to attend and pay for all sessions. Therapists must be particularly alert to prospective members' ability to attend the meetings. As a good deal of therapeutic leverage is achieved through therapeutic factors mobilized by an optimally rapid-forming cohesive group, repeated absences undermine the therapeutic work for all.

The literature regarding dropouts from time-limited or short-term groups suggests that therapists not begin with less than six members. Extrapolating from our knowledge of dropouts in long-term groups, we can predict that one or two members may drop out. That, combined with the probability of occasional absences, means that such groups might meet for a substantial part of their group life with too few members to gain the benefits of group therapy.

Leading a Time-Limited Group

Leaders of psychodynamic time-limited groups must reexamine their responses along the axes of leader roles and foci (see Chapter 9). While all positions on these axes still apply, the limit of time presumes certain aspects of role and focus.

Leadership Roles

Activity and Nonactivity. Whereas in open-ended groups the leader can wait and allow the process to unfold, in time-limited groups the leader must be somewhat more active and offer earlier interventions. Dies (1985), describing leadership functions, states, "Thus the group therapist is characterized as actively monitoring, prompting, shaping, and explaining group interactions to increase the likelihood that group members will accomplish their mutually contracted goals" (p. 437).

Activity serves to keep the therapist present as a real object and diminishes regression that occurs with a less active therapeutic stance. Cohesion and the therapeutic alliance are enhanced through a more interactive stance that sets the stage for interpretations which offer opportunities for self-reflection and understanding. Therapist activity is relative, and as such may be a problem for clinicians who are not comfortable with short-term formats. We believe that in most dynamically oriented groups, the leader's activity may diminish during the middle phases of the treatment. Nevertheless, the emphasis remains on group interaction and on following, rather than initiating, group process.

Transparency and Opaqueness. The blank screen role does not transfer well to time-limited therapy. Indeed, there is reason to believe a true "blank screen" role for the therapist is neither desirable nor possible in *any* form of treatment. In time-limited therapy it is the "lack of time" that primarily drives transference and regression. Therefore, even the most traditional psychodynamic therapist does not need to remain opaque in order to assist. One recommendation, requiring careful consideration is that therapists, in the service of maintaining the therapeutic focus, share their responses in the here and now. This strategy is advocated particularly in single-issue groups.

Gratification and Frustration. Affect remains a primary tool in time-limited therapy. Thus, the therapist's natural positioning along this axis is impacted by the increased activity, which may be gratifying for some members. However, the reduced time frame often stimulates patients' dependency needs and increased wishes for magical solutions, and so may pressure the therapist to become a gratifying object. Therapists' decisions along this axis are influenced by the assessment of the alliance and the recommendation by some that a positive therapeutic relationship is necessary in order to prevent the group from becoming mired in working on negative transferences.

Leadership Foci

The focus of the therapist's attention, which remains psychodynamic, is affected by reduced time. For groups with specific goals, leaders strive to keep the focus in mind and often will redirect or reorient the members when the discussion becomes diffuse or unfocused. This remains within the dynamic framework of following patients' leads, but the attention to focus in the context of the group goals is one of the significant differences in leadership style between time-limited work and open-ended long-term groups.

Past–Here and Now–Future. Here-and-now behaviors, feelings and interactions are stressed in time-limited groups. R. H. Klein (1985) states that the therapist's "job is to determine how he can best aid a particular set of patients to work most effectively on the agreed-upon work tasks" (p. 320). For groups with very limited time frames (6–12 sessions), the clinician may focus almost exclusively on the here-and-now interactions. In such groups it would be unlikely that meaningful working through of past conflicts could take place, and it would be the members' tasks to accomplish that work following termination.

In groups with a more interpersonal focus and a longer time span (12–24 sessions), linking in-group behaviors to emotionally significant events in the person's current life and/or to historic antecedents helps start the process of working through and provides a model for patients to use when their treatment is "completed."

Group-as-a-Whole–Interpersonal–Individual. While in the early and terminating meetings group-as-a-whole interpretations may be especially useful, in time-limited groups the focus of the therapist's attention is often on the interpersonal and individual dynamics. The leader may focus more quickly on the individual's contribution to the group focus than is done in open-ended groups. Yet, as we have emphasized, whole-group processes are invariably at work, and interpersonal transactions may be a product of these dynamics (i.e., scapegoating) and should not be neglected. After working with several individuals' particular foci, the therapist may be able to identify a theme—a group-as-a-whole intervention that engages all members and reinforces the patients' sense of mutuality and cohesion (Horwitz, 1977a).

In-Group and Out-of-Group. On this axis the focus of the leader's attention is a matter of personal leadership style. Some time-limited group therapists limit their focus to in-group data, feeling that the press of time precludes examination of out-of-group data. Others feel that the press of time proscribes the depth of in-group relationships and therefore requires more attention to out-of-group data. Patients generally can develop beginning bonds through commonalities in their out-of-group experiences, and if sufficient time is available and members demonstrate the capacity, exploration of in-group transactions is in order. Optimally, patients would benefit from linking in-group and out-of-group behaviors. There is no prescribed pathway in achieving this integration, because some patients begin with understanding out-of-group behavior and spontaneously recognize the same in-group pattern. The reverse process is also likely.

Affect and Cognition. The primary data of psychodynamic work remain affective, no matter the duration of treatment. Nevertheless, many clinicians incorporate more cognitive elements in their work with time-limited groups. Information may be provided regarding particular aspects related to the group focus. For example, in single-gender groups information about differences in social development between boys and girls may provide a useful frame to help the members understand themselves, and themselves in relation to the other gender.

Process and Content. For groups working in a psychodynamic model, the process provides more of an insight into the unconscious than does the content. As groups search for common content as a way of becoming cohesive or addressing termination, members may tell "stories." The clinician may listen to the content as a metaphor for the process. For example, in approaching termination, patients may seem to spend an inordinate amount of time discussing a member's distress about the terminal illness of a family member or several individuals may tell about past or anticipated losses. The process meaning would be linked to unconsciously determined concern about the "death" of the group.

Understanding and Corrective Emotional Experience. While neither in-depth understanding nor a true corrective emotional experience can be consistently obtained in a time-limited treatment, both of these foci remain important. As we have addressed earlier, a good deal of therapeutic benefit accrues from the experiences of sharing, of feeling that one's problems are not unique and are understood. The experience of a genuine emotional relationship can serve to restabilize an individual, and that may be sufficient to allow growth to proceed in the absence of additional treatment.

With properly selected individuals, therapists are able to effectively interpret the transferences both to the peers and the therapists. Insight into current behaviors or feelings gained in the group may be sufficient for some patients. It may be unnecessary to achieve integration of historical, extragroup, and intragroup experiences for a positive and useful therapeutic experience.

EXAMPLE OF THE DIFFERENCES BETWEEN LEADING A TIME-LIMITED GROUP AND AN OPEN-ENDED GROUP

A group of eight women meet for the first time in a 10-week group focused on social shyness. The leader begins the group: "We are here because each of you has identified a pattern of shyness that is interfering with your personal life. We will meet for 10 weeks. Each of you has agreed to attend all 10 meetings, to use the relationships for therapeutic rather than social reasons, to protect the names and identities of the members, to actively work on the problems that brought you, and to pay your bill." The leader then falls silent.

Abby, a vivacious redhead, begins at once: "I am *so* shy. I just cannot open my mouth in public. It is very painful. It is also surprising. My parents said I was very outgoing as a child."

The group all nod knowingly, but no one speaks. After a painful 3-minute silence, Barbara says, "You did not seem to have much anxiety about speaking *here*. I'm terrified. I am not sure I will be able to keep my commitment to come for 10 weeks." The other women quickly identify with Barbara.

Abby is very uncomfortable and pleads, "No, I am *really* shy!"

At this point the leader says, "The group is dealing with shyness right now. You are all meeting new people, and each of you is confronted with the anxiety this situation arouses." The members nod, and several speak of how uncomfortable they are. The common theme seems to be "Nothing that I have to say would be of worth to the group."

The leader (knowing something of the history of each of the patients) decides to help the group begin to consider the roots of their shyness by asking Abby, "When did you stop feeling outgoing?" Abby says, "Oh, I don't know . . . about 13, I guess." "So," the therapist continues, "you were not shy until boys and sexuality entered the picture?"

Abby seems genuinely stunned. "It's true. I can talk easily with groups of women, but if a man is in the environment, I simply cannot speak." The other members, while still implying that Abby's shyness is not as paralyzing as their own, now feel they can talk to Abby and identify with her pain. The group begins discussing when each of the members began to feel shy.

* * *

In an ongoing group, the therapist would not have so quickly intervened with an individually focused question. Further, the therapist's attention would have been on how the members were saying "hello" to one another and assessing the relative safety of this group situation. The time-limited framework, along with the homogeneous group composition, freed the therapist to *assume* that a degree of trust and cohesion was present (i.e., universalization) and that he could begin to help the patients become curious about the sources of their difficulties. The quick assumption that Abby's shyness had to do with sexuality, even if incorrect, would have served to help the members become curious about possible historic roots of their current difficulties.

Countertransference in Time-Limited Groups

Clinicians trained in the model of long-term treatment may have difficulty with the transition to leading time-limited groups. They may experience conscious and unconscious feelings about the necessary change in their leadership style and treatment goals. One source of countertransference is the therapist's guilt that the time limitation prevents anything meaningful from happening or that insufficient therapy is being offered. These feelings may be intensified near termination when both patients and the therapist see a potential for further gains only to have to stop treatment.

The need for increased therapist activity and what may seem like having to make interventions based on minimal clinical information in order to keep the group focused may evoke the therapist's resentment of the model and stimulate countertransferences such as feeling controlling or manipulative (Dies, 1985). Similarly, concerns about patients responding primarily out of the wish to please or by compliance may complicate a therapist's capacity to alter his/her style. Clinicians may become impatient with individuals who do not seem to make rapid progress. The potential for creating a scapegoat is substantial (Poey, 1985). Conversely, there may be an overidentification with members who exhibit behaviors that promote group movement (a "favorite child"), with a consequent failure to attend to their deficits.

Several systemic and cultural elements contribute less directly to clinicians' states of mind. The recurrent task of selecting patients and forming a new group can be stimulating but often contains a modicum of frustration. The pressures of finding sufficient candidates and the repetitive screening and preparing of patients has an intrinsic degree of stress because of the general cultural bias against group therapy. The result may be dulling of the clinician's curiosity, routinization of the tasks, and a mechanical approach to the work—the symptoms of therapist burnout (see chapter 12, the section on "The Therapist's Needs").

Developmental Issues in Time-Limited Groups

The fact that time-limited groups are of reduced duration does not preclude the powerful impact of development on the group process. Indeed, the limit on time may hasten developmental stages, while not providing sufficient time to work with these elements in great depth.

In a 10 week group, for example, it can be safely assumed that the first three sessions will demonstrate "early development" issues such as trust building; the middle four sessions will approximate a "working-through" period; and the final three meetings will be devoted to the ending. Further, the therapist can often clearly sense when the "point of no return" has passed (in this example, the sixth meeting), because themes of death, dying, and leave-taking will inevitably enter the process.

Termination in Time-Limited Groups

Time-limited groups are especially useful in helping people deal with endings, since the ending is part of the entire experience. Furthermore, this is an enforced termination, unlike open-ended groups where individuals decide when it is time for them to stop treatment. Since most endings in life (including moving to a different city and death) are enforced endings, there is much to be learned about how to negotiate such terminations.

Typically, time-limited groups begin dealing with the ending (often unconsciously) from the moment the group begins, but this escalates at about the halfway point in the life of the group. At that point the leader will usually begin hearing material about good-byes, dying, leaving, etc. Furthermore, time-limited groups offer the members an opportunity to deal with feelings about "not having enough time." Often it is useful for the leader to "count down" the final meetings in order to enhance these feelings. For example, the leader could say, "In 4 more weeks this group will never meet again." In time-limited groups termination has more to do with saying good-bye and less to do with "Is this the right time to leave?"

Advantages of Time-Limited Group Therapy

Time-limited groups offer some unique advantages:

1. From a purely pragmatic point of view, they are economical of time and money.
2. They can provide treatment for specified symptoms or developmental tasks without the development of long-term dependence.
3. Homogeneous groups can provide more rapid development of cohesion and mobilize therapeutic factors of support, self-revelation, and learning (see Chapter 4).
4. Patients appreciate the structure and the therapist's helping to keep a focus as an aid in accomplishing their tasks (Poey, 1985).
5. For some patients, knowing that a time limit exists assists in their keeping focused and addressing important personal problems without the fear of being mired in a long-term commitment.
6. The use of time clarifies the end point and highlights issues of separation and loss.
7. Patients can be treated in segments without having to accomplish everything at once.

Disadvantages of Time-Limited Group Therapy

There are also some disadvantages to time-limited groups:

1. There may be a limited number of suitable candidates, creating difficulty in forming dynamically oriented time-limited groups.
2. In managed-care situations there is often insufficient time to select and prepare potential members, possibly resulting in premature terminations or dropouts.
3. Because of the limitations of time, patients are often restricted to working with more superficial aspects of their problems, leaving deeper conflicts or character problems relatively untouched.
4. In single-symptom or focused groups, there is a tendency for patients to identify with their symptom or the focus, thereby limiting what can be achieved.

5. There is little information regarding dropouts in time-limited groups, which could lead to too few members in "closed" time-limited groups.
6. Therapists may experience significant countertransference difficulties derived from the format.
7. There is a significant underestimation of the amount of time (i.e., cost) required to evaluate and select patients.
8. Alliance with the organization or clinic in which groups are conducted also requires time and is often not cost accounted.
9. Some patients simply do not improve and require extended treatment (Mackenzie, 1996).

Piper and Joyce (1996) reviewed research on the the outcome of time-limited, short-term group therapy (TSGT) and state, "There was clear evidence of clinical benefit for TSGT of different theoretical and technical orientations across a diverse range of patients, and approximately equivalent results for group and individual therapy" (p. 318). Nevertheless, in an early direct comparison of four treatment formats (short-term individual, short-term group [24 session over 6 months], long-term-individual, and long term-group [96 sessions over 2 years]), short-term groups produced the weakest results (Piper, Debbane, Bienvenue, & Garant, 1984). Another study comparing 15-session individual and group therapies reported equivalent outcomes (Budman, et al., 1988). In this study, however, a more careful assessment through patient interviews revealed that patients assigned to the short-term group were dissatisfied with their assignment and 34% of the patients of those assigned to groups failed to attend any sessions. This was in contrast to only 6% of those assigned to dyadic therapy. Budman and colleagues (1988) observe that patients subjectively felt they benefited more from their individual therapy, despite the nearly equivalent measures of outcome in group therapy (p. 81). This report is a continuing reminder of the general cultural preference for individual treatment, and the necessity of careful selection and preparation of patients for groups.

SUMMARY

It is too simplistic to argue that "longer is better." There has been entirely too little study into the meaning of time in psychotherapy. Carstensen, Isaacowitz, and Charles (1999) argue that "boundaries on time provide the framework within which individuals select and prioritize goals. When time is perceived as expansive, long-term goals are chosen over others because they optimize future possibilities. . . . When time is limited, however, short-term goals, such as social connectiveness, social support, and emotional regulation assume highest priority" (p. 178).

For individuals who are not initially ready to commit themselves to an open-ended group, time-limited groups offer a viable treatment alternative. It is not unusual for such individuals to profit greatly from their group experience and then feel ready to work more extensively on the issues they unearthed in an ongoing group.

The changing culture and the general dissatisfaction with time-extensive treatment provided the impetus for exploring the use of time-limited treatments. Groups organized in such a manner have been helpful in the quest for more efficient treatment methods, and the results are encouraging. We have enumerated the advantages and disadvantages of time-limited groups, but we feel it is still too early to delineate the most effective composition, structure, and theoretical stance that will prove to be most effective. The plethora of approaches is a clear indication that no one approach will fit all needs.

SIXTEEN

Termination in Group Psychotherapy

Nothing so difficult as a beginning . . . unless
perhaps the end.
—GEORGE GORDON, LORD BYRON, *Don Juan*

Termination of psychotherapy is an extremely complex process. It is further complicated in therapy groups. In dyadic therapy the leave-taking is between two individuals and it can be modified to suit the situation. Barring unusual circumstances the patient has the option of returning to the therapist in the future, if needed. It is occasionally useful to terminate the therapeutic relationship gradually, by meeting less and less often and thus giving the patient the opportunity to "try it out" before a final termination occurs.

In group therapy, leave-taking is more public and more complicated because the member is leaving many individuals, not just one. Leave-takings tend to be final. When a patient terminates group therapy, it is unlikely that the group will remain unchanged should the patient need or desire further treatment. Also, it is more difficult in groups to modify terminations to suit the needs of individual patients because this flexibility would adversely affect the therapeutic process where members need continuity and consistency in order to accomplish their work.

HISTORICAL REVIEW OF THE CONCEPT OF TERMINATION

How do we know when termination is appropriate? The criteria by which to judge the time to terminate therapy have varied. In the earliest days of psychoanalysis, when Sigmund Freud and Josef Breuer were involved in hypnosis, termination was based on the topographic theory of mental functioning. According to this theory, therapy was finished when the unconscious was made conscious. This goal implied the lifting of repression but did not address the possibility of evaluating changes in psychic structure.

The theoretical picture was altered by Freud's discovery of transference neurosis. Transference, as one element of the repetition compulsion, implies the existence of a stable, organized mental agency with characteristic defenses. This perspective added a new criterion by which to evaluate treatment completion: the transferential attachment to the analyst had to be resolved. Such resolution was seen as a concomitant of change in mental structures. However, Firestein (1976), in a study of successful training analyses, found that simply reentering the interview situation reawakened the old transferences, though in mild and manageable form. This study suggests that even in a healthy population, transference neurosis is by no means obliterated or eliminated.

Further modifications in termination criteria followed the development of ego psychology. Successful psychotherapy was correlated with the emergence of higher-level defenses, greater appropriateness in the use of defenses, greater flexibility in defensive style, and improvement in the ego's capacity for autonomous functioning. The outgrowth of this shift in perspective to the level of ego functioning led directly to questions of internalization and structuralization, that is, to an interest in how new or regained ego capacities are integrated into the mental apparatus.

Another important contribution to the conceptualization of termination came from the object relations school, which postulated that the primary human drive is to find objects (relationships). Criteria for termination were associated with the individual's capacity to develop object constancy, the ability to hold a reliable internal image and memory of others. This capacity was operationalized through examination of the patient's ability to find and form meaningful relationships with appropriate persons while tolerating ambivalent feelings.

The work of Kohut (1971, 1977) suggested yet another set of criteria for termination. Viewed from the perspective of self psychology, the individual in therapy develops a reliable capacity to experience others as separate individuals who have their own needs and wishes and are not present solely to fulfill a missing function of the self. Self psychologists believe that the attainment of appropriate goals, ambitions, pride, and self-esteem is the result of maturation of infantile grandiosity and that the acquisition of appropriate values and ideals results from maturation of infantile idealization. Closely linked to these steps is increased empathic capacity.

CURRENT CRITERIA
FOR APPROPRIATE TERMINATION

There is some disagreement among those writers who discuss termination criteria for patients with preoedipal pathologies, in contrast to patients with classical oedipal conflicts. The classical criteria for termination for all pathologies have included the following:

- The transference neurosis and resistances are analyzed, with the resulting development of a more mature superego and ego ideal.
- Defenses are freer.
- Drives are discharged in a more socially acceptable manner.
- The patient internalizes the therapist's analyzing capacity.
- The patient develops the capacity for intimacy.

Blanck and Blanck (1974) have summarized termination criteria that seem most applicable to those patients with earlier developmental deficits and arrests:

- Identity, differentiation between self and object representations, and the capacity to retain the representation of the object independent of the state of mind are attained.
- Higher levels of integration are reached, indicating that structuralization has proceeded.
- Object relations approach object constancy.
- A more competent defensive capacity is acquired.
- The ego exercises more and more of its own functions.

Kohut (1971) suggested that in disorders of the self the development of a stable, cohesive self may be sufficient for the individual to restart the thwarted growth process and spontaneously move through oedipal developmental stages. In a more controversial formulation, Kohut (1971) also emphasized the development of structures in either the grandiose or idealizing axis to compensate for major organizational deficits in the opposite axis.

TERMINATION IN GROUPS

All of the aforementioned criteria are adequate means of judging the therapeutic process. More often than not, therapists will use a variety of criteria chosen according to their theoretical orientation. Fieldsteel (1996), describing an optimal, mutually agreed upon termination, asserts that

> Planned termination occurs when patients understand their own symptoms and character structures and have developed a coherent narrative of their historical origins. Behavioral changes are relatively well-established and the patient has made corresponding changes in his or her defensive systems. There is expanded self awareness and persistent transference distortions have been interpreted and modified. (p. 30)

In addition, we link judgments about the suitability of termination to the original group agreements, in which patients agree to remain in the group until they resolve the problems they bring to the group. This is a complicated judgment because many original problems have not been "cured" or eradicated but may have been resolved to the satisfaction of the patient. One example is the patient who comes with the specific goal of gaining the interpersonal attributes necessary to form a loving relationship, marry, and become a parent. Such a patient might terminate when he or she has been able to form a stable and successful loving relationship even though that is only the first step in the original design.

One dilemma in linking termination to the original goals of therapy is that almost universally patients discover *more* or *different* problems in the course of their therapies. Is termination appropriate if the patient resolves the problems that brought him/her but not the other problems that became apparent during the treatment?

The most important single criterion for determining the appropriateness of termination has to do with the question, "Has this patient gained the most that can be gained from this group at this time?" The answer will be quite different for different patients, and the group agreements can function as a rough guideline for termination. Patients may use the agreements in a positive fashion, but they may also defensively invoke the agreements as a rationale for leaving. Under the latter circumstance the therapist must work with the resistance to further therapy.

When individuals decide to stop treatment, they terminate from the real and the fantasied relationships with their group colleagues, therapist, and the group-as-a-whole. This is an active process, and the form it takes depends on the group norms, which define the way terminations are managed, and on a person's prior experiences with separations. Typically, termination evokes at least three major affective components: feelings about death and mortality, feelings about separation and/or abandonment, and hope (a new beginning). The degree to which each or all of these components are emphasized in particular terminations is a function of the individual and the prior group process.

Many different kinds of terminations occur in groups. Most members terminate successfully (though rarely with the kind of "perfection" therapists might fantasize). However, some members drop out before engaging in treatment, others quit prematurely, and still others leave for external reasons or with significant but incomplete gains. Some people quit with advance notice; others just disappear.

Life is filled with good-byes, so the capacity to bear the affect surrounding loss is a necessary skill if one is to attain intimate relationships. Each and every termination from a group offers all the members another opportunity to learn more about the experience of saying good-bye. Since loss and death are such painful experiences, members often resist experiencing the emotions surrounding terminations. Because they try to avoid these affects, their responses are often either totally hidden or are expressed metaphorically.

The therapist, functioning in the role of norm setter, should help draw the members' attention to the feelings surrounding loss. The therapist's attitude and willingness to confront these feelings increases the members' capacities to study their inner worlds. The therapist also tries to establish norms regarding proper termination procedures, including appropriate notification to the group and setting a termination date far enough in advance to allow for sufficient exploration of the feelings evoked.

There are at least four interacting factors in any termination:

- The Developmental Level of the Group
- The Type of Termination
- The Process for the Departing Member
- The Process for the Therapist

Though these dynamics and affects are intimately intertwined, we will attempt to separate them for heuristic purposes.

The Developmental Level of the Group

Dropouts in Early Group Development

In most instances of termination within the first few weeks or months of a group's existence, the person has not committed him/herself to the group. Frequently these terminators will simply disappear, or they will summarily announce, "This is my last session." The group response may be one of surprise or anger, but even in situations where there have been prior indicators of stopping treatment, the overall responses are somewhat muted.

In newer groups, members have not had time to establish relationships or to understand themselves or others, and they are more preoccupied with their own safety than with separations or abandonment. Indeed they may not know much about the internal or interpersonal world of the departing person. Furthermore, since the overall safety of the group has not yet been established, members may unconsciously want to keep open the opportunity to exit. The combination of these elements may limit members' abilities to consider consciously or unconsciously the impact of the departure upon themselves or the group.

If the leader or the group pays exclusive attention to an individual member who is departing, this misses other important dynamics at work. Powerful regressive forces are activated when new groups form, and the interplay between these forces and the individual is generally what prompts a person to drop out. For example, if a group has developed a norm for instant intimacy, this may produce very premature terminations. Furthermore, when a group does not recognize the frail but courageous efforts of certain members to become more engaged, the resulting painful narcissistic injury is covered in either a raging, stormy departure or a perplexing, sudden, unannounced disappearance (Stone, Blase, & Bozzuto, 1980). Some groups, in their pressure for rapid engagement, may become angry with silent members, precipitating dropouts. (These groups have not developed a capacity to self-reflect or to appreciate their tendency to scapegoat.) Other group processes that contribute to early departure are scapegoating, avoidance of in-group conflict, and insistence on immediate and intense expression of feelings (Bernard & Drob, 1989; Connelly, Piper, DeCarufel, & Debbane, 1986).

Dropping out presents a particular therapeutic problem in new groups because there is insufficient safety to allow unacceptable affects to emerge and be examined in an accepting atmosphere. These affects include guilt, shame, and envy. Guilt is almost universal. Members' defenses against engagement include distancing, controlling, or rejecting behaviors. When a dropout occurs, these patients' responses are "responsibility" and guilt. Shame may arise from the belief that not enough was done to prevent the dropping out—that one's feelings or behaviors toward the departed member were insufficient to prevent the departure. The regressive nature of these affects parallels those of small children who feel that they are the cause of a parental divorce or death.

Competitive strivings further contribute to the feelings of shame and guilt. Each departure represents a victory in that there is one less person with whom to vie for the group's attention or with whom to compete for the therapist's favor. Guilt over the victory and shame for having such wishes are likely to remain hidden in a new group.

Envy is also a powerful and frequently expressed feeling. Since it can be assumed that there is a part of every member that wishes to avoid belonging to a group and experiencing the difficult task of growing, all remaining members feel envious of the departed member. This feeling is often covered by a reaction formation, with those remaining avowing their increased dedication to and optimism about the group.

The absence of overt affect about an early dropout should not be mistaken for a genuine lack of interest in the event. Sometimes no mention is made of an early dropout until someone else leaves, and then a flood of previously unexpressed sentiments emerges. It is not at all unusual for a significant discussion of an early departure to occur months later, evoked by something in the current process of the group. The therapist must attempt to tactfully help the newly forming group explore their reactions to an early dropout, even in the face of considerable resistance.

At times the therapist can invite other members to address their own unspoken and unacknowledged wishes to drop out, thus reducing the press on one member to bear that wish.

On the other hand, when *several* members drop out early, concern about the group's continued existence emerges and members become preoccupied with the future, often asking about newcomers and the future plans of the therapist. The therapist has the task of balancing the discussion of the group's future with the more immediate feelings of discouragement and despair.

Dropouts in More Mature Groups

In more mature groups the premature departure of a recently added member stimulates many of the same feelings and dynamics that are found in new groups. However, the affects will be more available for discussion and exploration. In addition, the therapist may be the object of anger for having selected such an individual, since the old members are acutely aware of the disruptive effect of having someone enter and depart so quickly. In the process of group development they have acquired the capacity to explore their affects in the here and now of meetings and are in a position to retrospectively examine some of their own fears of joining and their wishes to flee. Compared to members of a newly formed group, they may be more empathic toward the departed member and more introspective about the processes that may have contributed to the quitting. This, of course, does not mean that all new members will remain in an established group—only that members of mature groups will have more access to the feelings evoked by the departure and more capacity to utilize those feelings for learning. Established groups are in fact not damaged or slowed down nearly as much by the premature departure of a new member as are less mature groups.

The Type of Terminations

Incomplete Treatments

Incomplete treatments are those in which a member has become engaged in the group process, accomplishes some therapeutic gain, and then terminates. In most instances the termination is initiated by the patient (see Chapter 14 for instances of therapist removal of patients). What is incomplete treatment from one perspective may be sufficient from another. However, the label "incomplete" should be considered from several different perspectives: that of the departing patient, that of the clinician, that of the other members.

A subtle countertransference may be present with such individuals, as the therapist may feel misled or shamed for not having predicted such a response. Actually, the clinician most likely had hoped that such a person would be willing to do the hard work necessary for resolution of personality problems.

As we emphasized earlier, it is important to maintain a view that ultimately it is the patients' decision when to leave. They may be in the best position to determine that they have gained what they wanted or achieved the most they can at the time. Such individuals may be well aware that there is more work to do but still choose to leave. These differing perspectives can become a source of considerable tension.

The dynamics surrounding such departures are generally those of more advanced stages of the group process. The remaining members in such groups are usually ready to explore their feelings of hurt, disappointment, envy, and rage at the one who left without finishing his/her work. Angry reactions to the loss of members are much in evidence in such groups, and considerable therapeutic gain is possible for members as a result of freeing up angry affects. Beneath the anger is often a deep-seated feeling of personal or group-wide failure to help or more deeply engage the departing member. Such departures evoke past hurts and grievances and lost loves. They also create shifts in the group system (Schermer & Klein, 1996). These painful affects, along with the associated depressive feelings, also can be examined in a therapeutically productive fashion.

Maturing groups also include persons who can recognize the personality limitations of the departing person and appreciate that the timing of his/her departure coincides with his/her ability. Their perspective balances some of the more painful and disruptive aspects of such loss to the group. Finally, mature groups are acutely aware that any termination means ultimately a new "hello" must be said and that the group will be changed. We will now examine several types of "incomplete" treatment.

The Curative Fantasy. Some patients enter treatment with a curative fantasy that is an organized wish for what they hope to gain in therapy (Ornstein & Ornstein, 1977; Stone, 1983). It cannot be expressed through a set of agreements because the curative fantasy contains both conscious and unconscious elements; instead, it is expressed in the process of the treatment. These patients use the group relationships to strengthen a sector of their personalities. When this has been accomplished, some of these patients terminate, leaving the therapist and other members bewildered. Although they seemingly have not fulfilled the agreements, they depart quite satisfied.

CLINICAL EXAMPLE

Alexis, married to a highly successful entrepreneur and experiencing an "empty nest" syndrome, entered group to address feelings of discouragement and withdrawal from social relations. She described a history of feeling that her contributions to the family or in the community had never been appreciated. In the group she appeared socially adept. The other members appreciated her contributions to their work, and they commented positively upon her effectiveness in certain areas of her life. On several occasions, when she seemed to have withdrawn, the therapist was able to recognize and empathically comment upon a subtle narcissistic injury that had preceded her withdrawal. In this context the patient rather abruptly announced that she would soon terminate.

*   *   *

In the theory of self psychology and the curative fantasy, the members' "mirroring" and the clinician's empathic responsiveness were sufficient to help Alexis regain a sense of inner balance. The disruption in her self-equilibrium had been precipitated by her children's departure and had left her feeling depleted. She had not examined the sources of her vulnerable self. In retrospect, her curative fantasy had been fulfilled and she terminated. In more traditional formulations, Alexis would have been described as having a "transference cure." However, we believe that explanation inadequately explains Alexis's experience in the group and her early departure.

Limited Capacity Patients. Another group of individuals who "prematurely" terminate make important personal gains and derive considerable benefit from their treatment, yet manifest continuing difficulties in several aspects of their lives or in their internal functioning. Often considered "difficult" patients, these individuals, who may have been in the group for extended periods, unilaterally announce they are going to terminate. They have potential for further gains, but that is unlikely to occur easily or in the foreseeable future. We differentiate these individuals from those who have made gains and yet remain relatively unaware of additional difficulties. Those patients (resistant patients) will be discussed in the next section.

Although from many perspectives the therapy may be "incomplete," when assessing the patient's strengths and limitations and determining that he/she is intent on leaving, the therapist should be able to respectfully help the patient depart. This is not an easy achievement for a clinician, who initially may be unprepared for such an announcement. Often the other members react with surprise, disbelief, anger, or withdrawal, associating to present and prior losses and abandonments. Some members are able to understand that, despite one's own assessment, this is each person's decision and must be respected.

CLINICAL EXAMPLE

Brenda, a childless, divorced woman, suffered recurrent major depressions and phobias. Her depressions were moderately responsive to pharmacotherapy, but she remained isolated, angry, and unable to form a loving relationship. Brenda viewed herself as only becoming involved with abusive men. She entered a group to address these problems.

She slowly engaged in the group and initially referred to the meetings as a "class." She attributed any improved sense of well-being to her medication. During her first year in the group, Brenda complained bitterly about her boss, several of her coworkers whom she saw as receiving special treatment, and her social isolation. Her few friends were several decades older than herself. Her difficulties at work continued, and she was threatened with dismissal; her annual salary increase was the least of anyone in her position.

Brenda seldom understood emotions in herself but could identify feelings in others. This was seen as helpful, and she formed positive alliances with several members. She kept distant from the therapist but gradually referred to the group as the more helpful aspect of her treatment, while not depreciating the medications. Her austere dress and generally self-righteous presentation modified, and she reported socializing with colleagues from work. Her efforts to form romantic relationships, however, remained unsuccessful.

Brenda's improvement was concretely actualized the following year when she received the largest raise among her peers. Soon thereafter she announced her plans to leave the group. She knew that she had more therapeutic work to do but chose to stop treatment. She gave 4 weeks notice, and then decreased the time to 3 weeks. The others had little time to react. They showed a range of responses, from direct angry confrontations of her remaining "deficits," to sadness that she was leaving.

At her final session, Brenda reported a dream from the preceding night: She was walking with a man holding hands. It felt very good. The scene changed and she was working on a puzzle and was having difficulty finding the last piece. A man was helping her, but they could not locate the missing piece.

*   *   *

The dream clearly signified the gains she had made (not only she was holding hands with a man, but a man was trying to be helpful to her). Brenda could not make any connections to the missing piece in relationship to unfinished therapeutic work, and she could not make a connection of the relevance of the dream to her experiences in the group.

The Resistant Patient. Incomplete treatments provide an opportunity to examine the differences between terminations that are the result of fate or external factors and those that at first seem to be the result of external factors but are later understood to be the final product of resistance to, or acting out against, the therapy. If there is sufficient time—and if the departing individual has not burned all of his/her bridges—this examination may even prevent the premature leaving.

In attempting to help prematurely departing patients examine the unconscious aspects of leaving, the therapist might review their initial complaints and symptoms with the idea linking the present wish to stop treatment to familiar behavioral patterns. The leave-taking may also be the result of newly exposed conflicts or of interpersonal clashes within the group that are fueled by historic conflicts. The therapist might state quite directly that the work of therapy is incomplete and that this is not the most propitious time to terminate. Of course, this should always be done with tact and empathy and in full recognition of the fact that patients are free agents. On occasion, however, a forthright statement about the incomplete therapeutic work will encourage a redecision. In some instances the entire process is an unconscious test of the therapist or group, a test designed to discover whether or not the therapist or group cares enough to fight to have the patient stay. It is also worth remembering that, ultimately, no one "resists" treatment or changing. What people resist is anticipated pain.

To focus solely on the individual in question is usually insufficient to understand fully what is occurring. It is useful to encourage the patient to be curious about why the decision to leave occurs at a particular point in the group's life. Attention to the group processes, which may be similar to those described for dropouts (e.g., scapegoating, pressure for emotional closeness, empathic unavailability, narcissistic injury, or perceived failure), may be precipitants for termination. By understanding a decision to leave in the context of the group process, the tendency to focus solely on the departing member is diminished. This not only provides the member with a more complete understanding of the impetus for wishing to leave, but it also makes it easier for him/her by offering a face-saving reason to remain in the group.

CLINICAL EXAMPLE

Ron, a never-married 40-year-old man who still lived with his elderly parents, reentered a group 2 years after his prior treatment ended when the group terminated. Ron made little gain in his previous group and upon entry into the new group he announced that he wanted to be open and honest and forgo his "people-pleasing" ways. His saccharine sweetness was immediately apparent in the new group. Indeed, the therapist often wondered about his judgment in accepting Ron because of the rigidity with which he interacted with others.

In the new group, Ron was often critical of the therapist—he was paid to take it—but he smoothed over conflict among members and almost invariably commented in a manner that would ingratiate himself with others. Ron avoided opportunities for improving his career because he didn't like change. His social life was limited to bowling and card playing. His few dates were filled with anxiety that he would be sexually impotent. Ron did manage to leave his parents and buy his own home. Soon thereafter he announced he was going to terminate because he could no longer afford the fee. His new home had depleted his finances more than anticipated. The group's response was mixed, with some members quite angry about his departure and others relieved because Ron had frequently interfered with their work. In his final session Ron acknowledged that he was choosing to leave because of the pressure for increasing intimacy and his discomfort with the others' abilities to tolerate angry exchanges.

*   *   *

Ron was a very resistant patient. He owned little responsibility for his problems. While he set as his overt goal improving his social life, it would appear that his unconscious goal was to move away from his parents. In this he was successful, and it would accomplish little at this point to push him to accomplish more.

In every premature termination there are some members, focusing only on the gains and overlooking the continuing difficulties of the departing patient, who are in initial complete agreement with the decision to leave. Thus, the resistance to continuing treatment or exploring the conflict may be a groupwide resistance. In these circumstances an exploration of the resistance in the members who sided with the announced departure may assist the potentially departing member in assessing his or her own resistances.

External Reasons. In a number of circumstances, individuals terminate their treatments for a variety of external reasons: they move (in some mental health clinics even a move to a suburban county makes a person ineligible for treatment), their jobs require extensive travel, and/or their finances change (including changes in insurance coverage).

Clearly not all external reasons are unencumbered with inner meaning and conscious or unconscious resistances. People do have choices about taking or remaining in jobs that require a move. Nevertheless, in many instances external factors create a substantial "reality."

Departures under these circumstances often are bittersweet. Real therapeutic gains and the need for additional work are both acknowledged. Such terminations carry with them the added dimension of a lost opportunity. In a way, such a termination allows for more direct expression of negative feelings because it was not the individual's choice. In a truncated way, forced terminations reawaken old experiences of death and of separations that occurred without the participants' volition.

Finally, such premature terminations highlight the very real limitations of control and power one person has over another. The opportunity for the remaining members to discover and deal with that reality can be a very important opportunity and can be distinguished from a neurotic feeling of helplessness or giving up. To believe genuinely that a member would be in error by terminating at a particular point in time and to make every effort to communicate that conviction to the member and still have the termination occur is to face both the real and existential limitations of life.

Complete Treatment

Successful terminations from groups are usually moving and powerful experiences for all concerned. Unlike terminations from dyadic therapy, terminations from groups are witnessed, felt, and shared by a number of people.

The optimal process for termination is set forth in the original group agreements (see Chapter 8). The agreement to "remain in the group until the problems that brought you have been resolved" implies a great deal about what constitutes appropriate termination; that is, patients are expected to stay until a particular goal or set of goals has been achieved. Furthermore, at the time of negotiating the agreements, the procedure for termination is explained; prospective members are told that they should terminate when they have finished their work and that termination includes exploring their decisions in the group, after which they should continue to attend the group for as long as it takes to deal with the important process of saying good-bye. The therapist should help the departing patient set a termination date far enough in advance for the group to deal with and learn from the related feelings. Generally, the process will be facilitated if the departing member has had the opportunity to observe a spectrum of terminations before saying his/her own good-byes.

In most successful terminations, the therapist and many of the members will sense that a termination is coming. The quality of the interactions, along with reports of improved functioning outside the group, provides ample data upon which to build awareness that the work is approaching a conclusion. One indicator of successful therapeutic work is a patient's ability to resolve his/her conflicts more rapidly and with diminished intensity. In most instances neurotic or character problems do not completely disappear, but these traits are accepted more lovingly. Angers and hurts which lasted weeks or months in the initial phases of treatment may be experienced less intensely and addressed more rapidly and effectively (Rubovitz-Seitz, 1998). One hallmark of a successful termination is the agreement of almost everyone in the room that the time is right (though many may be bitterly disappointed or angry about it).

When a member announces plans to terminate, major emotional responses are inevitable. Each patient has the right to determine when termination is in order. Termination is not the result of a group vote. Nonetheless, successfully terminating patients will allow and encourage input from their colleagues about the advisability of termination, and they will examine this decision as they have learned to examine all important decisions. Some terminating members will announce steadfastly, "I have decided to terminate," and will state the date of the last meeting they will attend. Others invite more groupwide participation in the decision. The approach can be appropriate or inappropriate, depending upon the individual and the situation. Sometimes an individual will make a hard-and-fast decision and set a date for the final meeting as a way of avoiding the power of the feelings regarding separation and loss. On the other hand, an individual who desires to forestall the inevitable leaving will appear to require groupwide approval of the decision to terminate, thereby delaying the implementation of a decision that has inwardly already been made. The important point is to make every possible effort to allow sufficient time and opportunity to explore the relevant affects that lead to and result from the decision of a member to terminate.

No stereotypical rule governs the length of time the termination process should take, but the most common error is allowing too little time to experience and learn from the feelings. Therapists and patients alike are hesitant about fully facing the feelings evoked by important good-byes. Time is needed for the group to come to grips with the idea of the termination. We prefer to have the discussion of the idea of termination precede setting an actual departure date. After the discussion, a departure date should be set far enough in the future to allow for full exploration and elaboration of the event. As a rough guideline, this entire process might take 1 month for each year that the patient has been in the group, though for members who have spent many years in a group this may be too protracted a guideline.

Following an announcement of the intention to terminate, members generally respond with important derivative material, frequently by associating to other important losses. This should not be viewed as a resistance to dealing with the leave-taking but, rather, as an integral part of mourning. By associating to powerful previous good-byes, the other patients are communicating how deeply this loss will be felt. The current loss also provides an opportunity for a more complete grieving of earlier, insufficiently mourned losses. As the actual departure date approaches, the group will deal more and more directly with the here-and-now feelings about saying good-bye to the departing individual.

In the termination process an appraisal of the departing member's growth, changes, and unresolved conflicts is commonly undertaken. Previous intragroup conflicts, incompletely resolved, will often resurface. Regression takes place, often affecting many in the group, and the emotional responses may include intense efforts to dissuade the member from leaving. Sometimes the terminating member succumbs to the pressure, or to his/her ambivalence, and considers not terminating therapy. Again, envy of the success of a colleague may be in evidence, but often reaction formation clouds the feelings by overidealizing the terminating member. These regressions are usually short lived, with all members realizing the archaic nature of their responses. Indeed, the members gain satisfaction from recognizing that they can experience old feelings and conflicts and rapidly regain their balance.

It is important to appreciate that not all the pressures to prevent or delay a departure are transferential. In the place of a senior, mature, and contributing member, the group will gain a neophyte who will initially take much more than he/she gives. Furthermore, there are also real relationships between human beings that will be missed.

CLINICAL EXAMPLE

Yola announced her termination after 5 years of extremely productive work in her group. The members responded with dismay, many suggesting that this was an inappropriate time for Yola to leave treatment. This surprised the therapist, who felt Yola's plan to terminate was entirely reasonable.

Over the ensuing weeks, members associated to the deaths of siblings and very close friends. Jerry was especially poignant, weeping as he recalled the death of his beloved mentor. JoAnn angrily associated to the birth of her younger sister when she was 13: "She was nothing but a burden to me."

Gradually the group was able to bid Yola a loving good-bye, having acknowledged that they fully agreed with her decision but found it hard to imagine the group without her. Furthermore, as with JoAnn's remembering her sister's birth, they were not the least bit excited about replacing such a powerful member as Yola with a newcomer.

*   *   *

Once a definite date for leaving is set, the departure becomes a reality. The termination date should not coincide with another disruption, such as the therapist's vacation or the addition of a new member. Each major disruption requires careful attention, and to confuse the successful termination of a member with another disruption diminishes the poignancy of the loss. Maintaining continuity in the face of loss furthers appropriate grieving.

Setting the final date underlines the group's awareness that the individual in question will soon be leaving and will ultimately be replaced by someone else. The focus on the future also concerns the departing member, and members will often ask, "What will you be doing on this night in the future?" and "What will it be like in group without you?" Members also turn their attention to their own futures, often wondering how many more months or years will be required before they too can successfully leave the group. In this process they may review their progress, and under the influence of the positive atmosphere they may work on their problems with new resolve.

As the final session approaches, it is usually increasingly difficult for the members to tolerate the feelings; thus, there is frequently a proposal made for action—a social gathering or the purchase of a group gift to commemorate the termination. These discussions can generate considerable enthusiasm, and much energy and effort can go into the planning of a "last supper." It is difficult under these circumstances for any single member to refuse to join in, and great therapeutic skill is required to handle these situations. When confronted with such plans for action, therapists should tactfully remind the members that the agreement is to share feelings verbally rather than to act on them. Such proposals for action attempt to set a norm that homogenizes all terminations, thereby diminishing the often painful reality that people are missed and mourned differently. Moreover, there is always—in addition to the genuine wish to send the successful patient off with good cheer—the opposite envious or angry side.

CLINICAL EXAMPLE

The therapist entered the office for the final group meeting with Zelda, a patient terminating successfully after many years. To his surprise and dismay, the therapist found that the room resembled a New York deli, with cold cuts, potato chips, wine, and all the utensils spread around in a decorative fashion. The group was in a festive mood, each member sitting with a plate brimming with food. The therapist was instantly greeted by Mildred, who offered to pour him some wine and make him a sandwich.

The therapist was confronted with a delicate therapeutic task. Clearly, great effort had gone into this lavish display, and the members obviously felt they were honoring the termination of Zelda. They had no conscious awareness of the denial implied in their party atmosphere. For the therapist to focus only on the resistant elements of the "celebration" would have been to miss part of the point. On the other hand, to have participated in the party would have been an even more serious error since doing so would have meant altering the fundamental agreements.

In this instance the therapist simply noted, "The group certainly seems to be celebrating Zelda's departure," and placing the glass of wine that he had been handed on an end table beside his chair, he said, "but I think there is a wide range of feelings to be expressed and explored on such an important evening." As the members realized that the therapist was not going to eat or drink, the plates and glasses slowly were placed on the floor or on tables. Mildred was the last to give up the hope that this last meeting with Zelda could be given over to eating and drinking and laughing. She angrily accused the therapist of being a "spoilsport" and wondered, "What shall I do with all this food I brought?" A prolonged and painful silence followed, punctuated by tears as various members began to experience Zelda's loss. Suddenly Mildred burst into tears, saying, "My God! I'm doing what I did at my mother's funeral. I catered that affair; I fed everyone. I never left myself time to cry."

*   *   *

Endings evoke very important feelings, and therapists should resist the temptation to alter the fundamental operation of the group when terminations occur. On the other hand, they must be able to respond creatively and not stereotypically. When a terminating member brings a gift, for example, there is no simple rule about whether to accept it. For some patients, the gift represents their continuing worry that without a physical reminder the group and the therapist will not remember them. If the therapist judges this to be the impetus, the gift usually should be tactfully interpreted and not accepted. In other cases a gift simply represents a wish to give something to commemorate the experience and accompanies feelings amply expressed verbally as well; in this case not accepting the gift might well result in a final narcissistic injury.

It is a rather common occurrence at termination for members to exchange addresses and telephone numbers with the aim of remaining in touch with the departing member. Sometimes members will inquire, "Is this a breach of our agreements?" We believe that the agreements hold only for members who are in the group and that what transpires between members and ex-members is not included. That is not to imply, however, that this wish to continue a relationship should not be explored like any other wish. Sometimes the wishful intention represents an avoidance of the termination and unwillingness by a member to acknowledge a loss. Clinical experience has shown that most efforts to establish or maintain relationships among members and former members do not last. The continuing member will report a number of meetings, but then the relationship fades (Fieldsteel, 1996). On occasion, members of a group may marry following termination. We do not know of any data describing the outcome of such marriages.

No separation or loss is complete. We all carry the images and memories of the departed individual and of his/her interactions with us, and the hope to say a complete and final good-bye is a fantasy. Successful terminations are painful and joyous occasions mixed together, and the therapist should make every effort to help the members explore all aspects of this very important experience.

The Termination Process for a Departing Member

Individuals terminate from groups in a wide variety of ways. Some simply never return, disappearing without even a good-bye. But when individuals remain in groups for any protracted period of time, it is more likely they will engage in at least some formal leave-taking.

Terminations from groups are somewhat different from terminations from dyadic therapy. In groups there is less time, because of the presence of the other members, for a detailed discussion of all the associations and memories that are stirred in the terminating patient by the leaving. Although, as in all human endeavors, there is a wide range of individual responses, individuals terminating from groups seem to experience less regression than do those terminating from individual therapy.

In successful terminations from a group there is a useful tendency on the part of the departing member to reminisce aloud about the treatment. Indeed, therapists can facilitate reminiscing if this does not occur spontaneously. The rich and varied interactions that occurred between members and the leader are remembered and discussed. Typically, departing members review incidents that illustrate their developing ego capacities and their abilities to manage conflict and tolerate affects. Although they may also discuss areas that require further attention and conflicts that remain unresolved, they convey an ability to master rather than be dominated by these incompletely resolved problems. As one departing member said, "I still get extra angry, but now I can stop it and try to work it out rather than just blame the other person." Another said, "I still tend to take care of people too much, but I don't let myself be used all the time anymore." The goal is not perfection but the capacity to recognize, accept, understand, and forgive one's own weaknesses and vulnerabilities and to own and recognize one's strengths.

Departing members may give credit to others who were able to see things well before they could see them for themselves. Moreover, they may comment on the unique opportunities the group provided them to genuinely understand someone else. During the development of a group there is a growing feeling of mastery in members as they learn to appreciate what is going on beneath surface appearances. In other words, members who terminate groups successfully no longer take the position of an external observer of the other members. They have developed or expanded the capacity to empathize, and for many patients this is a highly significant step.

Finally, almost all those who terminate indicate that they will miss the camaraderie, affection, and work of the group. On follow-up reports of factors facilitating therapeutic change, "intermember bonding is often more important than the relationship between the therapist and group members" (Dies, 1994, p. 136). Departing members often wonder aloud if they will be missed or remembered. Since the group has become an important part of their lives, it is natural for them to speculate on whether the remaining members and therapist will think of them, recall their contributions, and in some fashion indicate that they have made an enduring impact upon someone.

The Termination Process for the Group Therapist

The therapist is by no means immune to the effects of members' departures. Just as there are reverberations among the members of themes of separation and loss, so too are memories and affects of these themes stirred in the therapist, potentially producing powerful countertransferences. Therapists may find numerous unconscious reasons to interfere with a patient's departure, paralleling their own separation problems. Similarly, they may be uncomfortable with the wide range of intense affects evoked by terminations and therefore may avoid interpreting the resistance and acting out that are part of termination.

In the case of premature terminations the therapist may suffer the narcissistic hurt of not having been successful or loved. This is much more likely when a therapist is conducting just one group. There is no question that it would be exceedingly difficult for a dyadic therapist to gain therapeutic distance and perspective if he/she had only one patient. Likewise, the feelings of hurt, failure, or discouragement when someone leaves a therapist's only group can be intense. Such situations are always powerful, but if the therapist has other groups that are going well he/she is somewhat protected from severe narcissistic injury. Whenever a therapist's personal issues with loss keep him/her from fully exploring the issues of termination, patients lose opportunities to grow. The most common dilemma for the therapist may well be how to help a patient terminate well when the therapist does not agree that this is the best time to terminate. At these times we might do well to remember the words of John Updike: "Perfection is the enemy of creation, as extreme self-solitude is the enemy of well-being." The goal of the treatment process is not the creation of some "perfect" specimen of mental health, but rather to impart to our patients the tools necessary for them to attain better relationships and to better understand psychodynamic processes.

In especially difficult groups the therapist may harbor the fantasy that if one member quits, the others will also do so and thereafter he/she will not be burdened with the problem group. Unfortunately, this occasionally comes to pass, particularly for neophyte therapists and those who have not had the experience of successful terminations. As with those who learn long-term individual psychotherapy, only a few trainees in group therapy have the good fortune to be in a training placement long enough to experience the successful conclusion of an intensive therapy.

When there is a successful termination, the therapist has the narcissistic gratification of a job well done. At the conclusion of successful dyadic psychotherapy, the therapist often has the opportunity to state quite openly some of what the treatment experience has been like from his/her point of view. In a group the emotional connection from the therapist to the patient is no less powerful, but other patients are privy to and are participating in the good-bye. For some members the overt statement of caring from therapist to departing patient would be overstimulating, but most patients are significantly helped by observing the genuine relationship that has developed among the members, the terminating patient, and with the therapist.

In sum, therapists should feel free to state the same things to terminating group patients that they would state to terminating individual patients. However, they should be acutely aware of the impact of such statements on the remaining patients.

WHOLE-GROUP TERMINATIONS

Terminating an entire group may be predetermined, as in time-limited therapy, or a census inadequate to keep the group alive. However, it may also result from a life event of the therapist or some external event. In such a case, all members must struggle with termination at the same time. Homogeneous groups, organized around a particular symptom, crisis, demographic variable, or diagnosis, are usually planned to last a specific amount of time.

Time-Limited Groups

Though many patients in time-limited groups achieve their goals and are ready to stop at the specified time, this is not the universal situation. The dynamics that ensue are the reverse of those in effect when individuals prematurely drop out of groups. This time the group is quitting "too soon." The entire termination process is complicated because the overt and covert resentments about the loss are difficult to elicit when the group's ending was originally agreed upon. Kauff (1977) described the group fantasy of the destructive witch/mother in forced whole-group terminations or transfers. This reawakening of primitive fantasies surrounding the termination is consistent with the patients' deep-seated fears that their basic needs will remain unmet.

As time-limited groups reach the midpoint of their life expectancy, themes of good-bye, separation, and loss become more and more dominant. The therapist has the important and difficult task of keeping the group's attention on the impending termination. There is a great temptation, aided and abetted by the patients, to discount the importance of the approaching ending. The process of exploring the forthcoming separation and loss is complicated by the fact that members have more therapeutic work to do. Thus, a balance needs to be struck between these two elements. Usually, through clarification of metaphors such as death, divorce, and graduation, the therapist can help the patients understand how they are managing their feelings about the group's demise. As the ending approaches, certain patients may demonstrate a high rate of absenteeism. At the end of each meeting for the last 4 or 5 weeks, the therapist may, as a reminder, announce to the group the number of meetings that remain.

As in other effective terminations, initially the members of a time-limited group will typically resonate to the theme of saying good-bye and will deal with issues from their own personal histories. This is often a time when some excellent work is done on unresolved grief. As the end point comes closer, the group begins dealing with the here-and-now good-byes to the various members, to the leader, and to the group itself.

It is almost never in the best interests of the members of time-limited groups to alter the agreed-upon ending date. Inexperienced therapists occasionally take a vote of the members about whether or not to continue. In the usual scenario a substantial portion, if not all of the members vote to continue the group, but those who felt coerced may quit immediately or soon after the original deadline. In the diminished group, morale is undermined and effective therapy ceases. If a group was formed with the agreement that it would terminate on a specific date, it should do so. In time-limited groups the therapist should help members evaluate the need for continued therapy, but members should understand that they have fulfilled their group agreements and have no responsibility for joining another group. Members wishing to continue therapy may opt to join a new group, perhaps even an open-ended one (see Chapter 15 for a more extensive treatment of time-limited groups).

TERMINATION BY THE GROUP THERAPIST

Therapist Unavailability

Two scenarios exist when a group is terminated because the therapist is no longer available: (1) a sudden, unexpected event, and (2) events which are planned and provide an opportunity for advance planning. The central dynamic is whether or not there has been time to process the ending with the clinician. Although career-ending emergencies are rare, clinicians should have some plan in place to care for their patients. This includes having a therapist or therapists in mind who would take over the group. That person(s) should have access to the therapist's files and be in a position to contact the patients. When the clinician's absence is sudden, it is probably advisable to individually contact the patients and to meet as a group to process the members' responses to their loss. Of course, this is dependent upon the willingness and abilities of the replacement therapist. In these circumstances Sharpe (1991) states, "The new conductor [therapist] needs to 'read' the personality of the group and merge with and adapt to it. He or she should follow the process and be aware that he or she may be experienced as a sudden and perhaps unwelcome intruder" (p. 164). The dynamics are those of any traumatic event, with denial, anger, grief, and resolution occurring in a variety of combinations. However, at times the group dynamics may magnify the feelings—the process of emotional contagion—making it very difficult for the new therapist to maintain his/her balance.

A less traumatic but still difficult circumstance is when the clinician knows in advance that he/she will no longer be available to lead the group. Here the dynamics of grief can be worked with directly by the abandoning object, the departing therapist. In this process we believe it is important to make arrangements with the members and the group regarding their wishes for the future: to continue the group with a new therapist, to terminate or (for those who so choose) either to find another group or individual treatment. Nevertheless, the primary task is to say good-bye as effectively as possible.

Groups That Are Too Small

On rare occasions groups get started and along the way suffer from debilitating decrease in membership. This may be caused by the inability to replace early dropouts or the inability later in the life of the group to replace terminated members. A therapist may have a particularly hard time making the decision to stop the group, even in the face of very strong evidence that new referrals will not be forthcoming. The investment of time and energy that goes into forming a group is a strong incentive not to let the enterprise fail. If the group has been going on for an extended period, this is even more problematic. However, for some therapists the course has been rocky, with frequent absences and with patients dropping out or simply disappearing, and so the therapist may be relieved to end. In some circumstances, it is possible to "save" the group by arranging for its transfer or combination with another group that may need additional patients.

In well-developed groups a decision to terminate may be the result of an inability to find new members. Sufficient time to process the group's termination is respectful of patients, despite the prominent wish to "get it over with" (quickly terminate). In similar circumstances with newly formed groups, there is usually little overt reaction, although underlying disappointment is always present. Nevertheless, powerful feelings are often expressed in metaphors, and the clinician should be alert to subtle references to absences, loss, or death. Sometimes there are significant critiques of authorities, reflecting the disappointment in the therapist's ability to continue the group.

In long-running groups there may be real mourning for what is lost. A period of reminiscing about difficult and wonderful experiences is to be expected, and if not spontaneous, the therapist may introduce the process. Other processes typical of termination also may surface. The therapist in such circumstances may choose to share his/her grief with the members. They are all in the process together, and it is unlikely and probably countertherapeutic for the therapist to keep his/her emotions hidden.

SUMMARY

As we have discussed, termination is a complex process that stirs mixed emotions in all participants. A successful termination is often remembered as an important achievement for the individual and the group. Patients also decide to terminate their group experience "early." The reasons for such a departure vary across a spectrum from "reality" to fears stirred by participating in the process. Exploring the feelings of everyone and attending to the impact of group dynamics may clarify some enactment of prior experiences, and the patient may choose to remain. However, as we have clearly indicated, the decision to leave is ultimately the patient's and that decision deserves respect.

Whole group terminations may be planned, the result of census problems or of decisions by the therapist. Such group endings are replete with a spectrum of feelings, and sufficient time should be allowed to work with the feelings to the extent possible.

The therapist too undergoes important emotional experiences with terminations. The potential for countertransference enactment is enhanced by the presence of contagion and unresolved feelings of loss and separation from the clinician's own past.

It is our hope that the ideas presented in this book will facilitate the successful termination of many group patients.

References

Abse, D. W. (1974). *Clinical Notes on Group Analytic Psychotherapy*. Charlottesville: University of Virginia Press.

Ackerman, N. (1949). Psychoanalysis and group therapy. In J. Moreno (Ed.), *Group Therapy* (Vol. 8, Nos. 2–3, pp. 204–215). Boston: Beacon House.

Adler, G. (1996). Transitional objects, selfobjects, real objects and the process of change in psychodynamic psychotherapy. In L. E. Lifson (Ed.), *Understanding Therapeutic Action: Psychodynamic Concepts of Cure* (pp. 69–84). Hillsdale, NJ: The Analytic Press.

Adler, G., & Buie, D. H. (1979). Aloneness and borderline pathology: The possible relevance of, child development issues. *International Journal of Psycho-Analysis, 60,* 83–96.

Agazarian, Y. M. (1989). Group-as-a-whole system theory and practice. *Group, 13,* 131–154.

Agazarian, Y. M. (1997). *Systems-Centered Therapy for Groups*. New York: Guilford Press.

Allport, G. (1965). *The Nature of Prejudice* (2nd ed.). Cambridge, MA: Addison-Wesley.

Alonso, A., & Rutan, J. S. (1996). Separation and individuation in the group leader. *International Journal of Group Psychotherapy, 46,* 149–162.

Alonso, A., & Rutan, J. S. (1990). Common dilemmas in combined individual and group treatment. *Group, 14,* 5–12.

Alonso, A., & Swiller, H. I. (1993). Introduction: The case for group therapy. In A. Alonso, H. I. Swiller (Eds.), *Group Therapy in Clinical Practice* (pp. xxii–xxiii). Washington, DC: American Psychiatric Press.

American Psychiatric Association. (1994). *Diagnostic and Statistical Manual of Mental Disorders* (4th ed.). Washington, DC: Author.

Ashback, C., & Schermer, V. L. (1987). *Object Relations, the Self and the Group: A Conceptual Paradigm*. New York: Routledge & Kegan Paul.

Astrachan, B. M. (1970). Towards a social systems model of therapeutic groups. *Social Psychiatry, 5,* 110–119.

Atwood, G., & Stolorow, R. (1984). *Structurees of Subjectivity: Explorations in Psychoanalytic Phenomenology.* Hillsdale, NJ: Analytic Press.

Bacal, H. A. (1985). Optimal responsiveness and the therapeutic process. In A. Goldberg (Ed.), *Progress in Self Psychology* (Vol. 1, pp. 202–226). Hillsdale, NJ: Analytic Press.

Bacal, H. A. (1998). Notes on optimal responsiveness in the group process. In I. N. H. Harwood & M. Pines (Eds.), *Self Experiences in Group: Intersubjective and Self Psychological Pathways to Human Understanding* (pp. 175–180). London: Kingsley.

Bach, G. R. (1954). *Intensive Group Psychotherapy.* New York: Ronald Press.

Bader, B. R., Bader, L. J., Budman, S., & Clifford, M. (1981). Pre-group preparation model for long-term group psychotherapy in a private practice setting. *Group, 5,* 43–50.

Balint, M. (1957). *The Doctor, His Patient and The Illness.* New York: International Universities Press.

Battegay, R. (1972). Individual psychotherapy and group psychotherapy in combination. *ACTA Psychiatrica Scandinavica, 48,* 43–46.

Battegay, R. (1977). The group dream. In L. Wolberg & M. Aronson (Eds.), *Group Psychotherapy 1977: An Overview* (pp. 27–41). New York: Stratton Intercontinental Medical Books.

Benne, K., & Sheats, P. (1948). Functional roles of group members. *Journal of Social Issues, 4,* 41–49.

Bennis, W. G., & Shepard, H. A. (1956). A theory of group development. *Human Relations, 9,* 415–437.

Berger, M. M. (1969). Notes on the communication process in group therapy. *Journal of Group Process and Psychoanalysis, 2*(1), 29–36.

Berman, A., & Weinberg, H. (1998). The advanced-stage therapy group. *International Journal of Group Psychotherapy, 48,* 499–518.

Bernard, H. S., & Drob, S. L. (1985). The experience of patients in conjoint individual and group psychotherapy. *International Journal of Group Psychotherapy, 35,* 129–146.

Bernard, H. S., & Drob, S. L. (1989). Premature termination: A clinical study. *Group, 13,* 11–22.

Binstock, W. (1979). The psychodynamic approach. In A. Lazare (Ed.), *Outpatient Psychiatry: Diagnosis and Treatment.* (pp. 19–70). Baltimore: Williams & Wilkins.

Bion, W. R. (1960). *Experiences in Groups.* New York: Basic Books.

Birdwhistle, R. L. (1970). *Kinesics and Context.* Philadelphia: University of Pennsylvania Press.

Birk, L. (1974). Intensive group therapy: An effective behavioral–psychoanalytic Method. *American Journal of Psychiatry, 131,* 11–16.

Blanck, G., & Blanck, R. (1974). *Ego Psychology: Theory and Practice.* New York: Columbia University Press.

Borbely, A. F. (1998). A psychoanalytic concept of metaphor. *International Journal of Psycho-Analysis, 79,* 923–936.

Borriello, J. F. (1979). Group psychotherapy with acting-out patients: Specific problems and techniques. *American Journal of Psychotherapy, 33,* 521–530.

Bowlby, J. (1973). *Separation: Anxiety and Anger.* New York: Basic Books.

Bowlby, J. (1991). Postscript. In C. M. Parkes, J. Stevenson-Hinde, & P. Marris (Eds.), *Attachment Across the Life Cycle* (pp. 293–297). London: Tavistock/Routledge.

Bratter, T. E. (1981). Some pre-treatment group psychotherapy considerations with alcoholic and drug-addicted individuals. *Psychotherapy: Theory, Research and Practice, 18*(4), 508–515.

Brenner, C. (1988). Working through, 1914–1984. *Psychoanalytic Quarterly, 56,* 88–108.

Brook, D. W., Gordon, C., & Meadow, H. (1998). Ethnicity, culture, and group psychotherapy. *Group, 22,* 53–80.

Brown, D. (1992). Bion and Foulkes: Basic assumptions and beyond. In M. Pines (Ed.), *Bion and Group Psychotherapy* (pp. 192–219). London: Tavistock/Routledge.

Brown, D., & Pedder, J. (1979). *Introduction to Psychotherapy: An Outline of Psychodynamic Principles and Practice.* London: Tavistock.

Buchele, B. J. (1997). The development of an analytic perspective in the group leader: Some basic thoughts. *Group, 21,* 303–311.

Budman, S. H. (1994). *Treating Time Effectively* [Videotape and monograph]. New York: Guilford Press.

Budman, S. H., Bennet, M. J., & Wisneski, M. (1981). An adult development model of group psychotherapy. In S. H. Budman (Ed.), *Forms of Brief Therapy* (pp. 305–342). New York: Guilford Press.

Budman, S. H., Cooley, S., Demby, A., Koppenaal, G., Koslof, J., & Powers. T. (1996). A model of time-effective group psychotherapy for patients with personal disorders: The clinical model. *International Journal of Group Psychotherapy, 46,* 329–355.

Budman, S. H., Demby, A., Redendo, J. P., Hannan, M., Feldstein, M., Ring, J., & Springer, T. (1988). Comparative outcomes in time-limited individual and group psychotherapy. *International Journal of Group Psychotherapy, 38,* 63–71.

Budman, S. H., Demby, A., Soldz, S., & Merry, J. (1996). Time-limited group psychotherapy for patients with personality disorders: Outcomes and dropouts. *International Journal of Group Psychotherapy, 46,* 357–377

Budman, S. H., & Gurman, A. S. (1988). *Theory and Practice of Brief Therapy.* New York: Guilford Press.

Budman, S. H., Simeone, P. G., Reilly, R., & Demby, A. (1994). Progress in short-term and time-limited group psychotherapy: Evidence and implications. In A. Fuhriman & G. M. Burlingame (Eds.), *Handbook of Group Psychotherapy: An Empirical and Clinical Synthesis* (pp. 319–339). New York: John Wiley.

Butler, T., & Fuhriman, A. (1980). Patient perceptive on the curative process: A comparison of day treatment and outpatient psychotherapy groups. *Small Group Behavior, 11,* 371–388.

Carstensen, L., Isaacowitz, D. M., Charles, S. T. (1999). Taking time seriously: A theory of socioemotional selectivity. *American Psychologist, 54*(3), 165–181.

Cartwright, R. D., & Zander, A. R. (1960). *Group Dynamics.* London: Tavistock.

Chiang, E., & Beck, B. I. (1988). The effects of therapist turnover in a training group: The core group phenomenon. *International Journal of Group Psychotherapy, 12,* 127–134.

Christ, J. (1975). Contrasting the charismatic and reflective leader. In Z. Liff (Ed.), *The Leader in the Group* (pp.104–113). New York: Aronson.

Cohen, S. L. (1997). Working with resistance to experiencing and expressing emotions in group therapy. *International Journal of Group Psychotherapy, 47,* 443–458.

Cohen, Y. A. (1961). *Social Structures and Personality.* New York: Holt, Rinehart & Winston.

Comstock, B. S., & McDermott, M. (1975). Group therapy for patients who attempt suicide. *International Journal of Group Psychotherapy, 25,* 44–49.

Concannon, C. (1995). The dynamics of the cotherapy relationship: A symposium— the senior–senior team. *Group, 19,* 71–78.

Connelly, J. L., Piper, W. L., DeCarufel, F. L., & Debbane, E. G. (1986). Premature termination in group psychotherapy: Pretherapy and early therapy predictors. *International Journal of Group Psychotherapy, 36,* 145–152.

Conyne, R. K., Wilson, R. W., & Shi, K. (1999). Cultural similarities and differences in group work: Pilot study of U.S.–Chinese task group comparison. *Group Dynamics: Theory, Research and Practice, 3*(1), 40–50.

Cooper, A. M. (1987). Changes in psychoanalytic ideas: Transference interpretation. *Journal of the American Psychoanalytic Association, 35,* 77–98.

Cooper, L., & Gustafson, J. P. (1979a). Planning and mastery in group therapy: A contribution to theory and technique. *Human Relations, 32,* 689–703.

Cooper, L., & Gustafson, J. P. (1979b). Toward a general theory of group therapy. *Human Relations, 32,* 967–981.

Correale, A., & Celli, A. M. (1998). The model-scene in group psychotherapy with chronic psychotic patients. *International Journal of Group Psychotherapy, 48,* 55–68.

Corsini, R., & Rosenberger, B. (1955). Mechanisms of group psychotherapy: Processes and dynamics. *Journal of Abnormal and Social Psychology, 51,* 406–411.

Counselman, E. F. & Gans, J. S. (1999). The missed session in psychodynamic group psychotherapy. *International Journal of Group Psychotherapy, 49,* 3–17.

Crouch, E. C., Bloch, S., & Wanlass, J. (1994). Therapeutic factors: Interpersonal and interpersonal mechanisms. In A. Fuhriman & G. M. Burlingame (Eds.), *Handbook of Group Psychotherapy: An Empirical and Clinical Synthesis* (pp. 269–315). New York: Wiley.

Dalal, F. (1997). A transcultural perspective on psychodynamic psychotherapy: Addressing internal and external realities. *Group Analysis, 30,* 203–215.

Dalal, F. (1998). *Taking the Group Seriously.* London: Kingsley.

Davanloo, H. (1979). Techniques of short-term dynamic psychotherapy. *Psychiatric Clinics of North America, 2,* 11–22.

Davanloo, H. (1980). *Short-Term Dynamic Psychotherapy.* New York: Aronson.

Day, M. (1981). Process in classical psychodynamic groups. *International Journal of Group Psychotherapy, 31,* 153–174.

DeChant, B. (Ed.). (1996). *Women and Group Psychotherapy: Theory and Practice.* New York: Guilford Press.

Demarest, E. W., & Teicher, A. (1954). Transference in group therapy: Its use by cotherapists of opposite sexes. *Psychiatry, 17,* 187–202.

Detrick, D. W. (1985). Alterego phenomena and the alterego transferences. In A. Goldberg (Ed.), *Progress in Self Psychology* (Vol. 1, pp. 240–256). New York: Guilford Press.

Dick, B. M. (1975). A ten-year study of outpatient analytic group therapy. *British Journal of Psychiatry, 127,* 365–376.

Dies, R. R. (1977). Group therapist transparency: A critique of theory and research. *International Journal of Group Psychotherapy, 27,* 177–200.

Dies, R. R. (1985). Leadership in short-term group therapy: Manipulation or facilitation? *International Journal of Group Psychotherapy, 35,* 435–455.

Dies, R. R. (1994). Therapist variables in group psychotherapy research. In A. Fuhriman & G. M. Burlingame (Eds.), *Handbook of Group Psychotherapy: An Empirical and Clinical Synthesis* (pp. 114–154). New York: Wiley.

Dies, R. R. (1997). Comment on issues raised by Slavson, Durkin, and Scheidlinger. *International Journal of Group Psychotherapy, 47,* 161–168.

Dohrenwend, B. P., & Dohrenwend, B. S. (1974). Social and culture influences on psychopathology. *Annual Review of Psychology, 7*(23), 417–452.

Dublin, R. A. (1995). The dynamics of the cotherapy relationship: A symposium—the junior–senior team. *Group,* 19, 79–86.

Durkheim, E. (1951). *Suicide: A Study in Sociology* (J. Spaulding & G. Simpson, Trans.). Glencoe, IL: Free Press. (Original work published 1897)

Durkin, H. E. (1981). The technical implications of general system theory for group psychotherapy. In J. E. Durkin (Ed.), *Living Groups* (pp. 171–198). New York: Brunner/Mazel.

Durkin, H. E. (1964). *The Group in Depth.* New York: International Universities Press.

Durkin, H. E., & Glatzer, H. T. (1973). Transference neurosis in group psychotherapy: The concept and the reality. In L. R. Wolberg & E. K. Schwartz (Eds.), *Group Therapy 1973: An overview.* New York: Intercontinental Book Corporation. (Reprinted in *International Journal of Group Psychotherapy, 47,* 183–199, 1997).

Durkin, J. E. (1981). Foundations of autonomous living structures. In J. E. Durkin (Ed.), *Living Groups* (pp. 24–59). New York: Brunner/Mazel.

Edwards, N. (1977). Dreams, ego psychology, and group interaction in analytic group psychotherapy. *Group, 1,* 32–47.

Ethan, S. (1978). The question of the dilution of transference in group psychotherapy. *Psychoanalytic Review, 65,* 569–578.

Ettin, M. F. (1994a). Links between group process and social, political and cultural issues. In H. I. Kaplan & B. J. Sadock (Eds.), *Comprehensive Group Psychotherapy* (3rd ed., pp. 699–716). Baltimore: Williams & Wilkins.

Ettin, M. F. (1994b). Symbolic representation and the components of a group-as-a-whole model. *International Journal of Group Psychotherapy, 44,* 209–231.

Ettin, M. F. (1997). A view from the other side and a call for cultural exchange: Discussion on paper by Eric van Schoor. *Group Analysis, 30,* 44–48.

Evans, N. J., & Jarvis, P. A. (1980). Group cohesive: A review and evaluation. *Small Group Behavior, 11,* 359–370.

Ezriel, H. (1973). Psychoanalytic group therapy. In L. Wolberg & E. Schwartz (Eds.), *Group Therapy 1973: An Overview.* New York: Stratton Intercontinental Medical Books.

Fairbairn, W. R. D. (1952a). *An Object-Relations Theory of the Personality.* London: Tavistock.

Fairbairn, W. R. D. (1952b). *Psychoanalytic Studies of the Personality.* London: Tavistock

Faris, R. E. L., & Dunham, H. W. (1939). *Mental Disorders in Urban Areas: An Ecological Study of Schizophrenia and Other Psychosis.* Chicago: University of Chicago Press.

Feldberg, T. M. (1958). Treatment of borderline psychotics in groups of neurotic patients. *International Journal of Group Psychotherapy, 8,* 76–84.

Fenster, A., & Fenster, J. (1998). Diagnosis deficits in "basic trust" in multiracial and multicultural groups: Individual and social psychopathology? *Group, 22,* 81–93.

Ferenczi, S., & Rank, O. (1925). *The Development of Psychoanalysis* (C. Newton, Trans.). New York: Nervous & Mental Disease Publishing.

Fieldsteel, N. D. (1996) The process of termination in long-term psychoanalytic group therapy. *International Journal of Group Psychotherapy, 46,* 25–39.

Firestein, S. (1976). Termination in psychoanalysis. *Journal of the American Psychoanalytic Association, 24,* 3–10.

Foulkes, S. H. (1948). *Introduction to Group-Analytic Psychotherapy.* London: Heinemann.

Foulkes, S. H. (1961). Group process and the individual in the therapeutic group. *British Journal of Medical Psychology, 34,* 23–31.

Foulkes, S. H. (1964). *Therapeutic Group Analysis.* London: Allen & Unwin.

Foulkes, S. H. (1973). The group as the matrix of the individual's mental health. In L. Wolberg & E. Schwartz (Eds.), *Group Therapy 1973: An Overview* (pp. 211–220). New York: Stratton Intercontinental Medical Books.

Foulkes, S. H. (1975). *Group Analytic Psychotherapy: Methods and Principles.* London: Gordon & Breach.

Foulkes, S. H., & Anthony, E. J. (1965). *Group Psychotherapy: The Psychoanalytic Approach* (2nd Edition). Baltimore: Penguin Books.

French, T. M. (1952). *The Integration of Behavior* (Vol. 1 & 2). Chicago: University of Chicago Press.

Frank, J. D. (1957). Some determinants, manifestations, and effects of cohesiveness in therapy groups. *International Journal of Group Psychotherapy, 7,* 53–63.

Freud, E. (1905). Fragment of an analysis of a case of hysteria. In J. Strackey (Ed. & Trans.), *The Standard Edition of the Complete Psychological Works of Sigmund Freud* (Vol. 7, pp. 1–122). London: Hogarth Press, 1957.

Freud, S. (1910). The future prospects of psychoanalytic theory. In J. Strachey (Ed. & Trans.), *The Standard Edition of the Complete Psychological Works of Sigmund Freud* (Vol. 11, pp. 139–151). London: Hogarth Press, 1957.

Freud, S. (1913). On beginning the treatment. In J. Strachey (Ed. & Trans.), *The Standard Edition of the Complete Psychological Works of Sigmund Freud* (Vol. 12, pp. 121–144). London: Hogarth Press, 1958.

Freud, S. (1914). Remembering and repeating and working through. In J. Strachey (Ed. & Trans.), *The Standard Edition of the Complete Psychological Works of Sigmund Freud* (Vol. 12, pp. 145–156). London: Hogarth Press, 1958.

Freud, S. (1915). Observations and transference love. In J. Strachey (Ed. & Trans.), *The Standard Edition of the Complete Psychological Works of Sigmund Freud* (Vol. 12, pp. 157–171). London: Hogarth Press, 1958.

Freud, S. (1921). Group psychology and the analysis of the ego. In J. Strackey (Ed. & Trans.), *The Standard Edition of the Complete Psychological Works of Sigmund Freud* (Vol. 18, pp. 65–143). London: Hogarth Press, 1955.

Freud, S. (1930). Civilization and its discontents. In J. Strachey (Ed. & Trans.), *The Standard Edition of the Complete Psychological Works of Sigmund Freud* (Vol. 21, pp. 57–145). London: Hogarth Press, 1961.

Freud, S. (1937). Analysis terminable and interminable. In J. Strachey (Ed. & Trans.), *The Standard Edition of the Complete Psychological Works of Sigmund Freud* (Vol. 23, pp. 209–253). London: Hogarth Press, 1964.

Fried, E. (1954). The effect of combined therapy on the productivity of patients. *International Journal of Group Psychotherapy, 8,* 76–84.

Fried, E. (1970). Individuation through group psychotherapy. *International Journal of Group Psychotherapy, 20,* 450–459.

Fried, E. (1971). Basic concepts in group psychotherapy. In H. Kaplan & B. Sadock (Eds.), *Comprehensive Group Psychotherapy* (pp. 47–71). Baltimore: Williams & Wilkins.

Fried, E. (1973). Group bonds. In L. Wolberg & Schwartz (Eds.), *Group Therapy 1973: An Overview.* Stratton International Medical Books.

Fried, E. (1982). Building psychic structures as a prerequisite for change. *International Journal of Group Psychotherapy, 32,* 418–422.

Friedman, L. (1988). *The Anatomy of Psychotherapy.* Hillsdale, NJ: Analytic Press.

Frost, J. C. (1990). A developmentally keyed scheme for the placement of gay men into psychotherapy groups. *International Journal of Group Psychotherapy, 39*(2), 155–168.

Fuhriman, A. (1997). Comments on issues raised by Slavson, Durkin, and Scheidlinger. *International Journal of Group Psychotherapy, 47,* 169–174.

Fuhriman, A., & Burlingame, G. M. (1994). Group psychotherapy: Research and practice. In A. Fuhriman & G. M. Burlingame (Eds.), *Handbook of Group Psychotherapy: An Empirical and Clinical Synthesis* (pp. 3–40). New York: Wiley.

Fulkerson, C. C. F., Hawkins, D. M., & Alden, A. R. (1981). Psychotherapy groups of insufficient size. *International Journal of Group Psychotherapy, 31,* 73–81.

Gabbard, G. O. (1993). An overview of countertransference with borderline patients. *Journal of Psychotherapy Practice and Research, 2,* 7–18.

Gans, J. S. (1990). Broaching and exploring the question of combined group and individual therapy. *International Journal of Group Psychotherapy, 40,* 123–137.

Gans, J. S. (1992). Money and psychodynamic group psychotherapy. *International Journal of Group Psychotherapy, 42,* 133–152.

Gans, J. S., & Alonso, A. (1998). Difficult patients: Their construction in group therapy. *International Journal of Group Psychotherapy, 48,* 311–338.

Gans, J. S., & Counselman, E. F. (2000). Silence in group psychotherapy: A powerful communication. *International Journal of Group Psychotherapy, 50,* 71–86.

Gans, R. (1962). Group co-therapists and the therapeutic situation: A critical evaluation. *International Journal of Group Psychotherapy, 12,* 82–87.

Ganzarain, R. (1991). The "bad mother-group": An extension of Scheidlinger's "mother-group concept". In S. Tuttman (Eds.), *Psychoanalytic Group Theory and Therapy.* Madison, CT: International Universities Press.

Garland, C. (1982). Group analysis: Taking the non-problem seriously. *Group Analysis, 15,* 4–14.

Garland, J. A., & Kolodny, R. L. (1973). Characteristics and resolution of scapegoating. In S. Bernstein (Ed.), *Further explorations in group work* (pp. 67–68). Boston: Milford House.

Gauron, E. F., & Rawlings, E. I. (1975). Procedure for orienting new members to group psychotherapy. *Small Group Behavior, 6,* 293–307.

Getty, C., & Shannon, A. M. (1969). Co-therapy as an egalitarian relationship. *American Journal of Nursing, 69,* 762–777.

Gibbard, G. S., & Hartman, J. S. (1973). The oedipal paradigm in group development: A clinical and empirical study. *Small Group Behavior, 4,* 305–354.

Giovacchini, P. (1979). *Treatment of Primitive Mental States*. New York: Aronson.

Glatzer, H. T. (1953). Handling transference resistance in group therapy. *Psychoanalytic Review, 40*, 36–43.

Glatzer, H. T. (1978). The working alliance in analytic group psychotherapy. *International Journal of Group Psychotherapy, 28*, 147–162.

Glatzer, H. T. (1989). Working through in analytic group psychotherapy. *International Journal of Group Psychotherapy, 19*, 292–306.

Goldberg, A. (1998). Self psychology since Kohut. *Psychoanalytic Quarterly, 67*, 240–255.

Goldberg, D. A., Schuyler, W. R., Jr., Branfield, D., & Savino, P. (1983). Focal group psychotherapy. *International Journal of Group Psychotherapy, 33*, 413–431.

Greenberg, J. R., & Mitchell, J. A. (1983). *Object Relations in Psychoanalytic Theory*. Cambridge, MA: Harvard University Press.

Greene, L. R., Rosenkrantz, J., & Muth, D. Y. (1986). Borderline defenses and counter transference: Research findings and implications. *Psychiatry, 49*, 253–264.

Greenson, R. R. (1967). *The Theory and Practice of Psychoanalysis*. New York: International Universities Press.

Greenson, R. R. (1983). *Object Relations in Psychoanalytic Theory*. Cambridge, MA: Harvard University Press.

Grinker, R. R., & Spiegel, J. P. (1944). Brief psychotherapy in war neurosis. *Psychosomatic Medicine, 6*, 123–131.

Grotjahn, M. (1975). The treatment of the famous and the "beautiful people" in groups. In L. Wolberg & M. Aronson (Eds.), *Group Therapy 1975: An Overview*. New York: Stratton Intercontinental Medical Books.

Grotstein, J. (1981). *Splitting and Projective Identification*. Northvale, NJ: Aronson.

Group for the Advancement of Psychiatry. (1975). Pharmacotherapy and psychotherapy: Paradoxes, problems, and progress. *GAP Report, 9*, 271–272.

Group for the Advancement of Psychiatry. (1992). *Psychotherapy in the Future* (Committee on Therapy, Eds.). Washington, DC: American Psychiatric Press.

Groves, J. E. (1992). The short-term dynamic psychotherapies: An overview. In J. S. Rutan (Ed.), *Psychotherapy for the 1990s* (pp. 35–59). New York: Guilford Press.

Grunebaum, H., & Kates, W. (1977). Whom to refer for group psychotherapy. *American Journal of Psychiatry, 132*, 130–133.

Grunebaum, J., & Smith, J. M. (1996). Women in context(s); The social subtext of group psychotherapy. In B. DeChant (Ed.), *Women and Group Psychotherapy: Theory and Practice* (pp. 50–88) New York: Guilford Press.

Guntrip, H. (1969). *Schizoid Phenomena, Object-Relations, and the Self*. New York: International Universities Press.

Gustafson, J. P., & Cooper, L. (1979). Unconscious planning in small groups. *Human Relations, 32*, 1039–1064.

Gustafson, J. P., & Cooper, L. (1992). After basic assumptions: On holding a specialized versus a general theory of participant observation in small groups. In M. Pines (Eds.), *Bion and Group Psychotherapy*. London: Routledge.

Gustafson, J. P., Cooper, L., Lathrop, N. C., Ringler, K., Seldin, F. A., & Wright, M. K. (1981). Cooperative and clashing interests in small groups: Part I. Theory. *Human Relations, 34*, 315–339.

Guttmacher, J. A., & Birk, L. (1971). Group therapy: What specific therapeutic advantages? *Comprehensive Psychiatry, 12*, 546–556.

Hahn, W. K., & Toman, K. (1997). Destructive and reparative transference in multiple levels of group psychotherapy. *Group, 21,* 239–253.

Hardy, J., & Lewis, C. (1992). Bridging the gap between long- and short-term group psychotherapy: A viable treatment model. *Group, 16,* 5–17.

Harwood, I. N. H. (1992). Group psychotherapy and disorders of the self. *Group Analysis, 25,* 19–26.

Harwood, I. N. H. (1996). Towards optimum group placement from the perspective of self and group experience. *Group Analysis, 29,* 199–218.

Harwood, I. N. H., & Pines, M. (Eds.). (1998). *Self Experiences in Group: Intersubjective and Self Psychological Pathways to Human Understanding.* London: Kingsley.

Herman, J. L., Perry, J. C., & van der Kolk, B. A. (1989). Childhood trauma in borderline personality disorder. *American Journal of Psychiatry, 146,* 490–495.

Hill, W., & Grunner, L. (1972). A study of development in open and closed groups. *Small Group Behavior, 4,* 355–381.

Hopper, E. (1996). The social unconscious in clinical work. *Group, 20,* 7–42.

Hopper, E. (1997). Traumatic experience in the unconscious life of groups: A fourth basic assumption. *Group Analysis, 30,* 439–470.

Horowitz, M. J. (1979). *States of Mind: Analysis of Change in Psychotherapy.* New York: Plenum Press.

Horwitz, L. (1974). *Clinical Predictions in Psychotherapy.* New York: Aronson.

Horwitz, L. (1977a). A group centered approach to group psychotherapy. *International Journal of Group Psychotherapy, 27,* 423–440.

Horwitz, L. (1977b). Group therapy of the borderline patient. In P. Hartocollis (Ed.), *Borderline Personality Disorders* (pp. 399–422). New York: International Universities Press.

Horwitz, L. (1980). Group psychotherapy for borderline and narcissistic patients. *Bulletin of the Menninger Clinic, 44,* 181–200.

Horwitz, L. (1994). Depth of transference in groups. *International Journal of Group Psychotherapy, 44,* 271–290.

Hulser, W. (1958). Psychotherapy with ambulatory schizophrenic patients in mixed groups. *Archives of Neurology and Psychiatry, 79,* 681–687.

Imber, S. D., Lewis, P. M., & Loiselle, R. H. (1979). Use and abuses of the brief intervention group. *International Journal of Group Psychotherapy, 29,* 39–49.

Jeffrey, N. A. (1999, January). HMOs face questions over push for group therapy. *Wall Street Journal,* pp. A25 & A28.

Johnson, D., & Howenstein, R. (1982). Revitalizing an ailing group psychotherapy program. *Psychiatry, 45,* 138–146.

Kadis, A. L. (1956). The alternate meeting in group psychotherapy. *American Journal of Psychiatry, 10,* 275–291.

Kadis, A. L., Krasner, J. D., Winick, C., & Foulkes, S. H. (1963). *A Practicum of Group Psychotherapy.* New York: Harper & Row.

Kanas, N., Deri, J., Ketter, T., & Fein, G. (1990). Short-term outpatient therapy groups for schizophrenics. *International Journal of Group Psychotherapy, 39*(4), 517–522.

Kanzer, M. (1993). Freud: The first psychoanalytic group leader. In M. Kanzer & J. Glenn (Eds.), *Freud and His Self Analysis* (p. 165). New York: Aronson.

Kaplan, S. R., & Roman, M. (1961). Characteristic responses in adult therapy groups to the introduction of new members: A reflection on group process. *International Journal of Group Psychotherapy, 11,* 372–381.

Karterud, S. W. (1998). The group self, empathy, intersubjectivity, and hermeneutics: A group analytic perspective. In I. N. H. Harwood & M. Pines (Eds.), *Self Experiences in Group: Intersubjective and Self Psychological Pathways to Human Understanding* (pp. 83–98). London: Kingsley

Katz, G. A. (1983). The non-interpretation of metaphors in psychiatric hospital groups. *International Journal of Group Psychotherapy, 33,* 56–68.

Kauff, P. F. (1977). The termination phase: Its relationship to the separation-individuation phase of development. *International Journal of Group Psychotherapy, 27,* 14–22.

Kauff, P. F. (1979). Diversity in analytic group psychotherapy: The relationship between theoretical concepts and technique. *International Journal of Group Psychotherapy, 29,* 51–66.

Kauff, P. F. (1993). The contribution of analytic group therapy to the psychoanalytic process. In A. Alonso & H. I. Swiller (Eds.), *Group Therapy in Clinical Practice* (pp. 3–28). Washington, D.C.: American Psychiatric Press.

Kauff, P. F. (1997). Transference and regression in and beyond analytic group psychotherapy: Revisiting some timeless thoughts. *International Journal of Group Psychotherapy, 47,* 201–210.

Kaul, T. J., & Bednar, R. L. (1994). Pretraining and structure: Parallel lines yet to meet. In A. Fuhriman & G. M. Burlingame (Eds.), *Handbook of Group Psychotherapy: An Empirical and Clinical Synthesis* (pp. 155–188). New York: Wiley

Kelman, H. (1963). The role of the group in the induction of therapeutic change. *International Journal of Group Psychotherapy, 13,* 399–451.

Kernberg, O. F. (1975). A systems approach to priority setting of interventions in groups. *International Journal of Group Psychotherapy, 25,* 251–275.

Kernberg, O. F. (1976). *Object Relations Theory and Clinical Psychoanalysis.* New York: Aronson.

Kibel, H. S. (1991). The therapeutic use of splitting: The role of the mother-group in therapeutic differentiation and practicing. In S. Tuttman (Ed.), *Psychanalytic Group Theory and Therapy* (pp. 113–132). Madison, CT: International Universities Press.

Kieffer, C. C. (1996). Using dream interpretation to resolve group developmental impasses. *Group, 20,* 273–285.

Klein, E., & Astrachan, B. (1971). Learning in groups: A comparison of T-groups and study groups. *Journal of Applied Behavior Science, 7,* 659–683.

Klein, M. (1946). Notes on some schizoid mechanisms. *International Journal of Psycho-Analysis, 27,* 99–110.

Klein, R. H. (1985). Some principles of short-term group therapy. *International Journal of Group Psychotherapy, 35,* 309–330.

Klein, R. H., & Carrol, R. A. (1986). Patient characteristics and attendance patterns in outpatient group psychotherapy. *International Journal of Group Psychotherapy, 36,* 115–132.

Kleinberg, J. L. (1991). Teaching beginning group therapists to incorporate a patient's empathic capacity in treatment planning. *Group, 15,* 141–154.

Klein-Lipschutz, E. (1953). Comparison of dreams in individual and group psychotherapy. *International Journal of Group Psychotherapy, 3,* 143–149.

Knapp, P. H. (1992). Emotion and the psychoanalytic encounter. In T. Shapiro & R. N.

Emde (Eds.), *Affect: Psychoanalytic Perspectives* (pp. 239–264). Madison, CT: International Universities Press.

Kohut, H. (1980). Reflections on advances in self psychology. In A. Goldberg (Ed.), *Advances in Self Psychology* (pp. 473–553). New York: International Universities Press.

Kohut, H. (1984). *How Does Analysis Cure?* Chicago: University of Chicago Press.

Kohut, H., & Wolf, E. S. (1978). The disorders of the self and their treatment: An outline. *International Journal of Psycho-Analysis, 59,* 413–425.

Kohut, H. (1971). *The Analysis of the Self.* New York: International Universities Press.

Kohut, H. (1976). Creativeness, charism group psychology. In J. E. Gedo & G. H. Pollock (Eds.), *Freud: The Fusion of Science and Humanism.* New York: International Universities Press.

Kohut, H. (1977). *The Restoration of the Self.* New York: International Universities Press.

Kris, E. (1956). The recovery of childhood memories in psychoanalysis. *Psychoanalytic Study of the Child, 2,* 54–88.

Krystal, H. (1974). The genetic development of affect and affect regression. *Annual of Psychoanalysis, 2,* 98–126.

Lane, R. D., & Schwartz, G. E. (1987). Levels of emotional awareness: A cognitive-developmental theory and its application to psychopathology. *American Journal of Psychiatry, 144,* 122–143.

Lang, E., & Halperin, D. A. (1989). Coleadership in groups: Marriage à la mode? In D. A. Halperin (Ed.), *Group Psychodynamics: New Paradigms and New Perspectives* (pp. 74–86). Chicago: Year Book Medical Publishers.

Lazare, A., Eisenthal, S., & Frank, A. (1979). A negotiated approach to the clinical encounter: Attending to the patient's perspective. In A. Lazare (Eds.), *Outpatient Psychiatry: Diagnosis and Treatment* (pp. 141–156). Baltimore: Williams and Wilkins.

Lazare, A., Eisenthal, S., & Frank, A. (1979). A negotiated approach to the clinical encounter: II. Conflict and negotiation. In A. Lazare (Ed.), *Outpatient Psychiatry: Diagnosis and Treatment* (pp. 157–171). Baltimore: Williams & Wilkins.

Lazerson, J. S., & Zilbach, J. J. (1993). Gender issues in group psychotherapy. In H. I. Kaplan & B. J. Sadock (Eds.), *Comprehensive Group Psychotherapy* (3rd ed., pp. 682–693). Baltimore: Williams & Wilkins.

Leary, T. F. (1957). *Interpersonal Diagnosis of Personality.* New York: Ronald Press.

LeBon, G. (1920). *The Crowd: A Study of the Popular Mind.* New York: Fisher, Unwin. (Original work published 1895)

Leff, J. (1988). *Psychiatry Around the Globe: A Transcultural View* (2nd ed.). London: Gaskell.

Leibovich, M. A. (1981). Short-term psychotherapy for borderlines? *Psychotherapy and Psychosomatics, 39,* 1–9.

Leighton, A. H. (1959). *My Name is Legion: Sterling County Study of Psychiatric Disorder and Sociocultural Environment* (Vol. 1). New York: Basic Books.

Leszcz, M. (1989). Group psychotherapy of the characterologically difficult patient. *International Journal of Group Psychotherapy, 39,* 311–335.

Leszcz, M. (1992). The interpersonal approach to group psychotherapy. *International Journal of Group Psychotherapy, 42,* 37–62.

Levine, B. (1979). *Group Psychotherapy: Practice and Development.* Englewood Cliffs, N. J.: Prentice-Hall.

Levinson, D. J., & Astrachan, B. M. (1974). Organizational boundaries: Entry into the mental health center. *Administrative Mental Health, 1,* 1–12.

Lichtenberg, J. D. (1989). *Psychoanalysis and Motivation.* Hillsdale, NJ: Analytic Press.

Lichtenberg, J. D., Lachmann, F. M., & Fosshage, J. L. (1992). *Self and Motivational Systems: Toward a Theory of Psychoanalytic Technique.* Hillsdale, NJ: Analytic Press.

Lichtenberg, J. D., Lachmann, F. M., Fosshage, J. L. (1996). *The Clinical Exchange: Techniques Derived from Self and Motivational Systems.* Hillsdale, NJ: Analytic Press.

Lieberman, M., Yalom, I. D., & Miles, M. D. (1973). *Encounter Groups: First Facts.* New York: Basic Books.

Lipsius, S. H. (1991). Combined individual and group psychotherapy: Guidelines at the interface. *International Journal of Group Psychotherapy, 41,* 313–327.

Loewald, H. W. (1973). On internalization. *International Journal of Psychoanalytic Association, 54,* 9–17.

Long, K., Pendleton, L., & Winter, B. (1988). Effects of therapist termination on group process. *International Journal of Group Psychotherapy, 38,* 211–222.

Luborsky, L. (1985). Therapist success and its determinants. *Archives of General Psychiatry, 42,* 602–611.

Luborsky, L., Mintz, J., Auerbach, A., Crits-Christoph, P., Bachrach, H., Todd, T., Johnson, M., Cohen, M., & O'Brien, C. (1980). Predicting the outcome of psychotherapy: Findings of the Penn Psychotherapy Project. *Archives of General Psychiatry, 37,* 471–481

Lundin, W. H., & Aronov, V. M. (1952). The use of co-therapists in group psychotherapy. *Journal of Consulting Psychology, 16,* 77–84.

MacKenzie, K. R. (1987). Therapeutic factors in group psychotherapy: A contemporary view. *Group, 11,* 26–34.

MacKenzie, K. R. (1988). Recent developments in brief psychotherapy. *Hospital and Community Psychiatry, 39,* 742–752.

MacKenzie, K. R. (1990). *Introduction to Time-Limited Group Psychotherapy.* Washington, DC: American Psychiatric Press.

MacKenzie, K. R. (1993). Time-limited group therapy and technique. In A. Alonso & H. I. Swiller (Eds.), *Group Therapy in Clinical Practice.* Washington, DC: American Psychiatric Press.

MacKenzie, K. R. (1994). The developing structure of the therapy group system. In H. D. Bernard & K. R. MacKenzie (Eds.), *Basics of Group Psychotherapy* (pp. 35–59). New York: Guilford Press.

MacKenzie, K. R. (1996). Time-limited group psychotherapy: Has Cinderella found her prince? *Group, 20,* 95–111.

MacKenzie, K. R. (1997a). Comments on issues raised by Slavson, Durkin, and Scheillinger. *International Journal of Group Psychotherapy, 47,* 175–181.

MacKenzie, K. R. (1997b). *Time-Managed Group Psychotherapy: Effective Clinical Applications.* Washington, DC: American Psychiatric Press.

MacLennon, B. (1965). Cotherapy. *International Journal of Group Psychotherapy, 15,* 154–165.

Mahler, M. S., Pine, F., & Bergman, A. (1975). *The Psychological Birth of the Human Infant.* New York: Basic Books.

Malan, D. H. (1976). *The Frontier of Brief Psychotherapy.* Cambridge, MA: Harvard University Press.

Malan, D. H., Balfour, F. H. G., Hood, V. G., & Shooter, A. (1976). Group psychotherapy: A long term follow-up study. *Archives of General Psychiatry, 33,* 1303–1315.

Mann, J. (1973). *Time-Limited Psychotherapy.* New York: Plenum Press.

Masterson, J. F. (1976). *Psychotherapy of the Borderline Adult.* New York: Brunner/Mazel.

McCullum, M., & Piper, W. E. (1999). Personality disorders and response to group-oriented evening treatment. *Group Dynamics: Theory, Research and Practice, 3*(1), 3–14.

McDougall, W. (1920). *The Group Mind.* New York: Putnam.

McGee, T. F. (1969). Comprehensive preparation for group psychotherapy. *American Journal of Psychiatry, 23,* 303–312.

McGee, T. F. (1974). Therapist termination in group psychotherapy. *International Journal of Group Psychotherapy, 24,* 3–12.

McGlasher, T. H. (1986). The Chestnut Lodge Followup Study: III. Longterm outcome of borderline personalities. *Archives of General Psychiatry, 43,* 20–30.

McRoberts, C., Burlingame, G. M., & Hoag, M. J. (1998). Comparative efficacy of individual and group psychotherapy: A meta-analytic perspective. *Group Dynamics: Theory, Research and Practice, 2*(2), 101–117.

Meissner, W. W. (1996). The therapeutic alliance and the real relationship in the analytic process. In L. E. Lifson (Ed.), *Understanding Therapeutic Action: Psychodynamic Concepts of Cure* (pp. 21–39). Hillsdale, NJ: Analytic Press

Meyer, D. J., & Simon, R. I. (1999). Split treatment: Clarity between psychiatrists and psychotherapists. *Psychiatric Annals, 29,* 327–332.

Meyers, S. J. (1978). The disorders of the self: Developmental and clinical considerations. *Group, 2,* 131–140.

Michaels, R. (1981). The present and the past. *Bulletin of the Association of Psychoanalytic Medicine, 20,* 49–56.

Middleman, R. R. (1980). Co-leadership and solo leadership in education for social work with groups. *Social Work with Groups, 3,* 30–40.

Mintz, E. (1965). Male–female co-therapists: Some values and some problems. *American Journal of Psychotherapy, 19,* 293–301.

Model, A. H. (1997). Reflections on metaphor and affects. *The Annual of Psychoanalysis, 25,* 219–233.

Morrison, A. P. (1990). Secrets: A self-psychological view of shame in group therapy. In B. E. Roth, W. N. Stone, & H. D. Kibel (Eds.), *The Difficult Patient in Group: Group Psychotherapy with Borderline and Narcissistic Disorders* (pp. 175–189). Madison, CT: International Universities Press.

Munzer, J. (1967). Acting out: Communication or resistance? *International Journal of Group Psychotherapy, 16,* 434–441.

Neri, C. (1998). *Group.* London: Kingsley.

Neumann, M., & Geoni, B. (1974). Types of patients especially suitable for analytically oriented group psychotherapy: Some clinical examples. *Israel Annals Psychiatry and Related Disciplines, 12,* 203–215.

Newton, P. M. (1973). Social structure and process in psychotherapy: A socio-psychological analysis of transference, resistance, and change. *International Journal of Psychiatry, 11,* 480–523.

Nitsun, M. (1996). *The Anti-Group: Destructive Forces in the Group and Their Creative Potential.* London: Routledge.

Ogden, T. H. (1979). On positive identification. *International Journal of Psycho-Analysis, 60,* 357–373.

Ormont, L. R. (1967). Group resistance and the therapeutic contract. *International Journal of Group Psychotherapy, 18,* 147–154.

Ornstein, P. H. (1978). The evolution of Heinz Kohut's psychonalytic psychology of the self. In P. H. Ornstein (Ed.), *The search for the self* (pp. 1–106). New York: International Universities Press.

Ornstein, P. H. (1991). Why self psychology is not an object relations theory: Clinical and theoretical considerations. In A. Goldberg (Ed.), *The Evolution of Self Psychology: Progress in Self Psychology* (Vol. 7, pp. 17–29). Hillsdale, NJ: Analytic Press.

Ornstein, P. H., & Ornstein, A. (1977). On the continuing evolution of psychoanalytic psychotherapy: Reflections upon recent trends and some predictions for the future. *Annual Psychoanalysis, 5,* 329–370.

Ornstein, P. H., & Ornstein, A. (1995). Some distinguishing features of Heinz Kohut's self psychology. *Psychoanalytic Dialogues, 5,* 384–391.

Pine, F. (1985). *Developmental Theory and Clinical Process.* New Haven, CT: Yale University Press.

Pines, M. (1981). The frame of reference of group psychotherapy. *International Journal of Group Psychotherapy, 31,* 275–285.

Pines, M. (1983). Psychic development and the group analytic situation. *Group, 9,* 24–37.

Pines, M. (1985). Psychic development and the group analytic situation. *Group, 9*(1), 24–37.

Pines, M. (1997). Centennial celebration to commemorate the birth and work of Norbert Elias: Foulkes and Elias. *Group Analysis, 30,* 475–476.

Pines, M. (1998). Psychic development and the group analytic situation. In *Circular Reflections: Selected Papers on Group Analysis and Psychoanalysis* (pp. 59–76). London: Jessica Kingsley.

Pines, M., & Hutchinson, S. (1993). Group analysis. In A. Alonso & H. I. Swiller (Eds.), *Group Therapy in Clinical Practice* (pp. 29–47). Washington, DC: American Psychiatric Press.

Piper, W. E. (1994). Client variables. In A. Fuhriman & G. M. Burlingame (Eds.), *Handbook of Group Psychotherapy: An Empirical and Clinical Synthesis* (pp. 83–113). New York: Wiley

Piper, W. E., Debbane, E. G., Bienvenue, J. P., & Garant, J. (1984). A comparative study of four forms of psychotherapy. *Journal of Consulting and Clinical Psychology, 52,* 268–279.

Piper, W. E., & Joyce, A. S. (1996). Consideration of factors influencing the utilization of time-limited, short-term group therapy. *International Journal of Group Psychotherapy, 46*(3), 311–328.

Piper, W. E., & McCallum, M. (1994). Selection of patients for group interventions. In H. S. Bernard & K. R. MacKenzie (Eds.), *Basics of Group Psychotherapy* (pp. 1–34). New York: Guilford Press.

Piper, W. E., McCallum, M., & Azim, H. F. A. (1992). *Adaptation to Loss Through Short-Term Group Psychotherapy.* New York: Guilford Press.

Poey, K. (1985). Guidelines for the practice of brief, dynamic, group therapy. *International Journal of Group Psychotherapy, 35,* 331–354.

Praper, P. (1997). A case of combined therapy: some developmental and object-relations phenomena. *Group Analysis, 30,* 331–348.

Pratt, J. H. (1906). The home sanatorium treatment of consumption. In H. Ruitenbeek (Ed.), *Group Therapy Today* (pp. 9–14). New York: Atherton Press.

Redl, F. (1963). Psychoanalysis and group therapy: A developmental point of view. *American Journal of Orthopsychiatry, 33,* 135–147.

Reiss, H., & Rutan, J. S. (1992). Group therapy for eating disorders: A step-wise approach. *Group, 16*(2), 79–84.

Rice, A. K. (1969). Individual, group, and intragroup process. *Human Relations, 22,* 565–584.

Rice, C. A. (1992). Contributions from object relations theory. In R. H. Klein, H. S. Bernard, & D. L. Singer (Eds.), *Handbook of Contemporary Group Psychotherapy* (pp. 27–54). Madison, CT: International Universities Press.

Rice, C. A. (1995). The dynamics of the cotherapy relationship: A symposium—The junior–junior team. *Group, 19,* 87–99.

Rice, C. A. (1996). Premature termination of group therapy: A clinical perspective. *International Journal of Group Psychotherapy, 46,* 5–23.

Roberts, J. (1991). Destructive phases in groups. In J. Roberts & M. Pines (Eds.), *The Practice of Group Analysis* (pp. 128–135). London: Routledge.

Rodenhauser, P. (1989). Group psychotherapy and pharmacotherapy: Psychodynamic considerations. *International Journal of Group Psychotherapy, 39,* 445–456.

Rogers, C. (1970). *Carl Rogers on Encounter Groups.* New York: Harper & Row.

Roller, B. (1989). Having fun in groups. *Small Group Behavior, 100,* 97–100.

Roller, B., & Nelson, V. (1994). Cotherapy. In H. I. Kaplan & B. J. Sadock (Eds.), *Comprehensive Group Psychotherapy* (3rd ed., pp. 304–312). Baltimore: Williams & Wilkins.

Roller, B., & Nelson, V. (1999). Group psychotherapy of borderline personalities. *International Journal of Group Psychotherapy, 49*(3), 369–385.

Rosenbaum, M. (1983). *Handbook of Short-Term Therapy Groups.* New York: McGraw-Hill.

Rosenberg, P. (1996). Comparative leadership styles of male and female therapists. In B. DeChant (Ed.), *Women and Group Psychotherapy: Theory and Practice* (pp. 425–441). New York: Guilford Press.

Roth, B. E. (1980). Understanding the development of a homogeneous identity-impaired group through countertransference phenomena. *International Journal of Group Psychotherapy, 30,* 405–425.

Roth, B. E. (1979). Problems of early maintenance and entry into group psychotherapy with persons suffering from borderline and narcissistic states. *Group, 3,* 3–22

Rothke, S. (1986). The role of interpersonal feedback in group psychotherapy. *International Journal of Group Psychotherapy, 36,* 225–240.

Rubovitz-Seit, P. F. D. (1998). *Depth-Psychological Understanding: The Methodologic Grounding of Clinical Interpretations.* Hillsdale, NJ: Analytic Press.

Rutan, J. S. (1992). Psychodynamic group psychotherapy. *International Journal of Group Psychotherapy, 42,*19–35.

Rutan, J. S., & Alonso, A. (1978). Some guidelines for group therapists. *Group, 2,* 4–13.

Rutan, J. S., & Alonso, A. (1979). Group therapy. In A. Lazare (Ed.), *Outpatient Psychiatry: Diagnosis and Treatment.* Baltimore: Williams & Wilkins.

Rutan, J. S., & Alonso, A. (1982). Individual, group, or both? *International Journal of Group Psychotherapy, 32*(3), 3–16.

Rutan, J. S., & Alonso, A. (1980). Sequential cotherapy of groups for training and clinical care. *Group, 4*, 40–50.

Rutan, J. S., Alonso, A., & Molin, R. (1984). Handling the absence of the leader. *International Journal of Group Psychotherapy, 32*(3), 3–16.

Rutan, J. S., & Rice, C. A. (1981). The charismatic leader: Asset or liability. *Psychotherapy: Theory, Research, Practice, 18*, 12–24.

Salvendy, J. T. (1993). Selection and preparation of patients and organization of the group. In H. I. Kaplan & B. J. Sadock (Eds.), *Comprehensive Group Psychotherapy* (3rd ed., pp. 72–84). Baltimore: Williams & Wilkins.

Savaray, S. (1975). Group psychology and the structural theory. *Journal of the American Psychoanalytic Association, 23*, 69–89.

Savaray, S. (1978). A psychoanalytic theory of group development. *International Journal of Group Psychotherapy, 28*, 481–507.

Scheflen, A. (1964). The significance of posture in communication. *Psychiatry, 27*, 316–331.

Scheflen, A. (1965). Quasi-courtship behaviors in psychotherapy. *Psychiatry, 28*, 245–256.

Scheidlinger, S. (1968). The concept of regression in group psychotherapy. *International Journal of Group Psychotherapy, 18*, 3–20.

Scheidlinger, S. (1974). On the concept of the mother-group. *International Journal of Group Psychotherapy, 24*, 417–428.

Scheidlinger, S. (1982a). *Focus on Group Psychotherapy: Clinical Essays*. Madison, CT: International Universities Press.

Scheidlinger, S. (1982b). On scapegoating in group psychotherapy. *International Journal of Group Psychotherapy, 18*, 3–20.

Scheidlinger, S. (1994). An overview of nine decades of group psychotherapy. *Hospital and Community Psychiatry, 45*, 217–225.

Scheidlinger, S. (1997). Group dynamics and group psychotherapy revisited: Four decades later. *International Journal of Group Psychotherapy, 47*, 141–159.

Schermer, V. L., & Klein, R. H. (1996). Termination in group psychotherapy from the perspectives of contemporary object relations theory and self psychology. *International Journal of Group Psychotherapy, 46*, 99–115.

Schutz, W. C. (1958). *Firo*. New York: Rinehart.

Segalla, R. A. (1998). Motivational systems and group object theory: Implications for group therapy. In I. N. H. Harwood & M. Pines (Eds.), *Self Experiences in Group: Intersubjective and Self Psychological Pathways to Human Understanding* (pp. 141–153). London: Kingsley.

Shane, M., & Shane, E. (1993). Self psychology after Kohut: One theory or many? *Journal of the American Psychoanalytic Association, 41*, 777–797.

Shapiro, E. (1998). Intersubjectivity in archaic and mature twinship in group therapy. In I. N. H. Harwood & M. Pines (Eds.), *Self Experiences in Group: Intersubjective and Self Psychological Pathways to Human Understanding* (pp. 47–57). London: Kingsley.

Shapiro, T., & Emde, R. N. (1992). General introduction. In T. Shapiro & R. N. Emde (Eds.). *Affect: Psychoanalytic Perspectives* (pp. ix–xiii). Madison, CT: International Universities Press.

Sharfstein, S. S., & Goldman, H. (1989). Financing the medical management of mental disorders. *American Journal of Psychiatry, 143*(3), 345–349.

Sharpe, M. (1991). Death and practice. In J. Roberts & M. Pines (Eds.), *The Practice of Group Analysis* (pp. 163–173). London: Routledge.

Shaskan, D. A. (1957). Treatment of a borderline case with group analytically oriented group psychotherapy. *Journal of Forensic Sciences, 2*(2), 195–201.

Sifneos, P. E. (1971). Two different kinds of psychotherapy of short duration. In H. H. Barton (Ed.), *Brief Therapies* (pp. 82–90). New York: Behavioral Publications.

Sifneos, P. G. (1972). *Short-term Psychotherapy and Emotional Crisis*. Cambridge, MA: Harvard University Press.

Skolnick, M . R. (1992). The role of the therapist from a social systems perspective. In R. H. Klein, H. S. Bernard, & D. L. Singer (Eds.), *Handbook of Contemporary Group Psychotherapy: Contributions from Object Relations, Self Psychology, and Social Systems Theories* (pp. 321–369). Madison, CT: International Universities Press.

Slater, P. E. (1966). *Microcosm: Structural, Psychological, and Religious Evolution in Groups*. New York: Wiley.

Slavinska-Holy, N. (1983). Combining individual and homogeneous group psychotherapies for borderline conditions. *International Journal of Group Psychotherapy, 33,* 297–312.

Slavson, S. R. (1950). *Analytic Group Psychotherapy*. New York: Columbia University Press.

Slavson, S. R. (1957). Are there group dynamics in therapy groups? *International Journal of Group Psychotherapy, 7,* 115–130.

Socor, B. J. (1997). *Conceiving the Self: Presence and Absence in Psychoanalytic Theory*. Madison, CT: International Universities Press.

Solomon, A., Loeffler, F. J., & Frank, G. H. (1953). An analysis of co-therapist interaction in group psychotherapy. *International Journal of Group Psychotherapy, 3,* 174–188.

Stein, A. (1963). Indications for group psychotherapy and the selection of patients. *Journal of Hillside Hospital, 12,* 145–155.

Stein, A. (1964). The nature of transference in combined therapy. *International Journal of Group Psychotherapy, 14,* 410–416.

Stern, D. N. (1985). *The Interpersonal World of the Infant*. New York: Basic Books.

Stern, D. N., Sander, L. W., Nahum, J. P., Harrison, A. M., Lyons-Ruth, K., Morgan, A. C., Bruschweiler-Stern, N., & Tronick, E. Z. (1998). Non-interpretive mechanisms in psychoanalytic therapy: The "something more" than interpretation. *International Journal of Psycho-Analysis, 79,* 903–921.

Stevenson, J., & Mears, R. (1992). An outcome study of psychotherapy for patients with borderline personality disorder. *American Journal of Psychiatry, 149,* 358–362.

Stockman, A. W. (1997). Crisis for community mental health: The use of groups in the struggle for survival. *Group, 21,* 17–28.

Stolorow, R. D. (1995). An intersubjective view of self psychology. *Psychoanalytic Dialogues, 5,* 393–399.

Stolorow, R. D., Atwood, G. E., & Brandchaft, B. (Eds.). (1994). *The Intersubjective Perspective*. Northvale: Aronson.

Stolorow, R. D., Brandchaft, B., & Atwood, G. E. (1987). *The Interpersonal World of the Infant*. New York: Basic Books.

Stone, A. (1999, January–February). Where will psychoanalysis survive? *Harvard Magazine*, pp. 35–39.

Stone, W. N. (1975). Dynamics of the recorder-observer in group psychotherapy. *Comprehensive Psychiatry, 16*, 49–54.

Stone, W. N. The curative fantasy in group psychotherapy. *Group Therapy Monograph, 10*.

Stone, W. N. (1988). Transferences in groups: Theory and research. In D. Halperin (Ed.), *Group Psychdynamics* (pp. 44–61). Chicago: Year Book Medical Publishers.

Stone, W. N. (1990). On affects in group psychotherapy. In B. E. Roth, W. N. Stone, & H. D. Kibel (Eds.), *The Difficult Patient in Group: Group Psychotherapy with Borderline and Narcissistic Disorders* (pp. 191–208). Madison, CT: International Universities Press.

Stone, W. N. (1992a). A self psychology perspective of envy in group psychotherapy. *Group Analysis, 25*, 413–431.

Stone, W. N. (1992b). The place of self psychology in group psychotherapy: A status report. *International Journal of Group Psychotherapy, 42*, 335–350.

Stone, W. N. (1996a). *Group Psychotherapy for People with Chronic Mental Illness*. New York: Guilford Press.

Stone, W. N. (1996b) Self psychology and the higher mental functioning hypothesis: Complementary theories. *Group Analysis, 29*, 169–181.

Stone, W. N. (1998) Affect and therapeutic process in groups for chronically mentally ill persons. *Journal of Psychotherapy Practice and Research. 7*, 208–216.

Stone, W. N., Blaser, M., & Bozzuto, J. (1980). Late dropouts from group psychotherapy. *American Journal of Psychotherapy, 34*, 401–413.

Stone, W. N., & Gustafson, J. P. (1982). Technique in group psychotherapy of narcissistic and borderline and narcissistic patients. *International Journal of Group Psychotherapy, 32*, 29–47.

Stone, W. N., & Klein, E. B. (in press). The waiting list group. *International Journal of Group Psychotherapy, 49*, 417–428.

Stone, W. N., Rodenhauser, P. H., & Markert, R. J. (1991). Combining group psychotherapy and pharmacotherapy: A survey. *International Journal of Group Psychotherapy, 41*, 449–464.

Stone, W. R., & Rutan, J. S. (1984). Duration of treatment in group psychotherapy. *International Journal of Group Psychotherapy, 34*, 101–117.

Stone, W. N., Schengber, J. S., & Seifried, F. S. (1966). The treatment of a homosexual woman in a mixed group. *International Journal of Group Psychotherapy, 16*, 425–433.

Stone, W. N., & Whitman, R. M. (1977). Contributions of the psychology of the self to group therapy. *International Journal of Group Psychotherapy, 27*, 343–359.

Stone, W. N., & Whitman, R. M. (1980). Observations on empathy in group psychotherapy. In L. Wolberg & M. Aronson (Eds.), *Group and Family Therapy 1980* (pp. 102–117). New York: Brunner/Mazel.

Strachey, J. (1934). The nature of the therapeutic action in psycho-analysis. In L. Paul (Ed.), *Psychoanalytic Clinical Interpretation* (pp. 1–41). New York: Free Press.

Sullivan, H. S. (1953). *The Collected Works of Harry Stack Sullivan*. New York: Norton.

Summers, H. (1994). *Object Relations Theory and Psychopathology: A Comprehensive Text*. Hillsdale, NJ: Analytic Press.

Swiller, H. J. (1988). Alexithymia: Treatment utilizing combined individual and group psychotherapy. *International Journal of Group Psychotherapy, 38*, 47–61.

Toffler, A. (1970). *Future Shock*. New York: Random House.

Toker, E. (1972). The scapegoat as an essential group phenomenon. *International Journal of Group Psychotherapy, 22,* 322–332.

Tuckman, B. W. (1965). Developmental sequence in small groups. *Psychological Bulletin, 63,* 384–399.

Truax, C. B., & Wargo, D. G. (1969). Effects of vicarious therapy pretraining and alternate sessions on outcome in group psychotherapy with outpatients. *Journal of Consulting and Clinical Psychology, 33,* 440–447.

Turquet, P. (1975) Threats to identity in the large group. In L. Kreeger (Ed.), *The Large Group* (pp. 87–146). London: Constable.

Tuttman, S. (1994). Therapeutic responses to the expression of aggression by members in groups. In V. L. Schermer & M. Pines (Eds.), *Ring of Fire: Primitive Affects and Object Relations in Group Psychotherapy* (pp. 174–197). London: Routledge.

Tuttman, S. (1997) Protecting the therapeutic alliance in this time of changing healthcare delivery systems. *International Journal of Group Psychotherapy, 47,* 3–16.

van Schoor, E. (1997). Socio-cultural aspects of British and American group psychotherapy. *Group Analysis, 30,* 27–43.

von Bertalanffy, L. (1966). *General System Theory and Psychiatry* (pp. 705–721). New York: Basic Books.

Waxer, P. H. (1977). Short-term group psychotherapy: Some principles and techniques. *International Journal of Group Psychotherapy, 27,* 33–42.

Weil, S. (1977). In G. A. Panichas (Ed.), *Simone Weil Reader* (pp. 332). Mt. Kisco, NY: Moyer Bell Limited.

Weiss, B. (1995, April). Managed care: There's no stopping it now. *Medical Economics,* pp. 2–10.

Weiss, J. (1993). *How Psychotherapy Works: Process and Technique.* New York: Guilford Press.

Weiss, J., Sampson, H., & the Mount Zion Psychotherapy Research Group. (1986). *The Psychoanalytic Process.* New York: Guilford Press.

Whitaker, D. S. (1989). Group focal conflict theory: Description, illustration and evaluation. *Group, 13,* 225–251.

Whitaker, D. S., & Lieberman, M. A. (1964). *Psychotherapy through the Group Process.* New York: Atherton Press.

Whitman, R. M. (1973). Dreams about the group: An approach to the problem of group psychology. *International Journal of Group Psychotherapy, 23,* 408–420.

Whitman, R. M., & Bloch, E. L. (1990). Therapist envy. *Bulletin of the Menninger Clinic, 54,* 478–487.

Whitman, R. M., & Stock, D. (1958). The group focal conflict. *Psychiatry, 21,* 269–276.

Winnicott, D. W. (1965). *The Maturational Process and the Facilitating Environment.* New York: International Universities Press.

Wogan, M., Getter, H., Anidur, M. J., Nichols, M. F., & Okman, G. (1977). Influencing interaction and outcome in group psychotherapy. *Small Group Behavior, 8,* 26–46.

Wolf, A., & Schwartz, E. K. (1962). *Psychoanalysis in Groups.* New York: Grune & Stratton.

Wolf, E. S. (1988). *Treating the Self: Elements of Clinical Psychology.* New York: Guilford Press.

Wong, N. (1979). Clinical considerations in group treatment of narcissistic disorders. *International Journal of Psychotherapy, 27,* 325–345.

Wong, N. (1983). Combined individual and group psychotherapy. In H. Kaplan & B.

Saddock (Eds.), *Comprehensive Group Psychotherapy* (2nd ed., pp. 73–83). Baltimore: Williams & Wilkins.

Woolf, V. (1929). *A Room of One's Own* (Chap. 2). London: Hogarth Press.

Wright, F. (1998). Discussion of "difficult patients." *International Journal of Group Psychotherapy, 48,* 339–345.

Yalom, I. D. (1966a). A study of group therapy dropouts. *Archives of General Psychiatry, 14,* 393–414.

Yalom, I. D. (1966b). Problems of neophyte group therapists. *International Journal of Social Psychiatry, 12,* 52–59.

Yalom, I. D. (1970). *The Theory and Practice of Group Psychotherapy* (1st ed.). New York: Basic Books.

Yalom, I. D. (1975). *The Theory and Practice of Group Psychotherapy* (2nd ed.). New York: Basic Books.

Yalom, I. D. (1985). *The Theory and Practice of Group Psychotherapy* (3rd Ed.) New York: Basic Books.

Yalom, I. D., Bond, G., Bloch, S., Zimmerman, E., & Friedman, L. (1977). The Impact of weekend group experience on individual therapy. *Archives of General Psychiatry, 34,* 399–418.

Yeomans, F. E., Gutfreund, J., Selzer, M. A., Clarkin, J. F., Hull, J. W., & Smith, T. E. (1994). Factors related to drop-outs by borderline patients: Treatment contract and therapeutic alliance. *Journal of Psychotherapy Practice and Research, 3,* 16–24.

Zaslavv, M. R., & Kalb, R. D. (1989). Medicine as metaphor and medium in group psychotherapy with psychiatric patients. *International Journal of Group Psychotherapy, 39,* 457–468.

Zetzel, E. (1956). Current concepts of transference. *International Journal of Psycho-Analysis, 37,* 369–376.

Zimmerman, D. (1976). Indications and counterindications for analytic group psychotherapy: A study of group factors. In M. Aronson, A. Wolberg & L. Wolberg (Eds.), *Group Therapy 1976: An Overview.* New York: Stratton Intercontinental Medical Books.

Zinkin, L. (1983). Malignant mirroring. *Group Analysis, 16,* 113–126.

Index